CW01064417

# The Doctrine of God

# The Doctrine of God

HERMAN BAVINCK, D.D.

*Translated, Edited and Outlined by*
*William Hendriksen, Th. D.*

The Banner of Truth Trust

THE BANNER OF TRUTH TRUST
3 *Murrayfield Road, Edinburgh* EH12 6EL
*P.O. Box* 621, *Carlisle, Pennsylvania* 17013, USA

\*

© *Wm B Eerdmans Publishing Company* 1951
*First Banner of Truth Trust edition* 1977
*Reprinted* 1979
*Reprinted* 1991

ISBN 0 85151 255 0

\*

*Printed in Great Britain*
*Photo-litho reprint by Mackays of Chatham* PLC, *Chatham, Kent*
*from earlier impression*

# Translator's Preface

"My learning does not help me now; neither does my Dogmatics; faith alone saves me."

These remarkable words, uttered by one of the greatest Reformed theologians, Dr. Herman Bavinck, should not be misinterpreted. They were uttered on his death-bed and did not imply that this humble child of God retracted anything that he had written or that he was trying to express regrets. The statement simply means that a system of doctrine, however necessary and valuable, is of no avail in and by itself. It must be translated into Christian living. There must be genuine faith in the Triune God as manifested in Jesus Christ. Now, Dr. Bavinck was, indeed, a man of faith, a faith which in his case was working through love.

He was born in Hoogeveen, in the province of Drenthe, The Netherlands. The date of his birth was Dec. 13, 1854. His life may be divided into three periods, as follows:

(1) Period of preparation, 1854-1881.

(2) Period of great activity, especially in the field of Reformed Dogmatics, 1881-1911.

(3) Period of activity with respect to many other spheres of life; particularly, psychology, education, and politics, 1911-1921. He died July 29, 1921.

The suggested division of his life into three periods must not be taken too literally, as particularly the second and the third overlapped to some extent.

During the second of these three periods, the period which chiefly concerns us, he started out on his distinguished career by serving as minister of the church at Franeker, Friesland, for a year. He was an orator of great fame. Because of his amiable character, reverence for the Word, genuine enthusiasm, and rare eloquence, people flocked to his services from every direction.

On Jan. 10, 1883 he was inducted into the office of professor of theology at the Theological School at Kampen. From 1902 until the end of his life he occupied a similar position at the Free University of Amsterdam.

Dr. Bavinck's life was by no means a path of roses. There were several factors which exerted their sinister influence upon himself, upon the circle of his intimate friends, and, in general, upon religious life in the Reformed churches in The Netherlands during the latter part of the nineteenth and the early decades of the twentieth century. When Dr. Bavinck changed his position with reference to a burning issue, he would be charged with lack of integrity. When he tried to express himself very cautiously, showing that there are two sides to most questions, he exposed himself to the accusation of being too lenient in his attitude to "the opposition." Now this tendency to express himself very cautiously was deeply rooted in his nature. It was, to a very considerable extent, a strong point in Dr. Bavinck. We are not ruling out the possibility that, in a lesser degree, it may at times have proved a slight weakness in the man and in his method.

Among the many factors that are enumerated as contributing their share to the total picture of religious life during the period which we are discussing mention is also made of the fact that certain curators aspired after positions as theological professors; see the biography by Dr. V. Hepp, p. 283.

Last but by no means least, there was the keen disappointment which Dr. Bavinck suffered in his attempt to secure synodical adoption of his plan to bring about an organic union or consolidation of the Theological School and the Free University.

Being a man of very sensitive temperament, who was generally mild in his criticism of others, it is easily understood how all these affairs affected him, especially when ecclesiastical matters were not always conducted in an altogether laudable and objective manner. He once remarked to a group of students: "Ordinary politics *sometimes* has its sordid side; politics in church-affairs *always* has." As a result, he at length withdrew to a large extent from ecclesiastical life in the restricted sense of the term.

However, he did not cease to exert a powerful influence upon the religious, social, political, and cultural life of The Netherlands. His influence was felt even outside of his own country and denomination, for he was a man of ecumenical sympathies. Also, he was a scholar of almost unbelievable erudition and literary activity. The titles of his published works fill several columns. They concern themselves mainly, though not exclusively, with theology, psychology, and pedagogy. He belonged to the Royal Academy of Sciences, and in 1911 he became a member of the Upper Chamber in the Dutch government. As a popular lecturer he was in great demand. He traveled widely. Some of the readers will probably remember his visits to our country.

Dr. Bavinck's *Gereformeerde Dogmatiek* is his magnum opus. The first edition was published in the years 1895-1899. The third edition, from which we translated, is a reprint of the second, and came forth from the press in 1918. It consists of four volumes. The first of these may be considered a treatise in Fundamental Apologetics. In the second volume Dr. Bavinck begins his Dogmatics proper with a discussion of *The Doctrine of God*. Of this locus we herewith offer a translation.

At the suggestion of the publisher and for practical reasons it was decided to include only the more important references to sources; and to provide room for them in the body of the work—as Dr. Bavinck himself often does—instead of in footnotes.

Not only the Dutch but also the Hebrew, Greek, Latin, and German sentences and paragraphs, in which the original abounds, were translated into English.

Page-headings and summarizing captions were supplied in order to furnish the reader with an easy guide to the contents and to remove the criticism, heard so often, that it is difficult to find one's way through Bavinck.

It was especially the careful, historical presentation of the various doctrines, the wealth of biblical material to support them, and the painstaking effort on the part of the author to do full justice to both sides of every issue and problem, that endeared this work to our mind and heart. Whether, in each instance, every Scripture-passage, to which reference is made, is relevant and proves the point that must be established, is an open question. Let thorough exegesis do its work, on the basis of the materials here furnished. Let us at least appreciate the fact that the author strives at all times to be entirely fair and balanced in reaching and stating his own conclusions. See, for example, his masterful discussion of Supra-lapsarianism and Infra-lapsarianism, in the present volume.

It is hoped that the reading of this translation of Dr. Bavinck's *The Doctrine of God* may be a spiritual treat and may create a desire for the rest of the work in English.

*Wm. Hendriksen*

# CONTENTS

# GOD'S INCOMPREHENSIBILITY

# CHAPTER I

## God's Incomprehensibility

### I. According to Scripture God Is Incomprehensible Yet Knowable, Absolute Yet Personal.

**A. Mystery is the vital element of Dogmatics; the believer cannot fully comprehend revealed truth.**

Mystery is the vital element of Dogmatics. It is true that the term "mystery" in Scripture does not indicate abstract-supernatural truth in Romish sense; nevertheless, the idea that the believer would be able to understand and comprehend intellectually the revealed mysteries is equally unscriptural. On the contrary, the truth which God has revealed concerning himself in nature and in Scripture far surpasses human conception and comprehension. In that sense Dogmatics is concerned with nothing but mystery, for it does not deal with finite creatures, but from beginning to end raises itself above every creature to the Eternal and Endless One himself.

**B. Reason: Dogmatics has throughout to do with God: the Incomprehensible.**

At the very outset Dogmatics is confronted with the Incomprehensible. It begins with him, for of him are all things. But also in the other loci, when it descends to the study of creatures, it views the latter exclusively in their relation to God even as they are of and through and unto him. Hence, the knowledge of God is the only dogma, the sole content of the entire field of Dogmatics. All the doctrines treated in Dogmatics — whether in regard to the universe, man, Christ, etc. — are but the explication of the central dogma of the knowledge of God. Everything is treated with God as center and starting-point. Under him all things are subsumed. To him all things are traced back. It is ever God and God alone whose glory in creation and redemption, in nature and in grace, in the world and in the church, it must meditate upon and describe. It is the knowledge of *him*, of him *alone*, which it must display and show forth.

**C. The fact that Dogmatics has for its object the knowledge of God does not render it dry, but instead very fruitful and practical.**

We must not suppose, however, that by reason of this very fact Dogmatics is rendered a dry, scholastic study, without practical value. On the contrary, the more it meditates on him, the knowledge of whom is its only content, so much the more is it transformed into worship and adoration. As long as it does not forget to think and speak about *matters* rather than about *words,* as long as it remains "a theology of facts," and does not degenerate into "a theology of rhetoric" it will be fruitful in the highest degree, inasmuch as it is a systematic description of the knowledge of God. Indeed, the knowledge of God in Christ is life itself, Ps. 89:15; Is. 11:9; Jer. 31:34; John 17:3. Hence, Augustine desired to know nothing else and nothing more than God and himself: "I desire to know God and my soul. Nothing more? No, nothing at all." Hence, Calvin begins his *Institutes* with the knowledge of God and of ourselves. And hence, *The Catechism of Geneva* answers the first question: "What is the chief end of human life?" with "That men may know God, their Maker."

**D. (Cf. B.) But how can Dogmatics throughout discuss God? How is knowledge of the infinite, incomprehensible God possible? Answer: God has revealed himself.**

But as soon as we take upon ourselves the task of speaking about God, the question at once arises: how can we? We are men, and he is the Lord our God. There does not appear to exist such a relationship and connection between him and us as would enable us to name him according to truth. There is between him and us a distance as between the infinite and the finite, as between eternity and time, as between being and becoming, as between the All-in-all and nothingness. However little we may know of God, even the slightest notion concerning him represents him as a being exalted infinitely high above the creature. Holy Scripture corroborates this as strongly as possible; yet it presents a doctrine concerning God which fully maintains his knowability. For example, the Bible never makes any attempt to prove the existence of God but assumes this; and it presupposes all along that man has an ineradicable idea of that existence, and that he has a certain knowledge of the being of God: an idea and a knowledge which are not the result of man's own study and research, but of the fact that God on his part has revealed himself both in an ordinary and in an extraordinary manner, has manifested himself in nature and in history, in prophecy and miracle. Accordingly, in Scripture the knowability of God is never represented as a doubtful matter. The fool may say in his heart, "There is no God"; he who opens his eyes receives from every side the testimony of his existence, of his eternal power and Godhead, Is. 40:26; Acts 14:17; Rom. 1:19, 20. The purpose of God's revelation according to Scripture is this very thing: that man shall learn to know God, and hence may have life eternal, John 17:3; 20:31.

**E. The content of this revelation is that there is one only God, personal yet highly exalted above nature, the Infinite, the Absolute, the All-powerful, and Omnipresent One.**

By virtue of this revelation it is first of all established that God is a person, a conscious and free-purposing being, not shut in by the narrow confines of this universe but highly exalted above nature. The pantheistic conception, which identifies God and the universe, is entirely foreign to Scripture. This personality of God appears everywhere so much in the foreground that the question may arise at times whether full justice is done to his unity, spirituality, and infinitude. Some Scripture passages seem to give the impression that God is a being greater and more powerful than man indeed, yet confined to certain places, and in his presence and activity always limited by geographical and political boundaries. Not only does Scripture ascribe human organs and qualities to God, as we shall see later on, but it also tells us that he walked in the garden, Gen. 3:8, that he descended at the building of the tower of Babel, Gen. 11:5, 7, that he appeared to Jacob at Bethel, Gen. 28:1 ff., that he gave his law on Sinai, Ex. 19 ff., that he dwelt in Zion between the cherubim, I Sam. 4:4; I Kings 8:10, 11. Hence, he is called the God of Abraham, Isaac, Jacob, the king of Zion, the God of the Hebrews, the God of Israel, etc.

These facts have led many later theologians to the conclusion that the oldest religion of Israel was polydaemonism; that Jehovah, of Kenitic derivation, was originally a stone- or mountain-deity, a god of fire or of thunder; that after the conquest of the land of Canaan he gradually became the god of the land and people of Israel; and that this henotheism later on developed into an absolute monotheism by means of the ethical view of his being, which we find in the prophets.

But this evolutionistic representation does not do justice to the facts of Scripture, and deems incompatible certain elements in the doctrine of God which according to the testimony of Scripture belong to that doctrine. A few remarks will suffice to make this clear. The creation of Adam and Eve, Gen. 2:7, 21, and also Jehovah's walking in the garden, Gen. 3:8, are indeed narrated in very simple and concrete fashion, but they are said to be the work of the same God who made the entire universe, Gen. 2:4b. The appearance of Jehovah at the building of the tower of Babel, Gen. 11:5, 7, is introduced with the explanation that he *descended,* that is to say: came down *from heaven,* which, therefore, is regarded as his real dwelling-place. In Gen. 28:11 ff., a passage which in modern books on the History of

Religion is regarded as a *locus classicus* (cf. also Joshua 24:26 ff.;
Judg. 6:20 ff.; I Sam. 6:14), not the stone but heaven is represented
as the dwelling-place of Jehovah; and in vss. 12 and 13 ff. (of Gen.
28) the Lord presents himself as the God of Abraham and Isaac,
promises to Jacob the land of Canaan and innumerable offspring,
and vouches to protect him whithersoever he goes: the idea of a stone-
deity is wholly absent. The stone is merely a memorial of the wonderful event that took place there. The localization of Jehovah on Sinai,
Ex. 3:5, 18; Judg. 5:4; I Kings 19:8, occurs not only in earlier books
but just as well in writings which according to modern criticism are
of later origin and definitely monotheistic, Deut. 33:2; Hab. 3:3; Ps.
68:8. On Sinai Jehovah *revealed* himself, but he does not *dwell* there
in the sense that he would be confined to it. On the contrary, he descends *from heaven* to the mount, Ex. 19:18, 20. In the same manner
Scripture speaks of a close relationship existing between Jehovah
and the land and people of Israel, but we find statements of that
character not only in the more ancient records, Gen. 4:4; Judg. 11:24;
I Sam. 26:19; II Sam. 15:8; II Kings 3:27; 5:17, but as well in those
which according to many critics had their origin in the monotheistic
period, Deut. 4:28; Am. 1:2; Is. 8:18; Jer. 2:7; 12:14; 16:13; Ezek.
10:18 ff.; 11:23; 43:1 ff.; Jon. 1:3; Ruth 1:15; cf. John 4:19. Jehovah
is the God of Israel by virtue of the covenant which he made with
Israel. Accordingly, in an unclean, heathen land he cannot be worshipped in the proper and prescribed manner, as the prophets testify,
Hos. 9:3-6; Am. 7:17, etc., but his presence and activity outside of the
land of Canaan is by no means denied. On the contrary, he accom-
panies Jacob whithersoever he goes, Gen. 28:15, is with Joseph in
Egypt, Gen. 39:2, in Zarephath uses Elijah as an instrument to raise
the widow's son, I Kings 17:10ff., is recognized by Naaman as the God
of all the earth, II Kings 5:17, etc.

Because of this close relationship existing between God and Israel in
the Old Testament dispensation, many texts do not express themselves,
as it were, in regard to the question whether any reality pertains to
the gods of the other nations. In the first commandment the Lord
himself says, "Thou shalt have no other gods before me," Ex. 20:3,
and elsewhere we read that the Lord is greater than all the gods, Ex.
15:11; 18:11. In Judg. 11:24 Jephtha expresses himself as if Chemosh,
the idol of Moab, had real existence, and in I Sam. 26:19 David *seems*
to say that banishment from the heritage of the Lord coincided with
the worship of other gods. But viewed in their context, these passages
exclude henotheism altogether. This is plain from the fact that next to
the first commandment, Ex. 20:3, we find the fourth commandment,

Ex. 20:10, which ascribes the creation of heaven and earth to the Lord, and in so doing confesses the clearest monotheism. Also according to the Jehovist, the Lord is the God of heaven and earth, the God of all mankind, Gen. 6:5-7; 8:21; 9:20; 18:1 ff., 18:25, etc. In Gen. 24:3, 7 he is called the God of heaven and earth, and according to Ex. 19:5 all the earth is his. In Judg. 11:24 just referred to, Jephtha merely accommodates himself to the person with whom he speaks, and in I Sam. 26:19 David is in complete harmony with the idea which we find expressed everywhere in the Old Testament, namely, that in that dispensation God assumes an extraordinary relation toward the land and people of Israel. In writings which even according to higher criticism are of more recent origin and which maintain a definite monotheism, the same expressions occur which we find in the older books: the Lord is a God of gods, and higher than all the gods, Deut. 3:24; 4:7; 10:17; 29:26; 32:12, 16; I Kings 8:23; II Chron. 28:23; Jer. 22:9; Ps. 95:3; 97:9, etc., cf. I Cor. 8:5 ff., 10:20.

Hence, the distinction between a lower and a higher deity in the O. T. — a distinction already favored by Gnosticism — does violence to the facts; and whenever it serves as a criterion for the determination of sources, it leads to hopeless confusion. Of course, there is a difference between the religion *of the people,* which often consisted in image-worship and idolatry, and the religion *which the Lord demanded of Israel* in his law and in the prophets; and in connection with this there is a difference between a history of the religion of Israel and a Theology of the O. T. (*Historia Revelationis*). Neither can it be denied that the various authors of the O. T. emphasize different aspects of the Divine Being. But the sources by no means justify the evolutionistic view according to which the religion of Israel developed from polydaemonism by way of henotheism into absolute monotheism. On the contrary, throughout the whole O. T. and with all its authors the doctrine of God comprises the following elements albeit that they occur in different books with varying degrees of emphasis:

(1) God is a personal being, self-existent, having the source of life in himself, self-conscious, and self-willing, not shut in by nature but exalted above nature, Creator of heaven and earth.

(2) This God can appear and reveal himself in definite places, at definite times, to definite persons: to the patriarchs, to Moses, to the prophets, in the garden, at the building of the tower of Babel, at Bethel, on Sinai, in Canaan, at Jerusalem, on Zion, etc.

(3) This revelation throughout the entire O. T., not only in the period before but also in the period of the prophets, is preparatory in character. It is given in signs, dreams and visions, by means of the

casting of the lot, Urim and Thummim, angels and the Mal'akh Yhwh; it usually occurs at definite moments, ceases and becomes a matter of the past. It is more or less external, stays outside of and above man, is a revelation *to* rather than *in* man, and indicates by means of this peculiarity that it serves to usher in and prepare for the highest and lasting revelation of God in the person of Christ and his continuous abode in the church.

(4) Accordingly, the O. T. does not give a *complete* revelation of God's being. It does indeed furnish a *true* and *reliable* knowledge of God, but not a knowledge adequate to his being. The stone at Bethel, the pillar of cloud and the pillar of fire in the desert, the thunder on Sinai, the cloud in the tabernacle, the ark of the covenant, etc., are so many signs and pledges of his presence, but they do not comprise him. Moses, unto whom the Lord spake as a man speaketh unto his friend, did not see God until he had passed by, Ex. 33:23. Man cannot see God and live, Ex. 33:20; Lev. 16:2. He is without form, Deut. 4:12, 15. He is unpicturable, Ex. 20:4. He dwells in darkness. Clouds and darkness are the indication of his presence, Ex. 20:21; Deut. 4:11; 5:22; I Kings 8:12; II Chron. 6:1.

(5) The same God who in his revelation limits himself, as it were, to definite places, occasions, and persons, is, nevertheless, exalted infinitely high above the whole realm of nature and every creature. Even in those parts of Scripture which stress his temporal and local manifestation the idea of his exaltation and omnipotence is not wanting: the Lord who walks in the garden is the Creator of heaven and earth. The God who appears to Jacob determines the future. Although the God of Israel dwells in the midst of His people in the house which Solomon builds for him, yet even the heaven of heavens cannot contain him, I Kings 8:27. He reveals himself in nature, and lives along with his people, as it were; but at the same time he is the Incomprehensible, Job 26:14; 36:26; 37:5, the Incomparable, Is. 40:18, 25; 46:5, the One who is exalted infinitely above time and space and every creature, Is. 40:12 ff.; 41:4; 44:6; 48:12, the *one* and *only* true God, Ex. 20:3, 11; Deut. 4:35, 39; 32:19; I Sam. 2:2; Is. 44:8. Although he, indeed, reveals himself in his names, no name expresses him adequately. He is without name. His name is wonderful, Gen. 32:29; Judg. 13:18; Prov. 30:4. The profundities of Deity are far too deep to be sounded by us, Job 11:7,8; Ecc. Sir. 43:34, 35. To summarize: throughout the entire O. T. these two elements are found side by side: (a) "God dwelleth with him that is of a contrite and humble spirit," and (b) he is at the same time "the High and Lofty One that inhabiteth eternity, whose name is Holy," Is. 57:15.

(6) In the N. T. we find the same combination of ideas: God dwells in light unapproachable; no man hath seen him nor can see him, John 1:18; 6:46; I Tim. 6:16. He is exalted above change, Jas. 1:17, time, Rev. 1:18; 22:13, space, Acts 17:27, 28, above all creatures, Acts 17:24. No one knoweth him but the Son and the Spirit, Matt. 11:27; I Cor. 2:11. But he has caused his fulness to dwell bodily in Christ, Col. 2:9. He dwells in the church as in his temple, I Cor. 3:16; and he makes his abode with him who loves Jesus and keeps his word, John 14:23. Employing the terminology of recent theological thought: God's personality and his absoluteness are found side by side in Scripture.

## II. Heathen Religions, Theology, and Philosophy Express Themselves in Regard to God's Incomprehensibility. By Some Our Ability to Know God Is Emphasized at the Expense of His Incomprehensibility; According to Many God Is not Only Incomprehensible but Unknowable: Agnosticism.

**A. Heathen religions generally regard God as knowable; prominent heathen philosophers, however, deny God's knowability; e.g., the Brahmans, Simonides, Protagoras, Carneades, Plato (to a certain degree), Plotinus, and the Gnostics.**

As soon as we leave the sphere of God's special revelation, we immediately notice that in all religious and philosophical systems the unity of God's absoluteness and personality is broken. Generally speaking, heathen people characterize themselves by the fact that knowing God they glorify him not as God, but change his glory for the likeness of an image of the creature. Against this attitude man's philosophical reflection usually begins to react, and the opposite extreme results: God's absolute character is emphasized, his personality denied. For the Brahmans God is the Unknowable, without names and attributes, known only by him who knoweth not. The Koran frequently resorts to grossly anthropomorphistic descriptions of Allah, but among the disciples of Mohammed many arose who interpreted these passages spiritually, and refused to ascribe any attributes to God. Greek philosophy also frequently taught a similar unknowability with respect to deity. According to a well-known story, the philosopher Simonides to whom the tyrant Hiero had put the question, "Who is God?" kept on asking for more and more time to frame an answer. According to Diogenes, the treatise of Protagoras *On the Gods* began as follows: "Concerning the gods I am not able to know whether they exist or whether they do not exist. For there are many things which prevent one from knowing; for example, the obscurity of the subject and the shortness of human life." Carneades of Cyrene not only subjected belief in the gods to a severe criticism but even denied the possibility of forming a conception of God. Plato rejected all anthropomorphic and anthropopathic descriptions of the Deity and declared in *Timaeus,* par. 28: "Now to discover the Maker and Father of this Universe were a task indeed; and having discovered him, to declare him to all men were a thing impossible." And similarly he declares in *The Republic* VI, 19 that the godhead or the idea of the good transcends not only whatever exists but "even essence itself." Philo connected this Platonic philosophy with the teaching of the O. T. and held that the name Jehovah was itself an expression of God's unknowableness. According to him God is not only exalted above the *imperfections* present in finite, changeable, dependent creatures, but also above their *perfections.* He is better than virtue, knowledge, beauty; purer than unity, more blessed than blessedness. In reality he is without attributes, "bare of quality," and without names. He cannot be described. He is unknowable as to his being. We can know *that* he is, not *what* he is. Existence is all that can be ascribed to him; the name Jehovah is the only one that indicates his being.

Plotinus is even more radical. Plato ascribed many attributes to God. Philo complemented his negative theology with a positive in which he defines God as a personal, perfect, omnipotent Being. But according to Plotinus nothing can be said of God which is not negative. God is an absolute unity, raised above all plurality. Accordingly, he cannot be defined in terms of thought, goodness, or being, for all these descriptive terms imply a certain plurality. God, as pure unity, is indeed the *cause* of thought, being, goodness, etc., but is himself distinct from any of these and transcends them all. He is unlimited, infinite, without form and so entirely different from every creature that even activity, life, thought, consciousness, and being cannot be ascribed to him. Our thought and language cannot attain to him. We cannot say what he *is,* but we can only say what he *is not.* Even the terms "the One" and "the Good," of which Plotinus makes much use, are not to be construed as descriptions of God's being, but only as indicative of his relation to creatures, and suggestive of his absolute causality.

Gnosticism makes the distance between God and the creature even greater. Between the highest God and the world it posits an absolute separation. A revelation not of God but of the eons only, was to be found in nature, in Israel, in Christianity. Hence, there could be no natural theology neither innate nor acquired, nor yet a revealed theology. For the creature the highest God was absolutely unknowable and unattainable. He was "unknown depth, ineffable, eternal silence."

**B. Christian theology made the idea of God's incomprehensibility and unknowability its point of departure: Barnabas, Justin Martyr, Irenaeus, Clement of Alexandria, Athanasius, Origen, Eusebius, Augustine, John of Damascus, and many others held agnostic or semi-agnostic views.**

This theory of God's incomprehensibility and of the unknowability of his being also became the point of departure and basic idea of Christian theology. God's revelation in creation and redemption fails to reveal him adequately. He cannot fully impart himself to creatures, inasmuch as in that case the latter must needs be God. Accordingly, adequate knowledge of God does not exist. There is no name that makes known unto us his being. No concept fully embraces him. No description does justice to him. That which is hidden behind the curtain of revelation is entirely unknowable. We cannot approach it by means of our thought, imagination, or language. In the letter of Barnabas the question is already asked, "If the Son of God had not come into the flesh, how then could men have beheld him, and have survived?" Justin Martyr calls God inexpressible, immovable, nameless. The words Father, God, Lord, are not real names "but appellations derived from his good deeds and functions." God cannot appear, cannot go about, cannot be seen, etc. Whenever these things are ascribed to God in the O. T., they refer to the Son, God's ambassador. Among many also Irenaeus presents the false and partly gnostic antithesis between the Father: hidden, invisible, unknowable; and the Son, who revealed him. With Clement of Alexandria God is "the One." Whenever we eliminate from our thought everything pertaining to the creature, that which remains is not what God *is* but what he *is not.* It is not proper to ascribe to him form, movement, place, number, attribute, name, etc. If, nevertheless, we call him the One, the Good, Father, Creator, Lord, etc., we do not thereby express his essential being but his power. "He is even exalted above unity." In a word, as says Athanasius, "He is exalted above all being and above human thought." With this agree Origen, Eusebius, and many other theologians of the first few centuries. A.D.

Augustine and John of Damascus also favor this representation. With Augustine the concept of being is basic to the definition of God. He is the self-existing One, even as his name Yhwh indicates. This is his real name, "the name that indicates what he is in himself," all other names are "names which indicate what he is for us," *Serm. 6 n. 4*; *Serm. 7 n. 7.* Hence when we say what he *is,* we are only stating what in distinction from all finite beings he *is not.* He is "ineffable." "It is easier for us to say what he is not than what he *is.*" He is not earth, sea, heaven, angel, etc. He is nothing of all that which pertains to the creature, what he is not is all that can be said, *Enarr. in Ps.* 85 *n.* 12; *De doctr. Chr. I, 6; De ord. II, 47.* "Our thought tries to reach a nature than which nothing better or more sublime exists," *De doctr. Chr. I, 7.* But we cannot think of him as he really is. He is far exalted above that which is corporeal, changeable, transient, *tract* 23 *in Ev. John n.* 9. "Who is there whose conception of God really corresponds to his being?" *quaest in Jos. VI, 29.* He is incomprehensible, and must needs be, "For if you comprehend him, he is not God," *Serm.* 117, *n.* 5. If we wish to say anything about him, we struggle with language, "for God is more truly thought than expressed and exists more truly than he is thought," *De trin, VII,* 4; *De doctr. Chr. I, 6; cf. De doctr. Chr. I, 6.* "Just as no intellect is able properly to conceive of God, so no definition is able properly to define or determine him," *De cogn. verae vitae, 7.* "God is known better when not known," *De ord. II,* 44. In like manner John of Damascus declares God to be "the ineffable and incomprehensible Divine Being." We speak about God in human fashion, and we know what God has revealed of himself; but God's being and the manner of his existence in everything we do not know. The fact that God exists is evident, but "what he is in his essence and nature is entirely incomprehensible and unknowable." When we say that God is unborn, immutable, without beginning, etc., we are only saying what he is *not*. To say what he *is*, is impossible. He is nothing of all that which exists, not because he does not exist, but because he is "exalted above all beings and above being itself." Whenever anything positive is stated in regard to God, this is not said with reference to his nature as such, but with reference to "the relations assumed by that nature."

**C. Pseudodionysius and Erigena are even more radical in their teaching on unknowability.**

Pseudodionysius (appealed to by John of Damascus) and Scotus Erigena held views concerning God's being which were even more agnostic. The Areopagite taught that there is no concept, expression, or word, by which God's being can be indicated. Accordingly, whenever we wish to designate God, we use metaphorical language. He is "supersubstantial infinity, supermental unity," etc. We cannot form a conception of that unitary, unknown being, transcendent above all being, above goodness, above every name and word and thought. We can only name him in accordance with his works, because he is the cause and principle of everything. Hence, on the one hand he is "without name," on the other hand he "has many names." But those positive names which we ascribe to God because of his works do not disclose his essential being to us, for they pertain to him in an entirely different manner than to creatures. Hence, negative theology is better than positive, for the former teaches us God's transcendence above the creature. Nevertheless, even negative theology fails to give us any knowledge of God's being, for in reality God is exalted above both "negation and affirmation."

Exactly the same trend of thought is met with in Erigena's works. God is exalted above everything that pertains to the creature, even above being and knowledge. We know only *that* he is, we do not know *what* he is. Whatever we affirm in regard to him is true of him in a figurative sense only; hence, in reality he is not what we declare him to be. Affirmative theology is figurative, metaphorical. It is excelled by negative theology. "For it is more correct to say that God is not that which is predicated concerning him than to say that he is. He is known better by him who does not know him, whose true ignorance is wisdom." Hence, the best way to supplement his predicates is to prefix "super" or "more than." He "transcends essence, truth, wisdom," etc. Indeed, so highly is he exalted above all creatures that the name "nothing" may justly be ascribed to him.

**D. Scholasticism was not quite as radical as were Pseudodionysius and Erigena; yet it affirmed the unknowability of God's essential being. This was the position of Anselm, Albertus Magnus, and Thomas Aquinas.**

Although scholasticism expressed itself with greater reservation on several points, and attached greater value to positive theology than was done by Pseudodionysius and by Erigena, nevertheless, it also was in thorough accord with the theory of God's unknowability. Anselm states that the names of God indicate his being "figuratively" only, that the relative attributes of his being cannot be predicated, and the absolute attributes can be predicated only in a quidditative, and not in a qualitative sense.

According to Albertus Magnus God is exalted above all being and thought. He cannot be reached by human thinking, "he can be touched but he cannot be grasped by our comprehension." There is no name which expresses his being. He is incomprehensible and inexpressible.

Thomas Aquinas discerns a three-fold knowledge of God: "immediate vision of God," "knowledge of God by faith," and "knowledge of God by means of natural reason." Man's knowledge by nature falls far short of "the vision of God," which can be obtained only by supernatural grace, and is reserved for heaven though it is very rarely granted on earth. However, even this vision never renders possible a *comprehension* of God. Here on earth knowledge of God is mediate. We cannot know God as he is in himself. We can only know him as "the first and most eminent cause of all things." We can arrive at the cause from the effects. The same is true with reference to "the knowledge of God by faith," derived from God's special revelation. We thereby know him more fully "according as more and more excellent of his effects are demonstrated to us." But even this knowledge does not give us any "knowledge of God's essence." There is no knowledge of God's being as such. We know only "his disposition to his creatures." There is no name which adequately expresses his being. His essence is highly exalted "above that which we know and say concerning God." Positive names may indicate God's being. They do so in a very imperfect manner, just as the creatures from which these names are derived imperfectly represent him. God is knowable only "inasfar as he is represented in the perfections of his creatures."

### E. Duns Scotus opposed Thomas Aquinas.

Due to the further development of scholasticism, however, this truth of God's incomprehensibility receded to the background. The doctrine of God received detailed elaboration. God's existence, names, being, persons, and attributes were so minutely analyzed that there was no room left for his incomprehensibility. The latter was made an attribute next to the others, and was given equally detailed and dialectic treatment. Over against Thomas Aquinas, Duns Scotus affirmed that there was indeed a quidditative, albeit imperfect, knowledge of God.

### F. The position of Nominalism, Mysticism, and Roman Catholic Theology with respect to God's knowability.

Against this view (of Duns Scotus) nominalism reacted. The latter adopted a more or less skeptical position. Durandus declared that there was no "abstract knowledge" of the Divine Being. And Occam stated, "Neither divine essence nor divine quiddity nor anything that pertains to the very nature of God nor anything that is in reality God can here be known by us in such a manner that nothing else than God presents itself to the reason."

Mysticism, having lost confidence in discursive reasoning, endeavored to obtain knowledge of God in a manner still different. Nic. Cusanus in his work *De docta ignorantia,* written toward the close of the Middle Ages, declared that by way of discursive reasoning one would never be able to arrive at truth; only *faith* could effect this result, faith interpreted in a mystical manner, as a new organ in man.

After the Reformation Roman Catholic theology returned to the position of scholasticism, and adopted the doctrine of the unknowability of God's being as advanced by Thomas Aquinas. At the Lat.

Council, convened by Pope Innocent III, the view: "God is ineffable" was sealed with the stamp of ecclesiastical authority.

### G. The Reformers taught God's incomprehensibility.

The theology of the Reformation did not bring about any change in this view. Luther in his work *De servo arbitrio* differentiated between "the hidden and the revealed God" between "God himself and the Word of God." In his later years he preferred to speak of God as revealed in Christ. He did not teach, however, that the fulness of God's being was revealed in Christ. On the contrary, there remains in God a dark, hidden depth, namely, "God as he is in his own nature and majesty, the absolute God." This hidden depth is "unknowable, incomprehensible, inaccessible."

Later Lutheran theologians did not differentiate so sharply between God's being and his revelation, but all teach that it is impossible to give an adequate definition of God or to ascribe an adequate name to him.

Reformed theologians were in agreement with this view. Their deep abhorrence of every kind of deification of the creature led them to differentiate sharply at every turn between that which pertains to God and that which pertains to the creature. More than any other theologians they emphasized the truth, "the finite cannot grasp the infinite." Said Zwingli, "Of ourselves we are as ignorant with respect to the nature of God as is the beetle with respect to the nature of man." Calvin deemed it vain speculation to attempt "an examination of God's *essence*." It is sufficient for us "to become acquainted with his character and to know what is conformable to his nature." Later theologians affirmed the unknowability of God's being in even stronger terms. As the finite cannot grasp the infinite, God's names serve not to make known to us God's being, but merely to indicate (in a measure and in a manner suited to our understanding) that concerning God which we need to know. The statements: "God cannot be defined; he has no name; the finite cannot grasp the infinite," are found in the works of all the theologians. They unanimously affirm that God is highly exalted above our comprehension, our imagination, and our language. E.g., Polanus states that the attributes ascribed to God in Scripture do not explain his nature and being. They rather show us, "what is not God's essence and character than what is God's essence and character. Whatever is said concerning God is not God, for God is ineffable. No divine attributes reveal sufficiently the essence and nature of God, for that is infinite. That which is finite, moreover, cannot adequately and fully reveal the infinite."

**H. Gradually, however, the significance of the doctrine of God's incomprehensibility was lost sight of also in those circles where the principles of the Reformation once flourished.**

But the theology of the Reformation soon lost sight of the significance of the doctrine of God's incomprehensibility. It was taught, indeed, but was made a doctrine by itself without further implications. The manner in which the doctrine of God was treated became wellnigh fixed. In other systems of religious thought the error was magnified. Socinianism did not concern itself with the question of God's knowability. It did not display the least interest in the knowledge of God's being. Knowing God was considered to mean knowing him as absolute Lord. Crell wrote a work *De Deo ejusque attributis,* wherein he proved the existence of God with various arguments, but refrained from discussing God's being, knowability, etc. Conr. Vorstius wrote *Tractatus de Deo s. de natura et attributis Dei,* 1610, in which he committed the same Socinian errors.

The Arminians also failed to see any need of discussing metaphysical questions, and warned against vain speculations. They urged simplicity. According to them knowledge of the will of God is the only knowledge strictly necessary. *"Worship* of God" was held to be far more necessary than *"knowledge* of God."

Rationalism considered itself to be certain of the existence of God, and attached little significance to the knowledge of his being. It seems that God's majesty and greatness was not recognized at all any more. Disregarding all metaphysical questions men pressed on to discover and to do the will of God. Eternal life, it was maintained, does not lie hidden in the knowledge of God, but in the doing of his will. Bretschneider considers entirely superfluous the question whether God can be defined.

**I. Definite Agnosticism was reasserted by Kant (Fichte and Schleiermacher) in Germany; by August Comte in France; and by H. Spencer (Hamilton and Mansel) in England; while Feuerbach and others assume an atheistic position.**

Philosophy, however, reaffirmed the truth of the unknowability of God's being, well-nigh forgotten by theology. Rationalism, with its proofs for the existence of God and its doctrine concerning God's attributes, imagined itself to be standing upon a firm, scientific foundation. But Kant, though still steeped in rationalism as evidenced by his doctrine of God, freedom, and immortality, brought about a great change in the presuppositions of this doctrine. Just as the forms of space and time are coexistent with "the sensible realm" and just as the categories are a priorily the concomitants of the mind, in the same manner reason also is based upon a priori, "synthetic principles and rules," especially this "principle" that it advances from "the conditioned to the unconditioned." Three transcendent ideas result: the soul, the world, God. But these three ideas cannot be objectively indicated, but are deduced subjectively from the nature of reason itself. We cannot discern the object of these ideas; hence, we cannot obtain any real knowledge of them. Judged scientifically, they are paralogisms, antinomies, ideals; our knowledge is limited to the sphere of experience. Hence, these ideas do not add anything to our knowledge; they merely regulate it. They systematize our concepts, and cause us thus to view everything *as if* God, the world, and the soul had real existence. Science can neither affirm nor deny the reality of these ideas. Accordingly, psychology, cosmology (teleology), and theology are no real sciences. The criticism of pure reason produces a negative result. Now it is true that "practical reason" forces us to accept the reality of these ideas. It is also true that Kant ascribes to God mind, will, and other attributes. Nevertheless, the being of God remains hidden. "Practical reason" recognizes, indeed, the objective reality of the three ideas, but further than that it cannot go. It does not add to the store of our knowledge. Speculative reasoning can use these ideas merely to regulate and purify our knowledge, and employs the idea of God to combat anthropomorphism, the source of superstition and fanaticism. Whenever mind and will are ascribed to God, this is "a practical knowledge of God," never a speculative knowledge. Abstracting anthropomorphism, only the term (God) is left. The idea of God does not pertain to a metaphysics, which does not exist, but to ethics.

Fichte at first agreed with Kant. In his *Versuch einer Kritik aller Offenbarung* he advances the postulates of reason as the foundation for belief in God, and ascribes to God definite attributes; as, holiness, blessedness, omnipotence, righteousness, omniscience, and eternity. But, according to Fichte, all this does not in itself give us a definite idea of God, neither a knowledge of his being "as such." Indeed, if it did, this would not benefit but rather injure pure morality. Religion always represents God anthropomorphically, as existing in space and time, even corporeally. As long as this representation does not conflict with morality and is not considered to have objective validity, it will do no harm. It should be taken as "condescension to our subjective need. Only such a revelation can be of divine origin, which presents the concept of an anthropomorphized God not as objectively but merely as subjectively valid."

Schleiermacher, though in many respects disagreeing with Kant and Fichte and adhering more closely to the views of Spinoza, agreed with them in the doctrine of God's unknowability. The idea of the unity of existence and thought, of reality and ideality (i.e., the idea of God), is the presupposition of all our knowledge, the foundation of our thought; but this idea itself cannot be comprehended by thought, and remains behind the curtain. As soon as we try to bring the Absolute closer to our level, we limit him in our thought, and we speak in metaphors. In a word, the Absolute is inaccessible to our knowledge. In his *Glaubenslehre* Schleiermacher advanced the same ideas in a less developed and more religious manner. God is the "Whence" of our "existence"; and as an absolute causality he cannot be the object of our intellectual comprehension, but is merely the content of our sense of absolute dependence.

More and more did the doctrine of God's unknowability afterward penetrate modern thought. Hegel, it is true, stood on different ground. Granting that the usual representation of God was inadequate and suited to the masses only, he was nevertheless convinced that philosophy was able to rid this idea of its sensuous form and to raise it to an adequate concept. According to his view, reason raises itself by degrees to absolute knowledge, sees truth face to face, and recognizes in reason, thought, the idea, truth's very essence. Philosophy, pure science, still more definitely *logic,* is the description of God "as to his essence." It comprehends the Absolute in the only proper and adequate form, as thought in the form of concepts. In the spirit of Hegel, many—Strausz, Biedermann, Ed. von Hartmann, Scholten and others—endeavored by purification and deepening of concepts to approach transcendent reality more and more closely.

But Hegel's philosophy caused others to arrive at a different conclusion. They affirmed that it would be entirely impossible to abandon all concrete representation in a description of God. Accordingly, they adopted atheism. Reasoning along this line Feuerbach stated that the personal God was nothing but the being of man, and theology nothing but anthropology. Whatever is predicated of God has been borrowed from the sphere of man, not only personality but all the attributes. Religion is merely a deification of man. Man can never transcend his own being. Accordingly, God always remains a physical human being, not only in Christian dogmatics but in philosophy as well. Many agreed with Feuerbach. They discarded not only every anthropomorphic representation of God but with it the idea of God itself.

To others, however, this atheism appeared too radical. Considering the limitations of man's preceptive faculty, which is always confined to that which is finite, these concluded that we should restrict ourselves to that which is given by observation (positivism), should abstain from expressing ourselves in regard to the supersensuous sphere (abstentionism), and with reference to the latter should confess our absolute ignorance (agnosticism). In France Auguste Comte limited the task of science to the systematic examination and explanation of phenomena, and in keeping herewith excluded theology from the domain of sciences. In England Herbert Spencer with all kinds of arguments combated the doctrine of God's knowability. And Germany, satiated with Hegel's panlogism, returned to Kant's critical philosophy. Thus, agnosticism in the latter half of the nineteenth century began to reign supreme. There was a general distrust of all metaphysics, and an aversion to speculation. Only such facts were considered established as pertained to the realm of exact sciences. Agnosticism overawed theology to such an extent that at present the latter hardly dares to make mention of any knowledge of God. It endeavors to avoid all metaphysics (though some reaction may be observed of late). It would restrict itself to that which pertains to practical religion. It is ashamed of its own name, and has allowed itself to be changed to a science of religion. For, although agnosticism in reality destroys theology, the latter was by many revived in another form. Kant salvaged by practical reason what he threw overboard by pure reason. Spencer allowed a religious adoration of the Unknowable. Even before him Sir William Hamilton and Dr. Harry Longueville Mansel had maintained that inasmuch as our thinking is ever limited by space, time, distinction, antithesis, etc., it can never penetrate to the Absolute, albeit that on religious grounds the idea of God as a personal Being must be affirmed. The Neokantians in Germany arrived at a similar dualism. At best, logical reflection may give us the idea of the Absolute. For religion this is not sufficient. Here we need a God like unto us, a person, a Father, who cares for his children. It is true that this religious representation is ever subject to the criticism of reason. It is not satisfactory, but nothing better can be obtained. In like manner others resort to humanism, moral idealism, spiritism, theosophy, Buddhism, etc., in order to receive compensation for what they have lost in Christian theology.

### III. Agnosticism Is Based on the Following Arguments:

(A) **The nature of all human knowledge is relative: Man is the measure of all things.**

(B) **The only objects of human knowledge are the facts of human experience, the phenomena. Ideas of God, world, soul are transcendent, and can never be objects of intellectual knowledge.**

(C) **God, being absolute, cannot be personal, neither knowable.**

(D) **Knowledge of the absolute is impossible because it is a contradiction in terms, for knowledge implies relation; absolute — absence of relation.**

**A. The nature of all human knowledge is relative: man is the measure of all things.**

Agnosticism is able to advance weighty arguments in support of its position. In the first place it can make use of the argument advanced formerly by the sophists and skeptics, against the possibility of all knowledge; namely, that all human knowledge is subjective and relative. Nothing in the universe stands by itself. Subject and object are interdependent. Things and their qualities obtain reality as soon as they assume a relation to someone's perception. A thing really becomes something by means of its relation to the senses. Accordingly, we can never say what a thing is in its essence, independent of our perception. We can only say that at a given moment something appears so or so to us. "Man is the measure of all things."

This argument is indeed of great significance, but proves too much. If it were valid, it would render impossible not only the knowledge of *God* but *all* knowledge, also that concerning man and the universe. Furthermore, whereas this idealism has been treated before, we can dismiss it here.

**B. The only objects of human knowledge are the facts of human experience, the phenomena. Ideas of God, world, soul are transcendent, and can never be objects of intellectual knowledge.**

But agnosticism has various arguments which are especially advanced against the doctrine of *God's* knowability. Philosophy and theology were indeed at all times convinced of the *inadequate character* of our knowledge of God, as we have abundantly shown. Negative predicates merely declare what God is *not,* and positive attributes pertain to him in a manner entirely different from that in which they pertain to the creature. The limited, finite, and anthropomorphic character of our knowledge of God was acknowledged by all. But in recent times the inadequate character of our knowledge of God was argued in a different and more radical manner. Subjectively, the limitations of man's cognitive faculty were pointed out; and objectively, the self-contradiction pertaining to every idea of God was indicated. The former was done by Kant. The latter by Fichte. Kant examined man's perceptive faculty and reached the conclusion that the forms of perception and the categories of the mind were inherent in the structure of the mind itself, had validity in the realm of phenomena, but were unable to give us any knowledge of the noumena. The transcendent ideas of God, world, and soul regulate our actions, and a moral person must needs conduct himself as if an objective reality attached to these three ideas; but this cannot be proved.

**C. God, being absolute, cannot be personal, neither knowable.**

Fichte added to this argument the further one to the effect that the ideas of absoluteness and personality can never be harmonized with each other. Spinoza already remarked that every qualification was a negation, that a thing would become finite and limited in the measure in which it was qualified and represented as concrete. By being qualified it ceases to be what other things are: a white substance cannot at the same time be red or black. Hence, God cannot be a definite something next to and distinct from creatures, but must be the substance of all creatures, the only, infinite existence, so that whatever *is* exists in him. This philosophical premise was by Fichte applied to the idea of personality. According to him personality and consciousness are things which we find in ourselves, and which cannot be thought of as existing without limitation and finiteness. As soon as we apply them to God we make him a finite, limited, human being. The only thing really essential in religion is the moral world-order. We have need of nothing else. A distinct and personal God is unnecessary for religion and cannot be proved, is even impossible and self-contradictory. Whoever desires such a God is still in the power of eudaemonism. In Fichte's works this reasoning is met with at every turn.

In essence this antithesis between absolute and personal was ever felt by Christian theology, and found expression in the terms *negative* and *positive, apophatic* and *cataphatic* theology. However much the arguments against the doctrine of God's knowability may differ as to form, in reality they are always the same and amount to these: man is limited by physical perception, and always derives the material for his thinking from the visible world. He does not perceive that which is spiritual, and he cannot rise to the world of spiritual things inasmuch as he is ever limited by space and time. His thinking also is material, finite, and limited. As the eagle is confined to the air (Hamilton) and a fish to the pond (Lange), in the same manner our thinking ever moves in the sphere of that which is finite.

**D. Knowledge of the Absolute is impossible because it is a contradiction in terms, for knowledge implies relation, absolute implies absence of relation.**

Moreover, thought by virtue of its very nature presupposes a distinction between subject and object; and whereas these are opposed to each other and limit each other, neither of them can be absolute. Hence, Hamilton said, "To think is to condition." Mansel, similarly, "Distinction is necessarily limitation." Accordingly, knowledge of the Absolute is a contradiction in terms. It would mean that one has knowledge of something that is absolute, i.e., without relation, though it is at the same time related by virtue of the fact that it is known. The nature of thought being as described, it follows that if, nevertheless, we claim that we have an idea or a certain knowledge of God, we invariably either lower the Absolute to the level of our finite existence, and make of God a personal, limited human being; or in our thinking we strive to transcend the limitations of space and time. We eliminate from our idea of God every similarity to the creature, and as a result we have left an empty, abstract idea, entirely valueless for religion. Even this empty, abstract idea will finally fade away, and thought itself will reduce the Absolute to zero. Absoluteness and personality, infinity and causality, immutability and communicability, absolute transcendence above and similarity to the creature are mutually incompatible. We are confronted with an irreconcilable antinomy. It seems as if we are forced to choose between out-and-out realism and vain idealism; between God viewed as a super-man and a cold abstraction which freezes and kills the religion of the heart.

## IV. Criticism of Agnosticism: The Doctrine of God's Unknowability Is Partly True, Partly False.

**A. The truth contained in Agnosticism: we cannot comprehend God.**

To a large extent we can agree with this doctrine of God's unknowability. Both Scripture and the church maintain with emphasis the unsearchable majesty and sovereign glory of God. There is no knowledge of God as he is in himself. We are men. He is the Lord, our God. No name fully expresses his being; no definition describes him. He is exalted infinitely high above our conception, thought, and language. He cannot be compared to any creature. All the nations are accounted by him as less than nothing and vanity. "God has no name. He cannot be defined." He can be apprehended; he cannot be comprehended. There is a "knowledge"; there is no "comprehension" of God. Thus both Scripture and Christian theology affirm throughout. And whenever superficial rationalism asserted the possibility of an adequate knowledge of God, Christian theology has always combated this view with all its power. According to Socrates, Eunomius, a disciple of Arius, declared that his knowledge of God was equal to that of himself. According to him God's essential being existed in his "ingenerate nature," the comprehension of which gave Eunomius (as he thought) a clear and adequate idea of the being of God. God's knowledge of himself was not any greater, and man's knowledge of God was not any less adequate than what was expressed by this attribute. Spinoza later on declared that his idea of God was just as clear as his idea of a triangle, although he did not mean to declare thereby that he knew God thoroughly. And in the nineteenth century Hegel taught that in conceptual philosophy the Absolute was raised to perfect self-consciousness and was known completely and adequately by the philosopher, and that our consciousness of God is nothing but God's self-consciousness. God has existence inasfar as he is known by us; i.e., inasfar as he knows himself in us. The Christian church combated and refuted this rationalism with all its power. A deep religious principle is involved, to which Augustine gave expression in the following words: "We are speaking of God. Is it any wonder that you do not comprehend? For if you comprehend him, he cannot be God. Let it be a pious confession of great ignorance rather than a rash profession of knowledge. To have a very slight knowledge of God is a great blessing. To comprehend him is altogether impossible." Because God is the Infinite, the Incomprehensible, for that very reason he is the sole object of all our love.

B. **The errors of agnosticism. Refutation of the arguments stated under III.** Kant says that our knowledge is confined to the realm of human experience, and concludes from this that we cannot know God intellectually. But if God has revealed himself, he thereby has entered the sphere of human experience. Hence, we can know him. If God cannot be known intellectually, he cannot be felt either. Feeling is as limited as intellectual knowledge. If pure reason cannot reach him, then neither can practical reason. Hamilton and Mansel, etc., wrongly define absolute as meaning: existing out of all relation, extended infinitely in all directions. If, because of God's absolute character, he is the Unknowable (Spencer, etc.), then it is wrong and illogical to ascribe attributes to him or even to posit his existence. Conclusion of the whole matter: By virtue of the mystery of revelation, we can have a relative knowledge of God though we can never comprehend him.

Though, therefore, Scripture and the church accepted the premises of agnosticism, and were even more thoroughly convinced of the incomparable greatness of God and of man's insignificance and limitations than were Kant and Spencer, they arrived at a different conclusion, a conclusion stated by Hilary in these words: "Perfect knowledge is so to know God that he is not viewed as unknown but that you know him as indescribable." The knowledge that we have of God is a very peculiar knowledge. It may be called *positive* inasmuch as it recognizes a being infinite and distinct from all creatures. On the other hand, it is *negative* because we cannot predicate anything concerning God in the manner in which we think of it as present in the creature. And it is an *analogical* knowledge because it is a knowledge of a being, unknowable in himself; nevertheless, able to reveal himself to creatures.

Now it is true that something of an antinomy is involved in the fact which we have just stated, or rather: agnosticism suffers from a confusion of concepts, and sees an irreconcilable contradiction in what is considered by Christian theology a glorious mystery. Entirely unintelligible to us is the fact that, and the manner in which, God, in a measure, reveals himself in the creature, eternity in time, immensity in space, infinity in finiteness, immutability in change, being in becoming, etc. This mystery cannot be comprehended. It can only be gratefully accepted. But mystery and self-contradiction are not synonymous. Pantheistic philosophy has made a self-contradiction of a mystery. When it identifies the absolute with the undefined, and calls every definition a limitation and a negation, it makes itself guilty of confusing concepts. There is a great difference between infinite and endless, between omnipotent and the sum of all power, between eternity and the sum of all moments of time, etc. In the same manner there is a great difference between the absolute and the undefined, the unbounded and the boundless. Pantheism begins by putting its own concept of God into these words. Having done this, it finds it easy to accuse theism of being out of harmony therewith. To say that God is the Infinite, who, nevertheless, is able to reveal and actually has revealed himself in finite creatures, is indeed to acknowledge the existence of an incomprehensible mystery, the miracle of creation, but does not amount to a palpable absurdity. We can maintain both God's infinitude and the existence of finite beings as long as we believe that God is the ground of the existence of these beings. In like manner, our knowledge is not a limitation of God, for it is grounded in him, is able to exist only through him, and has for its object and content the Infinite God. If, moreover, absoluteness precludes every limitation, and if every definition is a negation, it is not only wrong to ascribe *personality* to God, but equally wrong to call him the Absolute, Unity, Goodness, Essential Being, Substance, etc. Pantheism supposes that after it has removed from its idea of

God the contradictory elements of personality and self-consciousness, it has finished its task. And the theistic philosophers of the first half of the nineteenth century (e.g., J. H. Fichte, Sarus, Steffens, Weisse, Ulrici, etc.), by way of reaction attached too great significance to this idea of personality, and supposed that the idea of absolute personality amounted to an adequate description of the being of God. Many pertinent remarks have been made in opposition to pantheism to prove that personality is not inconsistent with the absolute being of God. As long as *absolute* is not considered to mean *boundless,* extended infinitely in all directions, it is difficult to see how personality would ever be in conflict with it. Rightly defined, all it implies is that God's self-consciousness is equally rich and deep, equally infinite as is his being. To be sure, in the case of human individuals, personality may *assert* itself as soon as it is contrasted with a non-ego. Yet it does not *originate* in this non-ego, but has its own root and contents in human nature itself. In the case of God personality is, and therefore can be, the eternal comprehension of himself within himself, the infinite self-knowledge and self-determination, and therefore it is not dependent on a non-ego.

Nevertheless, the remark of Johann Gottlieb Fichte: that personality is an idea borrowed from the human realm and when applied to God can never be fully adequate, is correct. The idea of personality when applied to God is indeed inadequate, and in principle not any better than all the other anthropomorphisms which we employ with reference to God. The Christian church and Christian theology have never used this term to designate the *being* of God, and in connection with the three modes of subsistence in that being, they have employed this word very hesitantly for lack of a better term. But at the same time it becomes apparent that pantheism has not gained its objective by having pointed out the incongruity of this concept. The antithesis between absoluteness and personality is in reality identical with that between positive and negative theology. Even if the word "personality" is wrong, nothing is gained thereby. The identical question returns again and again. If every definition is a negation, God may not be called Unity, the Existing One, or the Absolute either. In that case it is even wrong to think or speak of God at all. If we as human individuals may not speak of God in a human, analogical manner, we must needs be silent altogether. For, it certainly is impossible for us to think and speak of God in a divine manner. Now, this would mean the end of all religion. For, if God cannot be *known,* he cannot be *felt* or *experienced* either. Feeling is just as finite as is mind. Both limit and anthropomorphize God in the same manner. There is then no possibility of an objective divine revelation to creatures, neither are we then at all able by means of any organ whatsoever to apprehend God subjectively. All religion thus becomes sacrilege, and all theology blasphemy.

Herewith the question of God's knowability is reduced to the question whether God has been willing to reveal himself and has actually revealed himself to creatures. For, we fully agree with Kant that our knowledge is confined to the realm of experience. If God has not revealed himself, there can be no knowledge of him. But if he has revealed himself, there is something, however insignificant, which can be the object of our perception and therefore can lead to knowledge. Hence, it has become evident that the denial of God's knowability is identical with the repudiation of God's revelation to his creatures. Agnosticism is reduced to the error of ancient Gnosticism. God is "the unspeakable depth."

There is then no relation between him and his creatures. The entire universe is in the most absolute sense of the word "without God." No trace of God can be found anywhere. The world becomes the product of a lower deity: a demiurge. It becomes the product of chance. Man was not created in the image of God. He is but a product of nature and is without God in the world. Nothing is left either of natural or of supernatural theology and religion. God and the universe are conceived of as absolutely separate. Even more: agnosticism cannot escape the conclusion that God *cannot* reveal himself. It confines God to the sphere of his own being. It makes of him an unknown, invisible power, without consciousness and will, unable in any way to communicate himself, eternal "silence." Moreover, the universe is elevated to the position of a power next to and opposed to God—as is also done by Manichaeism—a power incapable of affording entrance to God in any way, a power completely unable to radiate any of the glory of God. Agnosticism in reality reduces itself to atheism. It is atheism with a nineteenth century name and form. Nevertheless, agnosticism usually refuses to admit this logical conclusion. It maintains indeed *the existence* of the Unknowable. But as soon as it adopts this position, it becomes guilty of self-contradiction. Augustine already remarked that the supposition that we know nothing of God presupposes an extended knowledge of him and hence implies a "verbal conflict." "For, whenever we call God ineffable we at the same time say something, say indeed very much concerning him, thus again denying that he is ineffable. For if even before we can know what *is* the nature of God, we already are able to know what *is not* his nature, this is not a small amount of knowledge." To know what God *is not* means to have an extensive and positive knowledge. It amounts to a considerable beginning of the knowledge of God. To say that he is nothing of all that which pertains to the creature is indeed saying very much. This applies directly to the agnostics. Spencer declares that our thinking requires us to accept the existence of an absolute being as ground of the universe though because of our finiteness and limitedness we cannot form an idea of that being. But if we are *so* finite and *so* limited, how do we ever arrive at the formation of an idea of such an absolute being? How dare we ever posit the existence of the Absolute? Conversely, if it be true that we must needs accept the existence of that being, then why would knowledge of that being be at all impossible? Every one will have to admit that there is indeed a great difference between having an absolute knowledge and having merely a relative knowledge concerning an absolute being. For finite man the former remains ever impossible. If the opinion of Eunomius were correct: that we either have an adequate knowledge of God or otherwise have no knowledge of him whatsoever, knowledge of finite things would also be impossible for man. God's revelation is the only source of our knowledge concerning him. Hence, we know him only to the degree in which finite man can apprehend him. Therefore, knowledge of God can be real and pure, but is always very relative, and does not include but excludes comprehension. Over against Eunomius, Basilius correctly declared, "The knowledge of God's essence consists in the discernment of his incomprehensibility." But this discernment is in itself a very extensive knowledge. Hence, in the final analysis, no agnostic is willing to admit a state of uncertainty. Thus, though Spencer declares again and again that we do not know the Absolute, yet he has an idea of it, proves its existence, and ascribes all kinds of attributes to it. He asserts that it is not a negative but a positive idea; that it is the cause of all things; that it is a power especially analogous to the will in man; that it is infinite, eternal, omnipresent, etc. Now this, to be sure, is no agnosticism, but a very definite knowledge of God, a well-defined idea of God. Agnosticism, untenable in itself, afraid of atheism, in the end serves to justify a pantheistic idea of God.

# GOD'S KNOWABILITY

# CHAPTER II

# God's Knowability

**I. Innate Knowledge of God. Knowledge of God Is Possible Because of God's Revelation. Due to this Revelation There Is a Necessary and Universal Knowledge of God, Supposed By Many to Have Been Created in Man (Doctrine of Innate Ideas). There Are no Innate Ideas in the Sense of Conscious Ideas of God Given at Birth. By "Innate Idea" Christian Theology Understands "That Aptitude in Man Which Naturally and Necessarily Issues in Some Knowledge of God."**

**A. Knowledge of God is possible because of God's revelation. God cannot and does not reveal himself fully to man, neither is man able to grasp the full content of God's revelation.**

Religion and the knowledge of God can have their origin only in revelation. If God does not reveal himself in his creatures, knowledge of him is evidently unattainable. But if it be true that he displays his virtues to creatures, God's knowability can no longer be disputed. Of course, the character and the degree of that knowledge is not hereby given. All those who teach God's knowability are willing to admit that this knowledge is of a peculiar and very limited character. For, though God to a certain extent becomes manifest in the creature, there remains in him an infinite fulness of power and of life which does not become manifest. His knowledge and power are not exhausted in the universe, neither are they effused thereon to their full extent. It is even impossible for God fully to reveal himself to and in his creatures, for the finite does not grasp the infinite. No one knoweth the Father save the Son, Matt. 11: 27; cf. Deut. 29:29. Moreover, that which God reveals of himself in and through creatures is so rich and so deep that it can never be fully known by any human individual. In many respects we do not even understand the universe of created beings, which again and again confronts us with enigmas and mysteries. How then should we be able to understand the revelation of *God* in all its riches and depth? But by admitting all this we by no means deny God's knowability. God's incomprehensibility, instead of abrogating his knowability, presupposes and affirms the same. The unsearchable riches of the Divine Being constitutes a necessary and important element of our knowledge of God. The fact remains that God is knowable to us in that manner and in that degree in which he reveals himself to us in creation.

**B. It is difficult to deny the fact of God's revelation. Scripture affirms it. Moreover due to the fact that this revelation is so clear and that religion is so deeply rooted in man's heart, there is no atheistic world, and there are no atheistic tribes. This fact is admitted by the pantheists when they declare that religion is necessary for the masses. There are practical and relative atheists.**

The fact that God has revealed himself in the universe is indisputable. Scripture does not leave us in doubt regarding this matter. It does not erect an altar to an unknown God, but sets forth the God that made the world, Acts 17:23, 24; whose power and divinity are perceived by the human mind through the things that are made, Rom. 1:19, 20; who created man in his image, Gen. 1:27; as his offspring, living and moving in him, Acts 17:28; who spoke to him in the prophets and apostles, especially in the Son, Heb. 1:1; and who now continuously reveals himself to and in him by means of his word and Spirit, Matt. 16:17; John 14:23; etc. According to Scripture, the entire universe is a creation and therefore a revelation of God. Nothing is atheistic in the absolute sense of the term. And this testimony of Scripture is verified on every side. There is no atheistic world; there are no atheistic peoples, neither are there atheistic human individuals. We cannot think of the world as existing "without God," as in that case it would not be a work of God but of an "anti-god." Now dualism, again and again recurrent in religion and philosophy, has indeed seen a demonic principle in matter, but with reference to the universe it has always acknowledged a combination of matter and idea, a struggle of light and darkness. No one can absolutely and logically deny God's knowability and hence his revelation in the universe. The very existence of agnosticism proves this point. Skepticism also is unable to maintain itself except with the help of that which it denies.

Moreover, whereas the world cannot be thought of as existing "without God," there are no atheistic and irreligious peoples, though this fact has been contradicted by Socinus, Locke, and more recently by Büchner, Darwin, and others. But their opinion has been sufficiently refuted and is now generally abandoned. Cicero's well-known statement, "There is no people so barbarous that it does not believe in the gods," has been confirmed throughout the ages. Now this fact is of great importance. That in which all men by virtue of their very nature agree cannot be false. "For, time destroys erroneous opinions, but it establishes the verdicts of nature."

Finally, even the existence of atheistic *individuals* must be denied. There is indeed much difference of opinion in regard to the *being* of God; there is little difference in regard to his *existence.* Of course, there is a *practical* atheism, a life without God in the world, Ps. 14: 1; 53: 2; Eph. 2:12. But conscious theoretical atheism in the absolute sense of the word is very rare, to say the least.

Now the word "atheism" is often used in a relative sense, not as a denial of any kind of the Deity, but as the denial of a very specific Deity. In that sense the Greeks charged Socrates with atheism. Cicero counted Protagoras and Prodicus among the atheists because they denied the existence of the national gods. Therefore also the Christians were often called atheists by the heathen. The former, in their turn, applied the name to all those who denied the God of revelation. Roman Catholics have counted Luther, Melanchton, and Calvin among the atheists. Voetius used the word in a very general sense, and applied it also to Descartes. In more recent times J. G. Fichte was openly charged with atheism because he identified the moral world-order with God. And even now the name "atheist" is applied to those who recognize no other power than matter; as, Feuerbach, Strausz, Büchner, Haeckel, Czolbe, Dühring. And indeed, when materialists recognize nothing but matter and evolution of matter, they *are* atheists, and are usually proud of the name.

But this is hardly ever the case. Taken in the absolute sense, as a denial of an absolute power, atheism is well-nigh unthinkable. In reality, all recognize a power which they worship as God. The reverence which Strausz requires for his material universe is equal to that which the believer asks for his God. Atheism and materialism are again and again reduced to pantheism, for the very obvious reason that man must acknowledge a highest power. Denying the true God, he at the same time fashions a false God. Man cannot do without a God because religion is too deeply rooted in his nature and God's revelation is too abundantly clear. Even when in some periods of history religious indifferentism and skepticism increase both in intensity and extensiveness, as in the age of Pericles, of emperor Augustus, of the Renaissance, and in our own age, religion reasserts itself in the end. Man would rather cling to the grossest kind of superstition than persist in cold and naked unbelief. But we can go a step farther: not only is it a fact that atheism in the absolute sense hardly ever occurs; but even as a denial of a *personal* God, who can claim our worship, it is rare. Naturalism, hylozoism, and pantheism, to be sure, occur again and again. But they are philosophical rather than religious tendencies. They are not dogmatical but critical; and they usually last but a short time and are limited to a definite group. A nation, a society, a church, or a congregation of this kind of naturalists and pantheists is inconceivable. Pantheists themselves admit this when they say that the common man must needs picture the objects of his religion, and that it is only the philosopher who can attain to the pure, abstract concept. Accordingly, belief in a personal God is both natural and normal, spontaneous and universal; but atheism, even taken in the sense of the denial of the existence of a personal God, is an exception. It is philosophy, not religion. There is truth in the cutting remark of Schopenhauer: "An *impersonal God* is no God at all but only a misused term, an erroneous idea, a contradiction in the adjective, a shibboleth for professors of philosophy, who, after they have had to give up the *idea,* endeavor to sneak through with a mere *term."* It requires a certain effort not to believe in a personal God: "No one disbelieves the existence of God except he to whom God's existence is not suitable." There are no atheists who are so thoroughly convinced of their unbelief that they would die the martyr's death in its defence. As atheism is unnatural and abnormal, not based upon intuition but upon protracted argumentation and fallible reasoning, it is never certain of its cause. The arguments for the existence of a personal God may be weak, they are stronger than those advanced for the denial. It is even impossible to prove that there is no God. To do so one would needs have to be omniscient and omnipresent; i.e., one would himself have to be God!

**C. This natural, universal, and necessary character of the knowledge of God has given rise to the opinion that it is created in man, that man is born with this knowledge: doctrine of innate ideas.**

This natural, universal, and necessary character of religion and the knowledge of God early led to the opinion that it was created in man by nature, that it was innate. It is a fact which cannot be denied that all men from their very earliest youth are conscious of a psychical, spiritual, invisible world as well as of a physical world. Indeed, though notions of true and false, good and evil, right and wrong, beautiful and ugly do not represent measurable and ponderable magnitudes, which can be perceived by means of the five senses, nevertheless, they constitute a reality which is even more firmly fixed in our consciousness than the reality of matter and force. Gravity, warmth, and electricity may be the only forces with which the materialist wishes to figure; faith, hope, and love are different realities, are powers which have governed mankind and have kept it from sinking away into utter bestiality. Augustine was correct when he stated that the existence of spiritual things is much better established than that of the physical universe: "Nothing could be more absurd than to say that the objects seen by our eyes have being, while those which we discern with our intellect do not; since only a fool would doubt the fact that the intellect has an incomparably higher rank than our eyes." The truths of mathematics and logic, the principles of ethics, jurisprudence, and religion, are universally fixed and established. Their natural, universal, and necessary character cannot be denied by anyone. As innate ideas they seem to be congenital and included in man's nature.

> **D. The views held by distinguished philosophers in regard to innate ideas: Plato does not need this doctrine. Aristotle and the Stoics approach it. Cicero introduces it. Descartes advocated it, and is the first to use the term "innate idea." Leibnitz further develops it. Kant greatly modifies it. In the philosophy of Fichte and Hegel it becomes a fundamental principle.**

The doctrine of innate ideas is rooted in Greek philosophy. The problem in regard to the possibility of the acquirement of knowledge was held to be very difficult of solution. Two possibilities presented themselves: either, we know something and therefore cannot learn it any more; or, we do not know it, but then the question arises: how is it that we strive to learn it? Plato solved this problem by means of his doctrine of reminiscences: before the soul was joined to the body it had beheld the ideas in all their beauty, and in its memory it had deeply stored away the imprints of these ideas. He proved this especially with reference to the system of mathematics, which our mind is able to construct entirely by itself, unaided by observation; and he furthermore maintained that all acquisition of knowledge is based upon the assumption of the preëxistence of the soul.

Aristotle considered sense-perception to be indeed the road to knowledge. Nevertheless, he maintained that certain very general principles were inherent in the very constitution of reason, axioms upon which all arguments are based, and which are acknowledged by all. The Stoics spoke of "common, natural ideas," and "ingrafted preconceptions," i.e., concepts which everyone derives from sensation due to the very nature of our thought-processes. None of the philosophers which we have so far discussed advanced the view of innate ideas in the strictest sense. Plato does not restrict the memory to a few innate ideas but views the entire realm of knowledge as its object; and Aristotle and others speak indeed of general principles but expressly teach that these are not to be conceived of as ideas given at birth but as obtained by means of sensation and reflection; in such a manner, however, that every normal human individual necessarily arrives at them.

Strictly speaking, Cicero was the first to broach the doctrine of innate ideas. He speaks of "notions impressed upon the mind, ingrafted or innate thoughts," and accepts a knowledge of various truths which precedes all experience and investigation. According to him there are "innate seeds of the virtues, faint notions of the most important things," which nature planted in the soul "apart from any previous instruction," an innate knowledge of God. "By nature we believe that the gods exist."

In more recent philosophy the doctrine of innate ideas was advanced by Descartes who was also the first to use that term, and hence gave to the term "idea" a connotation very unusual before his time. The doctrine of innate ideas as advanced by Descartes follows from his dualism of substances. Knowledge (intellectual) cannot be derived from sensation. The latter merely supplies the occasion in connection with which our mind forms the concepts and ideas "by means of an innate ability." Knowledge proceeds from a principle of its own, from innate ideas. Chief among these innate ideas is the idea of God. This is, as it were, the author's stamp impressed upon his work. But by the innate character of these ideas he means that the soul has by nature the power, the "ability" the "disposition" to produce them out of its own store. Hence, the ideas are not actually but potentially present in our soul.

According to Leibnitz also, the necessary and universal truths do not reach us from without, but originate in our own being. This is true with respect to ideas of substance, duration, change, causation, the truths of mathematics, and especially the idea of God. Altogether, these ideas comprise the natural light of reason. But the innate character of these ideas was explained more clearly and extensively by Leibnitz than by Descartes. The latter merely taught that the ideas were potentially present in our soul. Leibnitz, however, maintains that they are "virtually" innate, "in the sense in which inclinations, dispositions, habits or natural energies — but not in the sense in which actions — are innate." The human soul has not only the *ability* to know them, for in that case all knowledge could be called innate; but is itself the *source* of truths, "which it can furnish out of its own store." The ideas are antecedently present in man's soul. This is possible because imagination and reflection can exist without consciousness. They reach the conscious level as soon as perception by the senses occasions this. Accordingly, the virtually present ideas become actually present in our soul.

In the same manner Malebranche supposed that acquirement of knowledge by the human soul could be explained only on the presupposition that we see the ideas in God, and hence that God, as universal and infinite being, is directly present in our mind.

Analogously, Gioberti, Gratry, Ubaghs, etc., taught (in their ontologism) that man's mind directly perceives God as absolute being; accordingly, that there is an intuitive knowledge of God in man.

Kant greatly modified this doctrine of innate ideas. In connection with the terminology of Wolff he spoke of a knowledge a priori and a posteriori; he did not teach the existence of innate ideas as such, but he maintained the existence of innate forms: forms of perception; i.e., space and time; forms of the mind; i.e., the categories; and forms of reason; i.e., the ideas of God, virtue and immortality.

The idealism of Fichte and Hegel placed such emphasis on the doctrine of innate ideas that not only the knowledge of necessary and universal truths but *all* knowledge and indeed all being, the whole material universe, was derived from the thought-process.

> E. The doctrine of innate ideas is based on the following arguments:
>
> (1) Ability to acquire knowledge presupposes knowledge.
>
> (2) The universality of certain ideas proves their innate character.
>
> (3) Because of the dualism existing between soul and body ideas cannot originate in sensation. Hence, they must be antecedently present in the soul. — The Socinians, Locke, Hobbes, and others combat the doctrine of innate ideas. Herbert Spencer applies the theory of evolution to this doctrine.

The main arguments which are advanced in favor of this doctrine of innate ideas are the following: Our ability to acquire knowledge presupposes antecedent knowledge. Argumentation and reasoning are based upon self-evident and a priori principles. Experience merely furnishes "notions," contingent truths. Universal and necessary truths can originate in the human mind only.

The actual existence of universal and necessary truths is proved by *"the universal consent."*

Finally, the antithesis existing between the soul and body is of such a character that concepts and ideas cannot originate in sensation. They must originate either in the soul of man or in the Spirit of God, in whom man sees all ideas.

The doctrine of innate ideas was denied by the Socinians, who rejected natural religion, and especially by Locke, Hobbes, and others. They appealed to the following considerations: the doctrine of innate ideas is entirely superfluous inasmuch as the origination of these ideas can very well be explained in a different manner. History teaches that there is not a single concept or idea which does not vary with different individuals and peoples. Not even ethical principles are innate. There is the greatest possible divergence of opinion in regard to good and evil; and the existence of atheistic individuals and tribes is a sufficient argument against any doctrine of an innate idea of God. Children, idiots, and insane individuals know nothing whatever of innate ideas. Sensation is the source of all human knowledge: "There is nothing in the mind which was previously in the senses." [Nihil est in intellectu quod non prius fuerit in sensu.] This denial of innate ideas became widely prevalent in England and France during the eighteenth century, and nineteenth century materialism also rejected this doctrine.

Herbert Spencer brought about an important modification in the rejection of the doctrine of innate ideas. To him it seemed that by means of the doctrine of evolution the long struggle between empiricism and nativism could be brought to a close. He applied the law of development also to the human soul. According to him the soul did not come into existence all at once, neither had it been endowed from the very beginning with a fixed and definite set of potentialities, but it had gradually advanced to its present state of development. Hence, with reference to the first beginnings of the soul empiricism was right, for in that stage the soul was indeed a blank. But it did not remain a blank. On the contrary, the experience of several generations gradually changed the soul in such a manner that it may now be considered to possess various forms and ideas by means of which it is in and by itself adapted to its entire environment. And this is the truth of nativism, according to H. Spencer.

**F. Christian theology rejects the doctrine of innate ideas:**

(1) The church-fathers affirm, indeed, that the idea of God needs no demonstration: man naturally and necessarily arrives at this idea; yet it is not present in the soul at birth, i.e., before any reflection or observation, but is reached by means of meditation upon God's revelation in nature.

(2) The position of Augustine agrees substantially with that of the church-fathers before him, though to him the dependence of the soul upon sensation did not seem quite as great.

(3) Bonaventura, the representative of mysticism, accepts the doctrine of innate ideas in this sense: that by virtue of God's special grace certain definite individuals have a direct knowledge of God, a knowledge not dependent upon the senses.

(4) Scholasticism rejects the doctrine of innate ideas.

(5) Luther does not even recognize the element of truth in this doctrine. Later Lutheran theologians reject this extreme position.

(6) According to Calvin and all Reformed theologians, the seed of religion in man, by means of the observation of the revelation of God in his works, naturally develops into the conviction of the existence of God; but the doctrine of innate ideas, in the strictest sense, is to be rejected. Cf. the views of Voetius against Descartes.

It is important to know the attitude which Christian theology assumed with reference to the doctrine of innate ideas. Prof. Spruyt considered it strange that scholasticism had presented a well-nigh unanimous front against this doctrine, and held that there must have been a theological reason for this though he did not know which. Now, this is indeed the case, as will become plain. Although Christian theology as a whole held that there were truths known by nature and not as the result of revelation, truths obtained involuntarily and not by means of intentional study and reflection; nevertheless, it has definitely rejected the doctrine of innate ideas. True, in later times the advocates of this teaching: e.g., Thomassinus, Staudenmaier, Kuhn, Klee, and the onthologists: Malebranche, Gioberti, Ubaghs, etc., have appealed to the writings of some of the church-fathers, but this appeal was unjustified. Justin Martyr, to be sure, speaks of the idea of God as "the expression of man's innate opinion regarding an object that can scarcely be defined," but he does not make clear what he means by "innate." Irenaeus, indeed, in opposition to the teachings of the Gnostics, states that the universe was created by God, reveals God and makes him known; but he does not mention any innate knowledge. Clement of Alexandria affirms that the Father and Creator of all things is known "by nature and apart from any instruction," but he also states more than once that this knowledge is obtained by means of the observation of God's works. Tertullian emphasizes the natural knowledge concerning God. In peril or distress all men invoke the one true God in spite of their idolatry. This knowledge they obtained not from Moses or from the prophets but from their own soul. "For, from the very beginning a consciousness of God is given to the soul." This is true of every tribe and people. "By nature the soul is Christian." All Tertullian means by this is that certain truths (as the truth of the existence and unity of God) are known by nature and do not need to be obtained by means of special revelation: "For, some things are known even by nature. The immortality of the soul, for instance, is accepted by many; the knowledge of our God is possessed by all."

Somewhat more legitimate is the appeal to Augustine, who was influenced in many respects by Plato, as he himself acknowledges. It is true that he attaches much greater significance to thought than to sense-perception. The senses perceive transient objects only. Reason, though distinct in every individual, perceives and knows universal, necessary, immutable truths. This is due to the fact that in the case of each individual, reason sees these general truths in the *one* universal reason, the *one* immutable truth, namely, God himself. In the same manner Augustine states again and again that even as we see material objects by means of the light of the sun, so we perceive the intelligible truths in the light of God, *De civ. VIII, 7; De trin. XII,* 15. He is closer to us and easier to be found than creatures, *De Gen. add litt. V,* 16. He is "the truth presiding over all things," *Conf. X,* 41. He even states: "The God and Lord of all things directs the minds of men without any intervention of nature," *De musica VI,* 1. From this it appears that Augustine deems it a much easier and lighter task to reach God by means of meditating upon eternal truths than by means of the observation of the external natural universe. Nevertheless, it would be wrong to conclude from this that according to Augustine man's soul would be able to see God directly and immediately here on earth, and that it would be able to attain to the knowledge of eternal truths. For, elsewhere he states very plainly that the "vision of God" is reserved for heaven, *De trin. II,* 17; that on earth we are endowed with a shadowy knowledge, *De Gen. ad litt. IV,* 32; that a distinction must be made between the eternal truths known by man, and God as Truth personified, *De lib. arb. II,* 13; *Solil. I,* 5; and that by means of the perception of nature, logical reflection, and reflection in regard to the laws of reason, man advances to the idea of God, *Conf. VII,* 10; *De lib. arb. II, c.* 3-13.

Mysticism, however, appealed again and again to Augustine, and taught that originally man had received not only a "natural vision" and a "rational vision" but also a "contemplative vision" which, when it is restored by God's grace, enables man to see God at times even here on earth, and will enable him to do so to perfection in the glorious hereafter. Hence, Bonaventura rejects the statement, "All knowledge is derived from sensation." The soul knows itself and God without the aid of the senses. Nevertheless, mysticism, as represented by Bonaventura, though disagreeing with Thomas Aquinas, stays within definite bounds. "Although God is present, nevertheless, on account of the enshrouding blindness and darkness of our understanding we see him as if he were absent." To see God is given to some; e.g., to Paul, but as a gift of God's grace it is not given to all. And although Bonaventura calls the knowledge of "first principles" an *innate* knowledge, he adds, "because that light suffices unto the understanding of these principles, after the reception of the ideas, apart from any persuasion super-added because of its own value as evidence. For, though I have the natural light, which is sufficient to enable me to know that I must honor my parents, and that I must not hurt my neighbors, yet by nature I do not have an idea (image) of my father or of the neighbor impressed upon my mind." Though Bonaventura believes, therefore, that there are truths not arrived at by means of the senses but by means of inner contemplation and communion with God, even he does not believe in innate ideas in the real sense of the term.

Scholasticism was unanimous in its rejection of the doctrine of innate ideas. In distinction from this doctrine it taught that the essence of things is the real object of intellectual knowledge. Perception by the senses was considered the *beginning* of all knowledge. But when things are thus perceived, the mind is able to abstract the general principles, especially the so-called innate ideas. Hence, it should not be supposed that reason itself furnishes the latter in complete and finished form, but rather that, in accordance with the nature of the intellect, they are derived from observation. This is also true with respect to the idea of God. God is not the substance of things but their cause; hence, to a certain extent his existence and virtues can be known from his works, by means of perception and thought. We can speak of innate knowledge only in this sense; viz., that there has been created in our mind a natural inclination to proceed from the finite to the Infinite, from particulars to universals. The ontologism of Gioberti and Ubaghs was condemned at Rome on the 18th of Sept. 1861, and Sept. 21, 1866.

The Lutherans could not do justice to the truth contained in the doctrine of innate ideas. "Natural theology" both "innate and acquired" was not appreciated by them. Because of his rejection of the scholastic doctrine that "what pertains to Nature has remained unimpaired" Luther allowed himself to be led to an opposite extreme. According to him the image of God in man is entirely lost. "Apart from the Holy Spirit reason is simply without the knowledge of God. With respect to divine matters, man is completely in the dark." In reality the only thing retained by man is a "passive capacity or aptitude"; i.e., the possibility to be saved. For the rest, his mind, will, and affections are limited to "civil affairs." In regard to spiritual things he is entirely blind and dead. Luther, indeed, recognized the fact that God reveals himself in his works, that creation is a mode of divine revelation, a "mask or face of God"; but he teaches that man is no longer able to know God by means of this revelation. Luther at times goes to the extreme of calling sin "the essence of man," and man "nothing but sin"; expressions which we should not unduly stress but which, nevertheless, indicate his view in regard to the "innate and acquired knowledge of God." The same stand is taken by the Lutheran symbols and by some theologians; as, Flacius and Chemnitz, who rejected entirely the "knowledge of God derived from nature." This extreme position, however, was soon abandoned. Luther himself entertained a different idea at times, and exalted nature as the work of God.

Melanchton taught a "knowledge of God innate as well as acquired." Vestiges of God can be observed in all his works. These would be insufficient "if the mind did not also have a certain idea or preconception of God." Other theologians followed this example: Gerhard, Quenstedt, Hollatz, Calovius, Buddeus, and others treat "natural theology," and defend it against the Socinians. Jaeger and others even gave it a distinct and separate place in the system of dogmatics. The "innate knowledge of God" was variously defined by these theologians as "an ability or disposition or characteristic tendency or perfection or innate light on the order of a natural inclination or habitus." But they all agreed in this that it did not consist in "an idea impressed on the mind," present in man prior to any use of reason. Hence Descartes' doctrine of innate ideas was rejected, as was also the mystic doctrine of the inner light and of contemplation. Over against this the "innate theology" was described as a natural fitness and inclination created in the mind of man whereby he is able to attain to the knowledge of God "apart from any discursive reasoning or mental ratiocination," and to verify this knowledge by means of an undoubted, fixed, and certain testimony. "Previous to sense-perception there is nothing in the mind in the nature of an ideal representation of things; but there is, nevertheless, something in the mind in the nature of an inclination to knowledge."

Reformed theologians from the very beginning assumed a more favorable attitude to "natural theology." Calvin distinguished between common and special grace, and by means of the former he explained all the good still left in sinful man. More particularly, he held that "a sense of a Deity" was implanted in the human soul "by natural instinct." God has implanted in everyone "a sense of a Deity, the memory of which he renews frequently and insensibly," *Instit.* I, 3, 1. Another name he gives to this is "seed of religion," by means of which he explains the universality of religion, *ib.* The conviction that there is a God is "by nature innate." It is "indelible,"*I,* 3, 3. Notwithstanding, there is scarcely one in a hundred "who cherishes what he has received, and not one in whom the seed of religion grows to maturity," *I,* 4, 1. Now to this seed of religion is added God's revelation in his works, so that "whenever men open their eyes, they must needs behold God," *I,* 5, 1. "There is not an atom of the universe in which you cannot see some brilliant sparks at least of his glory,"*I,* 5, 1. In the first place, man himself as microcosm is an excellent workshop for the innumerable works of God, *I,* 5, 3, 4; but the latter is true also of the entire realm of nature. Hence, devoutly speaking, we may call nature *God.* We find this same view expressed in all the Reformed symbols and accepted by all Reformed theologians. Ursinus states that God reveals himself to man "not only by means of notions concerning himself impressed upon the mind of men but also by means of all created objects displayed as so many mirrors and evidences of his divinity"; and among the innate notions or conceptions he also figures the awareness of the fact that there is a God, as is proved by the universality of religion. Zanchius rejects the views of both Plato and Aristotle, and in agreement with the Stoics and Cicero teaches that the "ideas held by all are innate, not furnished by experience"; that children know at once: "Three is more than two," and, "There is a distinction between good and evil," etc. According to Polanus "right understanding" consists in "the true knowledge of the will and works of God as also of the divine order and judgment written upon the human mind by God," a knowledge the Author of which is the Logos, the forms and norms of which are the natural principles, and which is increased by means of the contemplation of the works of God. Nevertheless, in spite of this vigorous defence of "innate theology," Descartes' doctrine of innate ideas was emphatically denied by Voetius. The latter charges Descartes with three errors: (a) that he gives to the word "idea" an unusual meaning and hence falsifies it; (b) that he fails to indicate plainly what is to be understood by the term "innate idea of God," whether it pertains to "innate or acquired theology," whether it is an "ability" or an "activity," a "real or intentional entity," etc.; and (c) that he unduly minimizes the value and certainty of knowledge derived from the senses. The sense in which "innate theology" is to be understood is clearly described by Voetius. It is "an ability or power or inclination which pertains to the reasoning faculty, or a natural light so that the intellect is able to comprehend the truth of principles apart from any exertion, previous study, or reasoning; and, with necessary presuppositions, it actually thus comprehends, inclining itself toward the perception of and assent to the truth from a kind of natural necessity and with authority inherent in itself," in the same manner in which the will by virtue of a natural inclination strives after that which is good, and the eye of itself beholds the light and that which is visible. The well-known saying: "There is nothing in the mind which was not previously in the senses," is recognized as true in the sense that in some way or other, whether as direct object or as product or as part or as opposition, etc., the world round about us is needed in order to bring us to conscious knowledge.

**G. Reasons why Christian theology rejected the doctrine of innate ideas:**

(1) It leads to rationalism by making man independent of divine revelation.

(2) It leads to mysticism by making man independent of the visible world.

(3) It is contrary to Scripture inasmuch as it belittles the importance of the body and of the material universe.

(4) It is not in harmony with psychology, for as a matter of fact the soul here on earth does not see God directly, but obtains knowledge of God by means of the observation of God's revelation in nature and in Scripture. "The invisible things of him (are) . . . perceived through the things that are made," Rom. 1:20a, "we see in a mirror darkly," I Cor. 13:12a.

(5) It also contradicts the facts of history. History clearly indicates that moral, religious, and aesthetic ideas vary with different individuals and tribes. This could not be the case if these ideas were innate.

From all that has been said the reason why Christian theology was so unanimous in its rejection of the doctrine of innate ideas becomes plain. Fear of rationalism and mysticism caused her to assume this attitude. If man were born fully endowed (in his soul) with a clear and definite knowledge either of all ideas (Plato), or of God (Descartes), or of being (Gioberti), he would thereby become independent of the world; he would be able to obtain pure and perfect knowledge from the storehouse of his own soul, be self-sufficient; he would even be able to do without the revelation of God in his Word; it would be easier for him to find perfect knowledge in his own soul than in nature and Scripture.

Moreover, by means of the doctrine of innate ideas an unbridgeable chasm was produced between spirit and matter, between soul and body. The visible world was no longer looked upon as a creation and revelation of God, an embodiment of divine thoughts. Eternal truths, intellectual knowledge, could not be derived from it. Man could arrive at these by way of contemplation and reminiscence only, by means of separation from the world and introspection.

And herewith the ever-threatening danger of the doctrine of innate ideas has been pointed out. In Neo-Platonism and in the Christian (esp. in the Roman Catholic) Church Plato's dualism has led to a mysticism which indeed at first, in the earlier stages of meditation, makes use of God's revelation in nature and Scripture, but which, having once risen to higher contemplation, can do without all these eternal expedients, and needs only the inner word, the spiritual light, the vision of and communion with God in the innermost recesses of the soul. And the dualism of Descartes (connected with his doctrine of innate ideas), reasserted in more recent philosophy, has led Leibnitz and Wolff, and afterward Kant, Fichte, and Hegel to a rationalism which constructs the entire universe of being out of the contents of man's immanent reflection (thought).

Now it is clear as daylight that Scripture does not countenance this "independence" of man and contempt of the body and of the material universe. Scripture teaches that man is an image-bearer of God according to both soul and body, and that his body links him to the visible world. But these bonds by means of which man is connected with the visible world are not to be viewed as bonds of slavery. On the contrary, instead of leading man away from God, they lead him to God. The universe is a creation of God, a mirror of his virtues, a manifestation of his thoughts. According to the beautiful statement of Calvin, "There is not an atom of the universe in which one cannot see some brilliant sparks at least of his glory." And because Christian theology understood this, it has with one accord rejected the doctrine of innate ideas.

Psychology and history also raised objections to the doctrine of innate ideas. These objections were voiced by Locke and others. Empiricism defended a glorious truth over against mysticism and rationalism. These two religious systems meant well when they maintained that the essence, the idea of things, could not be reached by means of sense-perception, but could arise only in God (Malebranche), in the soul through "recollection" (Plato), or were the product of man's own soul (Descartes — Hegel). God is indeed the light of the soul. In his light we see light. The Logos is the light which lighteth every man, coming into the world. Nevertheless, it is true that here on earth we do not see face to face, that we walk by faith, that we see in a mirror, darkly. In order to obtain knowledge of God we need his revelation in nature and Scripture, Rom. 1:19, 20; I Cor. 13:12; II Cor. 3:18. Here on earth we cannot obtain a direct, an immediate knowledge of God and of his thoughts but only a mediate knowledge "by means of and in a mirror." Accordingly, the opinion of the mystics, rationalists, and ontologists is not theistic but pantheistic; it confuses the "light of reason" with the "light of God," the universal truths in us with the ideas in the consciousness of God, our "logos" with the "Logos of God," the order of being with the order of knowledge. In the order of being God is undoubtedly first. He is Creator and Preserver of all things. *His* thought and knowledge precedes the coming into existence of things. We are not to suppose that the world was first called into being, and that, as a result of this, God afterward learned to know it. On the contrary, the world exists because he first thought it and called it into being by an act of his will. But this does not mean that our thought follows the same course and is identical to this order of being: that we must first know God because of and by means of his idea in us, and that we do not proceed to the knowledge of the world until then.

We are creatures. We stand on the level of the creature. We know things *after* and *because* they have come into existence, and in our perception and thought we advance from the visible to the invisible things from the world to God. If ontologism considers itself strong over against idealism which denies the objective reality of objects, it is deceived by an illusion; for, on its own basis it cannot maintain that reality except by identifying the idea of God in us with the being of God, the logos in us with the Logos of God, thereby falling into the error of pantheism. Against this, Christian theology maintained the doctrine of Holy Scripture: that, whereas we cannot know God's being as such, all our knowledge of God is obtained indirectly and bears an analogical character. As a matter of fact no one ever arrives at the knowledge of the "first principles" or at the idea of God apart from the universe. The infant, born without consciousness, gradually receives various impressions and notions from the environment in which it is educated. In the case of the *first* man this may indeed have been different. All those who were born afterward were brought to a conscious and clear knowledge both of visible and of invisible things by their parents and by means of their environment. They did not gain this knowledge merely by means of individual study and opportunity and entirely apart from environment. Accordingly, there is no knowledge of the invisible except by means of visible symbols. He who lacks one of the organs of sense does not obtain an idea of the phenomena that correspond to that organ. A blind man does not know light, and therefore he does not understand the meaning of the phrase "God is light" except in the negative sense and by means of contrast.

Hence, it is also clear how it is possible that individuals and races can differ so much in regard to rights and morals, religion and art. This would be inexplicable if ideas as such were innate and were directly implanted in our soul by God himself. As it is, we notice that all men have indeed an idea of God, but express it in various ways; that there are people who say in their heart, "There is no God"; that the *difference* between good and evil is known everywhere, but that the *contents* of both are defined very differently; that opinions in regard to good and evil, beauty and ugliness vary very widely. In a word, there is not one ethical truth which is recognized everywhere, always, and by all. In the real sense of the word *natural theology* never existed, no more than natural right and natural morals.

**H.** **All this (G) is only one side of the question. We are indeed justified to speak of innate knowledge of God if we mean thereby: that potentiality (aptitude, etc.) and inclination (disposition, etc.) in man which naturally and necessarily issues in some definite**

**knowledge of God. Thus, the truth contained in both empiricism and in the doctrine of innate ideas is accepted; the respective errors are rejected.**

But this is only one side of the truth. There is another side, of equal importance. It must be admitted that in order to see we have as much need of the eye subjectively as of the light of the sun objectively. That men acquire knowledge and obtain ideas from their environment is a fact; but it presupposes that they come equipped with an ability, an inclination, a disposition to learn. We are taught to speak by the people in whose midst we are born, but this presupposes on the part of every individual a disposition and an inclination to speak. Thus it is in every sphere: in religion, art, morals, jurisprudence, science, etc. By nature the "seeds of the sciences" lie hidden in man. All knowledge is based on general principles, axioms. All knowledge rests in faith. Every proof presupposes a "principle of argumentation." There are logical, mathematical, philosophical, ethical, and in the same manner also religious and theological principles which are indeed very general and abstract, but which, nevertheless, are accepted by all individuals and throughout all centuries and which bear a natural and necessary character. The laws of thought are the same for all. Mathematics is everywhere the same. The distinction between good and evil is known by all. There is no people without religion and knowledge of God. This can only be explained when we accept "self-evident principles, ideas which all men have in common, eternal verities," with which the human soul is endowed by nature. In religion, whether we wish to or not, we are ever forced to acknowledge a "seed of religion, a sense of divinity, a divine instinct, an innate knowledge." Scripture takes the lead. It points out the fact that for man objective revelation in nature and in grace is indispensable; but at the same time it recognizes the fact that man is God's image and offspring, that in his "mind" he possesses the ability to see God in his works, and that he has the work of the law written in his heart, Gen. 1:27; Acts 17:28; Rom. 1:19, 20; 2:15. Everything depends on a right view of this original character of the "common ideas." They have received various names, and the adjectives "inborn, innate, impressed, ingrafted," have been applied to them. No one employs these terms literally: as soon as they are studied, nearly all hasten to declare that they do not mean that man is born fully equipped with these innate ideas as if he would bring them with him "ready and matured" and as if they would be present in consciousness as "ideas impressed upon the mind." In that sense there are no innate ideas. God does not cause man to enter the world full-grown in any respect, but he causes him to be born as a helpless child in need of

care. Moreover, that child would perish if it were not fed and cared
for by its environment. Nevertheless, the child is the father of the man.
This is the case in the intellectual, ethical, and religious sphere. "Innate
knowledge of God" does not mean that God has in such a manner
directly endowed man with knowledge that he can dispense with revelation. It does not indicate that man is able to obtain a conscious, clear,
and true knowledge of God from the storehouse of his own soul. But
it indicates that man possesses both the "capacity, aptitude, power,
ability" and the "inclination, tendency, disposition" to obtain some
definite, certain, and indubitable knowledge of God; a knowledge
gained in the normal course of development and in the environment in
which God caused him to see the light, and arrived at in a natural way;
i.e., without scholarly argumentation and reasoning." Accordingly,
the words "implanted, inborn, innate," do not indicate "that wherewith
a man is born," but merely state that the knowledge of God is obtained
in a natural manner, without intellectual argumentation (reasoning):
that it is inherent in the structure of the human soul itself. They are
not used to contradict the doctrine that man is born as a tabula tasa,
without definite material content as to his consciousness; but they are
used to contradict the idea that the knowledge of God is forced upon
man, by means of a definite revelation, by means of scholarly argumentation, artificially, as it were. That is the meaning which Christian
theology has always attached to these terms. Accordingly, these terms
are interchanged with "untaught, natural, apart from previous study,
apart from a laborious reasoning process," etc. "The knowledge of
God is said to be innate inasfar as by means of the principles with
which we are endowed from our very birth we can easily perceive that
God exists." Hence, Locke is wrong when he states that if by innate
ideas were meant only the ability to know, all knowledge could be
termed innate. For the "knowledge of God" is called "ingrafted or
innate" because every individual in the normal course of development
*must* arrive at it. Just as a person when he opens his eyes necessarily
sees the sun and by means of its light discerns objects, even so man by
reason of his very nature *must* needs believe that there is a God and
that there is a distinction between good and evil, etc. The moment he
hears these things he cannot do differently. He voluntarily accepts
these truths without asking for any proof; for, they are self-evident.
Hence, the knowledge of God is called innate, and hence also the term
innate *potentiality* or *faculty* was unsatisfactory. Over against the
doctrine of the "innate ideas," the term "innate cognition" expresses
the fact that man is not born fully equipped with the knowledge of
God, but obtains this knowledge through the influence of revelation

upon his consciousness. And on the other hand, over against empiricism, the term implies that this revelation of God speaks so clear a language and finds such a ready response in the soul of every individual that it may be looked upon as pertaining to man by nature and may be called innate. Thus theology does justice not only to Scripture but also to psychology and history. There is a revelation of God in all his works, not only in nature as such, but especially also in man. Indeed, man himself constitutes the most important object of God-revealing nature. Moreover, from the entire realm of nature (both within him and exterior to him) man receives impressions and perceptions, which, prior to all argumentation and discussion, imbue his consciousness with the idea of a Highest Being. It is God himself who does not leave any man without witness.

**II. Acquired Knowledge of God. The Difference Between Innate Knowledge of God and Acquired Knowledge of God Is This: In the Former Man Is Largely Passive; In the Latter Man Is Active. On the Basis of This Knowledge of God Acquired From Nature Many Have Tried to Prove God's Existence. Accordingly, We Have the Cosmological, Teleological, Ontological, Moral, Historico-Theological Arguments and the Argument From Universal Consent. These Should Not Be Considered Proofs but Evidences of the Reasonableness of the Christian Faith.**

A. The distinction between innate knowledge of God and acquired knowledge of God is not that the former originates in man himself while the latter has its origin in the world, and hence is acquired; for in reality, both are acquired. The distinction is this:

(1) in the former man is largely passive: God's revelation makes its impression upon him; one involuntarily obtains innate knowledge of God; while in the latter man is active; he makes a study of God's revelation: one obtains acquired knowledge of God by means of argumentation and reasoning;

(2) innate knowledge of God comprises general principles only; acquired knowledge of God is a far more detailed knowledge.

"Innate knowledge of God" and "acquired knowledge of God" may not stand directly opposed to one another; nevertheless, there is undoubtedly a distinction between the two. This distinction is often taken to mean that the former indicates the knowledge of God *inherent* in man; i. e., which he has at birth, while the latter refers to the knowledge which is not inherent but *derived* from the observation of the universe of nature. Thus, however, the distinction has not been plainly and accurately given. For, in the real sense of the term, knowledge, whether of God or of the world, is never inherent(innate). All knowledge enters man's consciousness from without. Only the ability to know is innate;

but this ability realizes itself in action by means of the influence which nature in and round about us exerts upon us. The seed of religion lies indeed in man, but in order to sprout forth it has need of the entire field of human activity. Even as man, though he has eyes at birth, nevertheless, is unable to see any object except in the light of the sun, even so the believer is unable to behold God except in his works. Furthermore, it has become clear to us that Christian theology never spoke of innate knowledge as conscious knowledge of God with which an individual is born, but employed this term to indicate that the knowledge of God is spontaneous, pertains to man by nature, and is not the result of compulsion or coercion, reasoning and compelling argumentation. Without any hardship the normal individual obtains a certain knowledge of God. Accordingly, the innate knowledge of God does not stand opposed to the acquired knowledge of God, for in a sense also the former may be called acquired. God's revelation precedes the "innate knowledge of God" as well as the "acquired knowledge of God." God does not leave himself without witness. With his eternal power and divinity he influences (acts upon) man from every direction, both from within and from without. God, as it were, goes out to meet man in the realm of nature and in the realm of humanity, in heart and in conscience, in prosperity and in adversity. Moreover, man, having been created in God's image, has been gifted with the ability to receive the impressions of this revelation, and by means of these to obtain some knowledge of the Eternal One. The "innate knowledge" as soon as it is "cognition, knowledge" and not merely "ability" but "activity" is always the result of the influence of God's revelation acting from within and from without, and hence in so far it is always "acquired."

For these reasons the distinction between innate knowledge of God and acquired knowledge of God used to be stated differently. A twofold distinction was made:

(1) The "innate knowledge of God" is obtained spontaneously, without any hardship or compulsion. The "acquired knowledge of God," on the contrary, is the result of reasoning and argumentation, of study and reflection. It is gained by way of causality, removal of limits, and negation. The former is original or "noetic." The latter is discursive or "dianoetic."

(2) This leads to the further distinction that the former comprises principles only, is general and necessary; while the latter is more detailed and developed, presents more concrete propositions, and hence is much more subject to doubt and denial. That there is a God, well-nigh everyone accepts as an established fact; but the proofs for the

existence of God have been discovered by the mind, and hence have been successively overestimated and underestimated.

Now this twofold distinction is correct. The difference is not that innate knowledge has its source in man, and acquired knowledge has its source in the world round about him. Even the moral proof is derived from the ethical consciousness of man. In the case of both it is the same revelation, the complete revelation of God, which brings knowledge of God to our consciousness. But in the case of the "innate knowledge of God" that revelation acts upon man's consciousness, makes impressions, and produces notions; while in the case of the "acquired knowledge of God" man studies God's revelation; his mind becomes active; he begins to reflect, and, fully conscious, he strives by means of reasoning and argumentation to reach God through the study of the created universe. Man cannot rest satisfied with impressions and notions, not in any sphere of knowledge. Merely to be conscious of something gives him no satisfaction. The fact *that* he knows does not satisfy him. He also desires to *know* that he knows. He tries to explain the "how" and the "why" of his knowledge. Hence, common, ordinary, empirical knowledge always tries to develop into real, scientific knowledge. Therefore, faith rises to the level of theology, and the "innate knowledge of God" becomes complete in the "acquired knowledge of God."

B. **The distinction between innate knowledge of God and acquired knowledge of God is usually applied to natural theology, which is then contrasted with revealed theology. This is wrong, for all theology is revealed. All knowledge of God from nature presupposes:**

   **(1) God's revelation in the universe,**

   **(2) A heart opened by God: a regenerated consciousness,**

   **(3) Scripture's interpretation of God's revelation in nature. For the Christian, the testimonies derived from the realm of nature have great value, as TESTIMONIES.**

The distinction between "innate" and "acquired" knowledge of God is usually applied to "natural theology" only, which is then distinguished from and often placed in opposition to "revealed theology." The erroneous character of this presentation has already been indicated. A distinct natural theology, obtained apart from any revelation, merely through observation and study of the universe in which man lives, does not exist. The knowledge of God called "natural theology" is not a product of human reasoning. It presupposes:

(1) God's revelation in his handiwork: man does not seek God but God seeks man, and he does this also by means of his works in nature.

(2.) On the part of man: a sanctified mind and an opened eye to see God, the true and living God, in his creatures. Man does not grasp God's revelation by means of the natural light of reason although all pagan religions are positive.

(3) God's own interpretation of his revelation in nature, which interpretation we find in Scripture.

(1) and (2) together would not be sufficient. Without (3) even the believer, even the Christian, would not be able to understand God's revelation in nature or to interpret it rightly. Scripture itself contains the knowledge of God from nature and explains it at length. Accordingly, the Christian follows an entirely wrong method if, whenever he treats natural theology, he severs himself, as it were, from special revelation in Scripture and from the illumination of the Holy Spirit. He commits an error whenever he attempts to discuss natural theology "without any presuppositions," and then proceeds to the discussion of revealed theology. Also as dogmatician the Christian from start to finish stands foursquare on the foundation of special revelation. He is a believer and a Christian not only in the "doctrine of Christ" but equally in the "doctrine of God." But standing on this solid foundation he looks round about through the spectacles of Holy Writ, and sees in the entire realm of nature a revelation of the same God whom he knows and confesses as in Christ his Father, his Father in heaven. Accordingly, it is incorrect to view the innate and acquired knowledge of God as the knowledge which we derive from creation apart from God's *special* revelation. From our earliest youth God's special revelation in Christ has exerted its influence upon us. We are born in the covenant of grace. Hence, we are born as Christians: all kinds of Christian influences have produced the knowledge which we now possess. They have affected us in a greater measure than God's revelation in nature. In the light of that *special* revelation we have learned to view nature and the world round about us. To God's *special* revelation in his Word we are all indebted for the knowledge of God derived from the realm of nature. If we had not heard God speaking in the work of grace so that we are now able to discern his voice in the work of nature, we would have been like the heathen for whom nature has nothing but sounds of confusion. But now that revelation of God in nature has great significance. It is the same God who speaks to us in nature and in grace, in creation and in redemption, in the Logos and in Christ, in the Spirit of God and in the Spirit of Christ. Nature and grace do not stand opposed to one another. We have *one* God, of whom and through whom and unto whom are both nature and grace.

What has been said is true both in regard to the innate and the acquired knowledge of God. We are indebted to Scripture for both. It is true that Scripture does not try to prove God's existence. It presupposes God's existence and assumes that man knows and recognizes God. It does not view man as fallen so deeply that before he can believe he needs proof. Man is even now God's image-bearer, God's offspring. He possesses a "mind" by means of which he is able to discern God's power and divinity in the work of creation. Scripture looks upon the denial of God's existence as a sign of folly, of deep moral corruption, Ps. 14:2. Such individuals form the exception, not the rule. As a rule Scripture figures with those who voluntarily and intuitively recognize God's existence. It does not make an appeal to the reasoning intellect, but it appeals to our rational and moral consciousness. It does not argue and analyze, but it shows us God in all his handiwork. Moreover, this it does very emphatically. To the consciousness of the believer heaven and earth and all creatures, herbs and grass, rain and drought, fruitful and barren years, meat and drink, health and sickness, riches and poverty, yea and all things declare God. There is not an atom of the universe in which God's power and divinity are not revealed. Scripture urges us to behold heaven and earth, birds and ants, flowers and lilies, in order that we may see and recognize God in them. "Lift up your eyes on high, and see who hath created these,'" Is. 40:26. Scripture does not reason in the abstract. It does not make God the conclusion of a syllogism, leaving it to us whether we think the argument holds or not. But it speaks with authority. Both theologically and religiously it proceeds from God as the starting point. It shows God's virtues in his works and it demands that we recognize him. "The ox knoweth his owner, and the ass his master's crib; but Israel doth not know, my people doth not consider." Is. 1:3. It never doubts the fact that God reveals himself in the work of creation, and that he does not leave himself without witness to anyone, Acts 14: 17; Rom. 1:19, 20. Moreover, because it regards the entire universe as a testimony and revelation of God, it contains the germs of all those proofs which were later elaborated in much detail and developed dialectically. There is truth in the remark of C. J. Nitzsch: "Scripture gives us a beginning and an analogy of the aetiological [cosmological] proof in Rom. 1:20, 'For the invisible things of him since the creation of the world are clearly seen, being perceived through the things that are made, even his everlasting power and divinity; that they may be without excuse'; of the teleological proof, in Ps. 8:9, Acts 14:17, 'And yet he left not himself without witness, in that he did good and gave you from heaven rains and fruitful seasons, filling your hearts with food and gladness'; of the moral proof, in Rom. 2:14, 'for when the Gentiles that have not the law, do by nature the things of the law, these, not having the law, are the law unto themselves'; and of the ontological proof in Acts 17:24, 'The God that made the world and all things therein, he being Lord of heaven and earth, dwelleth not in temples made with hands'; also, in Rom. 1:19, 32." We could add to this that Scripture in a very remarkable way concludes the being of God from the being of man. The wicked suppose that God does not see them, neither is able to see them, but the poet asks: "He that planted the ear, shall he not hear? He that formed the eye, shall he not see?" Ps. 94:9; cf. Ex. 4:11. The poet proceeds on the assumption that God made man in his image, and, therefore, that the faculties of man must also be present in God; just as Paul concludes that the Godhead is not like unto gold or silver or stone, from the fact that we are his offspring, Acts 17:29. Now when Scripture speaks thus, not in the language of dialectic but in the language of testimony, not with an appeal merely to the reasoning intellect but to the heart and conscience, to the entire rational and moral consciousness of man, it is never without power and influence. Also in this respect it is living and active, and sharper than any two-edged sword, and piercing even to the dividing of soul and spirit, of both joints and marrow, and quick to discern the thoughts and intents of the heart. Even though Scripture does not employ logical arguments and philosophical proofs, it is powerful in the testimony which it thus presents, because it is the Word of God and because it appeals to the rational and moral nature of every man. It is God himself, who does not leave himself without witness to any one. It is man himself, who, because he was created in God's image, must needs heed this testimony and assent to it. From this point of view we should consider the so-called proofs for the existence of God. Thus we shall be saved from falling into the error of overestimating or of underestimating them.

**C. History of the attempt to prove God's existence.**

(1) Heathen philosophers tried to prove God's existence.

(2) Christian theology accepted these proofs. Their value was soon overestimated, as is done by Rome even today.

(3) The Reformers regarded these proofs as testimonies for the believer.

(4) Soon, however, Protestant theology turned to rationalism, and again overestimated the value of the proofs.

(5) Kant showed their inadequacy for pure reason.

(6) At present there is much difference of opinion in regard to their value.

Already in the works of the ancient philosophers: Anaxagoras, Socrates, Plato, Aristotle, Plutarch, Seneca, and Cicero, we find the proofs adduced to demonstrate God's existence. The existence of a conscious, rational God was deduced from the presence of beauty, harmony, motion, purpose, and ,design in the universe; from reason and the innate idea; from the importance of religion for the state and for society; and from the concensus of opinion among the various races.

Christian theology accepted all these proofs, and preferred to dwell on them at length, and Augustine added the argument derived from the existence of general concepts. Theology did not scorn the support of heathen philosophy, and, rejecting dualistic Gnosticism and Manichaesism, it recognized in nature the work of God. Now this position of Christian theology is all the more remarkable in view of the fact that to a certain extent Christendom assumed a hostile attitude to the cosmos, and placed all emphasis on man's salvation. In spite of all asceticism, which forced its way into the church, Christian theology persisted in its view that the realm of nature is a work of the same God who revealed himself in Christ as Savior and Redeemer. It even began to overestimate the value and force of these proofs. Although some of the church-fathers openly declared that it was impossible for the heathen to derive a pure knowledge of God from nature and that for the sinner the way of the proofs is very difficult; nevertheless, gradually these proofs began to lose their religious character. They were severed from every moral condition. The "acquired knowledge of God" was separated from the "innate knowledge of God," and Christian theology became more and more convinced that the truths of "natural religion" were demonstrable in the same manner as those of logic and mathematics. They were not to be considered "articles of faith," but were, nevertheless, to be viewed as "preambles to the articles of faith." The ontological argument of Anselm's *Prologium*, though accepted by some (e.g., by Halesius and Bonaventura), was rejected by the majority. It was considered impossible to reach God except by way of the creature (creation). For the rest, however, much value was attached to the proofs, and much care was bestowed on them. The general view was that in natural theology one was standing on a rational, scientific foundation, apart from and before proceeding to faith. Even today Rome and R. C. Theology assume the same rationalistic position. The Vatican declared that man by means of the natural light of reason is able to know God with certainty through the work of creation.

Now the Reformers indeed, accepted this "natural theology" together with its proofs, but instead of treating it *before* the doctrine of faith, they included it *in* the doctrine. Calvin, proceeding on the basis of the "seed of religion," saw "signs and testimonies" of God's omnipotence in "every atom of the universe": in the starry heavens, in the human body, in the soul, in the preservation of all things, etc.; but, having stated this, he hastens to add that this seed of religion, though ineradicably implanted in man, can be choked and cannot bring forth good fruit: man no longer has an eye to see God; to do so he needs faith. Other Reformed theologians agree with him in this view of "natural theology."

But Protestant theology soon turned to rationalism. Though natural theology was at first considered to be a description, based on Scripture, of the knowledge of God which *the Christian* could obtain from the created universe, it was soon looked upon as an exposition of the knowledge which the *unbeliever* by his own reasoning could derive from the realm of nature. Natural theology became rational theology. Descartes considered the innate idea to be an irrefutable proof for the existence of God. Voetius was still able to discern the difference between rationalistic argumentation and the Reformed doctrine of "natural theology." Later theologians, however, more and more lost sight of this distinction. Rationalism began to triumph everywhere. Natural theology became the real, scientific, demonstrable theology, while revealed theology was pushed to the background and finally disappeared. The proofs were classified in detail: *metaphysical* proofs were divided into those pertaining to the motion, causality, and accidental character of the universe; *physical,* into those pertaining to the harmony, order, and purpose, in general of the universe, and in particular of sun, moon, stars, fire, light, earth, water, animals, plants, man, his body, the soul; ear, eye, hand, instincts, etc.; *historical,* into those pertaining to "universal consent," "society," arts, sciences, revelation, prophecy, miracle; *moral,* into those pertaining to conscience, freedom, morality, judgment, reward and punishment, etc.; and finally, there were the *mathematical* proofs.

This self-sufficiency of natural theology lasted till Kant. He subjected the proofs to a rigid criticism, endeavored to show that for theoretical reason they have no value in themselves, but afterward tried to establish the existence of God as a postulate of practical reason. Later on many philosophers and theologians discredited the proofs. Jacobi even regarded it an impossibility to prove the existence of God, as God would then become dependent upon the premises of a syllogism. Others saw the inadequacy of this reasoning, but have very little if any use for these proofs, have called them unnecessary for the believer and unprofitable for the unbeliever, and have come to the conclusion that they ought to be removed from dogmatics. But, however great the number of these critics has ever been, their attempt to eliminate these proofs from the doctrine of God (in theology and in philosophy) has never been crowned with success. They themselves give separate—at times detailed—treatment to all of them, if only to prove their lack of force. Moreover, philosophers and theologians, in steady procession, continue their detailed and lengthy discussion of the proofs for the existence of God.

There is, however, a great difference of opinion regarding the form in which these proofs should be presented, regarding their collective and respective force, and regarding the conclusion to which they lead. Hegel (in his philosophy) attaches greater value to them than does Kant; the former regarding them to be the self-demonstration of God in the soul of man, and, accordingly, attaching great value to the ontological proof. This ontological argument in the form given to it by Anselm and Descartes has been generally abandoned, but many try to maintain it in the form in which it was presented by Plato, Augustine, and Thomas Aquinas as a proof derived from the ideas and norms of the human soul. As a matter of course, the cosmological proof is presented in many different forms, for it has been justly remarked that if the existence of God is to be concluded from the existence of the universe, every blade of grass may serve the purpose. But also in regard to the force of this argument opinions are widely divided. According to some it does not lead to an absolute cause: according to others it only proves the *existence* but not the *nature* of the absolute cause of the universe; and according to still others it proves directly or indirectly the existence of a personal God. Due to Darwinism's denial of all purpose the teleological argument, as a proof derived from the order and purpose in the universe, is often pushed to the background; but according to the opinion of many it gains renewed force when, as an argument from design, it is based upon evolution itself, as a process, perceptible in the universe, which brings about the gradual coming into existence of life and the soul, science and art, religion and morality, etc., a process which evidences a goal, striving, will, purpose. Kant attached great significance to the moral argument, which is also presented in different forms. At present it is usually stated in this form: the autonomy of the spiritual over against the material universe—which autonomy is evident in all culture and especially in moral life and consciousness—proves the existence either of a moral world-order only, or of a personal God. Finally, the argument from universal consent is either presented in its traditional form or modified in such a manner that it derives its greatest force from the religious nature of man, which is established beyond doubt by historical, psychological, and philosophical research, and which—provided it is not an illusion—proves God's existence, revelation, and knowability.    •

According to many all these proofs serve to indicate that materialism and pantheism (naturalism and idealism) are unable to solve the problem of the universe, and that this entire universe in its origin, essence, and goal can be explained only on the basis of theism.

> **D. Summary of "proofs" for the existence of God:**
> (1) Two are based upon the nature of the universe: (a) cosmological, (b) teleological;
> (2) Two are based upon the nature of the human soul: (a) ontological, (b) moral;
> (3) Two are based upon history: (a) the argument from universal consent, (b) historico-theological.

We do not need a long discussion in regard to the classification of these proofs. For, though classifications differ as to name and form, they amount to the same thing. Two proofs deduce God's existence from the origin and purpose, respectively, of the natural universe (cosmological and teleological). Two are based upon the rational and moral nature, respectively, of man (ontological and moral). The remaining two are based upon history, and deduce God's existence from the unanimous testimony and from the history, respectively, of mankind (the argument from universal consent and the historico-theological argument).

> **E. THE COSMOLOGICAL PROOF.** This is an argument from effect to cause. It is presented in various forms. Argument: whereas all things have a cause, the universe must have a cause, even God. But considered as a proof this argument is inadequate:
> (1) The universality of causality is denied by Hume and Kant.
> (2) May not the universe have had an infinite series of causes?
> (3) Even granting that the universe must have a cause, and that an infinite series of causes is inconceivable, hence being forced to the conclusion that the universe must have one eternal, infinite, absolute cause; that does not yet prove that cause to be the PERSONAL GOD.

The cosmological proof is presented in different forms. It deduces a "first self-moving power" from motion (Aristotle); the unchangeable, from the changeable (John of Damascus); the absolutely perfect, from the relatively perfect (Boethius-Anselm); a "first efficient cause" from the "series of causes" which cannot be infinite (Thomas Aquinas); "a necessary entity" from the contingent existence of the universe; independent existence (aseity), from dependent existence (Richard Vict.); the existence of the absolute, from the existence of that which is relative (Spinoza, Hegel, Hartmann, Scholten); the absolute dependence of all creatures upon a higher, divine power, from the relative interdependence of all creatures (Lotze); etc. But in all these forms the cosmological proof deduces a cause from an effect. Now in itself such a conclusion is legitimate, the criticism of Hume and Kant notwithstanding. If we may no longer apply the law of causality, we can know nothing whatsoever. But the cosmological proof proceeds on certain assumptions which are not self-evident and accepted by all. It assumes not only that *the individual objects* existing in the universe are contingent, finite, relative, imperfect; but it also assumes the same in regard to the entire universe; it assumes that an "infinite chain of causes" is inconceivable; and that the law of causality should also be applied to the universe as a whole. Only in case all these assumptions should be justified, would the cosmological proof have any force. It is correct to reason that even as all individual objects have a cause, so also the universe as a whole—whereas it consists of these objects—must have a cause. But further than that it does not bring us. It tells us nothing about the character and nature of that cause. If anyone wishes to conclude that the universe must have had a cause, which itself also had a cause, he has done full justice to the force of this argument. That this cause is infinite, absolute, perfect, is not the necessary, logical consequence of the cosmological proof, but follows from other considerations. Now an infinite series of causes is indeed inconceivable and impossible. Nobody accepts such a series: all recognize an absolute ground, a first being, whether this being be called God or the Absolute, substance or force, matter or will, etc. If this supposition is correct—as is admitted by all—the cosmological argument brings us a step farther; viz., to an independent, hence infinite, eternal, absolute cause of the universe. But whether this cause be transcendent or merely immanent, personal or impersonal, conscious or unconscious, is still undetermined. Many have tried to derive something more from the cosmological proof, whether by way of direct or indirect inference. By way of *direct* inference some have deduced a personal, conscious, free being, at the same time the highest idea, the highest reason, from personality, consciousness, freedom, and the ideas present in the universe; considering that an effect cannot be greater than its cause. But against this reasoning the objection may be urged that the relation of cause and effect is then thought of as an emanation, and, applied to God, would also lead to the conclusion that he is material, corporeal, yea even impure and unholy. Others have therefore *indirectly* inferred that an infinite, absolute cause, a being having existence of, in, and through itself, must be a spiritual being, must be personal. But the objection is warranted that the cosmological proof does not tell us anything of the inner nature of such a first cause; that we have no right to apply the law of causality also to it; hence, that we can say nothing definite in regard to this first cause, Therefore, we are forced to the conclusion that at best, i.e., provided that we grant the impossibility of an infinite series of causes, the cosmological proof brings us to a first, independent, absolute world-cause.

**F. THE TELEOLOGICAL PROOF:** Argument: there is purpose in the universe; hence, there must be a purposer, even God. Objections:

(1) Materialism denies the presence of purpose in the universe.

(2) Pantheism denies the presence of CONSCIOUS purpose.

(3) Kant argues that even granting that there is conscious purpose in the universe, this brings us only to one or more World-ARCHITECTS, not to a World-CREATOR.

Answers to objections:

(1) Answer to Pantheism's objection: an unconscious purpose does not exist; the unconscious act of the instinct points back to a conscious purposer.

(2) Answer to Kant's objection: how must we conceive of a World-ARCHITECT who is not World-CREATOR?

(3) Result: everything depends upon the question whether purpose is really present in the universe.

The teleological argument deduces an intelligent cause from the order and beauty, the harmony and purpose evident in the universe as a whole and also in individual creatures, starry heavens, elements, the earth, man, animals, plants, the hand, the eyes, etc. Although the teleological argument never fails to make an impression and was mentioned with respect by Kant, nevertheless, many objections have been urged against it especially of late.

(1) Materialism maintains that there is no purpose present in the universe, and that the mechanical interpretation must take the place of the teleological.

(2) Pantheism affirms that the presence of order and purpose in the universe does not force us to accept a conscious, intelligent cause, as both in the case of every human individual and also in regard to the universe as a whole the unconscious functions with a greater degree of wisdom and certainty than conscious reflection and planning.

(3) Finally, Kant raises the objection that this proof leads to a World-*Architect* and not to a world-*Creator*.

Now there are many ways of answering these objections. Scripture everywhere recognizes purpose in creation, Gen. 1; Prov. 8:1; 1 Cor. 3:21-23; Rom. 8:28; etc. The teleological conception of the universe is honored by nearly all philosophers: by Anaxagoras, Socrates, Plato, Aristotle, etc. It forces itself upon the mind of every human individual in spite of the misuse to which it has been subjected especially in the eighteenth century. Purpose is evident in individual phenomena, in climate, the seasons, temperature of water, fertilization of plants, blood-circulation, organisms, the hand, the eye, etc., and also in the universe as a whole. All atoms obey one law. Everything is based on thought which can be grasped by man. To maintain that the universe was brought forth by chance would be about as logical as to affirm that the *Illiad* was produced by a promiscuous throw of letters. Moreover, the very fact that we are at times unable to point out purpose proves that where we are able to notice it, we observe aright.

Hence, of late many naturalists have returned to vitalism and also to teleology. Darwinism's doctrine of descent was characterized by its attempt to substitute cause for purpose everywhere; but, because the theory of natural selection endeavored to give an explanation of the presence of adaptation in the universe, it brought to light the indispensableness of the teleological view. Matter, force, and motion do not suffice; there must also be *direction*, which is inconceivable apart from purposefulnesss. Accordingly, of late G. Wolff, H. Driesch, and J. Reinke, and before them Fechner and K. E. von Baer, have admitted the reasonableness of teleology as well as of causality. Teleology and causality do not exclude each other: whoever sets up a purpose, afterward applies the means which lead to the attainment of that purpose. In the teleological conception of the universe there is even sufficient room left for mechanical causality. Only, the latter does not explain all phenomena of the universe. It cannot derive the conscious and spiritual as well as the material from matter and evolution. If the presence of order and purpose were accepted by all, so that a forceful and lengthy demonstration would be unnecessary, the teleological proof would indeed give us the right, from the beauty and harmony present in the universe, to deduce a *conscious* being, for an *unconscious* purpose does not exist. Von Hartmann has indeed tried to prove the contrary, but his arguments for the purposive activity of the unconscious lack force, because for a creature to act with a definite purpose is one thing, the discernment of a purpose in the unconscious act of a creature is quite another. Instinct operates unconsciously; nevertheless, one is able to discern a purpose in the unconscious act of the instinct; a purpose which points back to a conscious being who has produced the instinct. If there is purpose in the universe, it must have been premeditated. Granted that even then the teleological proof brings us to a World-*Architect* only, this proof would be of great significance. Even if it should not lead us to *one* intelligent being, but should leave room for the existence of *many* divine beings who together would have brought forth the world, it would not be without value. It would have indicated that the constitution of the universe demands (an) intelligent first cause(s), and thus this argument would have proved all that it could be expected to prove. Nevertheless, having once derived one or more World-Architects from this argument, the question would arise: how can a being that did not *create* matter, nevertheless, give to it form and appearance? Also how can more than one being be the first cause of the universe? Everything depends upon the presence of purpose in the universe. If that is established, the existence of the Highest Being and the fact that he possesses consciousness are thereby given.

**G. THE ONTOLOGICAL PROOF.** This argument deduces God's actual existence from his necessary existence in thought. This conclusion is correct, provided God exists!

The ontological proof is presented in three different forms:

(1) From the general ideas and norms present in the human mind, i.e., from *that* reason which transcends both our individual reason and that of the entire world, it concludes absolute reason: the sum-total of all these ideas and norms, absolute truth, goodness, and beauty, i.e., God (Plato, Augustine, Boethius, Anselm in his *Monologium*).

(2) Or, it derives the real existence of the highest, absolute idea (i.e., of God) from the necessary presence of that idea in thought; as otherwise it would not be the highest idea, the absolute idea, inasmuch as an idea which has real existence is greater and higher than one not having real existence (Anselm, *Prologium*).

(3) Or, it proves God's existence from the innate character of the idea of God (Descartes).

The forms differ, but the proof is *one* inasfar as it concludes *real* existence from existence in thought. Now everyone admits that this cannot be done in the case of creatures. They are contingent: without any logical contradiction they can be thought of as non-existing. Existence in *thought* and existence in *reality* are distinct categories, are two entirely different things. From the existence of a certain object in *thought*, e.g., a winged horse, *actual* existence cannot be inferred. Existence in reality is not a product of existence in thought. Hence, no one has ever meant this when he advanced the ontological proof. But the question is whether with reference to the idea of *God* it is not legitimate to derive existence in reality from existence in thought; and the answer is, in the first place, "Yes," but under one condition, viz., that God exists.

In the second place we answer that the existence of God can never be concluded from the fact that we conceive of him, not even from the fact that we *necessarily* conceive of him, because God's existence in reality can never be the product of his existence in thought. The universe of ideas and norms, including the idea of God, cannot be identified with God; it is something in us. Hence, given these ideas, God's actual existence has not thereby been proved. Whenever we conclude the existence of God from *the presence* of these ideas in our mind, we have not the ontological but the cosmological proof. But the existence itself, of the idea of God in us, however necessary this may be, does not and cannot prove God's actual existence. The ontological proof, therefore, is not a real "proof." It implies no more than the following: (1) that the universe of ideas and norms — hence also the highest idea — is not arbitrarily but necessarily present in our thought; and (2) that as soon as we think of this universe of ideas and norms — especially the idea of God — we must needs conceive of it as having existence in reality. The necessary existence of the idea of God in our mind also implies that we must conceive of that idea as having actual existence. Farther than this the ontological proof does not carry us. We remain in the sphere of *thought*. The chasm between thought and being is not bridged. This would be done only in case we should be able to deduce a being that created and maintained the ideas in our mind — himself the highest being — not from these ideas as such, but from the fact of their presence in our mind; yet, as has been said, we would then have a cosmological, not an ontological proof. The value of the argument lies in this: that it indicates the fact that man necessarily has an idea of God, and thinks of him as actually existing, and hence: that it places man before the choice of either trusting this necessary testimony or else despairing of his own consciousness.

H. THE MORAL PROOF. The moral argument derives the existence of a supreme Law-giver, even God, from the presence of moral law in the universe. Objections:

(1) Evolution: man's moral consciousness is a product of inclinations found even in the animal world.

(2) Fichte: man's moral consciousness proves a moral world-order only, not a personal God.

(3) The fact that evil is not always punished and virtue not always rewarded indicates the absence of a moral world-order.

(4) The natural and moral world-order exist side by side and point back to several higher powers.

Answers to objections:

(1) Evolution confuses goodness with usefulness.

(2) A moral world-order is inconceivable apart from a personal God.

(3) The disproportion evident in this life between evil and punishment and between virtue and blessedness does not prove the impossibility of the existence of a moral world-order.

(4) The fourth objection is too far fetched to require serious consideration.

Result: the moral argument is not a proof but it is a mighty testimony.

The moral proof deduces a moral being who created and maintains the entire moral world-order, from ethical phenomena present in man and mankind; as, conscience, responsibility, grief, reward and punishment, virtue and happiness, fear of death and of judgment, the triumph of goodness, etc. Some place special emphasis on the voice of conscience speaking in every man: on the moral law from whose authority no one can emancipate himself; and thus arrive at a highest, sovereign Lawgiver. Others notice especially the disproportion between virtue and happiness, between sin and punishment, and from this they conclude a being who will bring about righteous harmony in the hereafter. Again, the entire moral world-order in its inner relation and in its supremacy above the order of nature is considered, and from it a being who created the moral world-order and placed it above the order of nature is derived. In every case the argument is based upon the ethical phenomena in the universe, whence the idea of the highest ethical being is derived.

Objections have also been advanced against this proof.

In the first place, the doctrine of evolution has led some to advance the objection that the ethical (as well as the conscious) principle in man does not constitute a distinct order, but that it gradually developed, and hence varies. Man's moral consciousness, we are told, is not something absolutely new, but consists in a development of inclinations, which in their primitive stage are also found in the animal world. If animals had greater power of intellect, they, by grouping themselves together, would have developed the same or similar ethical ideas and emotions as are now possessed by man: for those actions which result from the social instinct are bound to harvest the praise and approval of the group, while egoistic actions are naturally disapproved of and punished. In man's consciousness the motive giving rise to an action has gradually become separated from the action itself, and the latter is viewed as either good or evil, hence, morality is a product of society: man, also as an ethical being, is a product of circumstances.

On the other hand, Fichte and after him all the advocates of independent ethics, raised the objection that man's moral consciousness does not prove the existence of a personal God but implies a moral world-order only, i.e., a world-order in which there is room for goodness, and in which virtue has an opportunity to maintain itself and to gain the victory.

Thirdly, the objection at once presents itself that it is often very difficult to discern any moral world-order: virtue is not always rewarded; evil is not always punished. On the contrary, the wicked often enjoy peace and prosperity, while the righteous are persecuted and afflicted.

Nature seems to be so indifferent in regard to good and evil that it afflicts the innocent with calamities and catastrophies.

Finally, even though there should be something of the nature of a moral world-order, no one is able to indicate its relation to the order of nature. That the former will triumph over the latter cannot be proved; and according to some much could be said in favor of the position that these two world-orders exist side by side and indicate the existence of different powers. Hence, polytheism would contain an element of truth which is ignored by monotheism.

Valid counter-arguments can be advanced against all these objections:

The doctrine of evolution has evidently not succeeded thus far in its effort to explain the origin and essence of man's moral consciousness; in attempting to do so it always confuses the good with the useful and the pleasant.

The idea of a moral world-order apart from a personal, righteous, and holy God is not easily conceivable and amounts to the apotheosis of the abstract power of goodness.

The disproportion between virtue and happiness in this life is indeed a serious difficulty in the way of the supremacy of the moral world-order, but it does not prove the unreality or impossibility of this moral world-order.

Moreover, the return to polytheism looks so much like a make-shift that it cannot be considered an earnest attempt to arrive at a solution.

But the objections mentioned indicate very clearly that, as was true of the other arguments, so also the moral argument for the existence of God lacks the value of a *proof*. When, therefore, this argument is treated with so much respect by Kant and by many others after him that the other proofs are made to recede entirely to the background, this is not due to its logical force, but to the irresistible testimony of man's moral consciousness. Even though it may be ever so difficult for any-one to detect a moral order in the world round about him, in his *conscience* every one, whether he wills it or not, feels that he is as much bound to this order as his mind and reason are to the laws of thought. This moral order asserting itself in the conscience of every man may not have sufficient logical force to compel anyone to recognize God's exis-tence; it remains, nevertheless, a powerful testimony to the fact that in this universe the brute forces of nature will not gain the final victory. Even though the entire universe rise in opposition, and the intellect raise ever so many objections, man will continue to maintain himself as a moral being; he will persevere in his belief in the existence and in the supremacy of the moral world-order; and this conviction will naturally and involuntarily result in the recognition of a righteous and holy God, who exercises sovereign power over all creatures.

**I. THE ARGUMENT FROM UNIVERSAL CONSENT. This proof deduces the existence of God from the universality of religion. Either the universal consent is true to fact, i.e., God exists, or it is the result of the pathological condition of man's mind. In the latter case, however, the human mind is untrustworthy in every respect.**

Of similar force is the argument from universal consent. Cicero regarded this argument of great value, and the study of religions has strengthened its force. Although some in the past have maintained the contrary, all authorities in the science of religion now agree that there are no tribes without religion; that religion is common to all mankind. The historical study in regard to the origin of religion has resulted in the acknowledgment that history is unable to show us any age in which man lived without religion; even in the earliest periods of which we have any record man was a religious being, and the question concerning the *origin* of religion, history is unable to answer. The psychological study of religion, which complements the historical research or is substituted for it, never leads to any other conclusion than that religion has not and cannot have resulted from a combination of non-religious elements, but is rooted in the essence of human nature itself. Entirely against their wish some philosophers of religion find themselves compelled to accept a "seed of religion" and to recognize the fact that man was created in God's image. Now history and psychology can only *exhibit* religious phenomena. They cannot *evaluate* them. Hence, of late the necessity of a metaphysics of religion has again dawned upon the minds of many, a metaphysics which will try to establish the objective validity of this important phenomenon. This it will not be able to do until it rises to a belief in the existence, revelation, and knowability of God.

Of course, against this "universal consent" one can always raise the objection that religion constitutes a chapter in the pathology of the human soul; whoever prefers to consider religion a passing fancy or illusion which will at length be put to flight by means of scientific enlightenment (just as so many errors have thus disappeared), cannot be compelled by any syllogism to abandon this idea. Nevertheless, the "universal consent" remains a fact of great importance, for it teaches us that religion is not an individual or particularistic but a universal phenomenon: that it is rooted in human nature itself. If human nature cannot be trusted in respect to *this* universal consent, it is untrustworthy *in every respect*. Accordingly, even though logical force is wanting, the decision between truth and fancy cannot be a doubtful one.

**J. THE HISTORICO-THEOLOGICAL PROOF. The facts of history indicate an upward trend in human culture and civilization, pointing to the realization of a plan and hence to a wise and omnipotent World-Ruler who made that plan. Objection: there are no statistics which would establish this progress all along the line: pessimism can appeal to the facts of history as well as optimism. Conclusion: we must choose between atheism and theism; moreover, it is not the mind but the heart that chooses.**

Finally, closely related to the last argument, there is the so-called historico-theological proof. Some derive this argument from the *facts* of history, while others base it upon the *idea* from which consciously or unconsciously our view and study of history proceed. The former appeal to the upward trend noticeable in human culture and civilization, science and art, schools and societies, and from this they conclude a plan, the striving after a goal, and that all this points back to a wise and omnipotent world-Ruler.

It cannot be denied, however, that serious objections may be urged against all these argumentations, objections so strong that they could easily shake one's faith in God's providence, if that faith had no other foundation to rest on. History again and again confronts us with insoluble enigmas: we receive no answer to the "why?" which issues from our lips at every turn. The "real" is so different from the "ideal" that pessimism as well as optimism can appeal to history for arguments in support of its theses. Even admitting that there has been progress in mental development and material culture, there remains the greatest difference of opinion regarding the question whether the human race is advancing *religiously* and *ethically,* and there is no science of statistics that would be able to answer this question.

Hence, it is all the more remarkable that every one in his study of history proceeds (often involuntarily) from the assumption that in it there is purpose and guidance, development and goal. It was also for this reason that the doctrine of evolution received such an enthusiastic welcome. Though belief in God's providence was rejected, evolution, nevertheless, seemed to furnish grounds for the hope of a better future. The idea of progress, though not of itself included in that of evolution—for even death and dissolution are evolutionary processes—is usually associated or even identified therewith. Thus it is evident that the historian cannot dismiss the idea of guidance, plan, and purpose. There is, to be sure, much difference of opinion in regard to the character of that guidance and the content of that plan and of that purpose. But whether one accepts the Christian or the humanistic, the positivistic or the historico-materialistic view of history. in any case one proceeds from the belief that history is not the product of fate or chance but that a mighty hand is leading it to a definite goal. Thought finds no rest until at the end of the history of the world it finds some satisfaction whether in a kingdom of God or in a kingdom of humanity or in a socialistic Utopia or even if need be in Nietzsche's "eternal recurrence" of all things. Logical reasoning cannot prove the correctness of this belief. If any one prefers to believe that this world is worthy of destruction only, no rational argumentation will be able to persuade him that the contrary is true. But very remarkable indeed is the fact that the belief in guidance and purpose in history is ineradicably implanted in the heart of man, and that it is an indispensable element in the philosophy of history. Such being the case, we are again confronted with the dilemma: appearance or reality, and in principle we are thereby again forced to choose between atheism and theism, and it is not the mind but the heart that chooses.

### K. Though all the foregoing arguments are weak as "proofs," they are strong as testimonies.

The fact that these arguments for the existence of God are called "proofs" is to be regretted. Not, however, for the reason given by Jacobi. Although "to prove" means to derive one proposition from another, proving the existence of God is not therefore a "contradiction in the adjective." The dependence of a conclusion upon the premises of a syllogism is something entirely different from dependence in reality. The "ground of knowledge" is not by any means to be identified with the "ground of existence." Although in a syllogism the existence of God may be the *conclusion,* as, in general, one argues from the deed to the doer, nevertheless, that existence is in reality *origin and ground* of the being of all things. As such it is even posited in the conclusion. But the term "proofs" for these arguments is a less happy one for this reason: the latter are thereby transferred to a category to which they do not belong; namely, to the category of logical, mathematical, exact, compelling demonstration; and are thus deprived of their ethical and religious character. We receive the impression that belief in the existence of God is based entirely upon these proofs. But indeed that would be "a wretched faith, which, before it invokes God, must first prove his existence." The contrary, however, is the truth. There is not a single object the existence of which we hesitate to accept until definite proofs are furnished. Of the existence of self, of the world round about us, of logical and moral laws, etc., we are so deeply convinced because of the indelible impressions which all these things make upon our consciousness that we need no arguments or demonstration. Spontaneously, altogether involuntarily: without any constraint or coercion, we accept that existence. Now the same is true in regard to the existence of God. The so-called proofs may convey greater clearness, they are by no means the final grounds of our most certain conviction that God exists. This certainty is established only by faith; i.e., by the spontaneous testimony of our consciousness in confirmation of the existence of God, a testimony which forces itself upon us from every side. The proofs, taken as real proofs, are not *sources* but rather *products* of faith.

Our faith tries to give an account of the religious impressions and notions which enter into our mind and remain there. Faith exerts its influence also upon the intellect, and the latter seeks to establish order in that chaos of impressions and notions: it arranges and classifies them and reduces them to a few definite genera. The universe of ideas conveys its impressions (ontological proof). The world of finite, contingent, transient objects contributes its quota (cosmological proof). So does also the sphere of beauty and harmony (teleological proof), the moral world-order (moral proof), and the speech and history of all mankind (argument from universal consent and historical argument). But although they may be thus classified, no one should conclude that these six proofs are the only and isolated testimonies which God has given us. On the contrary, to the believer the entire universe is a manifestation of God: the whole world is a mirror of his virtues. There is not an atom of the universe in which his everlasting power and divinity are not clearly seen. We have this testimony within ourselves, and it also reaches us from the world round about us. God does not leave himself without witness either in nature or history, in the heart or in conscience, in life or in destiny. Accordingly, this testimony of God is so powerful that hardly anyone denies it. All peoples and tribes have heard something of the voice of the Lord, and their universal consent confirms the fact that God has not left himself without witness: it is mankind's answer to the voice of God. These testimonies, which in the interest of man proceed from God and are evident in the entire universe, are arranged and classified in the proofs. Their syllogistic form does not give them greater force, however. But though they are weak as proofs, they are strong as testimonies. They do not force the mind of the unbeliever, but they are signs and testimonies which never fail to leave an impression on the soul of any person. Analyzed, isolated, taken separately and one by one they can be attacked at every point of reasoning; instead of promoting faith they retard it, for faith is spontaneous and unforced. But taken in the sense of testimonies, and proclaimed as the revelation of that God, of whose existence every person is by nature and apart from reasoning or study assured in the very depth of his soul, they are of great value. For, though, to be sure, objections and doubts will arise even when thus presented, these arguments are not thereby deprived of their significance. Just as no one

believes in the love of God *because* everything reveals his love, but
rather *notwithstanding* everything which causes doubts to arise, even
so every one is a priorily convinced of the existence of God: the
proofs do not produce one's faith, and the objections do not cause it to
suffer shipwreck. In every sphere difficulties multiply upon further
reflection, but no one will for that reason cast overboard as mere
foolishness the laws of ethics and of logic, of religion, of art, and of
science for the sole reason that his mind is not able to explain all the
acknowledged phenomena and to defend them against all objections.
Nevertheless reflection, though not conveying certainty in regard to
existing reality, does lead to greater clearness and perspicuity. For the
believer the so-called proofs for the existence of God account for his own
religious and ethical consciousness. They provide him with weapons
wherewith he is able to repulse the attacks of the opponent. who, to
say the least, is not better armed than he. They signify to the Christian that it is one and the same God who reveals himself in nature and
in grace; consequently, that creation and redemption, the natural and
the moral world-order do not exist side by side in Manichaean and
dualistic fashion; but that those excellencies of God which shine forth
in nature are also resplendent in the kingdom of heaven. Moreover,
altogether the testimonies of God which proceed into the world and
are manifest to us, being summed up in the so-called proofs, are nothing
else than the revelation of the *Name of the Lord* by means of which he
designates himself to the ear of his creatures giving us the right to
address him. Taken together they reveal to us God, a being necessarily present in our thought, and necessarily viewed as actually existing: the only, first, and absolute cause of all creatures, consciously
and purposively reigning over all things, and to whomsoever believeth
manifesting himself, especially in conscience, as the Holy One.

# GOD'S NAMES

# CHAPTER III

# God's Names

**I. In Character These Anthropomorphic Names Are Descriptive. Their Necessity Is Rooted in the Fact of Man's Creation in God's Image, etc. As to Their Value, The Knowledge Concerning God Derived From Them Is Inadequate, Finite, Limited; Nevertheless, Real and Sufficient.**

**A. In Scripture a name is a DESCRIPTION of the person bearing it: it is not a mere denotation, but a connotation.**

All that which can be known of God by virtue of his revelation is called by Scripture: God's *name*. The original meaning of the word *shēm* is probably sign, distinctive mark, signum; just as the Greek *onoma* and the Latin *nomen* are derived from the root *gno,* and hence indicate that characteristic by which something may be known, a distinctive mark. A name is an indication of the bearer, an appellation according to this or that attribute which he reveals and by which he may be known. Between the name and its bearer there is a certain connection, and this connection is not arbitrary. Even among us though names have for the most part become sounds without meaning, that connection is felt. A name is something personal: it is not a mere number. It is always more or less unpleasant to have one's name misspelled. Our name stands for our honor, our worth, our personality, our individuality. That connection between the name and its bearer was more evident when names still had a transparent meaning, when they actually revealed the bearer. Thus we find it in Scripture: Adam named the animals in accordance with their nature, Gen. 2:19, 20. Scripture often gives us the meaning of names, and also states why they were given; e.g., Eve, Gen. 3:20; Cain, 4:1; Seth, 4:25; Noah, 5:29; Babel, 11:9; Ishmael, 16:11; Esau and Jacob, 25:25; Moses, Ex. 2:10; Jesus, Matt. 1:21; etc. Often a name is changed or a surname is added when a person begins to function in a different capacity: Abraham, Gen. 17:5; Sarah, 17:15; Israel, 32:28; Joshua, Num. 13:16; Jedidiah, II Sam. 12:25; Mara, Ruth 1:20; Peter, Mark 3:16; etc. After his ascension Christ received the name which is above every name, Phil. 2:9; Heb. 1:4; and in the New Jerusalem a new name is given to believers, Rev. 2:17; 3:12; 22:4.

> **B. The same is true in regard to the name of God: it is a REV-ELATION of God, first in the O. T., even more in the N. T., where the Son, Jesus Christ, reveals God unto us. The richest revelation of the name of God awaits us in the New Jerusalem.**

The same is true in regard to God's name. There is a very close connection between God and his name. According to Scripture also *this* connection is not an arbitrary one, but established by God himself. Men do not give him a name; he gives himself a name. God's name is, therefore, most of all God's *revelation* of himself whereby he actively and objectively makes himself known. Furthermore, the name of God is identical with the virtues or excellencies which he reveals outwardly: with his glory, Ps. 8:1; 72:19; honor, Lev. 18:21; Ps. 86:11; 102:15; redeeming power, Ex. 15:3; 3:21, etc. The name is God himself as he reveals himself in one quality or another, Lev. 24:11, 16; Deut. 18:58. Hence, that name, being the revelation of God, is great, Ezek. 36:23; holy, 36:20; terrible, Ps. 111:9; a high tower, Ps. 20:2; a strong tower, Prov. 18:10. By means of proper names, especially by means of the name Jehovah, God made himself known unto Israel. Through the Mal'akh in whom his name abides, Ex. 23:20, he revealed himself to Israel. Through him he put his name upon the children of Israel, Num. 6:27. Through him also he recorded his name among them, Ex. 20:24: put his name among them and caused it to dwell among them, Deut. 16:11; 12:5; especially in the temple established for his name, II Sam. 7:13. In that temple his name now dwells, II Chron. 20:9; 33:4. By that name he saves, Ps. 54:1; and because of that name he cannot leave Israel, I Sam. 12:22; Is. 48:9, 11; Ps. 31:3; 23:3; 143:11 ff. Hence, Israel is forbidden to profane, desecrate, or take in vain that name, Ex. 20:7; Lev. 18:21; 19:12; 24:11. On the contrary, that name must be invoked, proclaimed, exalted, made known, confessed, feared, magnified, cherished, sought, sanctified, Gen. 4:26; 12:2; Ex. 9:16; Deut. 28:58; I Kings 8:33; Ps. 5:11; 34:3; 52:9; 83:16; 122:4; Is. 26:8; Matt. 6:9; John 12:28; etc.

In the N. T. God's name receives an even richer and deeper meaning; for the Logos, who was in the beginning with God and in the bosom of the Father, hath declared the Father unto us, John 1:18, and hath revealed his name, John 17:6, 26. Whereas no one knoweth the Father but the Son, only that person to whom the Son reveals the Father obtains a knowledge of God, Matt. 11:27. He who confesseth the Son hath the Father, I John 2:23; he who hath seen him hath seen the Father, John 14:9. Hence, the name Jesus Christ guarantees our true knowledge of God as well as all the benefits connected with that knowledge. His name is Jesus because he saves his people from their sins, Matt. 1:21: his is the only name given under heaven, whereby we must be saved, Acts 4:12. By his name miracles are wrought, Acts 4:7; we receive remission, Acts 2:38; the right to become children, John 1:12; and eternal life, I John 5:13. Where two or three are gathered in his name, he is in the midst of them, Matt. 18:20. Whosoever prayeth in his name is heard, John 14:13. Whosoever calleth on the name of the Lord shall be saved, Acts 2:21. The name Father, Son, and Holy Spirit signifies complete salvation for man. To be baptized in that name is a token and seal of communion with God. And in the New Jerusalem an even greater revelation awaits believers, Rev. 3:12, when God's name shall be upon the foreheads of all, Rev. 22:4.

**C. God's names as we find them in Scripture are not the revelation of his being as such but make God known unto us in his relation to creatures. Of course, God's revelation is true to his being. Because his names are a revelation of his relation to his creatures, particularly to man, it follows that Scripture is anthropomorphic. If God spake to us in Divine language, we would not be able to understand him. Hence, human attributes, organs, emotions, actions, etc., are ascribed to God.**

The *name* of God in Scripture does not designate him as he exists in himself, but in his manifold revelation and relation to the creature. Nevertheless, this name is not arbitrary, but God reveals himself as he *is*. Hence, God's name stands for his honor, glory, excellencies, revelation, and divine essence. Hence, whosoever receives a revelation of that name receives a special privilege, and is, therefore, under special obligations. Whereas God reveals himself by means of his name, he requires his creatures to call him in accordance with that name. The "name by which God reveals himself" becomes the "name by which we address him." In Scripture "to be" and "to be called" indicate the same thing viewed from different angles: God *is* that which he *calls* himself, and he *calls* himself that which he *is*. Whatever God reveals of himself is expressed in certain definite names. To his creatures he grants the privilege to name him and to speak to him on the ground of and in conformity with his revelation. The *one* name of God, as inclusive of his entire revelation both in nature and in grace, is for us resolved into many, very many names. Only in that way do we obtain a view of the riches of his revelation and of the deep significance of his name. We are indeed *privileged* to address him in accordance with all that is revealed of his being in creation and redemption. Nevertheless, whereas all these names which we use to address him are names of

*God,* we are obliged to sanctify and extol them. It is the *one* name, the full revelation, and in so far, it is the very being of God with which the names have to do. By means of his name God places himself in a very definite relation to us. Our relation to him ought to be in conformity with this relation which he assumes to us.

Hence, the names which we use in mentioning and addressing God are not arbitrary: they are not the mere inventions of our mind. Rather, it is God himself who in nature and in grace reveals himself consciously and freely, who gives us the right to name him on the ground of this revelation, and who has even made known to us in his Word the names which are based on that revelation. God's names, therefore, have this in common: they are all derived from God's revelation: there is not one name which is expressive of the being of God "in itself." The "revealed name" is the basis of all the "names by which we address God." Moreover, whereas God's revelation in nature and Scripture is definitely directed to man, God uses human language to reveal himself and manifests himself in human forms. It follows that Scripture does not merely contain a few anthropomorphisms; on the contrary, *all* Scripture is anthropomorphic. From beginning to end Scripture testifies a condescending approach of God to man. The entire revelation of God becomes concentrated in the Logos, who became "flesh." It is as it were *one* humanization, *one* incarnation of God. If God were to speak to us in divine language, no one would be able to understand him; but ever since creation, he, in condescending grace, speaks to us and manifests himself to us in human fashion. Hence, all the names with which God names himself and by means of which he allows us to address him are derived from earthly and human relations. Accordingly, in Scripture he is called El, the Mighty One; El-Shaddai, the Powerful One; Yhwh, the One who *is*; moreover, he is called Father, Son, Spirit, good, merciful, gracious, righteous, holy, etc., expressions which are based on human relations and are applied to God metaphorically. Even the so-called incommunicable attributes; e.g., immutability, independence, unity, eternity, omnipresence, etc., are derived by Scripture from forms and expressions which pertain to finite existence, and hence are expressed negatively. Thus, eternity must needs be presented to us as a negation of time. Scripture never even attempts to describe these divine perfections *positively,* that is to say: without indicating the relation to finite existence.

But Scripture is even more emphatic in its anthropomorphism. Whatever pertains to man, whatever pertains to creatures, is applied to God: especially "human organs, members, sensations, affections," etc. God has a soul, Lev. 26:11; Matt. 12:28; and a Spirit, Gen. 1:2; etc.

Mention is never made of God's body, although in Christ God assumed a real human body, John 1:14; Col. 2:17; and the church is called the body of Christ, Eph. 1:22; but all the terms expressive of bodily organs are applied to God:. mention is made of his countenance, Ex. 33:20, 23; Is. 63:9; Ps. 16:11; Matt. 18:10; Rev. 22:4; his eyes, Ps. 11:4; Heb. 4:13; his eyelids, Ps. 11:4; the apple of his eye, Deut. 32:10; Ps. 17:8; Zech. 2:3; his ears, Ps. 55:1; nose, Deut. 33:10; mouth, Deut. 8:3; lips, Job 11:5; tongue, Is. 30:27; neck, Jer. 18:17; arms, Ex. 15:16; hand, Num. 11:23; right hand, Ex. 15:12; finger, Ex. 8:19; heart, Gen. 6:6; the "yearning of his heart" (A. V.: "sounding of his bowels"), Is. 63:15; cf. Jer. 31:20; Luke 1:78; his bosom, Ps. 74:11; foot, Is. 66:1. Further, every human emotion is also present in God; e.g., joy, Is. 62:5; rejoicing, Is. 65:19; grief, Ps. 78:40; Is. 63:10; anger, Jer. 7:18, 19; fear, Deut. 32:27; love, in all its variations; e.g., compassion, mercy, grace, longsuffering, etc.; furthermore, zeal and jealousy, Deut. 32:21; grief, Gen. 6:6; hatred, Deut. 16:22; wrath, Ps. 2:5; vengeance, Deut. 32:35.

Further, human actions are ascribed to God, as, knowing, Gen. 18:21; trying, Ps. 7:9; thinking, Gen. 50:20; forgetting, I Sam. 1:11; remembering, Gen. 8:1; Ex. 2:24; speaking, Gen. 2:16; calling, Rom. 4:17; commanding, Is. 5:6; rebuking, Ps. 18:15; 104:7; answering, Ps. 3:4; witnessing, Mal. 2:14; resting, Gen. 2:2; working, John 5:17; seeing, Gen. 1:10; hearing, Ex. 2:24; smelling, Gen. 8:21; tasting, Ps. 11:4, 5; sitting, Ps. 9:7; rising, Ps. 68:1; going, Ex. 34:9; coming, Ex. 25:22; walking, Lev. 26:12; descending, Gen. 11:5; meeting, Ex. 3:18; visiting, Gen. 21:1; passing, Ex. 12:13; casting off, Judg. 6:13; writing, Ex. 34:1; sealing, John 6:27; graving, Is. 49:16; smiting, Is. 11:4; chastening, Deut. 8:5; punishing, Job. 5:17; binding up the wounds and healing, Ps. 147:3; cf. Ps. 103:3; Deut. 32:39; killing and making alive, Deut. 32:39; wiping away tears, Is. 25:8; wiping (out), II Kings 21:13; washing, Ps. 51:2; anointing, Ps. 2:6; cleansing, Ps. 51:2; decking with ornaments, Ezek. 16:11; clothing (with), Ps. 132:16; crowning, Ps. 8:5; girding with strength, Ps. 18:32; destroying, Gen. 6:7; laying waste (making a waste), Lev. 26:31; killing, Gen. 38:7; plaguing, Gen. 12:17; judging, Ps. 58:11; condemning, Job 10:2; etc. Furthermore, God is often called by names which indicate a certain office, profession, or relation among men. Hence, he is called bridegroom, Is. 61:10; husband, Is. 54:5; father, Deut. 32:6; judge, king, lawgiver, Is. 33:22; man of war, Ex. 15:3; hero, Ps. 78:65; Zeph. 3:17; builder, (architect) and maker, Heb. 11:10; husbandman, John 15:1; shepherd, Ps. 23:1; physician, Ex. 15:26; etc., while in connection with these mention is made of his seat, throne, footstool, rod, scepter, weapons, bow, arrow, sword, shield, wagon, banner, book, seal, treasure, inheritance, etc. In order to indicate what God is for his children language derived from the organic and inorganic creation is even applied to God. He is compared to a lion, Is. 31:4; an eagle, Deut. 32:11; a lamb, Is. 53:7; a hen, Matt. 23:37; the sun, Ps. 84:11; the morning star, Rev. 22:16; a light, Ps. 27:1; a torch, Rev. 21:23; a fire, Heb. 12:29; a fountain, Ps. 36:9; the fountain of living waters. Jer. 2:13; food, bread, water, drink, ointment, Is. 55:1; John 4:10; 6:35, 55; a rock, Deut. 32:4; a hiding place, Ps. 199:114; a tower, Prov. 18:10; a refuge, Ps. 9:9; a shadow, Ps. 91:1; 121:5; a shield, Ps. 84:11; a way, John 14:6; a temple, Rev. 21:22; etc.

Scripture calls upon the entire creation, i.e., upon nature in its several spheres, and especially upon man, to contribute to the description of the knowledge of God. Anthropomorphism seems to be unlimited. In order to give us an idea of the majesty and exalted character of God names are derived from every kind of creature, living and lifeless, organic and inorganic. Although in himself God is "anonymous, i.e., without name." nevertheless, in his revelation he is "polyonymous, i.e., possessing many names." Says Augustine, "All things can be said of God, but nothing is worthily said of him. Nothing is more wide-spread than this poverty of expression. Thou seekest a fitting name for him; thou canst not find it." Moreover to make clear why it is that so many names can be applied to God, Augustine used a striking illustration: our body has many needs; e.g., light and air, food and drink, clothing and a dwelling, etc. Now in the universe of nature all these things differ and occupy a separate place. So also our soul has many and various needs; but, instead of requiring several things to supply these needs, the One and Only Divine Being supplies them all. "On earth a fountain is one thing, a light is another. When thou art athirst, thou seekest a fountain, and to get to the fountain thou seekest light; and if it is not day, thou lightest a lamp to get to the fountain. God himself is both a fountain and a light: to the thirsting a fountain; to the blind a light. Let the eyes be opened to see the light, let the lips of the heart be opened to drink of the fountain; that which thou drinkest, thou seest, thou hearest. May God become all to thee, for he is to thee the whole of these things which thou lovest. If thou regardest things visible, neither is God bread, nor is God water, nor is God that light, nor is God a garment, nor is God a house. For all these things are visible and separate objects. What bread is, water is not; and what a garment is, a house is not; and what these things are, God is not, for they are visible things. God is all this to thee: if thou hungerest, he is bread to thee; if thou thirstest, he is water to thee; if thou art in darkness, he is light to thee; for he remains incorruptible. If thou art naked, he is a garment of immortality to thee when this corruptible shall put on incorruption, and this mortal shall put on immortality." Pseudodionysius says that God is "anonymous," i.e., "without name" and at the same time "polyonymous," i.e., "possessing many names." He is both all that exists and nothing of all that exists.

Says Thomas Aquinas: "God prepossesses in himself all the perfections of creatures, being himself simply and universally perfect." Bonaventura says even more beautifully: "In order that we may be able to extol and glorify God, and in order that we may advance to the cognition (knowledge) of God, we must needs transfer to the divine that which pertains to the creature. Now the ground or purpose of this transference is twofold. In the first place, it is necessary with a view to the glory of God; in the second place, with a view to the guidance of our intellect. God's glory requires this transference. For, since God is greatly to be praised, lest he should ever lack praise because of the scarcity of words, Holy Scripture has taught us that the names of creatures — indefinite in number — should be transferred to God, in order that just as every *creature* glorifies God, so also every *name* that is ascribed to creatures might glorify him, and in order that he who is so glorious that not one single name can do justice to him — for he excels, as it were, every name — might be glorified by all the names. This transference is also necessary with a view to the guidance of our intellect. For, since we arrive at cognition of the Creator through the creature, and especially in view of the fact that nearly all creatures possess certain noble characteristics which furnish a source for our understanding of God — e.g., the lion possesses fortitude; the lamb, meekness; the rock, solidity; the serpent, prudence, etc. — hence, it is necessary that many names be transferred to God."

Calvin agreed with this when he said, "There is not an atom of the universe in which you cannot see some brilliant sparks at least of his glory." God is immanent in all creation. The pure of heart see God everywhere. Everything is full of God. "I confess that the expression, 'Nature is God' may be used in a pious sense by a pious mind!"

Now all creatures are not of equal importance. On the contrary, an upward trend is clearly observable, and the importance and rank of each creature is determined by its relation to God. Something of God is manifest in each creature, but of all creatures man is endowed with the highest degree of excellence. The exalted title: image, son, child of God, is born by him alone. The name: God's offspring (Acts 17:28), is peculiar to man. Hence, most of the names of the Deity, particularly the most exalted ones, are derived from man. Nevertheless, man should

never be severed from the realm of nature; neither should any creature or any portion of the universe ever be given a separate place or
position next to or in opposition to God. Outside of and apart from
God there is no existence. This truth has been disregarded again and
again. Plato's dualism, Neo-Platonism, Gnosticism, and Manichaeism,
limited God's revelation, and posited a material substance, represented
as existing independently of and in hostile relation to God. In various
ways this dualism influenced theology; the same dualistic principle is
evident when Kant and Jacobi limit God's revelation to the religious
and ethical sphere; when only the *ethico-religious* content of Scripture
is recognized; when the seat of religion is confined to the heart or
conscience, mind or will. In this way the realm of nature with its
forces and energies, man in his social and political life, and also science
and art, are given a place outside of the sphere of God's revelation.
They become neutral spheres, and are viewed as existing apart from
God. Of course, a proper appreciation of the O. T. and of a large part of
the N. T. is impossible on this basis. Nature is deprived of its mes-
sage for the believer. The revelation of God in his Word loses all its
influence on outward life. Religion, altogether confined to the inner
chamber and to the innermost recesses of the heart, forfeits every
claim to respect. Dogmatics, and in particular the "doctrine of God,"
is reduced to a minimum; and theology is no longer able to maintain
its proper and important position: it is no longer able to speak about
God, because it no longer recognizes him as its source and goal. It
has no names for God. He becomes the Great Unknowable; and the
universe becomes first a sphere "without God," later on "an antigod."

> **D. The question, however, arises: what right have we to ascribe
> creaturely names to him who is exalted above all creatures?
> Answer: the universe is the work, the creation of God. It is not an
> independent power, or a force opposed to God. If it be improper
> to speak about God in anthropomorphic language, the only logical
> alternative is not to speak about God at all.**

Now the names wherein God reveals himself present a peculiar difficulty. In an earlier chapter we learned that God is incomprehensible
and exalted far above all finite creatures. In his names, however, he
descends to the level of the finite and of the creature. A solution of
this difficulty seems to be impossible. On the one hand God is "anonymous," on the other he is, nevertheless "polyonymous." Apparently we
try to salvage by the doctrine of God's names what we threw overboard by the doctrine of God's incomprehensibility. What right have
we to speak of God in anthropomorphic language, and to apply human
and creaturely names to him? With what reason are these names applied to him who is exalted above every creature and cannot be com-

prehended by any finite being? The reason is this: though the distance between creature and Creator is, indeed, infinite; nevertheless, the entire universe is God's handiwork. Therefore, there is a close relation between God and the universe. God and the world are not to be conceived of as two objects or forces opposed to each other; the universe is not independent of God: it is not a second God. On the contrary, it is entirely God's handiwork, having been created in order that it might reveal God. The entire nation of Israel was destined to show forth God's excellencies in all it laws and ordinances, offices and institutions, morals and characteristics. Christ's human nature was by the Holy Spirit endowed with power to declare the Father, and to make known his name among men; and the circle of apostles, with its diversity of gifts, talents, manner of preparation, and degree of education, must serve to proclaim the "mighty works of God." Hence, we have a right to speak of God in language which pertains to the creature. We have the right to use anthropomorphic language with reference to God because God himself has come to dwell with and in his creatures, and because it has pleased him to reveal his name in and through creatures. Accordingly, as we have already seen, anthropomorphism is not confined to a single term, e.g., personality. On the contrary, it is altogether impossible to say anything about God apart from the use of anthropomorphisms. We do not see God as he is in himself. We behold him in his works. We name him according to the manner in which he has revealed himself in his works. To see God face to face is for us impossible, at least here on earth. If, nevertheless, God wills that we should know him, he must needs descend to the level of the creature. He must needs accommodate himself to our limited, finite, human consciousness. He must speak to us in human language. Whosoever, therefore, objects to anthropomorphisms, thereby in principle denies the possibility of a revelation of God in his creatures. Strict logic will force him to a denial of creation itself, so that he is finally driven to the conclusion that there is an eternal dualism between God and the universe, between the Infinite and the finite. For, if the ascription of anthropomorphic names to God implies a limitation of God, ascribing creative activity to him, will *certainly* imply this. The result of this reasoning is that God, the Infinite One, is not able to bring forth any other being distinct from his own; that the universe is not a *manifestation* of God in any sense whatsoever; it is much rather a *means of concealing* the Deity; that a dualism is established between God and man; and that God is eternal "depth," nameless "silence," both with respect to himself and with respect to man. Knowledge of God is rendered altogether impossible. If anthropomorphic, creaturely names do injustice to the being of God, then it necessarily follows that we have no right to address him at all: we must needs be silent altogether, for every name by which we should wish to designate him would be sacrilege, an attack on his majesty, blasphemy.

> **E. Attempts have been made to evade this conclusion by differentiating between abstract ideas and concrete representations of God. But even the most abstract terms are anthropomorphic. We must choose between absolute silence or anthropomorphic language. Philosophy has always returned to a recognition of the rights of anthropomorphism.**

Attempts have been made to evade this very natural conclusion by distinguishing between concrete representations and abstract concepts. To arrive at the origin of this distinction we must go back to Plato himself. His example was followed by Neo-Platonism and Gnosticism. Hegel reintroduced the distinction. But it does not bring those who make it a step nearer to their goal. Even the most abstruse speculation and the most abstract philosophy must needs think and speak about God. Even though they banish all concrete representations and retain only pure and abstract concepts, they never thereby arrive at a point where they can dispense with the necessity of thinking and speaking in terms derived from the human and creaturely realm: they never reach the Infinite One himself. Even the most abstract names; e. g., essence, substance, the absolute, the one, spirit, reason, etc., are and ever remain anthropomorphisms. For man there are only two alternatives: absolute silence with reference to God, or speaking about him in a human way; either agnosticism, i. e., theoretical atheism, or anthropomorphism. Hence, philosophy has always returned to a recognition of the rights of anthropomorphism. If it had not done this, its only result would have been a negative criticism. Plato, Philo, Plotinus, Pseudodionysius, John of Damascus, and Erigena in the end ascribe several names to God. Positive theology builds up what negative theology has broken down. Spinoza's substance receives several attributes and modes. In the philosophy of Hegel God in the end becomes life, spirit, thought, reason, subject. Rauwenhoff allows the imagination to appear on the scene when reason must leave. Accordingly, many philosophers defend the rights of anthropomorphism. In this defense philosophy is in accord with the truth which Christian theology has always proclaimed. God condescends to our level: he treads "the path of the children of man," as the Jews express it. "Incomprehensible are the works and actions of God, neither would we be able to understand anything concerning them if Holy Writ in speaking about God had not used such terms as are nearest to our human realm. Therefore it pleases the Holy Spirit, the Author of the Scriptures, because of our feeble comprehension, to stammer after our fashion, and, by means of images and words, to deal with us in a manner more pleasing and humble than is due to so great a majesty."

**F. Having shown the necessity of these names, we now ask: What is their value? Answer: they do not give us an adequate, complete knowledge of God, but they do give us a true knowledge of him, for God himself has originated them.**

The propriety of these names having been established, the next question is: What is their significance? What kind of knowledge of the Divine Being do they give us? It is clear that they do not furnish adequate knowledge. Yet, although this knowledge is limited and finite, it is real and true. Adequate knowledge we have very little: everywhere and in every sphere we are confronted with mysteries: "the inner essence of things" escapes our observation. To be sure, we observe phenomena, and from them we deduce the essence. We learn to recognize properties, and by means of them we ascend to the substance; but the latter lies hidden behind its manifestation and is unknown to us as it is in itself. Science posits atoms, electrons, and units of energy as the final elements of material existence, but has not the least empirical knowledge of any of these. Only the very simplest matters can be defined. To give a complete and adequate definition of things belonging to a somewhat higher order of existence is altogether impossible. This is even true with respect to things which pertain to the *visible* realm. Hence, it holds with added emphasis in regard to objects that are invisible. Man is a corporeal, physical being. All his knowledge originates in and is derived from sense-perception. Our thinking is linked up with the senses just as our soul is united with the body. We never perceive spiritual realities directly or immediately but always through the medium of material things. We see everything "in a riddle." Not only God but also the soul and the entire spiritual world becomes known to us through the physical universe. Hence, names which have their primary significance in the visible realm are employed by us to designate spiritual entities. We denominate the soul in accordance with its manifestations in the body. In order to bring before our own consciousness and that of others the activities of the *soul,* such as, knowing, thinking, understanding, comprehending, judging, deciding, perceiving, etc., we make use of terms and expressions which in their original and primary signification designate *physical* activities. Hence, whenever we discuss spiritual realities, we do so metaphorically, figuratively, poetically. But this does not mean that all such thought and speech is contrary to truth. On the contrary, real poetry is truth, for it is based upon the resemblance, similarity, and relation which actually exists between the different groups of phenomena. All language and every figure and symbol presupposes as the foundation upon which it rests this penetration of the visible by the invisible. If speaking in symbols were contrary to truth, all our thinking and all our knowledge would be a delusion, and speech itself would be impossible.

The same is true in the sphere of religion and theology. There is no adequate knowledge of God. Of all his names not a single one describes him as he is in himself, i.e., in his inner essence. All these names are derived from the sphere of creation. But this does not mean that they are therefore simply the result of human fancy and imagination. It does not mean that they are contrary to truth and reality. Just as things in this world may be compared because they are related and resemble each other, for the same reason it is proper for us to speak of God in language derived from the sphere of the creature, for God is related to his creatures. Not only that, but, although temporally that is not first which is spiritual but that which is natural; logically and ideally that which is spiritual precedes that which is natural. That which is natural would never be able to reveal to us that which is spiritual if the former had not been produced by the latter. Plato considered the cosmos to be a realization of ideas. Scripture teaches that "all things were made through the Logos," and that "what is seen hath not been made out of things which appear," John 1:3; Heb. 11:3. God himself made the entire creation, including the material universe, subservient to the manifestation of his virtues. He was able to do this because he is the omnipotent Creator, and because as such he has absolute dominion over matter. Therefore, though we call God by names derived from the creature, God himself first established these names for the creature. Indeed, although we first apply to the creature the names which designate God because of the fact that we know the creature before we know God; *essentially* they apply first of all to God, then to the creature. All virtues pertain first to God, then to the creature: God possesses these virtues "in essence," the creature "through participation." As the temple was made "according to the pattern shown to Moses in the mount," Heb. 8:5, even so every creature was first conceived and afterward (in time) created. "Every fatherhood" is named from "the Father" who created all things—Eph. 3:15; cf. Matt. 23:9.

Scripture uses earthly hues and colors to picture heavenly realities. God himself comes to us in creation, and in the human nature of Christ he tabernacled among us. Now, to be sure, Christ's human nature was not an adequate organ of his Deity: the splendor of his glory was even concealed by its human manifestation. Nevertheless, the fulness of the Godhead dwelled in him bodily. Whosoever beheld him beheld the

Father. Hence, to say that our knowledge of God is inadequate, finite, limited, and nevertheless, to maintain that it is real, pure, sufficient is not at all illogical or contradictory. God reveals himself in his works, and the names by means of which we designate him are in accordance with this revelation. He allows us to speak of him in creaturely language because he himself has manifested his virtues and revealed them unto us through the creature. Hence, in reality, it is not *we* who name God; whence should we derive the right to do so? but it is God himself, who through nature and Scripture, has put in our mouth his glorious names. According to an old distinction, God's names are not the product of man's "subjective reasoning," but of "objective reason" given in God's revelation. God's self-consciousness is the arche-type of which our knowledge concerning God, derived from Scripture, is the ectype.

**G. The position defended in the former paragraph avoids, on the one hand, the extreme view of Roman Catholic theologians, of Spinoza, Hegel, etc., who consider adequate knowledge of God possible; and on the other hand, the opposite extreme of Schleiermacher, Pierson, F. A. Lange, etc., who maintain that there is no reality corresponding to the names of God: that these are merely the products of human imagination.**

Herewith the character which necessarily pertains to all knowledge of God as found among creatures has been indicated. Accordingly, two extremes must be voided. On the one hand there are those who regard essential, quidditative, adequate knowledge of God within the range of possibility, either by way of mystic contemplation—the position of Plotinus, Malebranche, the ontologists, and Roman Catholics, when they teach a vision of God's essence in the state of glory—or by way of logical thinking, the position of Eunomius, Duns Scotus, Spinoza, and Hegel. Over against all these we must emphasize the saying, "No man hath seen God at any time: the only begotten Son who is in the bosom of the Father, he hath declared him." Moses did not see God's glory until it had passed by. Only in a vision did the prophets see God. With reference both to the realm of nature outside of us and to our inner soul-life that which was created ever stands between God and our consciousness: innate ideas do not exist. We see in a mirror darkly and we walk by faith. Substituting the idea for the description, the language of thought for that of the imagination, negative for positive theology, the Japhetic-abstract for the Semitic-concrete conception ever results in the total loss of the knowledge of God.

On the other hand, the name "ectypal theology" also implies the rejection of the view of those who hold that although creaturely names that are used to designate God are unavoidable, they are, nevertheless, merely symbols—products of poetic imagination.　In a certain sense even John of Damascus and Pseudodionysius belong to this group. They claim that the divine names describe God merely as the cause of all things; e. g., the name "Wisdom" when ascribed to God merely indicates that God is the cause of all wisdom.　But Thomas Aquinas already countered with the valid objection that in that case the names gold, silver, sun, moon, body, etc., could just as well be ascribed to God, as he is the originating cause of all these things; furthermore, that we always mean more when we say "God" than when we merely say "the cause of goodness," and that not all God's virtues are revealed in all his creatures, nor revealed alike in each creature.　Nevertheless, Schleiermacher revived the opinion that God is merely absolute causality; that his attributes are subjective appellations; and that theology is not ectypal or analogical but symbolical in character.　According to this view religious representations of God are merely products of poetic imagination, ideals to be evaluated according to esthetic principles—thus Rauwenhoff, Pierson, F. A. Lange, etc. In some liberal circles the tendency is manifesting itself of late to continue to use Biblical and ecclesiastical terms as symbols of higher spiritual truths.

Nevertheless, this view of the character of theology is untenable.　The name "symbolic theology" may be properly applied only to that branch of theology which has as its object the explanation of symbols that occur in Scripture and in the realm of the church. Vitringa gives to this branch the name *Theologia Symbolica, 1726.*　But a symbol is always a sensible object or action by which a spiritual truth is indicated; while theology as such does not deal with symbols but with spiritual realities.　When consciousness, will, holiness, etc., are ascribed to God, no one thinks that this is meant in a merely symbolical sense.　No religious person views these descriptions as products of his own imagination comparable to works of art.　On the contrary, a religious person views these religious representations as objective truth, and his religion would languish and die if he would ever begin to doubt this fact.　If they are merely products of the imagination, their objective reality can not be maintained.　They may retain a certain degree of *esthetic* value; they have lost all *religious* and *ethical* worth.　Religion cannot be changed into art any more than it can be changed into philosophy.　Attempts to maintain these religious descriptions as symbols never satisfy. Those who follow Hegel in distinguishing between concrete representations and abstract concepts are not satisfied with the former, always try to attain to the latter, and afterward wish to return to the former viewed as mere symbols.　Those who regard theology as nothing more than a science of symbols reduce the names of God to a mere reflex of man's own inner life, deny the fact that there is a reality corresponding to these names, and seek the ground of the existence of these names in man's own "subjective reasoning." Man thus becomes the standard of religion: as is man, so is his God.

**H. Scripture combats both of these extreme views. It teaches:**
(1) that the universe indeed reveals God, for it was created by God;

(2) that of all creatures man especially reveals God, for he is God's image-bearer; hence, our right to use anthropomorphisms; and

(3) that, although this knowledge of God is real and true — having as its arche-type God's self-consciousness, and as its foundation his self-revelation — nevertheless, it is not adequate.

Scripture combats both of these views. In the first place it teaches that God is Creator of heaven and earth. "What is seen hath not been made out of things which appear," Heb. 11:3. On the contrary, the visible world existed and exists eternally as an idea in the mind of God. It has its origin in God. Hence, it sustains a certain relation to him and it is able to manifest God's virtues and to reveal them to the eyes of his creatures. Whereas the universe is God's creation, it follows that it also reveals and manifests him. There is "not one atom of the universe" in which his divinity does not shine forth. Secondly, Scripture teaches us that man has an altogether peculiar position among creatures. Whereas creatures in general exhibit "vestiges" of God's virtues, man on the contrary, is the very image and likeness of God; hence, our right to speak of God in creaturely, especially, in anthropomorphic terms. We know God because he knows us: I know because I am known (Von Baader). We have the right to anthropomorphize God because he himself theomorphized when he created man (Jacobi). And thirdly, notwithstanding all that has been said, Scripture throughout maintains God's absolute transcendence. Both God's transcendence and his immanence, both the essential distinction and the inner relation existing between God and the creature are implied in the fact of creation. Scripture everywhere speaks to us concerning the God "who dwelleth in the high and holy place, with him also that is of a contrite and humble spirit," Is. 57:15. Hence, theology is not merely symbolical, but rather ectypal or analogical. This implies:

(1) that all our knowledge is out of and through God, and rests upon his revelation, i. e., on objective reason;

(2) that in order to impart knowledge concerning himself to his creatures, God must needs accommodate himself to their consciousness;

(3) that the possibility of this "condescension" cannot be denied as it is implied in the very fact of creation and in the existence of any finite being;

(4) that, for this very reason, our knowledge concerning God must remain analogical in character (i. e., resting upon the analogy of that which may be perceived of God in the creature), having for its object not God himself according to his unknowable essence, but God in his revelation to us, in "the relations which his nature sustains to us," in his disposition toward his creatures; that this knowledge is, accordingly, merely a vague image or likeness of that perfect knowledge which God has of himself; and

(5) that, notwithstanding all that has been said, our knowledge concerning God is real, pure, and dependable, because God's self-consciousness is its archetype, and his self-revelation in the cosmos its foundation.

## II. The Names by Which We Address God. Definition and Meaning of God's Proper Names. DEFINITION: God's Names Are Those Appellatives Which Designate God and By Means of Which We Address Him as an Independent, Personal Being. MEANING: El, Elohim: Powerful One; Adonai: Ruler; El-Shaddai: The Omnipotent One (i.e., Able to Help); Yhwh: I Will Be That I Will Be, The Ever-Faithful One; Father: He Who Loves Us. etc., (esp. in N. T.)*

### A. Definition of God's proper names.

When we speak of God's names in the more limited sense of that term (i. e., in distinction from his attributes), we understand thereby those appellatives which designate God and by means of which we address him as an independent, personal being. Such names are found in every language. Though in himself God is without name, nevertheless, we must be able to designate him, and we can do this in no other way than by means of the use of names. "For unless you know the name, your knowledge of the objects which it indicates will perish."

### B. Generic names: theos, daimon, kyrios, God, Asura, Ahura.

Formerly the Greek word *theos* was held to be derived from *tithenai, theein, theasthai.* At present some philologists connect it with Zeus, Dios, Jupiter, Deus, Diana, Juno, Dio, Dieu. So interpreted it would be identical with the Sanskrit "deva," the shining heaven, from "div," to shine. Others, however, deny all etymological connection between

---

*(Note: in the original this section follows that on the classification of God's attributes.)

the Greek *theos* and the Latin Deus and connect the former with the root *thes* in *thessasthai* to desire, to invoke. In many languages the words *heaven* and *God* are used synonymously: the oldest Grecian deity Uranus was probably identical with the Sanskrit Varuna; the Tartar and Turkish word "Taengri" and the Chinese word "Thian" mean both heaven and God; and also in Scripture the words heaven and God are sometimes used interchangeably; e. g., in the expression "kingdom of heaven" or "kingdom of God."

Another Greek word *daimōn* is derived from *daiō* meaning: he who determines one's destiny.

The word *kyrios* from *kyros* characterizes God as the Mighty One, Lord, Owner, Ruler.

Our word "God" is of uncertain origin. Attempts have been made to prove its derivation from the word "good"; from the Avestan "khodâ": "independent in existence"; from the Sanskrit "gudha" or "gutha," *keuthō*, which would designate God as the "Hidden One," or from the root "ghu," Sanskrit "hû," meaning to invoke, so that God would be the One to whom invocations are made; or from a root *kodō*, *kosmos* to which the meaning: to arrange, to order, has been given; or from the Aryan "cuddhas," pure, good, etc., but all these derivations are uncertain.

The Indian "Asura" and the Persian "Ahura" designate God as the Living One.

**C. Scripture uses the word "name of God" in a very comprehensive sense, as including his attributes. Speaking of the names of God in the more limited sense Jerome enumerates ten.**

Scripture often uses the expression "God's name" in a very comprehensive sense. Hence, the Jews enumerated seventy names, and originally Christian theology included God's attributes under his names. Gradually, however, a distinction was made. Jerome limits the number of divine names to the following ten: El, Elohim, Eloha, Sabaoth, Elyon, Esher ehye, Adonai, Yah, Yhwh, Shaddai. Others followed his example.

**D. El: the Strong and Mighty One;  Eloha, Elohim: the Powerful One or He that is to be feared;  Elyon: the High and Exalted One;  Adonai: Ruler; etc.**

The most simple name by which God is indicated in Scripture and by the Semites in general is the name *'El*. Its derivation is not certain. Lagarde and others try to prove its derivation from the root *'ly* and the preposition *'el* (unto, to) indicating God as the One "to whom" the human soul aspires. Others regard this derivation just as improbable as the idea that *'El* is connected with *'ēlāh,* sacred tree. According to most philologists the word is derived from *'ûl,* and means the First One, Lord (Nöldeke) ; or the Strong and Mighty One (Gesenius). *Elōha,* pl. *Elōhîm,* is from the same root *'ûl,* to be first, or from the root *'lh,* to be smitten with fear, and therefore points to God as the Strong and Mighty One, or as the object of fear. The singular is of infrequent occurrence; it is poetical, Ps. 18:32; Job 3:4. Generally the plural is used; it is the usual name whereby God is indicated. This plural is not to be regarded as a plural of majesty (never used in Scripture of God), nor as an indication of the trinity (as it is interpreted by Lombard and by many after him) since it nearly always has a singular adjective or verb, nor as a remnant of polytheism (as held by modern critics) ; for, in the first place, as was just stated, the word is singular in construction with verbs and adjectives and in the second place, it is found outside of Israel as the name of a single God. It is rather to be regarded as a plural of abstraction (Eswald), or of quantity (Oehler), or as an intensive plural, serving to indicate fulness of life and power (Delitzsch). A few times *Elōhim* is constructed with adjectives or verbs in the plural: Gen. 20:13; 28:13ff.; 35:7; Ex. 32:4, 8; Josh. 24:19; I Sam. 4:8; 17:26; II Sam. 7:23; I Kings 12:28; Ps. 58:11; 121:5; Job 35:10; Jer. 10:10. We find a similar plural in the personal pronoun: Gen. 1:26; 3:22; 11:7; Is. 6:8; 41:22; in *Qedhōshîm.* Prov. 9:10; Hos. 12:1; in *'ōsîm,* Job 35:10; Is. 54:5; in *Bōr'îm,* Ecc. 12:1; and in *'Adhōnāy.* All of these plural forms designate God as a being full of life and power. Says Beck, "The name 'Elohim' describes the Divine Being in his original relationship and in his continuous causal relationship to the universe. It is a designation of relationship, not a designation of immediate, inner essence. Indeed, it expresses the idea of absolute transcendence with respect to the entire universe."

The name *Elyon,* LXX: *hupsistos,* designates God as the High and Exalted One; it is used by Melchizedek, Gen. 14:18; Balaam, Num. 24:16; the king of Babylon, Is. 14:14; cf. Mk. 5:7; Luke 1:32, 35; Acts. 16:17; and occurs especially in poetry. *'Adhōnāy,* Lord, in strengthened form "Lord of lords" and "Lord of all the earth," indicates God as the Ruler to whom everything is subject, and to whom man is related as a servant, Gen. 18:27. In an earlier period the name *Ba'al* was applied to God with the same signification, but later on this name was given an idolatrous meaning; hence, its use was discontinued.

**E. The names which we have so far discussed:**
   (1) **are not proper names in the strict limited sense of that term;**
   (2) **are Semitic (i.e. those under D) ; and**

**(3)** **describe God as the One who is exalted far above all creatures.**

Now the names discussed so far are not "proper names" in the restricted, limited sense of that term. They are also used with reference to idols, to men, and to the government, Gen. 33:10; Ex. 7:1; 4:16; 12:12; 21:5, 6; 22:7; Lev. 19:32; Num. 33:4; Judg. 5:8; I Sam. 2:25; Ps. 58:1; 82:1. Nevertheless, these names are the usual appellatives and designations of the Deity. Moreover, they are Semitic, and indicate God's transcendence above all creatures. The Semites prefer to call God "Lord," "King." They feel deeply dependent upon him, and as his servants they humbly and reverently bow before him. They do not use these names to give expression to philosophic theories concerning the being of God, but emphasize God's relation to his creatures, especially to man.

> **F. Whereas the names discussed so far emphasize God's transcendence, there are others that signify especially his immanence: his condescension to the level of the creature. First among these names is El-Shaddai: God, the Omnipotent One. The name Elohim differs in this respect from El-Shaddai that while the former indicates the God of nature and creation, the latter describes God as subjecting all the powers of nature, and making them subservient to the work of grace.**

Though high and exalted, in transcendence, nevertheless, God condescends to the level of the creature. Not only does he reveal himself through the work of creation to all nations, but in a very special sense he makes himself known to Israel. The first name by means of which, in his special revelation, God makes himself known is *Shadday* or *'El Shadday*. As such God reveals himself to Abraham when he makes him a father of a multitude of nations and institutes the sacrament of circumcision as a seal of the covenant, Gen. 17:1 ff. In the time of the patriarchs this name occurs again and again, Gen. 28:3; 35:11; 43:14; 48:3; 49:25; Ex. 6:3; Num. 24:4. Furthermore, it is found in Job, in a few psalms, and a few times in the prophets. The N. T. equivalent for the name is *pantokratōr*, II Cor. 6:18; Rev. 4:8, the Lord Almighty. Up to the present no one has been able to establish with certainty the origin of this name. Nöldeke tried to show its derivation from *shadh*, lord, but according to Gen. 43:14; 49:25, and Ezek. 10:5, the name is undoubtedly an adjective. Formerly it was held to be derived from *sh* for *'shr* and *day*, and then translated "the all-sufficient one"; or from *shdd*, meaning: to be strong, to destroy. It has also been connected with *shdh* or *'shr*, to pour out, designating God as the One who distributes bountifully. Wherever the name occurs the idea of power and invincible strength is in the foreground, and in Is. 13:6 this name is brought in connection with *shdd,* to destroy, even though this connection may be considered one of alliteration, cf. Joel. 1:15. Hence, this name makes God known to us as the One who possesses all power, and is able to overcome all opposition and to make everything subservient to his will. The name Elohim differs in this respect from El-Shaddai that while the former indicates the God of nature and creation, the latter describes him as subjecting all the powers of nature and making them subservient to the work of grace. In this name God's "divinity" and "everlasting power" is no more an object of fear and terror but a source of blessing and comfort. God gives himself to his people, and his invincible power is for them the guarantee of the fulfilment of his promises and of the fact that he will ever keep his covenant. Hence, from now on God is repeatedly called the God of Abraham, Gen. 24:12; of Isaac, Gen. 28:13; of Jacob, Ex. 3:6; of your fathers, Ex. 3:13, 15; of the Hebrews, Ex. 3:18; of Israel, Gen. 33:20; while Isaiah often calls him the Holy One of Israel. God is the Exalted One, the Creator of heaven and earth, the Omnipotent One, who, nevertheless, sustains a relation of favor toward his people.

G. **The name Yhwh (Jehovah).** Because of the Jewish dread to pronounce this name, its original pronunciation, derivation, and meaning were lost. Interpretations:

(1) Voltaire and others derive it from the Egyptian tongue. Ex. 5:2 contradicts this view.

(2) F. Delitzsch and others hold that the name is of Canaanitish origin. The evidence is lacking.

(3) In all probability the name Yhwh is from the root hwh or hyh.

a. Some regard it as a Hiphil; hence, Giver of Life: he who causes to be. However, there is nothing in Ex. 3 to suggest this meaning. Moreover, it has been pointed out that the Hiphil of this verb occurs nowhere.

b. It must be a Qal form. Even then different interpretations are given:

1. The church-fathers regarded the name as referring to God's aseity as such. This interpretation is too philosophical and is not supported by Ex. 3.

2. Smend and others interpret it as meaning "he whò shall be with you." If that were correct, the suffix "with you" would have been given as an integral part of the name.

3. The true meaning of the name is clearly indicated in Ex. 3:13-15: "I WILL BE THAT I WILL BE," i. e., the God who is unchangeable in his grace, the Ever-faithful Covenant God.

(4) The name Yhwh-Ç bha'ôth describes Jehovah as the King in the fulness of his glory, surrounded by organized hosts of angels, governing the entire universe as the Omnipotent One, and in his temple receiving the honor and adoration of all his creatures.

It is especially in the name *Yhwh* that the Lord reveals himself as the God of grace. The Jews regarded this name as God's name par excellence, the name descriptive of God's essence, God's proper name, the glorious name, the name of four letters, the Tetragrammaton, etc., and from Lev. 24:16 and Ex. 3:15 they concluded that it is wrong to pronounce that name. In Lev. 24:16 we read, "And he that blasphemeth the name of Jehovah, he shall surely be put to death; all the congregation shall certainly stone him: as well the sojourner as the home-born, when he blasphemeth the name of Jehovah, shall be put to death." In Ex. 3:15 the Jews read, "This is my secret name" (lit. "my name to be concealed") instead of, "This is my name forever," seeing that the Hebrew consonants for "to be concealed" and for "forever" are the same; they read *le'allēm* instead of *le'ōlām*. Just when this idea arose among the Jews we do not know. We do know, however, that the LXX already read Adonai for Jehovah; hence the translation *Kyrios*. Other translations followed this example; accordingly, the Latin has Dominus; English: the Lord; German: der Herr; Dutch: HEERE; the French has l'Eternal. Because of the Jewish dread of pronouncing this name its original pronounciation was forgotten. The church-fathers called it "the name that should not be spoken, the ineffable, the unutterable or unpronounceable name," in all probability not because they themselves held that the name should never be mentioned, but because the Jews were of that opinion, and because the correct pronunciation was lost. In Greek the four letters were written thus: IIIIII, or the words *Iaō* and *Iaē* served as a transliteration, as we learn from Diodorus Siculus and Origen. According to Jerome, the Hebrew word was translated *Yaho;* according to Philo Biblius, *Ieuō;* and according to Clement of Alexandria *Iaou*. Theodoret relates that the Jewish pronunciation was *Ai-ia;* the Samaritan, *Iabe*. It is probable that this indicates an ancient pronunciation: *Yahweh*. With an appeal to Jewish tradition some, e.g., Joachim of Floris in his *Evangelium Aeternum* pronounced the name: *Yewe*. Samuel B. Meir gives this vocalization, which was afterward defended by Hottinger, Reland, and others. The pronunciation Jehovah (*Yehōwāh*) is of recent origin; it was advocated by the Franciscan Peter Galatinus who was opposed by several, e.g., by Genebrardus. Later on Drusius, Amama, Scaliger, Vriemoet, and others, maintained that the pronunciation Jehovah could not be correct, and that this vocalization had been borrowed from the word Adonaï (Adhonay). Now it must be admitted that this interpunction is burdened with many and serious objections. In the first place, the word *Yhwh* is a k'ri perpetuum in the Hebrew Bibles, having at times the vocalization of Adonai; at other times that of Elohim. Furthermore, the form *Yehōwāh* is un-Hebrew and unanalyzable; and finally, this interpunction dates from a time when the idea that the name should never be pronounced had already become traditional.

If this vocalization is incorrect, the question arises: How must the name be explained? The idea that it is of Egyptian origin (Voltaire, Schiller, Wegscheider, Heeren, Brugsch) is contradicted by Ex. 5:2, and is no longer defended. The idea that it is of Canaanitish or Phoenician origin, and that after entering Canaan the Israelites copied this name from the inhabitants of Palestine is also untenable and has been sufficiently disproved. Nevertheless, on other grounds this view has been endorsed by Friedrich Delitzsch in his first edition of *Babel und Bibel*. According to his reading this name is an element of each of two compound proper names written on clay-tablets of the time of Hammurabi. The compounds referred to are *Ya-a'-we-ilu* and *Ya-u-um-ilu*. From this he concludes that the name *Yhwh* was originally Canaanitish, and that the tribe of Hammurabi carried it from Canaan into Babylonia. However, against this view the following objections have been advanced:

(1) The reading of Delitzsch is very uncertain; many regard it as either definitely erroneous or very doubtful, and consider the first part of these words to be a verb rather than a noun so that the entire word would mean: El protect me, or otherwise they interpret it to be the name of a Babylonian *Yahu* or *Yau*.

(2) Even if the reading of Delitzsch should be correct, his idea that the name *Yhwh* is of Canaanitish origin would remain untenable, for the Semitic origin of the Canaanites and the emigration of the tribe of Hammurabi from Canaan to settle in Babylon are unproved hypotheses, and nowhere is there any trace of a Canaanitish deity named *Yhwh*.

(3) It is possible, indeed, that the name *Yhwh* existed long before the time of Moses, and that it was known to the Semites and the Babylonians, but it is remarkable that, aside from the two aforementioned words of doubtful interpretation, there is no evidence to sustain this supposition. *Yhwh* was definitely the God of Israel, not only according to Scripture, e.g., Judg. 5:3, 4; but also according to the Moabite Stone (Mesha Stone). [Cf. line 18, "and I took thence the shrines of Jehovah and dragged them before Chemosh."] This stone dates from the ninth century B. C.

(4) Moreover, even if the Babylonians recognized a deity by the name of *Yhwh, Israel's Yhwh* is an entirely different God, and for *Israel* the name *Yhwh* has an entirely different meaning. According to Scripture *Yhwh* is *Israel's* God; the only true God, the Creator of heaven and earth.

As to the etymology of the name, it is commonly held to have been derived from *hwh* or *hyh*. The only difference of opinion concerns the question whether it is the third person imperfect of Qal or of Hiphil. (The pronunciation *Yaho* favored by Von Hartmann, merits no consideration.) Gesenius, Schrader, Lagarde, Schultz, Land, and Kuenen, regard it a Hiphil. Now in reality the only ground upon which they base this idea is their conviction that people living at the time of Moses were not sufficiently advanced to be able to entertain so exalted a conception of God as that expressed by the Qal form. Accordingly, the name *Yhwh* would not have the meaning "He who is" but "He who causes to be," the Giver of Life, the Creator. But Smend observes (correctly from his point of departure) that the name even when thus explained is too far advanced for the time of Moses, and he considers this interpretation incorrect also for this reason: that the Hiphil form of this verb occurs nowhere. Hence, as to the etymology of the name, the only remaining derivation is the one given in Ex. 3. Even then however, there is a difference of opinion in regard to the *meaning* of the name. The church-fathers regarded it as referring to God's aseity as such, and as indicative of the fact that God is the One who is possessed of being, eternity, and immutability, in contradistinction to "the absolute non-existence" of idols and "the relative non-existence" of creatures. Others, e.g., W. R. Smith, Smend, etc., appeal to Ex. 3:12 in order to sustain their opinion that the name means "He who shall be *with you*." Both of these explanations are untenable: the former, because it is too philosophical and not supported by Ex. 3; the latter, because the suffix "with you" would then have been given as an integral part of the name.

In Ex. 3:13-15 the meaning of the name *Yhwh* is clearly indicated. The full name is *'ehyeh 'asher 'ehyeh*, which signifies that he who now calls Moses and is about to deliver Israel, is the same God who had appeared to the fathers. He is that he is, the same yesterday, today, and forever. Verse 15 indicates the meaning of this name even more clearly: "Jehovah, the God of your fathers, the God of Abraham, the God of Isaac, and the God of Jacob, hath sent me (Moses) unto you: this is my name forever, and this is my memorial unto all generations." God does not call himself "the One who is" in the *abstract*. He gives no explanation of his aseity, but he declares very explicitly what he is and what is his character. Now what is he and what is his character? This cannot be expressed in a single word, but "he will be that he will be." Everything is included in this expression; to be sure this qualification is general and indefinite, but for that very reason it is so rich and so full of meaning: he will be what he has been for the patriarchs, what he is now, and what he will remain: for his people he will be everything.

The One who appears to Moses is not a new or a strange God, but is the God of the fathers, the Unchangeable the Immutable One, the Faithful One, the eternally Self-consistent One, the One who never leaves or forsakes his people but ever seeks his own and ever saves them, who is unchangeable in his grace, in his love, in his succor, who will be what he is, since he ever remaineth himself. Hence, in Isaiah he calls himself: "I, Jehovah, the first and with the last, I am he," Is. 41:4; 43:10, 13, 25; 44:6; 48:12. Of course, God's aseity is basic to this conception, but this is not the pre-eminent meaning: the name does not directly convey this idea.

The explanation which we have just given also makes clear whether and in how far the name *Yhwh* was known before the time of Moses. Ex. 6:3 does not tell us that this name was never used before the time of Moses, but that the Lord was not known to the fathers by that name. As a matter of fact we meet with this name again and again before we come to Ex. 6. It constitutes an element in many proper names; e.g., Jochebed, Ahijah, Abijah, I Chron. 2:24, 25; and if it had been a name altogether new and unheard of, the people would not have listened to Moses. For this very reason Moses approached the people in the name of the God of their fathers, Ex. 3:12. Hence, Ex. 6:3 must mean that the Lord now for the first time made known to Moses the significance and import of this name. The facts sustain this explanation, for before Ex. 3 we nowhere find an explanation of this name such as is given by the Lord himself: here, for the first time God indicates how this name must be interpreted, exactly what it implies. The name, indeed, existed in earlier times when the Lord himself used it more than once. Gen. 15:7; 28:13. Already in former days the Lord was invoked by this name, Gen. 14:22; 24:3; 28:16; 15:2, 8; 32:9; but an explanation of it had not yet been given. In the abstract it is even possible that the name *Yhwh* had an entirely different meaning etymologically than that ascribed to it in Ex. 3. Ex. 3 does not give an etymology of a word but an explanation of an idea. Just as in his special revelation to Israel God adopted and gave special meaning to various religious customs, e.g., circumcision, the sabbath, sacrifice, priesthood, etc., so also God gave a special meaning to this name. Hence, in Ex. 6 the Lord tells us what his name *Yhwh* signifies, entirely apart from its derivation or original meaning. From now on the name *Yhwh* implies and guarantees that God is and remains the God of his people, immutable in his grace and faithfulness. Before the time of Moses this full import of the name could not have been given: a long period of time was necessary to prove God's unchangeable faithfulness: a person's faithfulness is not proved at once but in the long run, especially in seasons of distress. Thus it was in the case of Israel. Centuries had elapsed since the time of the patriarchs. Israel was being oppressed and was in distress. Now God comes and says: "I am that I am, Jehovah, the One who keepeth faithfulness forever, the God of the fathers, your God also now, and your God forever." At this time God gives an entirely new meaning to an old name, a meaning which before this time would not have been understood. Hence we read in Hosea 12:9 and 13:4, "I am Jehovah thy God from the land of Egypt."

In the name "Jehovah" the O. T. revelation of God reaches its culmination: no new names are added. God's "proper name par excellence" is Jehovah: Ex. 15:3; Ps. 83:19; Hos. 12:6; Is. 42:8. This name is, therefore, not used of any other than Israel's God, and never occurs in the construct state, in the plural or with suffixes. Nevertheless, the form of the name is often modified and it often occurs in composition. Abbreviated forms of it, found especially in composition, are *Yāh, Yāhû, Yahaw*, whence the substantive *Yah* which occurs independently several times, Ex. 15:2; Ps. 68:4; 89:8; 94:7, 12; 118:14; Is. 12:2; 38:11; Is. 26:4 ("Jehovah, even Jah"), and constitutes an element in the exclamation "Hallelu-jah." Often the name *Yhwh* is found in connection with Adonai; e.g. Ezek. 23:12. The former receives added force when combined with *Çbha'ôth*, Ps. 69:6; 84:1; Hag. 2:7-9; Am. 9:5; I Sam. 1:3; 4:4; Is. 1:24; Ps. 80:4; 84:8; (Jehovah of hosts, Lord Jehovah of hosts, Jehovah God of hosts). Because of the fact that *Çbha'ôth* is found in connection with *Yhwh*, which does not admit of the construct state, and because of its connection with *Elōhîm* in the absolute state, Origen, Jerome and others came to the conclusion that *Çbha'ôth* was used in apposition; in this opinion they were strengthened by the fact that the LXX leaves *Çbha'ôth* untranslated, especially in I Sam. and in Isaiah, also in Rom. 9:29 and in Jas. 5:4. This opinion, however, lacks sufficient proof. In other cases *Çbha'ôth* is rendered "the Almighty" or "Lord of power," and the translation: "Jehovah who is *Çbha'ôth*" yields no intelligible sense.

It is, however, difficult to give the exact and definite meaning of *Çbha'ôth*. Some think it refers to the armies of Israel, and that it designates the Lord as a God of war. However, most of the passages quoted to support this idea, as, I Sam. 1:3, 11; 4:4; 15:2; 17:45; II Sam. 5:10; 6:2, 18; 7:8, 26, 27; I Kings 17:1; 18:15; 19:10, 14; II Kings 19:31; Ps. 24:10 prove nothing. Only three of them contain a semblance of proof; viz., I Sam. 4:4; 17:45; II Sam. 6:2; and one of them, II Kings 19:31 is rather unfavorable to this view. Furthermore, while the plural *Çbha'ôth*, indeed, is used to indicate the hosts of the *people* of Israel, the army of *warriors* of Israel is regularly indicated by the singular *Cbh'*, Judge. 8:6; 9:29; II Sam. 3:23; 8:16; 10:7; 17:25; 20:23; I Kings 2:25. And finally, all agree that in the prophets the name "Lord of hosts" no longer refers to God as a God of war; but they fail to explain how the meaning of this expression was changed. Others think the word "Hosts" refers to the stars, and they appeal to such passages as Deut. 4:19; Ps. 33:6; Jer. 19:13; 33:22; Is. 34:4; 40:26; Neh. 9:6. Smend makes the term even more comprehensive and looks upon it as a designation of the elements and forces of the cosmos, with an appeal to passages like Gen. 2:1; Ps. 103:21; Is. 34:2. Now it must be admitted that Scripture often calls the stars "the host of heaven," Deut. 4:19; and all creatures, taken collectively, "the host of heaven and earth," Gen. 2:1. But, in the first place, the singular and never the plural is then used. Further, the stars are, indeed, called the host of *heaven,* but never the host of *God.* Finally, the term "host" is, indeed, applied to all creatures, but is never used to designate the abstract concept "elements and forces."

The inacceptability of these more recent explanations causes us to think that the older interpretation, which finds in "hosts" a reference to the angels, deserves preference. This view is substantiated by Scripture. The name "Lord of hosts" is often brought in connection with the angels, I Sam. 4:4; II Sam. 6:2; Is. 37:16; Hos. 12:5, 6; Ps. 80:1, 4, ff.; Ps. 89:5-8; and the angels are repeatedly represented as a host that surrounds the throne of God, Gen. 28:12, 13; 32:2; Hos. 5:14; I Kings 22:19; Job 1:6; Ps. 68:17; 89:7; 103:21; 148:2; Is. 6:2. Although it is true that Scripture usually employs the singular and speaks of the *host* of angels instead of the *hosts,* this does not constitute a serious objection inasmuch as Scripture also often makes mention of several hosts of angels, Gen. 32:2; Deut. 33:2; Ps. 68:17; 148:2. This interpretation is in harmony with the meaning of the name, which has no warlike or martial flavor (as was erroneously inferred from I Sam. 4:4; 17:45; II Sam. 6:2), but is everywhere expressive of God's kingly glory, Deut. 33:2; I Kings 22:19; Ps. 24:10; Is. 6:2; 24:23; Zech. 14:16; 1:14. The angels magnify, exalt, and participate in the "glory" of God or of Christ, Matt. 25:31; Mk. 8:38; II Thess. 1:7; Rev. 7:11. Throughout Scripture the name *Yhwh Çbha'ôth* expresses the glory of God as King, full of splendor and majesty. *The name Elohim designates God as Creator and Preserver of all things; El-Shaddai represents him as the Mighty One, who makes nature subservient to grace; Jehovah describes him as the One whose grace and faithfulness endure forever; Jehovah Çbha'ôth characterizes him as the King in the fulness of his glory, surrounded by organized hosts of angels, governing the entire universe as the Omnipotent One, and in his temple receiving the honor and adoration of all his creatures.*

**H. N. T. Names. All the O. T. names are retained in the N. T. The name "Father" gains richer meaning in the N. T. The fullest name is the trinitarian: "Father, Son and Holy Spirit."**

All these O. T. names are retained in the N. T. We find the name "God" as the equivalent of El, Elohim. Elyon is translated "the Most High," Mk. 5:7; Luke 1:32, 35, 76; 8:28; Acts 7:48; 16:17; Heb. 7:1; cf. Luke 2:14. The appellative "the God of Abraham, of Isaac, and of Jacob" recurs in the N. T., as is true also of the name "God of Israel," Matt. 15:31; 22:32; Mk. 12:26; Luke 1:68; 20:37; Acts 3:13; 7:32, 46; 22:14; Heb. 11:16. More often, however, "God" (*theos*) is constructed with the genitives "my," "thy," "our," "your," for in Christ God is the God and the Father of his people, and of each of his children, Heb. 8:10; Rev. 7:12; 19:5; 21:3. In the N. T. the name Jehovah is explicated a few times by "the Alpha and the Omega," "who is and who was and who is to come," "the first and the last," "the beginning and the end," Rev. 1:4, 8, 17; 2:8; 21:6; 22:13. For the rest the LXX is followed, which substituted Adonai for it, which has been rendered "Lord" (*Kyrios*) in the New Testament, derived from *Kyros* strength. *Kyrios* characterizes God as the Mighty One, the Lord, the Possessor, the One who *legally* exercises authority (in distinction from *despotēs* the one who *actually* possesses power), and is used not only of God, but also of Christ. The combinations Jehovah Elohim, Jehovah Elohim Çbha'ôth, are also found in the N. T. and are translated "the Lord God," Luke 1:16; Acts 7:37; I Peter 3:15; Rev. 1:8; 22:5 and "Lord God, the Almighty," Rev. 4:8; 11:17; 15:3; 16:7; 21:22; whereas we find Çbha'ôth untranslated in Rom. 9:29; Jas. 5:4.

The N. T. seems to introduce a new name "Father." But this name is even applied to the Deity in heathen religions, and it occurs repeatedly in the O. T., Deut. 32:6; Ps. 103:13; Is. 63:16; 64:8; Jer. 3:4, 19; 31:9; Mal. 1:6; 2:10; while Israel is often called God's son, Ex. 4:22; Deut. 14:1; 32:19; Is. 1:2; Jer. 31:20; Hos. 1:10; 11:1. The name "Father" expresses the special theocratic relation which God sustains to his people Israel. In a wonderful manner he formed this people out of Abraham. In the more general sense of Origin and Creator the name Father is used in the N. T., in I Cor. 8:6; Eph. 3:15; Heb. 12:9; Jas. 1:18; cf. Luke 3:38; Acts 17:18. In other places the name is expressive of the deep, ethical, individual relation which in Christ God sustains to all his children, of which the relation which according to the O. T. existed between God and Israel is a type and shadow. In the N. T. the name "Father" becomes the common name by which God is addressed. The rendering "Lord" (*kyrios*) for Jehovah is insufficient. It is supplemented by the name "Father." This name is the highest revelation of God, God is not only the Creator, the Almighty One, the faithful One, the King and Lord; he is also the Father of his people. A kingdom of the Father who is in heaven takes the place of Israel's theocratic kingdom. The subjects are also children; the citizens are members of the family. The N. T. presents to us the complete realization of both righteousness and love, of both the state and the family. We find here the *perfect* Kingship; for, here is a King who is at the same time Father, who does not *force* his subjects to obey him, but creates and protects them. As his children they are born of him; they bear his image; they constitute his family. This relationship has been realized through Christ, the Father's own, only-begotten, and beloved Son. Through the Holy Spirit believers partake of and become conscious of this adoption as children, John 3:5, 8; Rom. 8:15 ff. God has revealed himself in the richest manner in the name of "Father, Son, and Spirit." There is a gradual unfolding of the fulness which from the beginning was in Elohim, and this fulness has become most gloriously manifest in God's trinitarian name.

# GOD'S INCOMMUNICABLE ATTRIBUTES

# CHAPTER IV

# God's Incommunicable Attributes

**I. Classification of the Attributes. There Are Objections Against All of Them. The Division Into Incommunicable and Communicable Attributes Is Here Followed.\***

**A. Scripture never discusses God's being apart from his attributes. According to the Bible God is what he reveals himself to be.**

Scripture contains many names whereby God is indicated, but never speaks about the being of God in the abstract, and never emphasizes one of God's attributes at the expense of the others. Now the one, then the other attribute is placed in the foreground, but a perfect harmony exists among them all. Scripture strives to do full justice to each of God's perfections. Just as the person of Christ does not represent a definitely one-sided character or temperament though Christ is, nevertheless, a very real and living person, even so God ever unfolds and reveals all his virtues harmoniously. God's being in the abstract is nowhere discussed. The Hebrew word *tûshiâh* from the root *yâshâh,* to exist, to be, arab. III: to help, to establish, indicates that which has existed, that which is of a lasting or enduring character, that which is profitable, true wisdom and happiness, Job 5:12; 6:13; 12:16; 26:3 (cf. 30:22); Prov. 2:7; 3:21; 8:14; Is. 28:29; Mic. 6:9; but in none of these passages does it signify the being of God. Neither do the N. T. words "Godhead," Col. 2:9; "divinity," Rom. 1:20; "form of God," Phil. 2:6; "divine nature," II Pet. 1:4; cf. Gal. 4:8, indicate the being or nature of God apart from his attributes, as Polanus erroneously assumes. God's being is revealed to us in his names. These names are designations of God's "excellencies or virtues," *aretai,* I Pet. 2:9, a mode of expression which is in harmony with Is. 42:8, 12; 43:21; 63:5, where the LXX rendering of the Hebrew *tehillâh,* praise, honor, is *aretē;* cf. Hab. 3:3; Zech. 6:13. The church is called upon to "show forth God's excellencies"; i.e., to praise him because of his glorious revelation in all his works. Scripture nowhere discusses God's being apart from his attributes. Of course, this teaching of Scripture regarding God's being does

(\*Note: in the original this section precedes that on God's proper names).

not imply that it would be wrong to speak about God's nature. On the contrary, Scripture leads the way in doing this. Moreover, with a view to pantheism, which identifies God and the universe, it is of the highest importance to emphasize the fact that God has an altogether distinct nature, an independent being, an essence distinct from that of the universe. But we must never lose sight of the fact that Scripture nowhere teaches that the human mind becomes acquainted with the being of God by means of mere reason and apart from revelation. Scripture never separates God's ontological existence and his economical manifestation, even less does it represent these two as standing in antithetic relation to each other. God is what he reveals himself to be: in his names he himself becomes known to us. Though he is indeed exalted infinitely high above his creatures so that the knowledge which we have of him is analogical and not adequate, nevertheless, his several attributes exhibited by means of his revelation bring before our consciousness the fulness of his being, of which now one phase is displayed, then another.

**B. In harmony with this biblical representation early Christian theologians never discussed God's being in the abstract, but conceived of it as inclusive of all his perfections and attributes. Soon, however, a distinction was made between God's being in the abstract and his attributes. One of God's attributes was usually viewed as basic to all the others:**

**(1) Some described God as absolute essence: Plato, Philo, Origen, Athanasius, Augustine, R. C. theologians, Reformers, etc.**

**(2) Some emphasized God's will: Socinians, Remonstrants, rationalists, etc.**

**(3) Some stressed God's personality: Jacobi, Ulrici, etc.**

**(4) Some defined God as absolute reason, pantheistically conceived: Hegel, etc.**

**(5) Some looked upon God's moral attributes as fundamental: Ritschl, etc.**

**(6) Some gave undue prominence to the attribute of veracity: Jansenius, etc.**

**Thus, by emphasizing one attribute the harmony existing between all was destroyed.**

The early Christian theologians were indeed conscious of this fact. They used the term "names of God" as a summary of whatever was known concerning God. It was used to indicate not only the "proper names" but also—to use the terminology of a later period—the "attributes" and even the persons in the divine essence. Accordingly, God's attributes were at once included in the idea of God. Augustine speaks, indeed, of God's "essence," but he views this essence as fulness of divine existence and as inclusive of all the attributes: simplicity, eternity, goodness, wisdom, etc. The *Confessions* often speak of God in the same manner, without any attempt to distinguish between being and attributes or to classify the latter. Moreover, many of the theologians of later date refuse to enter into these distinctions. Consequently, they discuss God's attributes apart from any previous inquiry into God's nature.

Nevertheless, a distinction was soon made. It resulted from a consideration of the question which divine attribute at once distinguishes God from the creature; from an attempt to discover the basic idea in regard to God's essence. The question was asked, "In the doctrine of God which attribute constitutes the starting point from which we should proceed in our discussion of all the others?" To be sure, it was admitted that each attribute was in itself the being of God, but the question was asked whether among all these attributes there was not one which expressed God's being in the most fundamental manner, one attribute from which all the others, as it were, could be derived.

Now Platonic philosophy had already viewed essence as fundamental. Philo had indicated the connection between this attribute and the name Yhwh: the only name that does not refer to a divine operation or energy but to the being of God itself. Accordingly, he often called God "he who or that which has being." Christian theology accepted this definition of God's being. Irenaeus often describes God as absolutely simple and even calls him "inconceivable" and "unsubstantial"; nevertheless, in opposition to Gnosticism he especially emphasized the fact that God is the Creator of all things and that he has revealed himself in his works. But Origen, Athanasius, and John of Damascus conceive of God as the One, as essence. They even speak of him as the One who transcends all essence, as "he who has being, he who has the source of his existence in himself, that which has being." Moreover, in agreement with Philo they derive this description from and connect it with the O. T. name Yhwh.

In the West these definitions were copied. Augustine constantly defines God as "supreme essence, supreme goodness, truth, beauty," etc. God is a substance, for that which is not a substance does not exist. But whereas the word "substance" is often used in contradistinction to the term "accident" (i.e., that which inheres in the substance and of which the substance is the bearer), therefore with reference to God Augustine prefers to use the word "essence," "what is called 'ousia' by the Greeks" and is sometimes called "nature." For, with reference to God we cannot distinguish between substance and accidents. His being is not the bearer of the attributes, but his attributes are identical with his essence. God is the highest, best, most beautiful, most perfect essence, "than whom nothing better can exist or can be thought." He is "God, above whom there is nothing, outside of whom there is nothing, apart from whom there is nothing, supreme life, supreme truth, supreme blessedness, supreme wisdom, supreme essence."

Augustine appeals to the name Yhwh in order to justify his description of God. This description was copied by many. We find it in the works of Hilary, of Pseudodionysius — although he sometimes proceeds from the idea of goodness, which, according to him, is even broader in scope than essence — of Anselm, Lombard, Thomas Aquinas, Bonaventura, and many others. Roman Catholic theologians in their discussion of the doctrine of God usually proceed from this description of God's being.

Nevertheless, there were and are those who regard one of the other attributes as fundamental and basic to all the remaining. Some regard infinitude rather than "absolute essence or aseity" as constituting in itself the fundamental notion in the concept of Deity. Hence they give the preference to the definition of God as "an infinite being." Duns Scotus arrived at this conclusion and contended that essence as such was attributable univocally to God and to creatures, but that the characteristic distinction between God and creatures consisted in this: that God was an "infinite being" while creatures were finite beings. Now, while all of these proceed from the idea of absolute essence and regard some incommunicable attribute — e.g., aseity, infinitude, eternity — as the fundamental element in the concept of Deity, others preferred to emphasize God's intellectual nature and to proceed from the idea of personality rather than from the concept of absoluteness. Accordingly, they described God as an "intelligent being," and among themselves they differed with respect to the question whether knowledge in the abstract, i.e., spirituality, or actual knowledge, was to be regarded as the "constitutional principle" of the divine essence.

The Reformation brought about little change. Now the one, then the other previously mentioned description was adopted. Reformed theologians at first generally copied the definition given by Augustine and Thomas Aquinas. They proceeded from the idea of "aseity" or "independence" and described God as an "independent being." Besides this definition we also find descriptions of God as "the uncreated spirit, the most simple spirit, the spirit existing of itself," to which at times was added the trinitarian formula "one in essence, three in persons." Lutherans used the definition "an infinite spiritual essence, a spiritual being subsisting of himself, an independent spirit."

Socinianism, however, proceeded from a different viewpoint. Disregarding all metaphysical questions, it placed the entire emphasis upon the *will* of God. Knowing God is tantamount to knowing his will. Religion loses all mysticism and is reduced to a cult. God is banished farther and farther away from the universe and from mankind.

Remonstrantism, rationalism, and English deism continued along this line.

Philosophy in turn reacted against this cold moralistic conception of the Deity. Spinoza returned to the idea of essence; viewed God as "the sole, infinite, and necessarily existing substance, the absolutely infinite being, the absolutely first and immanent cause"; and once more spoke of God's intellectual love as the source of the highest happiness.

To be sure, rationalism and deism continued to reign after the days of Spinoza, but about the middle of the eighteenth century men grew tired of it. Great thinkers, e.g., Goethe, Lessing, Herder, etc., were inclined to agree with Spinoza, and his pantheistic philosophy soon won the day. Kant already undermined the foundations of rationalism although he continued to call himself a deist. Fichte contended against the ideas of God and immortality and looked upon these as products of eudaemonism. In his exaggerated moralism God was equal to the simple ego, the moral world-order. He contended that it was wrong to view God as essence or substance, and described God as absolute activity. Later on he altered his opinion to a certain extent and arrived at a position approximating that of Spinoza. Schleiermacher's view resembled that of Spinoza even more closely. God and the universe are correlates; God is the "Whence of our receptive and self-active existence." Schelling's view differs from that of both of these philosophers inasmuch as he not only takes into account spiritual reality, i.e., religion and morals, but also objective nature. It was his purpose to enhance the importance of natural science and to deliver it from the deplorable condition in which he found it. Accordingly, he views the spiritual realm and the natural realm as twin brothers: nature is visible spirit; spirit is invisible nature; in both he sees a continuous organic revelation of the Absolute, who transcends all opposites; the One, simple, eternal, without predicates; the unity of the Infinite and the finite, of God and the world; "the One and the All." Finally, it was Hegel who transformed this theory into a system of logical idealism. Nature and history are a logically necessary self-unfolding of the idea. Everything partakes of reason; everything is embodied thought or idea. Reason is the absolute substance. In itself it is God, for God is nothing else than the one living idea of the universe developing into self-consciousness. Accordingly, in the philosophy of Hegel God is indeed reason, thought, spirit (mind), subject, but this does not mean that God enjoyed a distinct life previous to and apart from the universe. On the contrary, "Apart from the world God is not God": the universe is an essential element or moment in the life of God.

But objections were also raised against this form of pantheism. Theistic philosophers, many in number, arrayed themselves against pantheism, showed its inconsistent character, and defended the rights of theism. In their arguments they proceeded from the concept of absolute personality, connected this with the idea of growth and development, and thus introduced into the concept of Deity a theogonic process, either unitarian in character — thus, Jacobi, Herbart, Drobisch, Rothe, Lotze, Ulrici, Carrière, etc. — or trinitarian — thus, Baader, Schelling, J. H. Fichte, Weisse, Dorner, etc.

But this theistic speculation also had its day. Separation between theology and philosophy, between religion and metaphysics became the watch-word. Science [Dutch: wetenschap, German: Wissenschaft, i.e., systematized knowledge in any field] by degrees withdrew from the domain of religion and theology. It became exact, positive science. Religion, on the other hand, more and more attempted to free itself from science and to banish all metaphysics and all philosophy. The result for the "doctrine of God" was that ethical goodness began to be considered the essence of God. The Groninger theology placed in the foreground God's fatherhood and love. Scholten, indeed, proceeded from the idea of God's absolute sovereignty, but the advocates of moralistic liberalism rejected his speculative intellectualism and monistic determinism, and viewed God as Father, as the moral idea, as the power of goodness and of holiness. In Germany Ritschl's Neo-Kantianism in the same manner arose in opposition to the speculative theology of the mediating school. Ritschl denies that religion is a judicial relation. He points out that according to Duns Scotus, Socinianism, and Arminianism, God is the absolute Sovereign, who treats men with fairness although they have no rights in relation to him. In their theory arbitrariness, "unlimited dominion," constitutes the essence of God and the law of the universe. God has a right to do the one thing as well as the other. The relation between God and man is a private-rights relation and is illustrated by the slave-holder who is fair to his slaves. According to the orthodox Protestants, on the other hand, God's relation to the world is determined by justice. Man has a right to eternal life if he keeps God's law; if not, he deserves punishment. This is a public-rights theory. It owes its origin to the O. T., especially to Pharasaism, was accepted by Paul, and consequently also by the Christian church. Nevertheless, both of these theories are erroneous. Religion is not a matter of rights. On the contrary, religion and rights oppose each other. It is wrong to view God's justice and his grace as contraries. We must banish forever that entire abstract, Areopagitic conception of the Deity, which posits a God who sustains merely a negative, transcendent relation to the world, and which does not make

allowance for communion between God and man. Religion is a moral
relation, and Christianity is "the perfectly spiritual and absolutely
moral religion." God's relation to man is neither that of a master
toward his servant nor that of a government toward its subjects but that
of a father toward his children. It is a relation exemplified in the
family. Accordingly, God must be regarded as Love. Nothing should
be considered as equal in value to the concept of love. Hence, the
Christian theologian should not follow the synthetic method and discuss
various metaphysical abstractions concerning God as the Absolute, nor
should he begin with so-called natural theology, which does not exist,
nor with the idea of personality or with the attribute of holiness, but
he should proceed from the concept of love, from which he should try
to derive everything: creation, providence, redemption, justification.

This criticism of the traditional treatment of the doctrine of God
received a hearty applause, and the position that in the description of
God one should proceed from the concept of love was accepted by many.
Reischle even opined that Ritschl's method consistently applied would
lead one to proceed from the idea of the Kingdom of God rather than
from the concept of love. From the idea of the Kingdom of God he
derived two other theories; namely, that God is love and that he is
personality. Moreover, even outside of the sphere of his own immediate
disciples Ritschl's views were accepted to the extent that some, e.g.,
Cremer and Von Oettingen, frowned upon the idea of the Absolute as
irreligious. But over against this stands the fact that others, even
among those who belong to the school of Ritschl, regarded this concept as an indispensable element in the doctrine of God. Kaftan, e.g.,
is of the opinion that Ritschl's objection to the word "absolute" —
namely, that its etymological meaning is "loosened" — is unfounded
because the meaning of a word is determined by its use. He adheres
to the idea of the Absolute and around it as a center he constructs the
Christian doctrine of God. Moreover, in the treatment of this doctrine
he emphasizes the idea of God as "transcendent, personal Spirit." Although Kaftan begins with a destructive criticism of the manner in
which the doctrine of God is treated in traditional works on dogmatics
and although he regards the absolute concept of being or essence to be
irreconcilable with the idea of divine personality, in the end he is himself confronted with the same difficulty and fails to give a different and
better solution. The same is true in regard to Wobbermin, who also
clings to the idea of the Absolute and who supposes that the unity which
he is trying to find is attained when God is defined as "the Archetype
and unitary totality of spiritual-personal life." Thus, theology continues
to struggle with the difficulty of giving a somewhat satisfactory description of the being of God. Accordingly, one defines God as "that which

has being, absolute essence, absolute substance"; another, as Sovereign, Lord, Supreme Being"; another as "infinite Spirit, absolute causality, absolute personality"; and still another as "Father, Love, personal and omnipotent loving-desire, goodness," etc. To proceed from the principle of the harmony of all God's virtues, and consistently to adhere to this principle is indeed very difficult, for we are constantly confronted with the problem of equally maintaining God's absoluteness and his personality, his incommunicable and his communicable attributes, his absolute transcendence above and his immanence in the universe. Moreover, we are all limited in our view and prone to emphasize one divine attribute at the expense of another. Jansenius emphasized God's veracity; Francois de Sales, his love; Vincent, his goodness; Saint Cyran, his omnipotence, Nevertheless, it remains the task of theology in harmony with Scripture to bestow equal honor upon each divine attribute.

> C. Relation between being and attributes: correct view and deviations:
>
> (1) Correct view: every one of God's attributes is identical with his being: God's attributes do not differ from his essence nor from one another.
>
> (2) Deviations: polytheism personifies and deifies the energies that operate in the creature; Plato ascribed independent existence to the ideas; Gnosticism regarded its emanating aeons as divine beings. Cf. also the views of Philo, Jewish theology, Arianism. Some Christian theologians distinguish between determinative and super-additional attributes.
>
> (3) Objections to the views of those who deny God's simplicity:
>
> a. Those who do not regard God's being as identical with each of his attributes differ among themselves in such a manner that what is viewed by one as a divine attribute is ascribed by another to God's essence.
>
> b. This view results in an impoverished conception of the Deity: the less fundamental attributes, e.g., love, are not viewed as present in God in as absolute a manner as the determinative attributes.
>
> (4) The objection which is presented against the Christian view and the answer to that objection:
>
> a. Objection: The Christian theologian is guilty of the same error when he, in harmony with the philosopher, takes as his starting-point the attribute of essence.
>
> b. Answer: When the Christian theologian speaks of God's essence he is not speaking of one fundamental attribute from which the others are derived, but he refers to an essence which is identical with supreme life, supreme wisdom, supreme love, etc. Furthermore, the Christian theologian does not have in mind the abstract, contentless essence to which the philosopher refers but the infinitely rich, intensive, concrete essence, an infinite and unbounded ocean of essence, the sum-total of all reality. The philosopher arrives at his concept of essence

**by means of a process of elimination or subtraction; the Christian theologian arrives at his concept of essence by means of addition.**

Now, Christian theologians have always been more or less conscious of this calling. On the whole their teaching has been that God is simple, exalted above all composition, and that there is no real distinction between his being and his attributes. Every attribute is identical with God's being. He *is* what he *has*. When we speak about creatures, we distinguish variously between what they are and what they have; e.g., a human being remains a human being even though he has lost the image of God and has become a sinner. But when we speak about God, we must maintain that each of his attributes is identical with his being. God is all light, all mind, all wisdom, all logos, all spirit, etc. In God "essence is the same as wisdom, the same as goodness, the same as power. One and the same thing is said whether it be stated that God is eternal or that he is immortal or good or just." Whatever God is he is completely and simultaneously. "God has no properties but merely is essence, God's properties are really the same as his essence: they neither differ from his essence, nor do they differ materially from one another."

By means of this doctrine of God's simplicity Christian theology was kept from falling into the error of regarding God's attributes as separate from and more or less independent of his essence. In a certain sense polytheism is guilty of this error inasmuch as it personifies and deifies the various energies that operate in the creature. But philosophy and theology have at times deviated from the truth in a similar manner. Plato ascribed independent existence alongside of God to the ideas viewed as archetypes of existing objects. Gnosticism indeed defined God as the Unknowable and the Inexpressible, but it changed the Platonic "ideas" into "aeons" which emanated from God and separated themselves from him in a decreasing series of emanation. The terms "idea, mind, reason, life, wisdom," etc., were used to describe these aeons, which in reality were nothing but divine attributes personified, emanating from God, and viewed as divine beings. Philo, influenced by Plato, also frequently personified the divine energies; especially, goodness, power, and the logos. Jewish theology accepted many hypostases; as, Metatron, Memra, Shekinah, Ruach, Bath-kol, and in the cabala the ten sephiroth or divine attributes are described as emanations from the divine essence. Even in later times this Gnostic and cabalistic philosophy exerted great influence. A faint trace of Gnosticism is evident in Arianism inasfar as it accepts a gradation with reference to the divine persons. As soon as monotheism is severed from belief in the trinity it loses its purity: on the one hand there is the threatening danger of pantheism or monism; on the other, that of polytheism or pluralism. Of late many are beginning to ascribe independent significance to certain things which in actual life are even substituted for God; such as, the state, science, art, industry, fate, and fortune; while some, not even satisfied with this position, boldly advocate their polytheistic sympathies.

Even Christian theologians have at times forgotten to exercise the necessary prudence in determining the relation between God's essence and his attributes. Thus, in the middle ages Gilbert Porretan distinguished between the essence or nature of God, i.e., "divinity," and "God himself." He viewed "divinity" as something distinct from God, i.e., as the form by virtue of which God is God. "God is divine, but divinity is not God." Duns Scotus indeed denied that there was a "real distinction" between being and attributes, but he maintained, with an appeal to Augustine and John of Damascus, that the attributes were "formally" distinct from God's being and from each other. Socinianism spoke of "accidents" (non-essential elements) pertaining to God and held that a separate conception and description of each attribute was necessary for the subject. Moreover, of late many are even beginning to accept an objective distinction in God at the expense of his simplicity and immutability. Accordingly, Doedes first treats those attributes which are directly implied in the idea of Deity: oneness (unity), incommunicability, incomparability, incomprehensibility, independence; etc., and then those attributes which pertain to the Divine Being in addition to the former. These are only five in number: omnipotence, wisdom, goodness, love, and holiness. Similarly, F. A. B. Nitzsch first discusses certain "fundamental determining attributes of the divine nature," and he views these as constituting the substratum of the other attributes which he treats after the doctrine of creation. In like manner C. Pesch uses the term "superadditions to the divine substance" as descriptive of the attributes.

This conception, however, does not do justice to the Christian view which regards *all* the divine attributes as identical with God's being. It is wrong to distinguish between determinations which are implied in the idea of God and attributes which are viewed as super-added. The theologians who make this distinction and whose names were mentioned in the preceding differ among themselves to such an extent that one regards as an attribute that which is viewed by another as pertaining to the essence, and vice versa. But there is still another objection to this method of distinguishing between being and attributes: it results in an impoverished rather than an enriched conception of the Deity, inasmuch as it easily leads to the conclusion that the attributes, e.g., divine love, are not present in God in as absolute a manner as, e.g., infinitude, and that they merely result from the outward influence of creation upon God. But Christian theology by means of its doctrine of simplicity has carefully avoided this error inasmuch as it impairs the absolute, divine character of all the attributes. To be sure, there have been some who have tried to make it appear as if theology, proceeding from the description of God as the highest essence, were in perfect agreement with philosophy, which regards God as the Absolute and is satisfied with an abstraction. But there is a great difference between the theological and the philosophical description of God, a difference which must not be overlooked. When the church-fathers in their attempt to determine the character of God's being chose as their starting-point the name Yhwh, they were not thinking of God's being apart from his attributes but of his being in all its fulness as it exists and is revealed in the attributes. Accordingly, the essence which was ascribed to God was no abstraction but a living, infinitely rich, concrete essence, a "supreme essence" at once identical with "supreme life, supreme truth, supreme wisdom, supreme love," etc., as Augustine constantly asserted; in other words, "an infinite and unbounded ocean of essence." The description of God as essence was employed in order to indicate that he was the sum-total of all reality. It certainly did not mean that he was abstract, contentless essence, the Absolute in the philosophical sense of the word. Although it is very well possible that in the description of God as essence theology is influenced by philosophy; nevertheless, theology and philosophy do not mean the same thing when they speak of God's absolute essence. Philosophy arrives at this concept by means of subtraction or elimination; i.e., by subtracting from existing objects whatever pertains to them distinctively, so that only essence, bare existence, common to all things, remains. Moreover, even that bare existence does not pertain to all objects similarly. The existence which we ascribe to bodies differs from the existence which we attribute to spirits. In like manner, one kind of essence pertains to substances, another to accidents; one to ideas, another to objects; one to that which is possible, another to that which is real. Nevertheless, the most simple and elementary concept of essence is common to all. It is immediately evident, however, that this concept of being or essence, which is the result of a process of continued subtraction or elimination, is nothing else and nothing more than an empty concept. It lacks all content and has no objective, independent reality. On the other hand, when *theology* speaks of God as essence, it arrives at this concept not by way of subtraction or elimination but by the opposite process, namely, by addition, i.e., by ascribing to God all creaturely perfections in an absolute sense and by viewing him as absolute reality, the sum-total of all essence, "most pure and simple actuality." The essence which theology ascribes to God is at once the richest, most complete, and most intensive essence and the most determined and concrete, the absolute, only, and simple essence.

> D. In the description of God's being some theologians proceed from the idea of divine personality. This deserves no recommendation; for,
>
> (1) it is confusing: the term "person" is used in a definite, technical sense in the doctrine of the trinity;
>
> (2) it tends to do injustice to God's tri-personality; and
>
> (3) personality (in the abstract, formal, modern sense of that term) is not distinctive of God.
>
> Others proceed from the idea of love. This is also objectionable; for
>
> (1) love presupposes consciousness, will;
>
> (2) righteousness and holiness are equally fundamental. Christian theology proceeds from God's aseity in the sense of absolute essence, not conceived of as standing apart from the other attributes and separated from them, but as inclusive of them all.

Hence, when Christian theology rejected this distinction between God's being and his attributes, this was not done with the intention of denying the fact that God has a being, nor with the purpose of forbidding the use of this word (being) in the doctrine concerning God. On the contrary, it took this position in order to make clear that nothing unreal pertains to God: that in all his attributes he is pure being, absolute reality. Moreover, Christian theology needs this word "being" in its doctrine concerning God in order to distinguish between God's nature and its three modes of subsistence. But even aside from that, in the doctrine of God's attributes we must needs speak of God's being, for whereas God is pure *essence*, the absolute, perfect, only, and uncomposed being, no definition can be given of him: there is no genus to which he belongs, and there are no specific characteristics by means of which he may be differentiated from other beings which belong to the same genus. Even existence as such, which, let us say, he has in common with all creatures, does not pertain to him in the same sense as it does to creatures, but pertains to him analogically. Nevertheless, name him we must: in religion and in theology we need a description of him in order that we may be enabled to distinguish him from whatever is not God. At this point we are confronted with the difficulty that God is on the one hand "anonymous; i.e., without name," but on the other hand "polyonymous; i.e., having many names." We do not need to concern ourselves with the question whether God has more attributes than those which he has revealed in the work of creation and of redemption. According to Spinoza the number of attributes pertaining to any object varies directly with its degree of reality; hence, God, as infinite reality must be infinite in the number of his attributes, though only two of these are known to us; viz., extension and thought. And according to Reinhard it is very probable that God might possess "a great multitude of attributes (properties) of which we have no conception, seeing that it is altogether impossible for infinite Perfection to unite with himself all resemblances within the narrow confines of our own creaturely existence." However this may be, the number of those divine attributes which have been revealed to us is so great that it is entirely impossible to mention them all. Hence, we must either refrain from giving any description of them, or we must limit our discussion to a select number of all God's attributes.

This final selection depends upon our theological presuppositions. We do not need to discuss all the descriptions of God which have been given. Two of them, however, deserve our attention, especially because of late they have found favor with many:

(1) theistic philosophers preferred to proceed from the idea of divine personality, which they considered to be the correct designation of God's being. And, indeed over against the pantheistic conception of God their view was right. From every other point of view, however, their idea is not deserving of commendation; for,

(a) it is confusing, inasmuch as the term "person" is used in a definite, technical sense in the doctrine of the trinity;

(b) it easily leads to an undervaluation of God's tripersonality and to the idea that he is a unipersonality; and,

(c) there is in the abstract, modern, and formal conception of personality nothing that distinguishes God, as such, from man.

(2) Others proceed from the idea of love. Now this is also open to objections; for,

(a) love presupposes personality, consciousness, and will; and

(b) love is indeed the essence of God, but it is such only in the sense in which all attributes are identical with God's essence. Hence this view tends to do injustice to other divine attributes; as, righteousness and holiness.

Christian theology has endeavored to avoid this one-sidedness by means of placing God's *aseity* (his absolute essence) in the foreground. We need the idea of absoluteness in order to designate God as *God,* and to distinguish him from all that is not God. However, it is necessary that we attach the right meaning to the word "absolute." To say that it signifies a philosophical conception and does not indicate a religious idea, is erroneous. On the contrary, it would be far easier to defend the thesis that the word "absolute" as used by philosophers bears a religious character. For although there is a difference of opinion in regard to the validity of the arguments for the existence of God, and in regard to the logical propriety of concluding the absolute from the relative, this uncertainty of reason never results in actual doubt concerning the existence of the absolute in the sense of the fundamental cause of the existence of all things. Man's metaphysical, religious need must assert itself. Hence, religion and theology require the idea of the absolute. Of course, theology is not concerned primarily with the *word*, but with the *thought* — *the idea*. For religion and for theology God must ever remain *God,* distinct from and exalted above all things, Creator and Ruler of all existence, on whom the believer can rely in seasons of difficulty and of distress. Otherwise God ceases to be *God* for him. It is in that sense that we speak of God as the completely independent, only, *absolute* Being. In that sense this was formerly understood. Absolute essence was not conceived of as *abstract* essence, free from every property and relation, and deprived of all contents; but it was looked upon as the real, the only essence, of infinite fulness, by reason of this very fact: that it was absolute (i.e., independent) essence, having the ground of its existence in itself. "Absolute is the same as not depending upon anything else."

From the beginning Christian theology connected this conception and description of God with the meaning of the name "Jehovah," as indicated in Ex. 3:14. Now, there may be a difference of opinion in regard to the question whether the idea of absolute essence is implied in this name, as we have seen in the previous chapter. One thing, however, is certain: God's distinctness from and absolute exaltation above every creature is emphasized throughout Scripture. Though he does indeed descend to the level of the creature, especially to the level of man, so that he is represented as walking in the garden, coming down to the earth to see the city and the tower, etc.; nevertheless, he is the Creator of heaven and earth, the First and the Last, of whom, through whom, and unto whom are all things, Gen. 1:1 ff.; Ps. 33:6, 9; 90:2; Is. 41:4; 43:10-13; 44:6; 48:12; John 5:26; Acts 17:24 ff.; Rom. 11:36; Eph. 4:6; Heb. 2:10; Rev. 1:4, 8; 4:8, 11; 10:6; 11:17; etc. In this doctrine of Scripture is implied all that Christian theology meant by its description of God's being as absolute essence: God is the real, the true essence. the fulness of essence, the sum-total of all reality and perfection. the totality of essence, to which all other essence owes its origin, an ocean of essence, unbounded and immensurable, the absolute Being, the only Being who has the ground of his existence in himself. This description of the being of God is to be preferred above that of love, personality, fatherhood, etc., because in it all God's attributes are included, and by it they are all ascribed to God in an absolute sense; i.e., by this description God is recognized as *God* in *all* his perfections. Of course, merely by means of *logic* we cannot derive all these attributes from the idea of absolute essence: the only means whereby we know God's nature and his attributes is *revelation* in nature and Scripture. Nevertheless, it is only because these attributes pertain to God in an *absolute,* altogether unique sense, that they are *divine* attributes. Hence, in that respect aseity (absolute essence) may be called the primary attribute of God's being. By means of God's revelation—not by means of a priori reasoning—we are even able to prove that because of God's aseity all those attributes are present in God which nature and Scripture make known to us. The very fact of God's divinity (i.e., of his eternal and absolute essence) implies that all those perfections of which there is a reflex in man pertain to God; e.g., that he is absolute in wisdom and goodness, in righteousness and holiness, in power and blessedness. Because he exists of and through and unto himself, he is fulness of essence, "the independent, most perfect Being."

> **E. From the doctrine of God's simplicity (cf. C) some concluded that we are not justified in making a distinction between the attributes severally (Eunomius, the Nominalists, Schleiermacher, etc). We maintain, however, that although every attribute is identical with God's being, nevertheless, distinctions must be made: the attributes do not differ in substance; nor. on the other hand, is the difference a merely verbal one; they differ in "thought", i.e., each attribute expresses a distinct something. Grounds:**
>
> **(1) God's names, i.e., the designations of his attributes, are not of our invention but God himself has revealed them unto us.**
>
> **(2) God's simplicity does not imply abstract essence; i.e., essence without attributes; on the contrary, it implies fulness of life.**
>
> **(3) From the fact that man was created in God's image it follows that God has many attributes.**
>
> **(4) Though in God holiness and righteousness are identical, nevertheless, we distinguish them in thought.**
>
> **(5) There is no name or attribute which adequately expresses God's being; hence, many names or attributes serve the purpose of giving us an impression of his eminent majesty.**

The fact, however, that we cannot distinguish between God's being or essence and his attributes, inasmuch as every attribute is identical with the essence, does not imply that there is only a nominal and subjective distinction between the attributes, a distinction which has no real basis. It is necessary to emphasize this fact because many have drawn this erronous conclusion. Eunomius, like Aetius before him, reasoned as follows: God is simple, i.e., he is not composed; consequently, the attributes which we ascribe to him are identical with his being and they cannot be distinguished from one another except *subjectively,* i.e., in our conception. Furthermore, our knowledge of God must be an adequate knowledge; otherwise it would be false. Now the idea of agennesia (lit. unbegottenness, the state of being ingenerate) furnishes us with an adequate knowledge of God's being. Consequently, all the other attributes — e.g., goodness, wisdom, power — must be "materially" identical with this concept. All divine attributes are "synonyms." Moreover, inasmuch as agennesia constitutes the essence of God, it follows that the Son, who was *begotten* by the Father, cannot be very God.

In the Middle Ages Gilbert Porretan, bishop of Poitiers, who died in 1159, taught a real distinction between being and persons, between Godhead and God, and perhaps also — although this is not certain — between being and attributes and between the attributes in relation to each other. According to the Nominalists, especially according to Occam, the attributes differed only "in subjective reason, having a connotation with respect to diverse effects"; i.e., with a view to the relation which they severally assume to the works of God. The concept of any one attribute was held to be included in that of any other attribute, "The one is involved in the other." Hence, according to this reasoning when we ascribe goodness to God, we thereby ascribe to him justice, power, etc. The Scotists preferred to say that the attributes differed not "objectively or in objective reason nor subjectively or in subjective reason but formally." The Palamites of the fourteenth century, named after Gregory Palamas, an archbishop of Thessalonica, even believed in an emanation and represented the divine activities of creation and providence, etc., as well as the attributes of omnipotence, goodness, wisdom, etc., as eternal radiations from the unknowable divine essence, really distinct from that essence, and to be regarded as a kind of lower deities. Similarly, the Arabic and Jewish philosophy frequently presents a merely subjective conception of God's attributes. Spinoza defined an attribute as "that which the intellect perceives as constituting the essence of the substance." Whether he regarded the attributes as subjective conceptions of the mind or as objective, real properties of the substance depends on the question whether one places the emphasis upon the first or second part of this definition. Pantheism, introduced into philosophy by Spinoza, has no place for the divine attributes. God has no essence apart from the universe. He has no life of his own. His attributes are identical with the laws of the universe. Accordingly, Schleiermacher describes them as existing subjectively only; as "something peculiar in the method of referring to God the feeling of absolute dependence." As he sees it, their origin is to be traced to religious-poetic invention: they lack speculative content. They neither express God's image, which is unknowable, nor his relation to the world, as this would imply that God assumed more than one relation to the world. They are merely subjective conceptions without any objective ground. Accordingly, in his writings, the doctrine of the attributes is not treated as a separate doctrine but is scattered here and there throughout his dogmatics.

Over against this conception of the names of God we maintain on the basis of God's revelation that although every attribute is most certainly identical with God's being, nevertheless the attributes are to be distinguished from each other. Thus Basil and Gregory of Nyssa taught in their writings against Eunomius. On the one hand they maintained that the attributes did not differ in "substance," as God is simple and exalted above all composition; nevertheless, on the other hand they held that the distinction between these attributes was more than a merely "verbal" one. Avoiding both of these extremes they judged that the names of God differed in *thought;* that in our mind we possess different "ideas, thoughts, considerations," of one and the same Divine Being; accordingly, that with reference to the different attributes, such as goodness, wisdom; etc., we not only use different *names* but we really entertain different *thoughts.* There is not a single name which adequately expresses God's being, but there are many names, properties, ideas, dignities by means of which "some characteristic of God is revealed to us." Gregory of Nyssa even spoke of the "substance or essence" of God as the *"subject"* and of "different qualities or properties" pertaining to that essence. Accordingly, the ideas which we associate with the names of God differ the one from the other. It was considered an error to use the names of God interchangeably: they were not to be confused or used promiscuously. Each name could be viewed in distinction from all the others. So, for example, God is indeed identical with the attributes "divinity, goodness, wisdom, paternity," etc., but this does not mean that each of these attributes is identical in conception to all the rest. One property is not involved in the other in the sense that one cannot be conceived of apart from the other. Rather, each attribute expresses a distinct something. Augustine emphasizes the fact that every attribute is identical with God's being and insofar with every other attribute, "For whatever seems to be predicated with respect to qualities is to be understood with respect to the substance or essence." "Moreover, in God *to be* is the same as *to be strong* or *to be just* or *to be wise,* etc." Neither do the attributes differ the one from the other, "That which is justice is also itself goodness, and that which is goodness is also itself blessedness. His greatness is the same as his wisdom, for he is not greater in size but in virtue; and his goodness is the same as his wisdom and his greatness; and his truth is the same as all of these; and with respect to him it is not one thing to be blessed and another thing to be great or wise or

true, or to be good, or, in general, to be himself." He even expressly
states that these "predicates or qualities" when attributed to God are
really "affections" of our own spirit. "Whichever of these you affirm
concerning God, not only is it wrong to suppose that one ascription
refers to one thing and another to quite another thing, but it is also
wrong to suppose that anything is affirmed worthily, i.e., adequately,
because these ascriptions pertain to souls which, in a measure, are
filled with that Light and affected by it in accordance with their own
qualities, just as when this visible light begins to shine upon physical
objects. If it be withdrawn, all these objects have the same color;
rather: they have no color. But when it has been produced and has
illumined these objects, then, although this light itself is of one kind,
nevertheless it suffuses the objects with a luster which varies in accordance with their diverse qualities. Consequently, these affections
pertain to our own souls, which are wondrously affected by that Light
which is not affected, and are formed by that which is not formed."
Nevertheless, in spite of these strong assertions, Augustine fully maintains that all of these "predicates" are certainly and correctly ascribed
to God. God *is* whatever he *has*: he *is* whatever is *ascribed* to him in
his names. Accordingly, in discussing "God's simplicity" Augustine
is not trying to deprive God of anything, but on the contrary, he tries
to conceive of God in the fulness of his essence. It is with this object
in view that he speaks of God's *"simple multiplicity"* or of his *"multifold simplicity"*; and for the same reason he says that God's wisdom is
*"simply-manifold and uniformly-multiform."*

In later times the distinction of "subjective and objective reason"
was used in order in some measure to solve the problem which presents
itself in connection with the doctrine of the attributes. It was necessary
so to conceive of the distinction between one attribute and another that
the unity, simplicity, and immutability of God's essence remained unin-
paired, while at the same time this distinction was not viewed as a
merely subjective, arbitrary, and untrue conjecture of the human mind.
Hence, it has been correctly remarked that the distinctions are based on
God's revelation itself. For, the names which we use to address God
are not of human invention. We do not discover them. On the contrary, left to ourselves we would be altogether silent with respect to
God: we would try to forget him and we would deny every one of his
names. We have no delight in the knowledge of his ways. We continually protest against all his names or attributes: against his independence, his sovereignty, his justice, and his love; and we set our face
like a flint against all his perfections. But it is *God himself* who reveals
all his excellencies and puts his names upon our lips. It is *he* who gives
himself these names, and it is *he* who defends them against every attack.

It will not help us any to deny his righteousness, for the events of every single day of history declare this virtue. The same is true with respect to all the other attributes. In spite of ourselves God reveals them. The goal of all his ways is that his name may shine forth in all its glory and that it be written upon the foreheads of all, Rev. 22:4. Therefore, in order to address him we employ the names which he himself has revealed.

Moreover, it is not true that the distinctions between the attributes are in conflict with God's simplicity, for God's "simplicity" does not indicate that he is an abstract and contentless essence. On the contrary, it signifies that he is absolute fulness of life. And it is for this very reason that God cannot reveal himself to finite creatures except by means of many names. God's essence is infinitely rich; hence it cannot be seen at a glance. Just as a child cannot conceive of the value of a coin of high denomination until its worth is counted out to him by means of a number of coins of lesser denomination, even so we are not able to conceive of the infinite fulness of God's essence unless it is revealed to us in this, then in another relation, now from this then from another angle. God remains eternally and immutably the same, but he assumes different relations to his creatures and they enter into various relations with respect to him. Light remains the same in essence even though in the spectrum it is broken up into various individual colors (Augustine). Fire does not change whether it warms, illumines, or burns (Moses Maimonides). And grain remains grain whether, in accordance with the different relations which it assumes, we call it fruit, seed, or food (Basil). In addressing God we use various names because of the "various effects" of his ever unchanging essence upon creatures. In this connection we must not forget the close relationship which exists between God and his creatures. It is for this reason that God is able to assume many different relations and that so many different names are used to address him. 'If it were not for this relationship, all names would be untrue. But now in the creature there is an analogy of that which is present in God. The names not merely refer to God as the cause of things, but they give us a conception, however feeble and inadequate, of the divine essence. Accordingly, when we employ these names in addressing God, we speak in an imperfect, finite, limited, human manner. Nevertheless, we do not speak falsely or untruly. For, although in God knowing and willing, justice and grace are *one*, and although they are always identical with his full and complete essence; yet in these excellencies God so reveals to our eyes that one and only, rich essence that these virtues appear to lie alongside of each other and seem to follow each other. Although it is always the same being that is disclosed to us in these names, yet each name gives us some knowledge of what that being really is, of what it is in infinite fulness. Although in God holiness and righteousness may be the same essentially; *nevertheless,* on the basis of God's revelation we distinguish them in *thought.* There is no name or attribute which adequately expresses God's being. Hence, many names or attributes serve the purpose of giving us an impression of his all-transcending majesty.

F. Classifications of God's attributes:
(1) Negative and Positive, for these attributes either deny the applicability of creatural limitations to God, e.g., God is not changeable; or, they ascribe to God certain attributes of which there is a reflex in man, and which pertain to God as infinite perfections; e.g., righteousness. This classification is based on the theory of the three (really two) ways of knowing God: negation, eminence, causality. This classification is unobjectionable providing we bear in mind that the two divisions overlap.
(2) Communicable and Incommunicable. Of the former there is a reflex in man, of the latter not. We should remember, however, that the communicable attributes as they exist in God are just as incommunicable as those called "incommunicable."
(3) Quiescent and operative; indwelling and outgoing. This classification found favor among the Lutherans.
(4) Attributes which may be referred to man's feeling of dependence, entirely apart from any consciousness of sin; e.g., eternity; attributes which presuppose a consciousness of the opposing power of sin, e.g., holiness, righteousness; attributes which are "experienced" when the opposing power of sin has been conquered; e.g., love, wisdom. This is Schleiermacher's classification. It is based upon a subjective conception of the attributes.
(5) Attributes based on God's relation to the universe in general; e.g., omnipresence; to the ethical universe; e.g., holiness; and to the ethico-physical universe; e.g., blessedness.
(6) Attributes derived from the ontological argument for the existence of God; e.g., aseity; from the cosmological argument; e.g., causality, etc. Dorner's classification.
(7) Attributes which describe God as he is in himself: the metaphysical attributes; those which describe God's relation to the universe; those which describe the result of God's being and of his life; e.g., blessedness.
(8) The attributes which describe God's relation to the universe (cf. 7) are divided variously, into:
    (a) intellectual, volitional, emotional;
    (b) intellectual, ethical, dynamical;
    (c) physical and moral;
    (d) psychological attributes and attributes of holy love.

As stated in the preceding, whatever one was able to think or say about God was formerly subsumed under his *names.* But the ideas which were grouped under this heading soon became so numerous that organization of all this material became a necessity. Accordingly, the term *"the names of God"* was soon used exclusively to indicate the *proper* names; i.e., the names which we use to *address* God; e.g., God,

Lord, etc. Furthermore, the doctrine of the trinity was soon treated as an independent unit, either before or after the doctrine of the attributes. It was given a terminology which distinguished it from the other doctrines. Again, the attempt to give a description of God made it necessary to place one definite virtue in the foreground (e.g., aseity, personality, etc.) and to treat it separately, so that at times a chapter bearing the heading *God's Essence* and preceding the sections in which the other attributes would be discussed, was devoted to this single attribute. The division or classification of all the others which very readily suggested itself and which is also the oldest was that which referred to the attributes as *negative* and *positive*. Reflection upon the origin of the terms used to indicate the divine attributes resulted in the conclusion that they were derived from the realm of created objects either by way of *negation* or by way of *excellence* (or *eminence*) and *causality*. We already meet with this classification and this two or threefold way or method of gaining knowledge concerning God in the works of Philo and Plotinus. The church fathers regarded God as both unknowable and knowable; unknowable in his essence, knowable in his revelation. Hence, it was held that on the one hand it is true that one can only say what God is *not;* but that on the other hand it is also true that something, be it ever so little, can be affirmed concerning God *positively,* though defectively and inadequately. Pseudodionysius, John of Damascus, and Erigena constructed upon this idea a classification, a twofold theology: the *negative* and the *positive.* Pseudodionysius, describing the three ways of gaining knowledge concerning God, uses the very terms already mentioned when he says that we attain to the knowledge of God "via the *remotion* or *subtraction* of all things [i.e., by describing God in terms that indicate that he is *removed* from all creaturely limitations; e.g., he is unchangeable], and via *excellence* or *eminence* [i.e., by *removal of limits*: ascribing to God in a super-eminent degree those attributes of which there is a reflex in the creature] and by means of describing him as the *cause* of all things."

And scholasticism, especially since Durandus de S. Porciano, began to speak of the three "ways" which lead to the knowledge of God: the "way (method) of *negation, of "removal of limits,"* and of *"causality."* Until this very day these three "ways" have found favor with theologians. Roman Catholic, Lutheran, and Reformed theologians have accepted the theory of the three "ways," and at times dwell on them at great length. Nevertheless, they have often been subjected to severe criticism. Spinoza rejected "the way of eminence or excellence by remarking that a triangle, if it could speak, would say that "God is eminently triangular." Kant held that the usefulness of "the way of causality" was limited to the sphere of the phenomena.

Schleiermacher rejected the "way of negation and of removal of limits" and retained only "the way of causality." And others have entirely rejected the method of reaching God by way of the creature, and have sought to discredit it by asserting that we should not try to reach God by taking our starting-point in the universe, but that we should try to reach the universe by taking our starting-point in God.

Now with reference to all these remarks we should recognize the fact that the knowledge of God's attributes existed a long time before these three "ways" had been discovered; accordingly, that the theory of the three "ways" arose much later and was the result of reflection upon attributes already well-known and defined. Furthermore, it cannot be denied that "the way of excellence or eminence" and "the way of causality" are really *one*, and together may be viewed as "the way (method) of *affirmation*" over against "the way (method) of *negation*." And finally, the fact that "the theory of cognition" should not be confused with "the theory of being" admits of no doubt. In reality not the creature but God is first. He is the Archetype, the Original; the creature is the ectype, the likeness. In God everything is original, absolute, perfect; in creatures everything is derived, relative, limited. Hence, in reality God is not named on the basis of that which is present in creatures, but creatures are named on the basis of that which exists in God in an absolute sense. Nevertheless, on the other hand, one should bear in mind that there is no knowledge of God except that which has its origin in his relation to the universe. Since here on earth we walk by faith and not by sight we have only an analogical and proportional knowledge of God. We do not have a "direct or proper idea" of God, but an "indirect or derived idea," an idea which is derived from the creaturely realm, but which, though inadequate, is not untrue, inasmuch as the creature is *God's* creature and hence reveals something of his excellencies. When we bear this in mind, we can say that both of these "ways" may safely be traveled. In its epistemology Scripture, which is theological from beginning to end and derives everything from God, in spite of this fact, rather because of it, ascends to God *from the plane of the universe*, Is. 40:26; Rom. 1:20. Just because everything is *from* God, everything points back *to* God. Whoever wishes to think or speak about God must needs operate with forms and images borrowed from the world round about him, whether he prefers the positive or the negative way. On the one hand we withhold from God all those imperfections and limitations which we encounter in the creature; and on the other hand we ascribe to God as absolute attributes all those perfections of which there is a reflex in the creature. But these two paths are not separated by a wide chasm. They do not even run parallel, neither can one travel the one and not the other.

In order to reach our goal both methods must be employed continuously and simultaneously. When we make use of "the way (method) of negation" and withhold from God (i.e., deny with respect to him) all imperfections which pertain to the creature, this presupposes that we have a positive awareness of him and conceive of him as the absolute being, even though we may not be able to express that awareness in so many words: the confession of his incomprehensibility is a proof of his knowability. Conversely, whenever we, "by way of affirmation" ascribe to him the excellencies which are found in the creature, we always do it in such a manner that we at the same time make use of "the way of eminence." We ascribe these excellencies to him only in a super-eminent sense; i.e., our very *affirmation* implies a *negation,* for we deny that these excellencies are present in God in the same sense in which they pertain to the creature. Hence, it is correct to say that all attributes are ascribed to God and withheld from him at one and the same time. God is wise and good and holy and glorious but not in the manner in which creatures are. This way of speaking about God found great favor with the mystics, who asserted that God was exalted above all wisdom, goodness, holiness, life, essence, being, yea even above all godhood. Nevertheless, they did not mean to deny that God was all this, but they meant to point out that God was all this in a sense which completely transcends our thought. God is at once *"panonymous"* (the possessor of all names) and *"anonymous"* (without a name). He who does not know him, i.e., he who regards him as exalted above that which can be conceived in thought, knows him best. The superlatively transcendent Light dwells in thick darkness, Ex. 20:21. Accordingly, Pseudodionysius called God "the affirmation of all things and the negation of all things, the cause or principle exalted above all affirmation and negation."

The classification of the divine attributes stands in close relation to these two ways of reaching God. This division of the attributes (into negative and positive) has a very ancient origin, was soon accepted everywhere, and is really presupposed by all other and later classifications. We already meet with it in the works of Philo, Plotinus, and the church-fathers; of John of Damascus, Anselm, Thomas Aquinas, Petavius, and many others. With Roman Catholic theologians this is the most usual representation, while some Lutheran and Reformed theologians have also adopted it. On the basis of this classification several other distinctions are introduced. Augustine already remarked that some attributes (names) belong to God *"properly,"* others *"meta-phorically,"* and still others *"relatively."* Accordingly, the "negative names or attributes" were subdivided into those properly negative and those relatively negative; while the "positive names or attributes" were subdivided into "the proper and the metaphorical."

Alongside of this division of the attributes into negative and positive there arose another one. Plato already taught that God is good in and by himself while creatures are good by "participation." This idea produced many fruits in Christian theology, a fact which is especially apparent in the works of Augustine. Over against Pantheism it was maintained that the essence of God is incommunicable, and that the soul was not a "particle of God." But it was also maintained that all creatures are related to God and particularly that man is God's image and likeness. Creatures resemble their Creator. This view led to the division of the attributes into *"communicable and incommunicable."* At first these terms were used in the doctrine of the trinity; for, the *being* or *essence* of God was "communicable": by means of generation it was communicated by the Father to the Son; while the *persons* and *personal attributes,* e.g., "fatherhood" were "incommunicable." These same terms were later on applied to the attributes in order that justice might be done both to God's transcendence and to his immanence. Reformed theologians eagerly adopted this classification, especially because it afforded them an opportunity to attack the Lutheran doctrine of ubiquity. Nevertheless, all agree that the communicable attributes when taken in the absolute sense, i.e., as they exist in God, are as incommunicable as are the others.

Generally speaking, among the Lutherans another division of the attributes found favor; namely, that into *"quiescent* and *operative,"* or that into *"indwelling* and *outgoing* attributes." This classification was resorted to in defence of the doctrine of the "communication of attributes." Under the first group (negative, incommunicable, metaphysical, quiescent) the following attributes were usually discussed: oneness, simplicity, independence, immutability, eternity, and omnipresence. The second group (positive, communicable, operative, personal) was usually subdivided into attributes of mind, will, and power.

In recent years many new classifications have been added to the older and more usual ones. Schleiermacher views the attributes as merely subjective conceptions, as grounded in "subjective reason." Consequently, he grouped them according to the relation in which, for our consciousness, God stands to the universe, to sin, and to redemption. Thus, first of all there are attributes which may be referred to man's feeling of dependence, entirely apart from any consciousness of the opposing power of sin; e.g., eternity, omnipresence, omnipotence, omniscience. Then, there are attributes which presuppose a consciousness of the opposing power of sin; e.g., holiness, righteousness. Finally, there are those attributes which are experienced when the opposing power of sin has been conquered; e.g., love and wisdom. Closely related to this is the classification which distinguishes the attributes according to the relation in which God stands to the world, i. e. to the universe in general (infinitude, eternity, omnipresence); to the ethical universe (holiness, righteousness, grace, lovingkindness); and to the ethico-physical universe (wisdom, blessedness).

Among those who base their division of the attributes entirely upon God's relation to the universe is also Dorner, but he does this by connecting God's attributes with the arguments for the existence of God, and by deriving a group of attributes from each argument. Thus, the ontological argument makes us think of God as the One who has being, essence, the One who *is;* hence, it furnishes us with the idea of the absolute, and it gives us the attributes of oneness, simplicity, and infinitude. The cosmological argument describes God as the causality of all things; hence, as the One who is in himself absolute Life, etc.

There are others who think that to the group of attributes which we learn to know on the basis of God's relation to the universe there should be prefixed those which describe God as he is "in himself." These latter attributes are called metaphysical attributes or attributes of essence, of the absolute, of absolute personality, of "the Spirit, all-glorious in himself, who conditions every living object," etc. Again, there are different methods of classifying the attributes which are referred to the second group (those based on God's relation to the universe). By some these are subdivided into *intellectual* and *volitional* attributes to which Hase adds the *emotional* attributes; by others they are subdivided into *intellectual, ethical, and dynamical* attributes; by still others into *physical* and *moral* attributes; while at times they are all grouped under the heading *psychological attributes* or *attributes of holy love.* Some add a third group of attributes to the two already mentioned. This third group contains the attributes which describe the result of God's being and of his life, and reveal his blessedness and his glory. Finally, there are those who have given up the attempt to classify the attributes according to a definite scheme, and who follow some kind of an order merely for the sake of convenience in treatment.

**G. The same fundamental objection may be advanced against every one of these classifications; the division into communicable and incommunicable attributes has in its favor that it maintains both God's transcendence and his immanence; i.e., that it avoids the error of pantheism as well as of deism.**

Now in appearance these different classifications vary widely. To be sure they differ in terminology; in reality, however, they amount to the same thing. Whether one speaks of negative and positive, or of incommunicable and communicable, or of quiescent and operative, or of absolute and relative, or of metaphysical and psychological, or of substantial and subjective attributes; in reality the order of treatment is the same. The same main objection may be advanced against every one of these classifications: they all seem to divide the being of God into two halves. They all seem to treat first God's absoluteness, then his personality; first God's being "as such," afterward his relation to creation: they all seem to imply that the first group of attributes bears no relation to creation while the second group is derived from creation; and that, consequently, all harmony among the several attributes is wanting: that they do not form a unity. Now Scripture certainly teaches that God is unknowable as to his inner essence, and that all God's names presuppose revelation and creation. We know nothing concerning God apart from creation, for the simple reason that we ourselves are and ever remain creatures. This is clear in regard to God's relative, metaphorical, and positive names. The *relative* names — such as Lord, Creator, Preserver, Savior; etc. — are his on account of the work of creation: no one is called "lord" if he has no servants. Hence, these relative names became applicable to God *after* he created the universe, not *before;* for man is not from eternity but was created in time; hence, in time God became our Lord. These names, therefore, presuppose creation. That this is also true in regard to the *metaphorical* names is very evident, especially when we consider the fact that the anthropomorphisms are included in this class. In the same manner also the *positive* names — such as, good, holy, wise, etc. — have meaning for us because of these qualities there is a reflex in the creature. But on the other hand, all these names (whether relative, metaphorical, or positive) clearly indicate something which is *absolute* in God, and which, therefore, pertains to him in a sense differing from that in which it pertains to the creature. Augustine tried to make clear that although God becomes Lord in time, *he* is, nevertheless, unchangeable, whereas the change which takes place really pertains to the creature. "Accordingly, that which begins to be spoken of God in time; that which was not spoken of him before, is manifestly spoken of him relatively; yet not according to any accident of God, as if anything had happened to him, but clearly according to some accident of that in respect to which God begins to be called something relatively."

The opposite is true in regard to the second group of names (attributes), whether these be called negative, incommunicable, quiescent, or absolute; for although these deny certain limitations to God which pertain to the creature, nevertheless, in a certain sense they are all positive, communicable, transeunt, relative. If they were completely incommunicable, they would also be absolutely unknowable. The very fact that we are able to name them proves that in one way or another they were revealed by God in creation. Hence, the negative attributes have a positive content: though we need the idea of time in order to obtain a conception of God's eternity, and that of space in order to form an idea of his omnipresence, and that of finite, changeable creatures in order to become aware of his infinitude and immutability; nevertheless, these negative attributes furnish us with a very important positive knowledge concerning God. Thus, even though we cannot comprehend eternity in any positive sense, nevertheless, to know that God is exalted above the limitations of time is very important. By means of that knowledge we are constantly correcting our ideas concerning God; we speak of him in human terms, we ascribe various human attributes to him, but while we are doing this we are ever conscious of the fact that all these properties pertain to him in a sense entirely different from that in which they pertain to creatures. The fact that we *know* that our knowledge concerning God is inadequate causes this knowledge to be, nevertheless, true, analogical, and ectypal. Hence, the classification of God's attributes in such a manner that we have on the one hand the negative, incommunicable, quiescent, absolute, metaphysical perfections, which describe God's being "as such" apart from his relation to the universe; and on the other hand the positive, communicable, operative, relative, psychological attributes, which are derived from God's relation to the universe, will ever remain open to criticism, and will never give complete satisfaction, for all these perfections are at the same time both absolute and relative. Nevertheless, we can name God only in accordance with that which he has revealed in creation, though in doing this we name him who is exalted far above all creatures. Hence, one would even be justified in saying that there is no classification which is objectively based upon the attributes themselves, because these perfections are in reality identical with God's being, and in God they are also identical with each other.

But, though we admit these difficulties, in order to treat the many names ascribed to God we must have a classification. When we summarize what God has revealed concerning himself in his names, the fact that there are two distinct groups of names aside from the group containing the attributes is readily noticeable. First, we have those names by which God is *addressed,* proper names which were specifically indicated as God's "names." Then, those attributes which do not pertain to God's being as such but to *the three persons* in that being form a second group and are called "properties, notions, notional properties personal properties, relative attributes." They are treated in the doctrine of the trinity. The third large group is composed of those *attributes which describe God's being.* These attributes, taken as a group, have received various names in theological science; such as, dignities, values, thoughts, ideas, concepts, properties, excellencies, notions, qualities, virtues, attributes, perfections, etc. It is extremely difficult to bring about order in the treatment of the numerous attributes which belong to this last group. However, the relation which God sustains to his creatures can serve as a "principle of division." The entire universe reveals God: there is no "atom of the universe" which does not manifest something of his virtues. Nevertheless, all creatures are not the same; each individual creature does not reveal all of God's virtues, neither does each creature show forth God's excellencies in the same degree and manner as do all the others. There is order and gradation; all creatures reveal traces or "vestiges of God," but of all creatures man, he alone, is the image and likeness of God. Not only has he *existence* in common with the *lower creation,* and *life* in common with *higher creatures,* but he is also related to *God* in a very special sense, having been created as prophet, priest, and king, in true knowledge of God, holiness, and righteousness. Hence, God, the source of all being, and man's arch-type, is himself all that which creatures share of essence, life, and spirit, of knowledge, of holiness and of righteousness. There is an analogy of God's being present in every creature, but especially in man. But whatever of perfections is found in creatures is present in God in a very unique, original manner; in each of God's virtues both his transcendence and his immanence shine forth; every attribute is in one sense incommunicable, and in another, communicable.

Scripture leads the way by maintaining both God's "transcendence above and his immanence in the world," and Christian theology followed the example by discussing first the negative (incommunicable) and afterward the positive (communicable) attributes. To be strictly correct one would have to indicate in regard to every positive attribute that it is at the same time negative; inasmuch as essence, life, spirit, knowledge, righteousness, holiness, etc., pertain to God in a different sense than to the creature; i.e., these perfections are independent, immutable, eternal, omnipresent, and simple in God. But this would result in constant repetition and would render impossible a separate and necessary treatment of these qualifications. We must needs discuss things consecutively, and an orderly discussion of God's attributes results in the old classification, whatever be the name given to it. The difficulty encountered in this classification is unavoidable and natural. In the doctrine concerning God we should throughout maintain both his transcendence and his immanence. When we do this, it matters less what names we shall use to indicate these two groups of attributes, whether negative and positive, quiescent and operative, incommunicable and communicable; or still others.

It may be said in favor of the division into incommunicable and communicable attributes that these names, preferred by Reformed theologians, safeguard Christian theism against both pantheism and deism. Hence, it is perfectly proper to speak of incommunicable attributes, if one remembers that these are really descriptions of the unique, absolute, divine manner in which the other attributes (viz., those of essence, life, and spirit, mind and will, love and righteousness, etc.,) exist in God. According to the usual order of classification there are four incommunicable attributes:

(1) "Independence, self-sufficiency, aseity"
(2) "Immutability"
(3) "Infinity, Infinitude"
 (a) "Eternity"
 (b) "Immensity, Omnipresence"
(4) "Oneness"
 (a) "Numerical Oneness, Unity"
 (b) "Qualitative Oneness, Simplicity"

From these incommunicable attributes we must distinguish those which affirm something positively (though analogically, proportionately) concerning the content of the Divine Being. The usual, suitable division, derived from the image of God as revealed in man, is as follows:

(1) Attributes which designate God as Life and Spirit:
 (a) "Spirituality"
 (b) "Invisibility"
(2) Attributes which describe God's being as perfect in self-consciousness:
 (a) "Knowledge, omniscience"
 (b) "Wisdom"
 (c) "Veracity"
(3) Attributes which indicate God's Ethical Nature:
 (a) "Goodness"
 (b) "Righteousness"
 (c) "Holiness"
(4) Attributes which designate God as Lord, King, Sovereign;
 (a) "Will"
 (b) "Freedom"
 (c) "Omnipotence"
(5) Attributes which summarize and complement the preceding, and reveal God's Absolute Blessedness:
 (a) "Perfection"
 (b) "Blessedness"
 (c) "Glory"

This classification is on the one hand related to the knowledge of God derived from the "vestiges of God" in creation, which is summarized in the so-called proofs for the existence of God; and on the other hand points forward to the image of God in man, especially in Christ. Apart from this revelation in creation there is no knowledge of God; hence, the latter ever remains analogical and ectypal. Nevertheless, because of this revelation our knowledge of God's incomprehensible and glorious being is real and true.

**II. Note Regarding Arrangement of Material. God's Independence. God's Independence Is a Scriptural Truth. Philosophy, Pagan Religions as Well as Christian Theology Accept This Truth in One Form or Another. Only God Is Independent, Yet There Is a Trace of God's Independence in the Creature.**

### Introductory Note regarding arrangement of material

Some theologians treat the doctrine of the trinity before the divine attributes; and Frank even raises objections to the opposite order. Now if the discussion of the attributes before the trinity owed its origin to the desire to ascend from "natural" to "revealed theology," from the purely natural to the Christian conception of God, it would indeed merit our disapproval. But this is by no means the case. In the discussion of God's attributes or perfections we are discussing the divine nature as it is revealed to us in Scripture, as it is confessed by faith, and as it exists in a threefold manner, to be set forth when we discuss the doctrine of the trinity. In order to understand what is meant when in the doctrine of the trinity we are taught that Father, Son, and Holy Spirit partake of the same divine nature, it is necessary that we know first of all what is comprised by that divine nature and wherein it differs from every created nature. Moreover, in adopting this order we are following the lead of Scripture. There God's *essence* is taught earlier and clearer than his trinitarian existence. The truth with respect to the trinity is not clearly revealed until we come to the N. T. The names Yhwh, Elohim, precede Father, Son, and Spirit.

#### A. Scripture throughout proclaims God's independence.

The first thing Scripture teaches us concerning God is that he has a distinct, free, and independent existence and life. He has a distinct being, a distinct "nature, substance, essence," not apart from his virtues, but revealed in all his virtues and perfections. He has proper names that do not pertain to any creature. Among all these names the name "Jehovah" stands out pre-eminently, Ex. 3:14. By means of this name he is designated as the One who is and will be what he was; i.e., who remains eternally the same in relation to his people. He has the ground of his existence in himself. He existed before all things, and all things exist through him, Ps. 90:2; I Cor. 8:6; Rev. 4:11. In the most absolute sense of the word he is "Lord" (*ādhôn, kyrios, despotēs*), Lord of all the earth, Ex. 23:17; Deut. 10:17; Josh. 3:13. He depends on nothing, everything depends on him, Rom. 11:36. He kills and makes alive; he forms the light, and creates darkness; he makes peace and creates evil, Deut. 32:39; Is. 45:5-7; 54:16. He doeth according to his will in the army of heaven, and among the inhabitants of the earth, Dan. 4:35, so that in his hand people are as clay in the hand of the potter, Is. 64:8; Jer. 18:1 ff.; Rom. 9:21. His counsel, his good pleasure, is the final ground of all that is and of all that happens, Ps. 33:11; Prov. 19:21; Is. 46:10; Matt. 11:26; Acts 2:23; 4:28; Eph. 1:5, 9, 11. He does everything for his name's sake and for his praise, Deut. 32:27; Josh. 7:9; 1 Sam. 12:22; Ps. 25:11; 31:3; 79:9; 106:8; 109:21; 143:11; Prov. 16:4; Is. 48:9; Jer. 14:7, 21; Ezek. 20:9, 14, 22, 44. He needs nothing and is all-sufficient, Job 22:2, 3; Ps. 50:18 ff.; Acts 17:25; he hath life in himself, John 5:26. Hence, he is the first and the last, the Alpha and the Omega, who is and who was and who is to come, Is. 41:4; 44:6; 48:12; Rev. 1:8; etc. absolutely independent, not only in his existence, but consequently also in his virtues and perfections, in all his decrees and deeds. He is independent as to his mind, Rom. 11:34, 35; as to his will, Dan. 4:35; Rom. 9:19; Eph. 1:5; Rev. 4:11; as to his counsel, Ps. 33:11; Is. 46:10; as to his love, Hos. 14:5; as to his power, Ps. 115:3; etc. Thus, all-sufficient in himself, and independent of all things he is the only source of all life and existence, of all light and love, the fountain of all blessings, Ps. 36:9; Acts 17:25.

**B. God's independence is generally recognized:**

(1) Heathen religions generally assume the existence of a supreme power on which everything else is dependent: chance, nature, fate, fortune.

(2) Philosophers prefer to speak of God as "the Absolute."

(3) Early Chr. theologians speak of God's aseity, all-sufficiency, independence, greatness, etc.

(4) The Scholastics and later R. C. theologians usually proceed from God's aseity.

(5) The Reformers also accepted this doctrine, but preferred to speak of God's independence rather than of his aseity because, whereas the latter designates God as self-sufficient in his EXISTENCE, the former characterizes him as self-sufficient in EVERYTHING.

Now, every one accepts God's independence, although the degree of emphasis placed on this doctrine varies with different individuals. To be sure, the heathen bring down whatever is divine to the level of the creature and teach a theogony; nevertheless, they often accept one power, conceived of as existing above and beyond their gods, to which all things are subject in the most absolute sense. Many speak of *nature, chance, fate* or *fortune* as if it were a power exalted above everything else, while philosophers prefer to speak of God as *the Absolute*. In Christian theology this divine attribute was called *self-sufficiency, aseity, all-sufficiency, independence, greatness*. In the East the following terms were used: *"God, the inoriginate, uncaused, ingenerate,"* and theologians preferred to speak of God as *"the self-generate, self-begotten, self-existent, self-divine, self-luminous, self-wise, self-virtuous, self-excellent,"* etc.

Whatever God is he is of himself. "By his own self" he is "goodness, holiness, wisdom, life, light, truth; etc." As remarked in the preceding, the churchfathers followed Philo in basing their description of God on the name Yhwh. That was considered to be God's essential name par excellence. God was the existing One. In his name *I WILL BE THAT I WILL BE* everything was included. All other divine attributes were derived from this one. God is "supreme essence, supreme goodness, supreme truth, supreme beauty." He is the perfect, the highest, the most excellent essence, "than whom no one better can exist or can be thought." Within himself he possesses all essence. He is an infinite and unlimited sea of essence. "If thou shalt have predicated of God that he is good, great, blessed, wise, or whatever such like quality thou shalt have predicated of him, it is summed up in this word, namely, that *he is*. For indeed, for him *to be* means *to be all these*. Even if thou addest a hundred such like qualities, thou hast not departed from essence; if thou shalt have predicated these things, thou hast added nothing; if thou shalt not have predicated them, thou hast subtracted nothing." Scholasticism concurred with this view. In its discussion of this attribute it at times gave to it the name "God's infinity or spirituality" or "God's aseity," a term which indicated that as "supreme substance" God "is whatever he is by his own self or of his own self." Later Roman Catholic theologians also usually proceeded from God's aseity or independence.

In this respect the Reformation did not bring about any change. Among those who, on the basis of the name Yhwh, describe God as absolute existence is also Luther. God is pure essence. Yet, Luther refuses to dwell at great length on abstract, metaphysical definitions. He soon passes from "the hidden God" to "God as he is revealed in Christ." In his *Loci* Melanchton defines God as "spiritual essence." Lutherans usually copy this definition, but add to it this further qualifying phrase "infinite, subsisting of himself, or independent." Among the Reformed this divine perfection receives even greater emphasis. even though the word "aseity" soon gave place to the better term "independence." "Aseity" merely expresses the fact that God is self-sufficient in his *existence*; but "independence" has a broader connotation, and indicates that God is self-sufficient in *everything*: in his existence, in his attributes, in his decrees, and in his works. Accordingly, while in general the name Yhwh used to serve as a starting point for the discussion of the attributes, at present divine "independence" is commonly viewed as the first of the attributes.

C. **God's independence, on the one hand, marks him as differing from all other beings, for every creature is dependent; only God is independent; yet, on the other hand, there is a faint trace of this independence in the creature; for, every creature, though absolutely dependent, has, nevertheless, a distinct existence and a striving toward self-preservation.**

When God in Scripture ascribes aseity to himself, he reveals himself as absolute essence. By virtue of this perfection God is absolutely different from every creature, for every creature is dependent "on another"; no creature has the source of its existence "in itself"; no creature possesses anything of itself, but all are absolutely dependent in their origin and hence also in their entire existence and development. But, according to this attribute, *God* has the source of his existence in himself: not in the sense of having caused himself, but in the sense of *being* (not becoming) what he is from eternity to eternity: he is absolute essence, fulness of essence, hence, eternally and absolutely independent in his existence, in his virtues, and in his works; the first and the last; the only cause and purpose of all things. This divine aseity, taken in the sense of having not merely existence "of himself" but also fulness of essence, implies all the other virtues: they are so many brilliant manifestations of it. The consideration of this attribute clearly indicates the unbridgeable chasm existing between the Creator and the creature; nevertheless, there is a faint trace of this perfection in the creature. Pantheism, indeed, does not admit this; but theism maintains that every creature, though absolutely dependent, has, nevertheless, a *distinct* essence. This essence has been endowed with a "striving toward self-preservation." Every creature, by reason of its very existence, fears death; even the smallest atom opposes every attempt to destroy it. In this we see a trace of God's independent, immutable essence.

**III. God's Immutability. God's Independence Implies His Immutability. This Truth Is Clearly Taught In Scripture. It Was Accepted By the Early Church as Well as By Later Theologians. It Is Partly Denied By Pelagians, Socinians, Arminians, and Rationalists. It Is Completely Rejected By Pantheism. Immutability Should Not Be Confused With Immobility.**

A. **God's independence implies his immutability. Scripture throughout proclaims God's immutability.**

God's aseity implies his immutability. Now at first it may seem that this immutability is unsupported by Scripture. The Bible everywhere represents God as being in very close contact with the world. In the beginning he created heaven and earth; hence, from the state of non-creative activity he proceeded to that of creative activity. Ever since that beginning he lives the life of the world, as it were; in a very special sense he lives the life of Israel; he comes and goes; he reveals himself and hides himself; he withdraws his countenance, and lifts up the light of his countenance. He repents, Gen. 6:6; 1 Sam. 15:11; Amos 7:3, 6; Joel 2:13; Jonah 3:9; 42; he changes his purpose, Ex. 32:10-14; Jonah 3:10; he becomes angry, Num. 11:1, 10; Ps. 106:40; Zech. 10:3; and he turns from the fierceness of his anger, Deut. 13:17; II Chron. 12:12; 30:8; Jer. 18:8, 10; 26:3. He assumes a different relation to the believer than to the unbeliever, Prov. 11:20; 12:22: with the pure he shows himself pure, and with the perverse he shows himself froward (a wrestler, an opponent), Ps. 18:25, 26; in the fulness of time he becomes flesh in Christ and through the Holy Spirit he comes to dwell in the church; he rejects Israel, and accepts the Gentiles. Similarly, the people of God experience at one time God's wrath, then again his love; at one time his absence, then again his closeness; at one time they are burdened with the consciousness of their guilt, at other times they rejoice because of forgiveness of sins. Notwithstanding all this, Scripture testifies that in all these various relations and experiences God remains ever the same. Though everything perishes, he endures; he remains what he is, Ps. 102: 26-28. He is Jehovah, who remaineth eternally the same. He describes himself as "Jehovah, the first, and with the last, I am he," Is. 41:4; 43:10: 46:4; 48:12. He is what he is, Deut. 32:39; cf. John 8:58; Heb. 13:8; the incorruptible God, who only hath immortality; he remains ever the same, Rom. 1:23; I Tim. 1:17: 6:16; Heb. 1:11, 12. Moreover, being immutable in his existence and essence, he is also unchangeable in his thoughts and will, in all his purposes and decrees; he is not a man that he should repent. He does what he threatens, Num. 15:29; 1 Sam. 15:29. The gifts and the calling of God are not repented of, Rom. 11:29. He does not cast off his people, Rom. 11:1. He perfects what he begins, Ps. 138·8; Phil. 1:6. Summing it up in one word: he, Jehovah, changes not, Mal. 3:6; with him there can be no variation, neither shadow that is cast by turning.

**B. This Scriptural representation of God's immutability runs counter to heathen mythology: the gods of Epicurus resemble changeable men. It is approached by heathen philosophers (Aristotle, etc.), was taught by early Christian theologians, by scholastics and later R. C. theologians, by the Lutherans and the Reformed. According to Socinians, Pelagians, Arminians and Rationalists, God is changeable, not in his being but in his will. Gnosticism and Pantheism (Fichte, Hegel, Schleiermacher, Scho-**

penhauer, Von Hartmann, etc.) deny God's immutability by representing him as eternally BECOMING. It should be noted:

(1) that Scripture teaches this doctrine very clearly, Deut.
32:4; I Sam. 2:2; Ps. 19:15, etc.;

(2) that the very idea of Godhead leaves no room for that of
"change": if God, according to his essence, can change, he cannot be God; and

(3) that the rejection of the doctrine of God's immutability
implies the rejection of all God's attributes: if God is changeable, he cannot be eternal, omniscient, etc.

On this foundation Christian theology constructed its doctrine of
"God's immutability." Mythological theogony was not able to raise
itself to this level, but philosophy often called and described God as the
only, eternal, immutable, undisturbed Ruler, who ever remains like unto
himself. According to Aristotle the perpetuity of motion in the universe presupposes a "first mover," an "eternal, immovable being," who
was *one* and everlasting, necessary, immutable, free from all composition, devoid of "matter, capacity or potentiality"; pure "energy or
activity," pure "idea or form," unadulterated essence, absolute form,
"the very nature of a thing, the primary substance." Philo called God
"unchangeable, consistent with himself, invariable, steadfast, firm, fixed,
unalterable." And Christian Theology was in thorough agreement with
this view. According to Irenaeus God is "ever the same, equal and
similar to himself." According to Augustine God's immutability ensues
from the fact that he is the highest, perfect essence. It is "naturally
and truly ingrafted in every creature that there is an altogether unchangeable and incorruptible God." This conception of an eternal
and immutable being is not produced by the senses, for every creature,
also man, is changeable; but within his soul man sees and finds that
which is immutable, better and greater than all those things which are
subject to change. If God were not immutable, he would not be God.
His name is *being,* and this name is "an unchangeable name." Whatever changes ceases to be what it was. But real *being* pertains to him
who does not change. That which really *is* remains. But that which
changes *"was* something and *will be* something"; "however, we cannot
say that it *is,* i.e., that it has *being,* for it is mutable." However, God,
who *is.* is not subject to change as every change would indicate a decrease in his being. Moreover, God is as unchangeable in his knowing,
willing, and decreeing as he is in his being. "The essence of God,
whereby he is, has nothing changeable, neither in eternity, nor in truthfulness, nor in will." As he *is,* so he *knows* and *wills,* i.e., in an immutable manner. "Thy essence knoweth and willeth unchangeably;
and thy knowledge is and willeth unchangeably; and thy will is and
knoweth unchangeably." Creation, revelation, and incarnation did not

bring about any change in God. God never made a "new plan." He has always had the one and only, immutable will. "By one and the same eternal and immutable will he effected with respect to the things which he created, both that formerly, so long as they were not, they should not be, and that afterward, when they began to be, they should come into existence." Whatever change there is, is wholly in the creature: the creature changes from non-being to being, from good to evil; etc. This same thought recurs again and again in the writings of the scholastic and Roman Catholic as well as in those of Lutheran and Reformed theologians.

Nevertheless, this doctrine of divine immutability met with much opposition from the side of both deism and pantheism. According to Epicurus the gods are in every respect similar to excellent men, who are continually changing with respect to place, occupation, thought: etc.; and according to Heraclitus and (at a later date) the Stoics God, as the immanent cause of the universe, was included in its perpetual flux. In Christian theology we encounter a similar trend of opposition to divine immutability. On one side we find pelagianism, socinianism, remonstrantism, and rationalism, which launch their attack chiefly against the immutable character of God's knowing and willing, making the will of God dependent upon the will of man. Especially Vorstius in his work *Concerning God and his Attributes* assailed the doctrine of God's immutability. He distinguished between God's *"essence,"* simple and unchangeable, and his *"will,"* which, being free, does not will everything *eternally* or *unchangeably*. But pantheism's opposition to the doctrine of divine immutability is even more serious. Common to all pantheistic argumentation is this, that the idea of *becoming* is applied to God, and thus the boundary line between Creator and creature is completely erased. The idea of God as "substance," as developed by Spinoza, was shown to be an abstract concept without content. In order to put life into that concept philosophy often replaced being by becoming. Of course, it makes a great difference whether we conceive of this process of becoming in a unitarian or in a trinitarian sense, whether we think of it as immanent in the being of God or transeunt in the universe.

Now, among the isms which deny God's immutability because they apply to God the idea of becoming we think first of all of Gnosticism; furthermore, of the theosophy of the cabala, and of Böhme, Schelling, Rothe, Hamberger, etc., which exerted its influence upon the doctrine of kenosis (self-emptying, cf. Phil. 2:7 ff.); and finally, we have in mind the pantheistic philosophy of Fichte, Hegel, Schleiermacher, Schopenhauer, Von Hartmann; etc. The elaborations may differ, the *basic idea* in all these systems is the same: God *is* not; he *becomes*.

Originally and purely "in and of himself" God is "unknowable depth," a purely abstract and potential being, mere nature, contentless thinking, a dark urge, a blind and a logical will; in a word, a being who is nothing but may become everything. But very gradually, by means of a lengthy process of emerging, God's potential existence develops into actual existence. God is his own creator. He produces himself. Very gradually he attains to personality and self-consciousness; he becomes mind, spirit. He is "his own cause." In more recent times under the influence of this philosophic idea of absolute becoming certain theologians have begun to reject or restrict God's immutability, and have spoken of God as "his own cause," as a self-actualizing energy. Says Luthardt, "God is his own deed." Others speak of "God's self-determination (self-establishment)." In a monograph Dorner tried to avoid both the deistic and the pantheistic or acosmismic errors, and to harmonize God's immutability with his vivacity. He imagines that he can accomplish this end by limiting God's immutability to the ethical sphere. Ethically God is unchangeable and ever self-consistent: he remains holy love. But for the rest Dorner imagines that creation, incarnation, redemption, etc., brought about a change in God; that he stands "in reciprocal relation" to man: that he is dependent upon the universe for his knowledge of reality; that also for him there is a past, a present, and a future; that he becomes angry, justifies, and, in general, that his disposition answers to that of man.

Finally, there are those who in their doctrine of God do not commit themselves with respect to this very important attribute, but who, in their discussion of creation, incarnation, or self-emptying (kenosis, cf. Phil. 2:7 ff.), give plain evidence of their rejection of God's immutability; e.g., Ebrard, Hofmann, Thomasius, Von Oettingen, etc.

Nevertheless the doctrine of God's immutability is of the highest significance for religion. The contrast between being and becoming marks the difference between the Creator and the creature. Every creature is continually becoming. It is changeable, constantly striving, seeks rest and satisfaction, and finds this rest in God, in him alone, for only he is pure being and no becoming. Hence, in Scripture God is often called the Rock: Deut. 32:4, 15, 18, 30, 31, 37; I Sam. 2:2; II Sam. 22:3, 32; Ps. 19:14; 31:2; 62:2, 6; 73:26, etc. On him man can firmly rely; he does not change with respect to his being, nor with respect to his knowing or willing; he ever remains himself. Every change is foreign to God. He transcends every change in time, for he is eternal; in space, for he is omnipresent; in essence, for he is pure being, whence Christian theology often called God "pure actuality." Aristotle so conceived of God's being as "the first (primary) Idea or Form," without any "potentiality," as "absolute energy or activity." Accordingly, scholasticism began to speak of God as "purest and simplest actuality," in order to indicate that he is perfect, absolute being without any "capacity" for non-being or for being different. Accordingly, Boëthius states that God does not change in essence "because he is pure actuality." Therefore, the application of the term "his own cause" to God was generally regarded with disfavor. The idea of absolute becoming was first clearly expressed by Heraclitus and recurs again and again in philosophy. Plotinus more than any one else made use of this concept, and he applied it not only to matter but also to that which he regarded as absolute being. He taught that God brought forth his own being, that he was active before he existed. Now, we grant, of course, that Christian theology spoke of God as "a being who exists *of himself*"; hence, of his "aseity." Moreover, Lactantius, Synesius, and Jerome used the term "his own cause"; and the latter wrote, "The God who always *is,* who does not have a beginning from elsewhere but is himself his own origin and the cause of his own substance, cannot be understood to have from elsewhere that which subsists." Nevertheless, this expression was always understood thus: that God is the ground of his own *being* or *existence,* not of his own *becoming* or *development.*

When at a later date René Descartes accepted the primacy of God's *will* rather than of his mind, and taught that the essence of all things was dependent upon that will, so that he even viewed God's existence as a product of his will, and said, "God is his own cause," he exists "of himself" not in a negative but in a positive sense, God is "the efficient cause of his own existence," he owes his existence to the real immeasurableness of his power, a few followers copied this expression, but the Reformed theologians insisted that the terms "his own cause," and "existence of himself" be understood in a negative sense only. A "cause of itself" in the positive sense is impossible, because in that case the very selfsame object is at one and the same time said to exist, inasfar as it produces itself, and not to exist inasfar as it is produced. Now we can easily understand why monistic philosophy has taken recourse to this idea of absolute becoming; namely, in order to give at least a semblance of an explanation of reality. But Herbart has rightly subjected this idea to a scathing criticism, and not without good reason have his followers expressed their surprise concerning the fact that this concept of becoming had met with such great success in speculative theology.

For, indeed, the idea of becoming or development predicated of the divine being is of no value whatsoever in theology. Not only does *Scripture* explicitly state that with God "there can be no variation neither shadow that is cast by turning," but a moment's *reflection* upon this matter leads to the same result. Becoming presupposes a cause, for there is no becoming without a cause. But absolute being leaves no room for a cause. Absolute being is because it is. The concept of deity of itself implies the idea of immutability. Both increase and decrease are absolutely inconceivable with respect to God. He can become neither worse nor better, for he is the absolute, complete, and *very* being. Becoming is an attribute of the creature. It is a form of change with respect either to time or to space. But God is the I WILL BE THAT I WILL BE, eternally transcendent above space and time and exalted far above every creature. He rests in himself, and for that very reason he is the goal and the resting-point of every creature, the Rock of salvation, whose work is perfect. He who predicates of God any change whatsoever, whether with respect to essence, knowledge, or will, belittles every one of his attributes: independence, simplicity, eternity, omniscience, omnipotence. He robs God of his divine nature and religion of its firm foundation and sure comfort.

**C. The fact that God is immutable does not mean that he is inactive: immutability should not be confused with immobility.**

Nevertheless, this immutability should not be confused with monotonous inactivity or immobility. Scripture itself describes God to us in his manifold relations to his creatures. Though unchangeable in himself, God lives the life of his creatures, and is not indifferent to their changing activities. Scripture must needs describe God in anthropomorphic language. Nevertheless, no matter how far this anthropomorphism is carried, the Bible very positively denies any change in God's being. There is change round about him; there is change in the relations of men to God; but there is no change in God. God's majesty and the glorious character of the Christian confession is apparent in this, that God, though immutable in himself, is able to create mutable beings; that he, though eternal in himself, is immanent in time; that he, though transcending all spatial relations, is present in every point of space; that he, though he is absolute essence, is able to give a distinct existence to transient beings. Completely absent from God's eternity is every moment of time; from his immensity, every point of space; from his being, every element of becoming. But conversely, it is God who is immanent in the creature; eternity, in time; immensity, in space; being, in becoming; immutability, in change. A deep chasm exists between *God's* essence and the essence which pertains to every creature. Because of his majesty divine, God is able to condescend to the level of the creature. Though transcendent, he is able to be immanent in every creature; while preserving himself, he is able to give himself; and likewise also, though absolutely maintaining his immutability, he is able to sustain an infinite number of relations to his creatures. Various illustrations have been employed to illustrate this truth. The sun remains the same, whether it scorches and singes, or warms and fosters; a coin remains a coin, whether it be called a price or a pledge (Augustine); the pillar remains standing, whether it be called the right or the lefthand column (Thomas Aquinas); an artist does not undergo a change when he gives expression to his conception by means of dissertation or song, by means of tone or color; neither does a scholar, whether he does or does not write a book. To be sure, not any of these comparisons is perfect; nevertheless, all make clear that an object may change in its relations, while it remains the same in essence. This is especially true with reference to God, because, while himself immutable, he is the only cause of whatever changes. We should not conceive of God's relation to the universe in such a way as if God in time established a relation between himself and an already existing creature, as if existence apart from God were ever possible for a creature. On the contrary, he causes all things to assume those bearings to himself which he himself immutably decrees; and he causes them to enter into those relationships at such a time and in such a manner as he himself eternally wills. No "before" and "after" should ever be ascribed to God, but to "things which before did not exist and afterward do exist." God's immutable "being" is itself the cause of the distinct existence and manifestation of all those things which "become," and more particularly, of their existence according to an altogether distinct law and order.

## IV. God's Infinity: Eternity and Immensity (Omnipresence). God's Infinity Is His Exaltation Above the Limitations of Finite Creatures. God Is Eternal; i.e., Exalted Above the Limitation of Time; He Is Omnipresent; i.e., Exalted Above the Limitation of Space.

A. God's infinity. Various meanings of the term "infinite":

(1) Unbounded, limitless, absolutely undetermined, unqualified. (Neo-Platonism, Cabala, Spinoza)

(2) Capable of becoming anything and everything. (Hegel). Theories (1) and closely related (2) are erroneous.

(3) Exalted above the limitations of finite creatures. God is
    (a) eternal; i.e., exalted above the limitation of time;
    (b) omnipresent; i.e., exalted above the limitation of space.

(4) Possessing every virtue in an absolute degree, perfect, God's infinitude is qualitative, not quantitative; intensive, not extensive; positive, not negative.

God's immutability applied to time is called eternity; applied to space it is called omnipresence. The name God's "infinitude" has been used in a sense inclusive of both. However, this concept is not clear in itself. Negatively it may be used in the sense of limitless, meaning: without *actual* — though not without *conceivable* — bounds. In philosophy the term has often been applied to God in that sense. Thus Neo-Platonism viewed God as a being limitless and formless, transcending every determination, "having no boundary, boundless, infinite"; etc., an overflowing fulness from which the universe emanated. Similarly, according to Cabalistic speculation God is *ên sôph,* the endless one, unbounded and without form; yet, according to this view, he created the ten Sephiroth or emanating intelligences as a transition from the infinite to the finite. Due to the philosophy of Spinoza this interpretation of God's infinitude afterward gained favor. Spinoza's "substance," God, is not a being distinct from the universe; it is that which constitutes the innermost essence of the creature; accordingly it is unbounded, an absolutely undetermined being. All determination is negation, deprivation, a denial of existence. God transcends every limitation and definition. He is infinite substance. One of his attributes is "extension."

Hegel gave a still different meaning to this concept, for he conceived of Spinoza's "substance" not as eternal and immutable being but as absolute becoming. God, according to Hegel, is infinite in the sense that he may become anything and everything, somewhat after the manner of Anaximander's "infinite atmosphere," which, although it was nothing definite in itself, was able to bring forth all manner of objects.

The error of this conception lies in the fact that by way of mental abstraction it reduces finite existences to their very lowest common denominator and then identifies the result with infinitude. The philosophy of identity was characterized by its attempt to derive the particular from the general, the definite from the indefinite, the finite from the infinite by means of a process. In himself God is infinite; he becomes finite, personal, conscious, and determinate in creation as his revelation. But this view is untenable. Infinitude is not a negative but a positive concept. Applied to God it does not indicate that he is not a distinct being, but it indicates that the limitations of finite creatures do not apply to him. Even then, however, the term may be used in a twofold sense: (a) If we wish to convey the thought that God is exalted above the limitation of time, infinitude coincides with eternity; if we wish to indicate that God transcends the limitations of space, infinitude is the same as omnipresence. Thus the term is often defined. But (b) it may also be used to indicate the fact that God is unlimited in his attributes, that in him every virtue is present in an absolute degree; in that case infinitude amounts to perfection. But also when so construed it is necessary that we properly conceive of this attribute. It is not an infinitude of magnitude — in the sense in which men sometimes speak of the infinite or endless dimensions of the universe — for God is incorporeal and the attribute of expansion must not be ascribed to him. Neither is it an infinitude of multitude — as in mathematics we speak of infinitely small or infinitesimal and of infinitely great — for this would conflict with God's unity and simplicity. But it is an infinitude of essence. God is infinite in his essence, absolute, perfect, limitless in the intensive, qualitative, positive sense. Thus interpreted, however, infinitude is synonymous with perfection; hence, we need not treat it as a distinct attribute.

**B. Infinity applied to time is eternity. Scripture represents eternity as duration without beginning and end. Eternity excludes beginning, and, succession. Time has no existence, in and by itself, yet it is not merely a subjective category of the mind, as Kant thought. It is an inseparable accompaniment of created existence. We should distinguish between extrinsic and intrinsic time. God's eternity is immanent in time.**

Infinity applied to time is eternity. Scripture nowhere speaks of a beginning or an end of God's existence. Though God is often represented as immanent in time, he is, nevertheless, transcendent above time. He is the first and the last, Is. 41:4; Rev. 1:8; he existed before the world, Gen. 1:1; John 1:1; 17:5, 24; and, regardless of all change, he remains forever, Ps. 102:26, 27. He is God from everlasting to everlasting, Ps. 90:2; 93:2. The number of his years is unsearchable, Job 36:26. A thousand years in his sight are but as yesterday, Ps. 90:4; II Peter 3:8. He is God eternally, Is. 40:28; Rom. 16:26; he inhabits eternity, Is. 57:15; living forever, Deut. 32:40; Rev. 10:6; 15:7; he swears by his life, Num. 14:21, 28; he is "God living and abiding," I Peter 1:23; incorruptible, Rom. 1:23; immortal, I Tim. 6:16; who is and who was and who is to come, Ex. 3:14; Rev. 1:4, 8. To be sure, in all these passages Scripture speaks of God in anthropomorphic fashion, and of eternity in the forms of time; but it, nevertheless, clearly indicates that God transcends time, and cannot be measured by means of the measure of time. Deism, however, defines eternity as time extended infinitely in both directions; according to it the difference between eternity and time is quantitative, not qualitative; gradual, not essential; the distinction is not that eternity excludes a succession of moments, but merely that it excludes a beginning and an end; past, present, and future are terms that should be applied to God as well as to man. The Socinians held this view, and so did many after them. Pantheism, on the other hand, also, confuses time and eternity. According to it God and the world are related as "nature begetting" and "nature begotten." Pantheists hold that eternity is not essentially distinct from time, but is the substance, the immanent cause of time; while time is the "mode," the "accident" of eternity, just as the waves are the manifestation of the ocean; and that God himself does not attain to complete self-realization apart from time. Thus Strauss made the statement, "Eternity and time are related to each other as the substance and its accidents"; and Schleiermacher defined eternity as "God's absolutely timeless causality which conditions all that is temporal and even time itself."

Also in regard to this divine perfection it is the task of Christian theology to avoid the errors of both deism and pantheism. Of course, it is true that one distinction between eternity and time is this, that the latter has a beginning and end, either actually or potentially, while the former has not. But this is not the only distinction. The concept "eternity" has three characteristics; namely, that it excludes "beginning," "end" and also "succession of moments." God is unbegotten, incorruptible, but also immutable, unchangeable. Between eternity and time there is a distinction not only in quantity and degree, but also in quality and essence. Aristotle already remarked that time is not to be *identified* with motion but stands in very close connection with it and with becoming; i.e., with the transition from the potential to the actual. According to him, however, a motion without beginning was conceivable. Augustine held that time exists there only where the present becomes past, and the future becomes present. "What, then, is time? If no one asks me, I know; if I wish to explain to him who asks, I do not know. Nevertheless, I confidently affirm that I know that if nothing passed away, there would not be past time; and if nothing were coming, there would not be future time; and if nothing were, there would not be present time." Time is not a separate substance, a real "something," but it is a mode of existence. If there were no creatures, there would be no time. That time began "with the creature" is more true than to say that "the creature began with time." On the other hand, time is not merely a subjective category of the mind, as held by Kant. A certain element of truth is, indeed, contained in this view, and Augustine reasoned that in order to measure and compute time a thinking mind is required; a mind which remembers the past, exists in the present, and expects the future, and in so far within itself measures the moments of time. But with this Augustine did not imply that there would be no measurable motion if there were no mind to do the measuring. But one should distinguish between "extrinsic time" and "intrinsic time." By extrinsic time we mean the standard employed to measure motion. In a certain sense this standard is casual and arbitrary. We derive it from the motion of the heavenly bodies, which is constant and universally known, Gen. 1:14 ff. Time, in this sense, shall cease, Rev. 10:6; 21:23 ff. But intrinsic time is something else.

It is that mode of creaturely existence by virtue of which beings have a past, present, and future, as so many parts or divisions which can be measured and counted. Now, whatever can be measured and counted is subject to measure and number, and limited thereby, for there always remains a measure and a number which is greater than that which was measured or numbered. Accordingly, the essence of time is not that it is without beginning or end but that it contains a succession of moments; that it is past, present, or future. From this it follows that time — intrinsic time — is a mode of existence of all created and finite beings. He who says "time" says motion, change, measurableness, finiteness, limitedness, that which can be numbered, created being. Time is the measure of creaturely existence. "Time is the measure of motion in the movable object." Hence in God there is no time. He is what he is from eternity to eternity. There is in him "no variation, neither shadow that is cast by turning." God is not an "eternally-becoming" being, but he is eternal essence. He is without beginning and end, and also without succession of moments; he cannot be measured or counted in his duration. A thousand years are with the Lord as one day. He is the eternal "I Am," John 8:58. Hence, God's eternity should rather be conceived of as an eternal present, without past or future. "With God all is present. Thy to-day is eternity. Eternity itself is the substance of God, to which pertains nothing that is mutable." Boëthius said concerning God's eternity that "God comprehends and at the same time possesses a complete fulness of interminable life"; while Thomas Aquinas described this eternity as "a complete and at the same time a full possession of interminable life." With this agree all the theologians, not only the R. C. but the Lutheran and the Reformed as well.

Nevertheless, we should not conceive of God's eternity as an eternally fixed, contentless moment of time. On the contrary, eternity is identical with God's essence; hence, it implies a fulness of essence. Not only is God eternal, but he is even "his own eternity." We do not have a true analogy of God's eternity in the case of the loafer, who wastes his time in idleness so that the days do not go but creep; nor in the case of the man who is confronted with imminent peril or overwhelmed with sudden grief so that the minutes seem like hours; but we have an analogy of God's eternity in the abundant and exuberant life of the cheerful laborer, who never even considers time, and whose days and hours speed by. From this point of view there is truth in the saying that in hell there is no eternity but only time, and that the more a creature resembles God and becomes God's image so much the more will he be victorious over the imperfections of time, and approach eternity. Hence, God's eternity does not exist in the abstract: it is not separate from time, but it is present and immanent in every moment of time. There is, indeed, an essential distinction between eternity and time; but there is also analogy and resemblance so that the former can be immanent in and exert influence upon the latter. Time is the concomitant of created existence; it has no origin in itself; eternal time in the sense of time without beginning is inconceivable. God, the eternal, is the only, absolute cause of time. In and by itself, moreover, time is not able to exist or to endure: it is a continuous becoming, and must needs rest in an immutable essence. It is God, who, by virtue of his everlasting power, bears the time, both in its entirety and in its separate moments. In every second the pulsation of his eternity is felt. God stands in a definite relation to time: with his eternity he fills time; also for him time is objective; by virtue of his eternal consciousness he knows time in its entirety and in the succession of all its moments. The fact that time is objective for him does not make him temporal, however. He never becomes *subject* to time, measure, number: he remains eternal, and inhabits eternity. But he uses time as a means for the manifestation of his eternal thoughts and excellencies; he makes time subservient to eternity, and thereby proves himself to be the "King of the ages," I Tim. 1:17.

### C. Infinity applied to space is omnipresence. Scripture gives us a very vivid description of this attribute.

Infinity applied to space is omnipresence. Also of this virtue Scripture gives us a very vivid representation. God is the Creator; he is and remains the absolute Possessor of all things. He is the Lord, the Possessor of heaven and earth, Gen. 14:19, 22; Deut. 10:14; and he is exalted above every creature and above all space. Heaven and earth cannot contain him, how much less an earthly temple! Cf. I Kings 8:27; II Chron. 2:6; Is. 66:1; Acts 7:48. Nevertheless, this does not mean that God is excluded from space. On the contrary, he fills heaven and earth; no one can be hid from his presence; he is a God at hand, and also afar off, Jer. 23:23, 24: Ps. 139:7-10; Acts 17:27; "in him we live and move, and have our being," Acts 17:28. Moreover, he is not present in the same degree and manner everywhere. Scripture everywhere teaches that heaven, though also created, has been God's dwelling and throne ever since it was called into being, Deut. 26:15; II Sam. 22:7; I Kings 8:32; Ps. 11:4; 33:13; 115:3, 16; Is. 63:15; Matt. 5:34; 6:9; John 14:2; Eph. 1:20; Heb. 1:3; Rev. 4:1 ff., etc. But from heaven God descends, Gen. 11:5, 7; 18:21; Ex. 3:8; walks in the garden, Gen. 3:8; appears often and at various places, Gen. 12, 15, 18, 19; etc.; and in a special sense comes down to his people on Mt. Sinai, Ex. 19:9, 11, 18, 20; Deut. 33:2; Judg. 5:4. While he suffers the nations to walk in their own way, Acts 14:16; he dwells in a special sense in the midst of his people Israel, Ex. 19:6; 25:8; Deut. 7:6; 14:2; 26:19; Jer. 11:4; Ezek. 11:20; 37:27; in the land of Canaan, Judg. 11:24; I Sam. 26:19; II Sam. 14:16; II Kings 1:3, 16; 5:17; in Jerusalem, Ex. 20:24; Deut. 12:11; 14:23, etc.; II Kings 21:7; I Chron. 23:25; II Chron. 6:6; Ez. 1:3; 5:16; 7:15; Ps. 135:21; Is. 24:23; Jer. 3:17; Joel 3:16; etc.; Matt. 5:34; Rev. 21:10; in the tabernacle and in Zion's temple, called his house, Ex. 40:34, 35; I Kings 8:10; 11:2; II Chron. 5:14; Ps. 9:12; Is. 8:18; Matt. 23:21; above the ark between the cherubim, I Sam. 4:4; II Sam. 6:2; II Kings 19:15; I Chron. 13:6; Ps. 80:1; 99:1; Is. 37:16. But again and again the prophets protest against the people's trust in this dwelling of God in the midst of Israel, Is. 48:1, 2; Jer. 3:16; 7:4, 14; 27:16; for the Lord is far removed from the wicked, Ps. 11:5; 35:10 ff.; 50:15 ff.; 145:20; but the upright shall behold his face, Ps. 11:7. He dwells with him that is of a contrite and humble spirit, Is. 57:15; Ps. 51:19. When the Israelites forsake him, he returns to them in Christ, in whom all the fulness of the godhead dwelleth bodily, Col. 2:9. Through Christ and through the Spirit sent by him he dwells in the church as in his temple, John 14:23; Rom. 8:9, 11; I Cor. 3:16; 6:19; Eph. 2:21; 3:17; until he will dwell with his people, and will be all in all, I Cor. 15:28; Rev. 21:3.

> D. **Different views with respect to God's omnipresence:**
> (1) **Polytheism, Gnosticism, and Manichaeism deny God's omnipresence.**
> (2) **Some of the early theologians accept the omnipresence of God's WILL, not of his BEING.**
> (3) **The Arminians usually refuse to commit themselves on this subject.**
> (4) **Deism confines God to heaven.**
> (5) **Augustine and others teach that God is transcendent above space — for space is a mode of existence pertaining to CREATURES — and immanent in space: filling every unit of space with the WHOLE of his being, not diffused through space like light or ether.**
> (6) **Later theologians, both Roman Catholic and Reformed, agree with Augustine.**

Polytheism, Gnosticism, and Manichaeism were not in a position to acknowledge God's omnipresence. But even in the Church there were many who, though willing to recognize the omnipresence of God's power, refused to accept the omnipresence of his being. The anthropomorphites were not able to conceive of God without a definite form and place. In order to safeguard God against too close a contact with material substance and with the impurity of the universe some of the church-fathers in opposition to the Stoics went so far as to maintain that God was "far off as to essence, but as near as possible in power," that he dwelt in heaven as the human soul dwells in the body. Yet they did not deny the essential omnipresence of God. Not until later was the doctrine of God's omnipresence definitely denied and assailed by Augustine Steuchus, bishop of Eugubium, d. 1550, in his commentary on Ps. 138, and by Crell, who accepted an "operative omnipresence" but rejected God's "essential omnipresence" which he limited to heaven.

The Remonstrants expressed themselves guardedly, said that the question was of little significance and, just as in the case of the doctrine of God's eternity, preferred to steer clear of a definite statement. Among others, Coccejus was accused of limiting God's omnipresence to "the most efficacious will of God sustaining and governing all things," but he defended his views in a few epistles to Anslar and Alting. The Cartesians held that God was omnipresent not by extension of being but by a simple act of his mind or by a powerful deed of his will, which were regarded as one with his being, and they denied the theory that "whereness" could be ascribed to God. Rationalists went still farther, and confined God's essential presence to heaven and separated it from the world. Deism accepted this limitation of God's omnipresence for fear of the pantheistic error of identifying God with the universe and of polluting the divine being with the moral and material impurity of created objects. And we must grant that this fear is not imaginary. The Stoics already taught that the divine essence permeates fire, ether, air, breath, and all things, also those which are ugly and filthy. Spinoza spoke of "substance," as "corporeal," described God as "an extended object," and taught a divine omnipresence which coincided with the essence of the universe. With Hegel God's omnipresence is identical with his absolute substantiality. Similarly, Schleiermacher defines God's omnipresence as "God's causality absolutely transcendent above space, determining space itself together with whatever is spatial." Biedermann likewise maintains that God's "existing-in-himself" is the very opposite of all space and whereness and to that extent is transcendent, but that as ground of the universe God is immanent in the universe, and that this relation of "being the ground" of the universe is his very essence.

Now also with respect to *this* doctrine Christian theology has steered clear of both deism and pantheism. And no wonder, for Scripture teaches emphatically that God transcends space and whereness, and that these cannot enclose or set bounds to his being, I Kings 8:27; II Chron. 2:6; Jer. 23:24. Even when Scripture speaks anthropomorphically and when, in order to give us a conception of God's being, it, as

it were, infinitely magnifies space, Is. 66:1; Ps. 139:7; Am. 9:2; Acts
17:24, this very representation presupposes that God transcends every
limitation of space. Accordingly, just as there is an essential difference
between eternity and time, so also between God's immensity and space.
Aristotle defined space or whereness as "the immovable limit of the
containing entity." But this definition proceeds from a conception of
space which is too external in character. For, to be sure, space is the
distance between one definite object and other fixed points. But suppose we imagine that there is only one object, even then space and
whereness would pertain to that object because of its relation to
imaginary points, capable of being conceived in thought. Therefore,
space and whereness is an attribute of all finite being. It is implied as
such in whatever is finite. As a matter of course whatever is finite has
its existence in space. Its very limitedness implies the idea of "whereness." It is always somewhere, and not at the same time somewhere
else. Regardless of every consideration with respect to measurable
distance from other objects, i.e., regardless of "extrinsic whereness,"
"intrinsic whereness" pertains to all creatures. Even spiritual beings
are not excepted. To be sure, in another dispensation distances may be
totally different from what we know them to be here on earth—steam
and electricity have already greatly altered our ideas of distance—
nevertheless, limited and spatial existence will forever pertain to all
creatures. Accordingly, space is not a form of perception, as was held
by Kant, but a form of *existence* which pertains to all created being.
And even less true is the notion that space is a form of *ex*ternal, time
a form of *in*ternal perception, so that the idea of space would be applicable only to the physical universe, that of time only to the spiritual.
On the contrary, both time and space are internal modes of existence
pertaining to all finite being. This leads to the conclusion that space, as
well as time, cannot be predicated of God, the Infinite. He transcends
all space. Philo and Plotinus already held this view, and Christian
theology also maintained that God "contains all things and is himself
alone uncontained." In his manichaean period Augustine thought that
like a fine ether God penetrated the whole mass of the universe and
the immeasurable and boundless spaces. Later on, however, he learned
to see things differently. God transcends all space and whereness. He
is not "somewhere"; yet he fills heaven and earth; he does not
permeate space as does the light or the air, but he is present at every
place with his whole being. He is "wholly everywhere, yet nowhere in
space." There is no place or measure of space which contains him
within its boundaries; hence, instead of saying that he is in all things
it were better to say that all things are in him. Yet, even when we say
that all things are in him, we must be on our guard, for we certainly

do not mean that he is space and that as such he contains the objects, for he is not a place. Just as the soul is present in its entirety in the body as a whole and also in every part of the body, just as one and the same truth is acknowledged everywhere, thus, by way of comparison, God is present in all things and all things are present in God. And in the works of the scholastics these thoughts of Augustine recur. Roman Catholic and Protestant theologians have added no essential element.

E. **Some of the implications of the doctrine of God's omnipresence:**
   (1) **God is transcendent above all space.**
   (2) **He is immanent in all space.**
   (3) **Space itself presupposes God's immensity.**
   (4) **God is not present in the same sense in every creature: we should distinguish between his physical and his spiritual immanence; also between his immanence in the wicked and in the believer; and between his immanence in the believer and in Christ.**
   (5) **Sin separates from God, not spatially, but spiritually.**

It is wrong to ascribe space or whereness to God. Space is a mode of existence pertaining to finite beings; immensity pertains to God, to him alone; not to any creature, not even to the human nature of Christ. Immensity implies first of all that God is transcendent above all space and whereness. "In himself he is everywhere with his entire being." In this sense it is just as correct to say that God is nowhere (Philo, Plotinus), for it is wrong to ascribe "whereness," a "place" to him. Nevertheless, the term "omnipresence" does not in the first place express this existence of God in and by himself; it rather signifies the definite relation that God assumed to space ever since he created it along with the universe. Of course, also in the discussion of this subject we must needs speak of God in human terms. Scripture makes mention of God's going, coming, walking, coming down. It uses anthropomorphisms, and so must we. "To find out where he *is,* is difficult; to discover where he is *not,* is even more difficult." It will serve a good purpose, however, whenever we take up the discussion of a new attribute, to remind ourselves of the fact that we are speaking of God in human language. The consciousness of the fact that God cannot be measured by time or space, even though purely negative, will keep us from denying to him his transcendence above the creature. The negation implies a strong affirmation. God's relation to space does not consist in this, that he is encompassed and shut in by space; i.e., that space stands over him as Uranos and Kronos were powers that stood over Zeus, for God is not a creature. "If he were confined to any place, he would not be God." He is neither a body extended or diffused through space and *circumscriptively* present in space; nor a finite, created spirit, bound to a distinct locality, and therefore *definitely* present in space. Neither should we conceive of that relation in such a way as if space were within him and surrounded by him viewed as a greater and infinite space, as some used to call God "the space in which the universe exists," and as Weisse speaks of infinite space as being immanent in God; for space is a mode of existence that pertains to finite creatures, and not to the Infinite, not to God. But the relation of God to space is such that God, the Infinite, having the ground of his existence in himself, is present in every point of space *repletively,* and sustains space by means of his immensity.

In connection with God's immensity we must avoid on the one hand the error of pantheism, namely, that God is really the substance of all things and that he is spatial; and on the other hand, the error of deism, namely that God is omnipresent in power but not in essence and nature. Though God is essentially distinct from his creatures, he is not separate from them. Every particle of matter and every point of space require God's immensity to sustain them in their existence. The deistic idea that God dwells in a place far distant from the world and thence governs all things by his omnipotence does injustice to the proper conception of the being of God. In reality this representation is in conflict with all of God's attributes: with his simplicity, immutability, infinity, etc.; accordingly, God becomes man, and creation becomes independent. It needs to be emphasized that God is not present in creation as a king in his realm or a captain aboard his ship. He does not act upon the world from a distance; but with his whole being he is present powerfully here and everywhere with respect to his essence and power. He is present in hell as well as in heaven, in the wicked as well as in the pious, in places of filth and darkness as well as in palaces of light. Because his essence, though omnipresent, is of a character different from that which pertains to creatures, he remains pure in the presence of all impurity. Hence, Anselm made the statement that it is more correct to say that God is *with* time and space, than that he is present *in* time and space.

However, God is not present in the same sense in every creature. There is a difference between his physical and his ethical immanence. Something analogous to this is found in the sphere of human beings; e.g., two persons may be physically near to one another, but far apart in sympathy and spirit, Matt. 24:40, 41. The soul is present in the entire body and in all of its several parts, yet in a different manner in each of these parts: it does not dwell in the mind in the same manner as in the heart, neither is it present in the hand in the same manner as in the foot. "The fact is that all these actions and energies belong to the one true God, who is a God in truth, who is wholly present everywhere, is confined by no frontiers and bound with no chains, is indivisible and immutable, and, though his nature has need of neither heaven nor earth, he fills them both with his presence and his power. Nevertheless, the Creator of every nature has so ordained that each of his creatures is permitted to have and to exercise powers of its own. Although apart from him they could not exist, their essence is different from his" (Augustine). God's immanence is not an unconscious emanence, but a conscious presence of his being in all his creatures. That is the reason why the nature of this divine presence varies in accordance with the nature of these creatures. To be sure, even the most insignificant creature owes its origin and preservation to God's power, to his being: God dwells in every creature; but this does not mean that he dwells equally in every creature. All things are indeed "*in* him" but all things are not "*with* him." God does not dwell on earth as he dwells in heaven, in animals as in man, in the inorganic as in the organic creation, in the wicked as in the pious, in the church as in Christ. Creatures differ according to the different manner in which God dwells in them. A creature's nature and essence is determined by its relation to God. Hence, though all creatures reveal God, they do so in different ways and along different lines. "With the pure thou wilt show thyself pure; and with the perverse thou wilt show thyself froward," Ps. 18:26. In all creatures God is present "by means of his essence," but in Christ alone dwelleth the fulness of the Godhead bodily. God dwells in Christ in a very special sense, "by means of union." In other creatures his immanence varies with the character of their essence; in some he dwells "by means of his nature"; in others "by means of his justice"; in others "by means of his grace"; in others "by means of his glory." There is endless variety, in order that all may reveal God's glory.

It is useless to deny this divine omnipresence. We experience it in our heart and conscience. He is not far from each one of us. The only thing which can separate us from God is sin. It brings about a spiritual, not a physical, separation between God and man, Is. 59:2. Going out from the presence of Jehovah, fleeing away from him, does not indicate physical separation, but spiritual incongruity. "It is not with respect to place but with respect to being unlike him that a man is afar from God." Conversely, approaching God and seeking his countenance does not require a pilgrimage, but penitence and humiliation. Moreover, he who seeks God, finds him; he learns that God is not far distant but close at hand; for in him we live and move and have our being. "To approach him means to become like unto him; to depart from him means to become unlike unto him." "Do not, therefore think that God is present in certain places: he is with thee such a one as thou shalt have been. What is that which thou shalt have been? Good, if thou shalt have been good; and he will seem evil to thee, if thou shalt have been evil; but a Helper, if thou shalt have been good; an Avenger, if thou shalt have been evil. There thou hast a Judge in thy secret place. When thou dost wish to do something evil, thou retirest from the public into thy house where no enemy may see thee; from those places of thy house which are open and visible to the eyes of men thou removest thyself into thy chamber; even in thy chamber thou fearest some witness from another quarter; thou retirest into thy heart, there thou meditatest: he is more inward than thy heart. Whithersoever, therefore, thou shalt have fled, there he is. From thyself whither wilt thou flee? Wilt thou not follow thyself whithersoever thou shalt flee? But since there is One more inward even than thyself, there is no place whither thou mayest flee from God angry but to God reconciled. There is no place at all whither thou mayest flee. Wilt thou flee from him? flee unto him."

## V. God's Oneness: Numerical Oneness Or Unity, Qualitative Oneness Or Simplicity. God's Unity Must Be Defended Against the Evolution Theory Applied To the O. T., Against Polytheism, and Against Pantheism. God's Simplicity Indicates that In God There Is No Composition of Any Kind. This Attribute Has Been Accepted By the Church From the Beginning. It Is Denied By Some, Misinterpreted By Others, and Ignored Entirely By Still Others.

A. God's unity: the fact that there is and can be only one God. This attribute must be defended against:

(1) The evolution theory applied to the O. T. We are told that monotheism was not taught in the earlier portions of the O. T. and that it was introduced by the prophets. Objections to this theory:

(a) The prophets were not conscious of introducing a new religion but admonished Israel to return to the old religion.

(b) Critics differ widely in regard to the character of Israel's religion before monotheism was "introduced."

(c) Even the theory of evolution itself, when strictly applied, demands the existence of monotheism in some initial stage before the time of the prophets.

(d) Monotheism is plainly taught in the earlier parts of the O. T., Gen. 18:25, etc.

(2) Polytheism. Over against this error the church appealed to Scripture, etc., and triumphed.

(3) Pantheism. Its "unity" is in conflict with Scripture and satisfied neither the heart nor the mind.

The last of the incommunicable attributes is God's oneness. This comprises both God's unity and his simplicity. By the first we mean that there is only one God, that his nature renders impossible the existence of several Divine Beings, and, consequently, that all other beings exist of and through and unto him. Accordingly, this attribute teaches God's absolute oneness and uniqueness, his exclusive, numerical oneness in distinction from his simplicity, which indicates the inner or qualitative oneness of the Divine Being. Scripture repeatedly emphasizes this attribute over against every form of polytheism. All agree that this is true with reference to the N. T. and the later O. T. writings. Many critics maintain, however, that monotheism is not taught in the earlier portions of the O. T. and that by means of the testimony and activity of the prophets it gradually developed out of polytheism prevailing formerly also in Israel. But this representation is handicapped with so many objections that its intenability is becoming more and more apparent. It is very evident that the prophets were not at all conscious of bringing to their people a new religion in the form of an ethical monotheism. On the contrary, they regard themselves as standing on the same religious foundation as the people of Israel: the foundation of Jehovah's election and covenant. They call idolatry apostasy, unfaithfulness, and breaking the covenant, and they admonish the people to return to the religion of Jehovah, which they have wantonly forsaken.

Moreover, critics differ widely in regard to the character of Israel's religion before monotheism had been "introduced" by the prophets, some declaring that the previous religion was animism, others fetishism, totemism, ancestor-worship, polydaemonism, while they are especially at a loss with respect to the question concerning the character of Jehovah. According to the one he was a fire-deity akin to Moloch; according to another he was a storm-deity of Sinai; while a third calls him a tribal deity who had already acquired certain ethical traits. With respect to the question of his origin there is a still greater diversity of opinion. Canaan and Phoenicia, Arabia and Syria, Babylon and Egypt have in turn been pointed out.

But apart from these divergent beliefs regarding Israel's ancient religion the question arises: if under the influence of the prophets polytheism developed into ethical monotheism, how did this happen? At this point a new difficulty presents itself. The evolution theory which underlies the opinion of the critics leaves no room for the idea that ethical monotheism was something entirely new, an invention of the prophets. The presupposition demands that long before this the ethical monotheism of the prophets was in process of preparation, and that in its initial stage it existed at a much earlier time. Hence, the critics are confronted with this dilemma: if they continue to deny the occurrence of ethical monotheism in the earlier portions of the O. T., they are baffled by the insoluble mystery of its sudden occurrence in the writings of the prophets; otherwise they must be willing to grant that monotheism existed long before the time of the prophets. Some have accepted the first alternative: they turn away from every further explanation, regard the ethical monotheism of the prophets an enigma, hide behind the now current expression "mystery of personality," and say with Wellhausen, "Even if we were able to trace the development of Israel's religion more accurately, fundamentally very little would have been explained. Why, e.g., did not Chemosh of the Moabites become God of righteousness and Creator of heaven and earth? A satisfactory answer cannot be given." Indeed, the prospect of a satisfactory answer has often been held out as a result of the new critical method. Others, regarding this position unsatisfactory, were forced to resort to the second alternative: they are willing to concede that monotheism existed long before the prophets, e.g., in the time of Moses and Abraham, but they ascribe it to the influence of the surrounding religions, to the "monarchical pyramids of the pantheon," already apparent among "the learned" in Syria, Palestine, and Canaan, and to the "ideas tending to monotheism" which penetrated into Canaan from Babylon and perhaps also from Egypt. Thus by means of the study of comparative religions the theory is advanced that from very ancient times polytheism rested upon a conscious or unconscious monotheistic belief, more or less after the same manner in which, according to Haeckel, the origin of life needs no explanation because life is not a new entity but something already inherent in inorganic substance and in all atoms. Thus one extreme position has taken the place of another. Nevertheless, the latter representation has this advantage over the former: that it is not forced by a preconceived idea of development either to deny the existence of monotheism in the earlier portions of the O. T. or to assign a much later date to them.

Now Scripture is monotheistic from beginning to end: monotheism is plainly taught in the earlier as well as in the later portions of the O. T. Notwithstanding the fact that Jehovah's intercourse with man is described in very vivid, concrete, and anthropomorphic language, nevertheless, Jehovah is the Creator of heaven and earth, the Maker of man, the Judge of all the earth. He destroys the human race by a flood, is present and active in all lands, and the call of Abraham prepares for the working out of his gracious purpose of election in Israel. Even though it is certainly true that revelation is progressive and that there is a gradual unfoldment of its ideas, nevertheless, the entire O. T. with its doctrine concerning the solidarity of the universe and of the human race, concerning the election of and the covenant with Israel and concerning religion and morals as described in the law is from beginning to end based upon the idea of God's unity. Jehovah is the Creator of the universe, Gen. 1 and 2; the Possessor and Judge of all the earth, Gen. 14:19, 22; 18:25; the only Lord, Deut. 6:4; who will have no other gods before him, Ex. 20:3. Besides him there is no God, Deut. 4:35; 32:39; Ps. 18:31; 83:17; Is. 43:10; 44:6; 45:5; etc., and the gods of the heathen are called "that which is not God," vanities, things of nought, wind and confusion, not Elohim (gods) but elilim (worthless idols), Deut. 32:21; Ps. 96:5; Is. 41:29; 44:9, 20; Jer. 2:5, 11; 10:15; 16:19; 51:17, 18; Dan. 5:23; Hab. 2:19; etc., and inasfar as real powers are worshiped as idols they are considered to be malign in character, Ps. 106:37; I Cor. 10:20. In the N. T. God's unity becomes even clearer in the person of Christ, John 17:3; Acts 17:24; Rom. 3:30; I Cor. 8:5, 6; Eph. 4:5, 6; I Tim. 2:5.

With this confession of the only true God the church made its appearance in the heathen world. To be sure, the official religion of heathendom was often the object of ridicule among the intelligentsia; nevertheless, polytheism was still a power to be reckoned with both in social and political life, and it retained this position in the mind of philosophers and of those who endeavored to rise to a syncretism above the religion of the people. Hence, from the very beginning the church was involved in a serious conflict and its spokesmen used not only defensive but also offensive weapons against polytheism. Christians eagerly confessed their monotheistic belief and derived arguments in support of their position not only from the Word of God but from every sphere of knowledge, from the entire universe. They appealed to the testimony of the human soul, to quotations from heathen philosophers and poets, to the solidarity of the universe and of the human race, to the coherent and unitary character of truth and of the moral law, and to the fact that the nature of God's being is such that it leaves no room for anything co-ordinate with itself. The church directed its attack not only against polytheism itself but against everything that stood in connection with it, whether directly or indirectly, against daemonism and superstition, magic and divination, deification of man and emperor-worship, theaters and games in honor of the gods. In this mighty struggle which lasted for centuries polytheism was vanquished and robbed of all its religious and political power. Nevertheless, various forms of polytheistic ideas and practices have become the vogue again and again and in recent times have begun to reassert themselves. When the confession of the only true God begins to weaken and to be denied, and the much longed for unity offered by pantheism satisfies neither the mind nor the heart, then the solidarity of the universe and of the human race, of religion, morals, and truth succumbs with it, and can no longer be maintained; consequently, nature and history break up into fragments and as a result of conscious or subconscious polytheistic leanings there is to-day a resuscitation of every kind of superstition and idolatry. The time in which we are living furnishes an abundance of evidence for this statement and for that very reason the open confession of the only true God is to-day even more vitally necessary than formerly.

> **B. God's simplicity.** By this we mean that there is no composition of any kind in the Divine Being: that every attribute is identical with God's being by reason of the fact that every one of God's virtues is absolutely perfect in God. According to Scripture God is light, love, wisdom, etc., Jer. 10:10; 23:6; John 1:4, 5, 9; 14:6; I John 1:5 etc.
>
> (1) The church-fathers (esp. Augustine) emphasized the doctrine of God's simplicity.
>
> (2) The scholastics, later Roman Catholics, Reformed and Lutheran theologians agree with the teaching of the early church.
>
> (3) Others either denied this doctrine, interpreted it erroneously, simply ignored it, or while confessing it held theories which were in conflict with it.
>
> (4) The doctrine of God's simplicity is denied especially on two grounds:
>
> > (a) that it is a metaphysical abstraction, and
> >
> > (b) that it is in conflict with the doctrine of the trinity.

God's oneness includes more than his numerical unity. It comprises also his simplicity. This becomes clear when one considers the fact that Scripture in giving us a description of the fulness of God's being uses not only adjectives but also nouns: it tells us not only that God is faithful, righteous, living, omniscient, loving, wise, etc., but also that he is the truth, righteousness, life, light, love, wisdom, etc., Jer. 10:10; 23:6; John 1:4, 5, 9; 14:6; I Cor. 1:30; I John 1:5; 4:8; and that every attribute is identical with God's being by reason of the fact that every one of his virtues is absolutely perfect. Theologians called this the doctrine of God's simplicity. Irenaeus calls God "all thought, all perception, all eye, all ear, the one entire fountain of all good things." Over against Eunomius the Cappadocians were compelled to defend the correctness of ascribing many names and attributes to God, but Augustine reverted again and again to the subject of God's simplicity. God is pure essence, without accident; compared to him all creaturely being is non-being. With creatures there is a difference between being, living, knowing, willing; there is a difference of degree among them; there are some creatures that have being only; others that have life also; still others that have a mind besides. But God is *one* in every respect. He *is* whatever he *has*. He is his own wisdom, his own life; being and life are one in him. After Augustine this doctrine was held by John of Damascus, the scholastics, and further by all Roman Catholic, Lutheran, and Reformed theologians.

Others, however, vigorously denied and opposed the doctrine of God's simplicity. Eunomius taught God's absolute simplicity, but drew the conclusion that the divine names were but hollow sounds and that God's being coincided with his "ingenerate nature." This one attribute was sufficient and rendered all the others superfluous and valueless. The extreme anthropomorphists of earlier and later date reject God's simplicity because they believe in his corporeity. The Arabian philosophers confessed God's simplicity, but used this truth as a weapon against the doctrine of the trinity. According to their view the three persons are "denominations added to the substance." Duns Scotus emphasized the doctrine of God's simplicity but came in conflict with it by teaching that God's attributes are "formally" distinct from his being. Nominalism even taught a real distinction between God's attributes severally. In the period of the Reformation this example was followed by the Socinians. On behalf of man's independence they brought God down to the finite level, and as a result were at a loss with the doctrine of God's simplicity. Socinus doubted whether it was Scriptural to ascribe simplicity to God. The Catechism of Rakow omits this attribute entirely. Schlichting, Volkelius, and others held that the attributes were distinct from God's being, and that a fulness of attributes was not in conflict with God's oneness. Vorstius agreed with this position and on the basis of the doctrine of the trinity held that with reference to the being of God we must distinguish between matter and form, essence and attributes, genus and differentiae. He appealed to Scripture, e.g., to Jer. 51:14, where we read, "Jehovah of hosts hath sworn by his soul," and I Cor. 2:11, which seems to imply that the Spirit is *in* God. Accordingly, he averred that there is a difference between knowing and willing, between the subject that lives, and the life that causes it to live. The Arminians were of the same opinion. In the second chapter of the *Apol. Conf.* they stated that Scripture does not contain even a single word or iota regarding God's simplicity, that it is purely a metaphysical doctrine and not at all necessary unto salvation. They stressed the objection that it is impossible to reconcile the freedom of God's will and the changing character of his disposition with his simplicity. Episcopius still was willing to include the doctrine of God's simplicity under the attributes, and held that the "relations, volitions, and free decrees" could be harmonized with it, but Limborch did not mention this attribute any more. By rationalism it was relegated to the background or even omitted entirely. Bretschneider says that the Bible knows nothing of these philosophical niceties. Neither was pantheism in a position to recognize or appreciate this doctrine. It identified God with the universe, while Spinoza, one of its exponents, even ascribed the attribute of extension to God. Thus the doctrine of God's simplicity has almost completely disappeared from theology; its importance is not recognized; at times it is vigorously denied. Schleiermacher did not co-ordinate God's simplicity with the other attributes, and viewed it merely as "the undivided and indivisible mutual inherence of all God's attributes and activities." Lange, Kahnis, Philippi, Ebrard, Lipsius, Biedermann, F. A. B. Nitzsch, Kaftan, Von Oettingen, Haering, Van Oosterzee, and others ignore this attribute entirely. Others oppose this doctrine vigorously, especially on two grounds:

(1)　that it is a metaphysical abstraction, and

(2)　that it is in conflict with the doctrine of the trinity.

**C. God's simplicity is, indeed, taught by Scripture: it is not a mere philosophical abstraction. It indicates that in God there is no composition of any kind, hence, that his attributes are identical with his being.**

Nevertheless, this "divine simplicity" is of the greatest importance for the knowledge of God. Not only is it plainly taught in Scripture, where God is called light, life, love, etc., but it is also implied in the very idea of God and in the other attributes. By simplicity is meant the quality of being uncompounded or incomposite. If God be composed of parts, as a body is composed of parts, of genus and differentia, substance and accident, matter and form, power and activity, essence and existence, his perfection, unity, independence and immutability cannot be maintained. On that basis he cannot be love in the highest sense of the term, for then there is in God a subject which loves, and love itself; the same would apply also to the other attributes. God is then not the One "than whom no better can be thought." We must, therefore, maintain God's aseity: that there is nothing above him; hence, wisdom, grace, love, etc., are identical with his being; he is absolutely perfect; he is the One "than whom no better can be thought." The same thing cannot be affirmed with reference to creatures. In their case there is a difference between existence, being, living, knowing, willing, acting, etc. "Whatever is composed is created"; no creature can be absolutely simple (uncompounded), for every creature is finite. God however, is infinite, and whatever pertains to him is infinite. All his attributes are *divine* attributes; hence, infinite: identical with his being. By virtue of this, God is and can be self-sufficient and perfectly blessed and glorious in himself. From this it is evident that God's simplicity is not a metaphysical abstraction. There is a very real difference between it and the philosophical idea of "absolute being, the One, simplicity," substance, the Absolute, etc., by means of which Xenophanes, Plato, Philo, Plotinus, and later on Spinoza and Hegel designated God.

The idea of God's simplicity is not the result of abstraction; i.e., it is not arrived at by eliminating from the concept of God all oppositions and distinctions which pertain to creatures, and by describing him as the being in whom there are no oppositions. On the contrary God's simplicity is the result of ascribing to God all creaturely perfections in the most complete and divine manner. By describing God as "simplest essence" we designate him as perfect essence; we ascribe to him an infinite fulness of essence; we confess that he is an infinite and unbounded "ocean of essence." Instead of being in harmony with pantheism this doctrine of God's simplicity is directly opposed to it. The great difference is evident from the fact that while pantheism teaches that God has no distinct existence and life apart from the universe —cf. for example, the fact that Hegel's Absolute, pure essence, thought, idea, etc., exists before the world only logically and potentially; and that descriptions of the Absolute are without any content: merely abstract, logical categories—Christian theology in describing God as "simplest essence" intends to convey the idea that God has a distinct, infinite, glorious life in himself, albeit that we must needs designate the Divine Being by means of creaturely names. Pantheism's Absolute, substance, highest essence, etc. (names preferred by pantheism to designate the Divine Being) is the result of abstraction: one by one the attributes pertaining to several objects are eliminated in thought until these objects have finally been reduced to their lowest common denominator: pure essence, unqualified existence. This essence is indeed an "abstraction," a concept without any reality; hence it would be wrong to give it any further description. Every further qualification would be a limitation, would make of this conception a distinct something, and would destroy its character of being the lowest common denominator. "Every definition is a negation." On the other hand, the essence which theology ascribes to God is a very extraordinary essence, an essence altogether distinct from that of the world. Christian theology does not designate God as that kind of essence which amounts to mere existence, but it describes him as the absolute fulness of essence; i.e., that kind of essence which implies a fulness of being. Hence, God's simplicity does not *exclude* the many names ascribed to him—as Eunomius thought—but *demands* them. God is so rich in majesty that in order to obtain a vague idea of his glory it must be revealed by means of many names. Every name designates the same Divine Being, but from a special angle, in accordance with God's revelation in his works. Hence, according to Augustine God is "simple" in his "multiplicity" and "multifold" in his "simplicity." Hence, every name used to designate God, and every qualification ascribed to him, is not a negation, but an enrichment of the knowledge of his being.

"The divine essence is self-determined, and differs from everything else in this respect that nothing can be added to it." Taken in that sense this simplicity is not in conflict with the doctrine of the trinity, for the term "simple" is not used as an antonym of "twofold" or "threefold," but of "compound." Hence, this simplicity does not conflict with the doctrine of the trinity, for the Divine Being is not composed of three persons, neither is each person composed of God's being plus the personal property; but the one and only uncompounded (simple) being exists in three persons; every person or personal property is distinct from God's being not "in the object" but "in reason"; every personal property is indeed a "real relation," but does not add "something real" to the "essence." The personal properties "do not compose but only distinguish."

# GOD'S COMMUNICABLE ATTRIBUTES

# CHAPTER V

# God's Communicable Attributes

**I. Attributes Which Indicate God's Spiritual Nature: Spirituality and Invisibility. God's Spirituality Is Proclaimed In Scripture: It Is Denied By Polytheism, Materialism, Deism, Pantheism, and Theosophy. Negatively, This Attribute Indicates that God Is Immaterial; Positively, that He Is the Ground of All Existence. God's Spirituality Implies His Invisibility, Likewise Taught By Scripture and Defended Against the Teaching of the Audians, Socinians, and, In A Sense, of the Roman Catholics.**

A. God's spirituality. God's simplicity implies his spirituality, for that which is incomposite is spiritual. Scripture teaches God's spirituality.

The incommunicable attribute which we discussed last, namely, God's simplicity, very naturally leads to the discussion of God's spiritual nature, since all corporeal things are composite. Although Scripture indeed describes God in anthropomorphic language, and ascribes to him various physical organs and actions, it does not do so indiscriminately. Of the inner organs of the human body only the heart and the "inward parts or bowels," cf. Phil. 1:8, etc., are ascribed to God. We are never told that digestive and reproductive organs pertain to him: Sight, hearing, and smell are ascribed to him, not taste and touch. Nowhere do we read that God possesses a body. Although the O. T. does not contain any passage which in so many words defines God as a Spirit; nevertheless, this spirituality, is everywhere implied. God is indeed Jehovah, who condescends to the level of his people, and who reveals himself in a human manner; but from the very beginning he is also Elohim far exalted above every creature. He has the ground of his existence in himself, Ex. 3:13; Is. 41:4; 44:6; he is eternal, Deut. 32:40; Ps. 90:1 ff.; 102:27; omnipresent, Deut. 10:14; Ps. 139:1 ff.; Jer. 23:23, 24; incomparable, Is. 40:18, 25; 46:5; Ps. 89:6, 8; invisible, Ex. 33:20, 23; unpicturable, Ex. 20:4; Deut. 5:8; since he is without form, Deut. 4:12, 15. God and man are related to one another as spirit and flesh, Is. 31:3. Though God often reveals himself by means of theophanies, dreams and visions, and to that extent becomes visible,

Gen. 32:30; Ex. 24:10; 33:11; Num. 12:8; Deut. 5:24; Judg. 13:22; I Kings 22:19; Is. 6:1; nevertheless, it is through his Spirit, hence in a spiritual manner, that he is present in creation, and that he creates and preserves all things, Ps. 139:7; Gen. 2:7; Job 33:4; Ps. 33:6; 104:30; etc. In the N. T. God's spirituality is even more clearly evident. Not only is it taught indirectly whenever eternity and omnipresence are ascribed to God, Rom. 16:26; I Tim. 6:16; I Peter 1:23; Rev. 1:8; 10:6; 15:7; Acts 17:29; Rom. 1:22; but it is also directly proclaimed by Jesus when he calls God a Spirit, and therefore demands that God be worshipped in spirit and in truth, John 4:24. Moreover, though the apostles do not repeat these very words, they present the same idea of God's being when they call him invisible, John 1:18; cf. 6:46; Rom. 1:20; Col. 1:15; I Tim. 1:17; 6:16; I John 4:12, 20; which is not in conflict with the vision of God in the state of glory, Job 19:26; Ps. 17:15; Matt. 5:8; I Cor. 13:12; I John 3:2; Rev. 22:4.

B. **Different views with respect to God's spirituality:**
(1) God's spirituality is denied by the heathen, cf. Rom. 1:23.
(2) Materialism considers the atoms of matter to be the final ground of existence.
(3) Deism changes God into a finite being, similar in essence to man.
(4) Epicurus ascribed to God an ethereal body.
(5) In the church God's spirituality was denied by Tertullian (at least in a sense), by Audius, by many fourth century Egyptian monks, by the Socinians, etc.
(6) Theosophy also ascribes a body to God; cf. its influence upon Böhme, Oetinger, Baader, Delitzsch, Auberlin, Hamberger, etc.
(7) Pantheism, both ancient and modern, fails to do justice to God's spirituality.

The heathen, however, underrate and even deny this spiritual character of God's being, Rom. 1:23. And even philosophy has not been able to divest itself from sensuous conceptions concerning God. Materialism regards the atom as the deepest ground of essence. Deism changes God into a finite being similar in essence to man. Epicurus pictures the gods and goddesses as a company of reasoning philosophers, with a body of thin ether. But pantheism also fails to do justice to God's spirituality. According to Heraclitus and the Stoics the first cause must be conceived of physically; God is the original energy which produces everything that exists, and to which every being strives to return. Now all these various schools exerted their influence upon the Church. They have been doing this to this very day. The realistic, eschatological theories which were widely current during the latter part of the second century were not far removed from the notion that, in a certain sense, God has a body. We are not able to say definitely whether Tertullian ascribed a material body to God. It is true that he states, "For, who will deny that God is a body although God is spirit? For spirit has a body of its own kind, in its own form"; but he seems to use the term "body" in the sense of "substance" when he says, "Everything that exists is a bodily existence of its own kind; nothing is incorporeal except that which does not exist," and elsewhere he speaks about the soul in terms just as realistic. Nevertheless, this identification of "body" and "substance" is significant; it proves that Tertullian could not conceive of any substance which was not a body. And elsewhere he explicitly affirms that affections pertain to God as well as to man albeit that in God they are present in a perfect manner. He even wishes to conceive of the "hands" and "eyes" which Scripture ascribes to God not in a spiritual but in a literal sense, although he asserts that also these pertain to God in perfect manner. Hence, Tertullian may be called the father of Biblical realism. The spiritualizing tendency of the Alexandrian school, a result of the allegorical method of exegesis, brought about a reaction in the direction of anthropomorphism. According to Origen, Melito, bishop of Sardes, ascribed a body to God, but we are not able to determine to what extent this report is true. During the fourth century Audius and his followers, as also many Egyptian monks, taught a similar anthropomorphism, against which especially the treatise *Contra anthropomorphitas,* a work ascribed to Cyril, directed its attack. Later on this ascription of a human form to God was renewed by Socinianism, which describes God as being merely a lord who exercises authority over us. No mention is made of his simplicity, infinitude, independence, and spiritual essence. Crell maintained that the term "spirit," when applied to God, to an angel, and to the soul, was not used "equivocally" and "analogically" but "univocally." And Vorstius expressed himself after the manner of Tertullian, "Truly a body should be ascribed to God if by body a true and complete substance is indicated." Furthermore, theosophy also holds that in a certain sense God has a body; hence, that also with respect to his body, man was created after God's image. In the cabala the ten Sephiroth, i.e., the attributes or modes whereby God reveals himself, are together called *Adhām Qadhmōn,* the archetypal man, i.e., the first heavenly man, since the human form is the highest and most perfect revelation of God, and God is thus pictured in Scripture. This gave rise to the view, advocated by Christian theosophists in connection with the doctrine of the trinity, that God, who is not a being at rest but rather an eternally developing life, not only inwardly ascends from darkness to light, from nature to spirit, but also outwardly surrounds himself with some kind of nature, corporeity, glory, or heaven, in which he assumes a form and glorifies himself. That is the representation of Böhme, Oetinger, Baader, Delitzsch, Auberlin, Hamberger, etc.

Finally, even modern pantheism fails to do justice to God's spirituality. Spinoza ascribed to substance the property of "extension." And in the philosophy of Hegel, Schleiermacher, Von Hartmann, and others the universe is an essential part or constitutive element of the infinite. "Apart from the world God is not God." God and universe are "correlates"; they give expression to the same essence, first as a unity, then as a totality. To be sure, this pantheism continues to speak of God as a spirit, and even prefers to describe him thus. But what this may mean is hard to determine. Hegel uses the term "spirit" or "mind" especially with reference to the final and highest "stage" in the development of the "idea"; i.e., the stage which by way of the realm of nature it reaches in man, especially in philosophy. "The logical develops into nature, and nature develops into spirit or mind." He still seeks the essence of mind or spirit in ideality, in "the simple being-in-oneself," in egoity, but God does not become spirit or mind except by means of a lengthy process in and by means of man. Others have begun to use the terms "spirit" or "mind" to indicate the final, immanent cause of things, without thinking of a distinct, independent existence and a personal, conscious life. Von Hartmann describes the unconscious as pure, unconscious, impersonal, absolute spirit or mind; hence, he calls his philosophy spiritualistic monism and panpneumatism.

**C. The character of God's spirituality: negatively, God's spirituality means that he is immaterial and invisible (as the human soul and the spirit of angels); positively, it indicates that he is the hidden and absolute ground of all creaturely, somatic and pneumatic, essence.**

Over against all these tendencies the Christian church and Christian theology have always maintained God's spirituality. It was not always treated as a distinct attribute, but was often included under God's simplicity, but it is defended equally by Roman Catholic, Lutheran, and Reformed theologians. The term "divine spirituality" was used to indicate that God is a substance distinct from the universe, immaterial, invisible to human eyes, and without composition or extension. The analogy of our human soul serves to give us a vague conception of the nature of that immaterial substance. Man has, however, no direct or immediate knowledge of the essence of his own soul: we deduce a spiritual substance from the psychical phenomena which we observe; but the soul's essence in and by itself escapes our observation. Besides, the "divine spirituality" has a very distinct character. The term "spirit" when applied to God is not synonymous with that same term when applied to an angel or to the human soul. This is evident from the fact that the spirit of human beings and of angels is composite in character; not, to be sure, in the sense that it is composed of elements of matter, but in the sense that it is composed of "substance" and "accident," of "power" and "activity," and is, therefore, subject to change. In God, however, there is no composition of any kind: he is pure essence. But it is also evident from this that God, as Spirit, is not only Father of spirits, Heb. 12:9, but also the Creator and Father of visible things. Also these visible things have not been made out of things which appear, Heb. 11:3; but have their origin in God as "Spirit." God, as a spiritual Being, is the author not only of all that is called "spirit" and "soul," but also of all that is called "body" and "flesh." Hence, by spirituality we understand that divine perfection which designates God negatively, as being immaterial and invisible, analogous to the spirit of angels and the human soul; and positively, as the hidden, incomposed (uncompounded, simple), absolute ground of all creaturely, somatic and pneumatic, essence.

This altogether distinct sense in which we apply the term "spirit" to God caused some to suggest that the spirits of angels and the souls of human individuals be called "bodies," and that the word "spirit" be reserved as a distinct characterization of the being of God; while others thought best to ascribe to God neither corporeality nor incorporeality, since he is exalted above both descriptions. But these suggestions are not deserving of recommendation, because they result in misunderstanding, and those who make them disregard the fact that although all knowledge of God is analogical, this analogy is more clearly evident in one group of creatures than in another, and more manifest in the universe of invisible reality than in the world of visible things. Equally erroneous is the idea of Descartes: that the essence of spirituality is "thought" and that God is a "thinking being" or "purest and most perfect intellection"; for this representation identifies God's spirituality with personality, as was done by Reinhard, Wegscheider, and others. Pantheism did not know what to do with God's spirituality, and made it a term without meaning. Therefore, it is of great importance to interpret God's spirituality as a designation of his "incorporeal substance." It does not as such imply personality, self-consciousness, and self-limitation; in God these are, of course, implied, whereas he is a simple being; but not in the idea as such. Animal consciousness and subconsciousness in man prove sufficiently that "spirituality" and "personality" are not identical. The meaning of personality will be discussed under the doctrine of the trinity while self-consciousness and self-limitation will be treated under the mental and volitional attributes. In this section we are dealing with the spiritual nature of God. That the belief in divine spirituality is, indeed, of

very great significance becomes clear when one considers that on it
rests the character of our worship of God. This divine spirituality,
rightly understood, is destructive of all image-worship.

> **D. God's invisibility. God's spirituality implies his invisibility.**
> **(1) Scripture clearly teaches this attribute.**
> **(2) The church was forced to defend the truth of God's invisi-**
> **bility against the teachings of the Audians, Socinians, etc.**
> **(3) Among those who accepted God's invisibility in the sense**
> **that he cannot be seen by physical eyes the question was raised,**
> **"Is direct spiritual vision of God's essence possible?" The con-**
> **sensus of opinion was that such a direct spiritual vision is im-**
> **possible here on earth. Roman Catholics maintain that it is**
> **possible in the state of glory. This direct spiritual vision of**
> **God's essence is in conflict with Scripture and with God's incom-**
> **prehensibility, and results in the deification of man.**

God's spirituality implies his invisibility. Scripture proclaims this
attribute very emphatically. Accordingly, there was very little difference of opinion in the early church in regard to the question whether
God can be seen by human eyes, which was generally denied both for
this dispensation and the next. A few, however, took exception to this
position; e.g., the Audians, Socinians, Vorstius, and some Lutheran
theologians: Quenstedt, Hollatz, Hulsemann, Majus, Jaeger, and others;
these appealed to the Reformed theologians Alsted and Bucanus.
Gerhard, however, leaves the question undecided, while Baier and Buddeus confined themselves to the "knowledge of the intellect." For the
rest, all held that God, being a Spirit, cannot be perceived by the
senses and that if we are at all justified in speaking of a vision of God
this must refer to seeing God with the eye of the soul or of the spirit.

In this connection, however, the question might present itself whether
a direct, immediate, face to face vision of God is possible. Was the
position of scholasticism correct; namely, that God can be seen "as he
is in himself, in his own substance or essence?" The consensus of
opinion was that such a "vision of God with respect to his essence" is
impossible here on earth and if possible at all is reserved for the state
of glory. At best by a very special act of God's grace this privilege has
been granted to Moses, Ex. 34; Isaiah, chap. 6; and Paul, II Cor. 12;
and even then only for a moment. By far the majority, however, held
that even the patriarchs, prophets, and apostles had only a mediate
vision of God, and saw him by means of a cloud, a token or a physical
manifestation. Consequently, the real discussion was limited to the
question whether in the state of glory there is a "vision of God with
respect to his essence." Now the church fathers often speak of a vision
of God that is reserved for heaven; but they do not mention an essential
vision. They simply agree with Scripture in affirming that believers

will see God "not in a mirror but face to face." To this they add that God is invisible but is able to make himself visible and to reveal himself to man. "It is not in our power to see him but it is in his power to reveal himself." Others, therefore, explicitly deny an essential vision of God in the hereafter; e.g., Chrysolt, Gregory of Nyssa, Cyril of Jerusalem, Theoldoret, Jerome, Isidore, etc. Roman Catholic theologians do not know what to do with the statements of these church fathers. Vasquez admitted openly, "If we wish to be honest, we are scarcely able to interpret these fathers in a favorable sense." Others, however, try to rob these statements of their true meaning and say that they refer to a perception of God by means of the senses or to a vision of God in this life or to the absolute knowledge of God which is and remains unattainable even in heaven.

Gradually, however, under the influence exerted by Neo-Platonic mysticism upon Pseudodionysius a different view of the vision of God began to prevail. The vision of God began to be interpreted as a contemplation of God's "inner essence." According to this view God does not descend to the human level but by a supernatural gift man is raised to the divine level and deified. Gregory the Great already remarked that God will be seen not only in his glory but also in his nature, for "his nature itself is its own perspicuity; perspicuity itself is his nature." Prosper spoke of the believers in heaven as "in the heavens contemplating within their hearts the substance of their own Creator." Bernard of Clairvaux states that God will be seen in all his creatures but that the trinity will also be seen "in itself, in very essence." And the council of Florence declared that the souls "would immediately upon their entrance into heaven obtain a clear vision of the one and triune God as he really is, nevertheless, in proportion with the diversity of their merits: the one more perfectly than the other." Scholasticism discovered that this subject offered abundant opportunity for divers speculations, and did not fail to exploit it for that purpose. In connection with the doctrine of "accessory gifts" ("super-added endowments") it was held that man as he is by nature is not able to attain to this vision of God, but that he needs a "special divine gift" that will complement his natural gifts and raise them to a higher level. That supernatural helping gift was usually indicated by the name "light of glory." But a great difference of opinion arose in connection with the question of the nature of this light, whether it was objective or subjective, the Word or the Spirit, a gift of the Holy Spirit or the Holy Spirit himself, although it was commonly held to be something created, bestowed upon the intellect, a disposition or state of the mind. For the rest it became the generally accepted doctrine that God can be seen in his essence, and that the redeemed in heaven see whatever is essential to the being of God, the attributes as well as the persons. But the Thomists argued that God's being cannot be seen apart from the persons, neither one attribute apart from the others, while the nominalists and Scotists adhered to the opposite view. Furthermore, all agreed that God himself, i.e., all that pertains to him essentially, is the object of such vision, but opinions varied with respect to the question whether that which is called into being by God's decree is included in this object. Usually this question was answered in the affirmative in order to justify the invocation of angels and saints, who according to this view, see in God whatever is going to happen and therefore are acquainted with the needs of believers on earth. Although it was indeed added that the vision of God is not a comprehension and that it differs according to merits, nevertheless, this doctrine resulted in the deification of man. On the basis of a supernatural gift the creature by his own merits raises himself to a higher level and becomes like unto God.

The theologians of the Reformation differed in their views with respect to the vision of God. The Lutherans were inclined to accept not only a mental but even a physical vision of God's essence. According to their view God is so great in power that he can illumine the saints so that they will be enabled to see God's essence with their physical eyes. Also a few Reformed theologians regarded such an essential vision of God as not altogether impossible. But most of them, clinging to the promise of a glory that passeth all understanding which is prepared for the believer, refused to consider the "obscure questions" of scholasticism or otherwise completely rejected an essential vision of God.

This reluctance to accept an essential vision of God is entirely in harmony with Scripture. The Bible does indeed teach that the blessed in heaven behold God, but it does not describe the nature of that vision and it maintains God's invisibility everywhere. The vision of God that awaits believers is called by Paul a "knowing as we are known." If God cannot be *known* perfectly, i.e., according to his essence, if, in other words, he is *incomprehensible,* as all accept, he is also *invisible in his essence,* for essential vision and "comprehension" are synonymous. Moreover, God is infinite and man is finite and remains finite even in the state of glory. Hence, man can never have anything higher than a finite, human vision of God. The object may indeed be infinite, its representation in the consciousness of man is and remains finite. The "vision of God" is therefore, not a vision "with respect to his essence." Every vision of God presupposes a divine "condescension," a revelation by means of which God descends to our level and makes himself known to us; Matt. 11:27 retains its force in heaven. The vision of God in his essence implies man's deification, the wiping out of the line of demarcation that exists between the creature and the Creator. This would be in harmony with the Neo-Platonic mysticism adopted by Rome, but not with the mysticism of the Reformation, especially not with that of the Reformed church and theology. By means of the "supernatural gift" Rome lifts man above his own nature, and makes of him a higher creature, a "supernatural and divine human being, a God-man"; but, no matter how glorious the Reformed theologians conceived heaven to be, in their opinion man will always remain man, exalted indeed "above his natural positon," but never "above his species and above that which resembles himself." Man's blessedness exists, indeed, in the "beatific vision of God" but this vision is adapted to man's finite nature. A vision of God as taught by Rome fits into the system of the Pseudodionysian hierarchy, but finds no support in Scripture.

**II. Mental Attributes: Omniscience, Wisdom, and Veracity. Scripture Teaches These Attributes. Pantheism Denies God's Distinct Consciousness, cf. Ed. Von Hartmann's Philosophy of the Unconscious. God's Knowledge Is All-Comprehensive, Simultaneous, Simple, Unchangeable, and Eternal. We Distinguish Between Natural Or Necessary Knowledge and Free Knowledge. The Doctrine of "Middle Knowledge" Is Unscriptural. Wisdom and Knowledge Compared. God's Wisdom Is Manifest In Creation, Redemption, and Providence. Relation Between God's Wisdom and the Doctrine of "Ideas." We Distinguish Between Metaphysical, Ethical, and Logical Veracity.**

A. **God's omniscience.** Scripture proclaims God's omniscience; namely, that God is light, and that his knowledge is eternal, all-comprehensive, and certain.

Scripture everywhere presupposes God's consciousness and knowledge. He is "light," and in him dwelleth no darkness at all, I John 1:5, dwelling in light unapproachable, I Tim. 6:16, the source of all light in nature and in grace, Ps. 4:7; 27:1; 36:10; 43:3; John 1:4, 9; 8:12; Jas. 1:17; etc. When God is called "light," he is designated as perfect in self-consciousness, perfect in the knowledge of his own being, so that nothing in his being is hid from his consciousness. In Scripture the word "light" is, to be sure, also symbolical of purity, chastity, holiness, and of joy, cheerfulness, blessedness, Ps. 27:1; 36:9; 97:11; Is. 60:19; John 1:4; Eph. 5:8; just as darkness is symbolical not only of error and ignorance, but also of unchastity and moral corruption, of suffering and misery, Ps. 82:5; Ecc. 2:13, 14; Is. 8:22; Matt. 4:16; 8:12; Luke 22:53; John 3:19; Rom. 3:12; Eph. 5:8 ff.; I Pet. 2:9; etc.; but the symbolical meaning of "light" which stands in the foreground is that of "knowledge." The reason for this is that the main function of light is that of revealing that which is hidden in darkness, and causing it to become manifest; light is "everything that is made manifest," Eph. 5:13. Hence, consciousness is called "light," Prov. 27:19; I Cor. 2:11; Matt. 6:22, 23. The moral signification of the word follows very naturally from its intellectual meaning, for just as we hide ourselves, and love the darkness, and do not dare to be made manifest, and do not see ourselves as we really are whenever we are polluted by sin; even so we regain the courage to see ourselves, we begin to love the light, and we walk in the light, whenever God through Christ, the true Light, shines in our hearts, to give unto us the light of the knowledge of the glory of God in the face of Jesus Christ, Gen. 3:8; John 1:5; 3:19; John 1:4; 5:8, 12; 9:5; 12:35; II Cor. 4:4, 6; Matt. 5:14, 16; John 3:21; Rom. 13:12; Eph. 5:8; Phil. 2:15; I Thess. 5:5; I John 1:7, etc. Hence, the word "light" when applied to God signifies first of all that God has a perfect knowledge of himself whereas his being is never polluted by sin; no darkness can dwell in him; he is nothing but light; moreover, God's trinitarian existence is one of perfect consciousness, Matt. 11:27; John 1:17; 10:15; I Cor. 2:10. Furthermore, God is conscious of and knows whatever has existence distinct from his being. Scripture nowhere gives any indication that there is anything unknown to God. Though God's method of obtaining knowledge is at times depicted in striking anthropomorphic language, Gen. 3:9 ff.; 11:5; 18:21; etc.; he is, nevertheless, represented as being omniscient. The very idea that there could be anything unknown to him is rejected: "He that planted the ear, shall he not hear? He that formed the eye, shall he not see?" Ps. 94:9. Again and again mention is made of his wisdom, might, counsel, understanding, knowledge, Job 12:13; 28:12-27; Prov. 8:12 ff.; Ps. 17:5; Rom. 11:33; 16:27; Eph. 3:10; etc. All creatures are the objects of this knowledge. God's knowledge is all-comprehensive; strictly it is omniscience. His eyes run to and fro throughout the whole earth, II Chron. 16:9; all things are known him, and are laid open before his eyes, Heb. 4:13. All things are known to him: things of least significance, Matt. 6:8, 32; 10:30; the most hidden objects, heart and reins, Jer. 11:20; 17:9, 10; 20:12; Ps. 7:10; I Kings 8:39; Luke 16:15; Acts 1:24; Rom. 8:27; thoughts and meditations, Ps. 139:2; Ezek. 11:5; I Cor. 3:20; I Thess. 2:4; Rev. 2:23; man, in his origin, being, and is all his actions, Ps. 139; the night and the darkness, Ps. 139:11, 12; Sheol and Abaddon, Prov. 15:11; wickedness and sin, Ps. 69:6; Jer. 16:17; 18:23; 32:19; the contingent, I Sam. 23:10-13; II Sam. 12:8; II Kings 13:19; Ps. 81:14, 15; Jer. 26:2, 3; 38:17-20; Ezek. 3:6; Mt. 11:21; and the future, Is. 41:22 ff.; 42:9; 43:9-12; 44:7; 46:10; the days that were ordained for us, Ps. 31:15; 39:5; 139:6, 16; Job 14:5; Acts 17:26; etc. He knoweth all things,

I John 3:20. This knowledge of God is not an a posteriori knowledge: it is not the result of observation, but it is a priori, eternal, I Cor. 2:7; Rom. 8:29; Eph. 1:4, 5; II Tim. 1:9. His knowledge is not capable of increase, Is. 40:13 ff.; Rom. 11:34; it is certain and definite, Psalm 139:1-3; Heb. 4:13; so that God's revelations are all true, John 8:26; 17:17; Tit. 1:2; and all his works make known to us his wisdom, Ps. 104:24; 136:5; Eph. 3:10; Rom. 11:33; and cause us to worship and adore him, Ps. 139:17 ff.; Is. 40:28; Job 11:7 ff.; Rom. 11:33; I Cor. 2:11.

**B. The entire church accepted God's omniscience. Pantheism denies God's distinct existence, hence also his distinct consciousness (Fichte, Schelling, Hegel, Schopenhauer). This gave rise to Eduard Von Hartmann's Philosophy of the Unconscious. V. H. points out the great significance of the unconscious in the life of a human individual. From this he derives the unconscious Absolute. But man's unconscious acts in which, nevertheless, a purpose is evident, prove a conscious, intelligent rather than an unconscious God. God's consciousness differs from ours for it is all-comprehensive, eternal, and infinite.**

God's knowledge of himself and of the universe is so definitely and clearly taught in Scripture that it has always been accepted by the church. But pantheism rejects this belief. Pantheism is not able to ascribe a distinct consciousness to God inasmuch as it does not attribute to him an essence distinct from the universe. To be sure, Spinoza spoke of thought as an attribute of the Deity and called God a "thinking entity," but he distinguished between thought and intellect and viewed the latter as a "certain mode of thinking" that pertains not to "nature begetting" but to "nature begotten," and further held that all together these modes of thinking constitute the eternal and infinite mind of God. Via Fichte, Schelling, Hegel, and Schopenhauer this pantheism led to Eduard Von Hartmann's *Philosophie des Unbewussten*. In the first volume of his work Von Hartmann sets forth at length the universal significance of the unconscious and then states that the unconscious is *one* everywhere. And although he would rather not call this unconscious being God, nevertheless, in his philosophy it takes the place of God. Now at times Von Hartmann views this unconscious being not as blind and alogical, as, e.g., Schopenhauer's "will" but rather as discerning and clairvoyant, as is instinct in man and animals, and as possessing an omniscient, all-wise "most consummate intelligence." Nevertheless, it remains unconscious, for consciousness consists in a distinction between subject and object and therefore always implies limitation individualization, and even a body. Consciousness, viewed absolutely, loses its form and becomes unconscious. If the Absolute had consciousness apart from the consciousness of individual beings, it would swallow these up immediately. Monism is incompatible with a conscious, Divine Being. Such a being would not be immanent in but separate from the world. The Absolute is indeed the cause of all consciousness but in itself it is not conscious. Especially is it erroneous to ascribe self-consciousness to the Absolute, for this presupposes a distinction between subject and object, a reflection concerning itself, something altogether impossible in the Absolute. Accordingly, pantheism ascribes to God neither "knowledge of the universe" nor "knowledge concerning himself, self-consciousness." Even when the Absolute attains to consciousness in the consciousness of the individual, he knows the world but never himself.

Now we grant nearly all that Von Hartmann says in regard to the importance and influence of the unconscious in the creature. It is indeed true that the unconscious plays an important role in the lives of men and animals. But it is all the more remarkable that Von Hartmann himself does not see that the wide range of the power of the unconscious presupposes an intelligent God. For, it is certainly true that there are many instances of unconscious actions that are nevertheless purposeful. But in these cases the unconscious in man or animal does not itself act with a purpose, but the conscious soul of man sees a purpose in that action, and its attention is thereby directed to a higher, supernal consciousness. Accordingly, Anaxagoras already accepted a "mind" possessing infinite knowledge in order to arrange all things in the best order. Socrates describes the Deity as seeing and hearing everything and being present everywhere. Plato's God is the World Architect, who creates all things in accordance with the ideas. Aristotle reasons that the Deity is the "first mover" absolute essence, "pure actuality," the absolutely incorporeal One. Hence, God is thought, mind, and is the content of his own thinking. He cannot derive the content of his thinking from a sphere outside of himself; he can only think what is best, which is himself. Accordingly, God thinks himself; he is the thinking of his thinking; thinking and its object are one in him; he is thought of thought. Even the Stoics, reasoning teleologically, derive an intelligent cause from the manifestations of purpose in the universe. Zeno reasons thus: "No part of anything void of sense is capable of perception; some parts of the world have perception; the world, therefore, is not void of sense; that which reasons is superior to that which does not; nothing is superior to the world; the world, therefore, reasons." He that does not acknowledge a purpose in the universe does not need a self-conscious God either but should be satisfied with materialism; but he who with Von Hartmann advocates a teleological philosophy must ascribe consciousness to God and will never be able to explain the conscious by means of the unconscious.

Surely, the effect cannot be greater than the cause. "He that planted the ear, shall he not hear? He that formed the eye, shall he not see?" A perfection in the creature points to a perfection in God. If a rational being excels all others in worth, if man's ability to think raises him above all other creatures although in other respects he may be frail as a reed, then it is impossible to conceive of God as unconscious. Both religion — which always and everywhere presupposes a personal, self-conscious Supreme Being — and philosophy protest against the theory of an unconscious God. Pantheism may be able to appeal to Spinoza and Hegel; theism is supported by all the ancient philosophers and even by such later ones as Descartes, Leibnitz, Kant, Schelling (second period), J. H. Fichte, Herbart, Lotze, Ulrici, Carrière, etc. Of course, the fact that God's self-consciousness differs specifically from that pertaining to man, and that the latter is but a faint shadow of the former, is raised above all possibility of doubt. In that sense there would be no objection in calling God "superconscious." But for that very reason it is wrong to make deductions concerning the character of God's knowledge from the finiteness of self-consciousness in man. In spite of all pantheistic argumentation concerning the finiteness, individuality, and sensuous basis as necessary prerequisites of self-consciousness, it is not clear that *God's* self-knowledge would be a limitation of his being. In our case self-consciousness is finite and limited because we ourselves are finite and because it is never commensurate with our being. We are conscious of less than what we really are. But God is eternal, pure being. And his self-knowledge has for its content nothing less than that full, eternal, divine essence. Being and knowing are one in God. He knows himself by means of his own being. With him consciousness is not the result of a gradual process of development, neither does he rise to a higher degree of self-consciousness at one time than at another. For in him there is no process of becoming and no development. He is pure being, pure light without any darkness.

**C. We distinguish between God's self-consciousness and his world-consciousness. God's knowledge is all-comprehensive, simultaneous, simple, unchangeable, and eternal.**

We distinguish between God's self-consciousness and his world-consciousness. Hence, theologians used to divide the "knowledge of God" into "natural or necessary knowledge or knowledge of simple intelligence" and "free or contingent knowledge or knowledge of vision." These two are not to be identified, as pantheism teaches, for if the Absolute is viewed as existing before the world merely logically and potentially, the universe is not thereby explained. God does not need the universe in order to become personal and self-conscious. Neither logic (Hegel) nor history (Schelling) are necessary to bring

him to full actuality (Von Baader). Nevertheless, God's self-consciousness and his world-consciousness are not two things so entirely separate
as theology formerly presented them to be. The two are organically
related. Out of the fulness of ideas present in his absolute self-consciousness God did not arbitrarily select a few in order to bring these
to outward realization; but in the actualization of these ideas he was
guided by the purpose of revealing himself in the universe in all his
virtues and perfections. Hence, "free knowledge" comprises those
ideas which in their realization are capable of revealing God in a creaturely manner. The "natural knowledge" cannot be imparted to creatures, of course. As God knows himself he cannot be known by
creatures, neither as far as the depth or breadth nor as far as the
manner of that knowledge is concerned. "Free knowledge," however,
comprises the knowledge of all that which is capable of realization and
is able to reveal God's virtues in creation. The "free knowledge" bears
the same relation to the "natural knowledge" as the ectype to the
archetype. Nevertheless, it should be remembered that in God this
"free knowledge is something entirely different from what it is in
creatures." Even though it is communicable, its nature and depth is
different in God from what it is in the creature.

Scripture teaches that God's knowledge is, in the first place, all-
comprehensive; nothing is outside of the sphere of his omniscience;
there is nothing that is not manifest in his sight; all things are
naked and laid open before the eyes of him with whom we have to do.
This truth has been admitted by all Christian theologians, Jerome excepted. In commenting on Hab. 1:13, he says that it is absurd to lower
the divine majesty by asserting "that God knows how many mosquitoes
are born each single moment and how many die; how many bugs, fleas,
and flies there are in the world; how many fishes swim in the water,
and how many of the smaller ones should constitute a meal for the
bigger ones." But this restriction of God's omniscience is not supported
by Scripture, and was rejected unanimously by Christian theology.
Furthermore this knowledge is not only all-comprehensive but also
intuitive, i.e., it is not derived from observation, but it is an inherent
possession. Our knowledge is posterior; it presupposes existence from
which it is derived. Exactly the opposite is true in regard to God's
knowledge: he knows a thing before it exists. Scripture expresses this
very plainly whenever it states that God knows all events before they
happen, Is. 46:10; Am. 3:7; Dan. 2:22; Ps. 139:6; Mt. 6:8; etc.
God is the Creator of all things: all things have been thought by him,
before they were called into being. "This world could not be known
to us unless it existed, but it could not have existed unless it had been
known of God." He has the ground of his existence in himself, hence,

his consciousness and knowledge cannot be dependent upon or determined by anything outside of himself. His aseity implies the absolute independence of his knowledge. His knowledge is not derived from the universe of created beings after these came into existence, for then they would have their origin in unconsciousness, as Schopenhauer and Von Hartmann taught; but he knows all things in, and of, and by means of himself. Hence, his knowledge is simple, undivided, immutable, eternal; he knows all things instantaneously, simultaneously, eternally; all things are eternally present in his mind.

**D. Strictly speaking, foreknowledge cannot be ascribed to God; nevertheless, we need this Biblical term in order to gain a correct idea concerning God's omniscience. But if God knows all things beforehand all freedom of action seems to be excluded:**

**(1) It was this difficulty which caused Cicero, Marcion, and the Socinians to deny God's all-comprehensive foreknowledge.**

**(2) The Jesuits tried to harmonize God's foreknowledge and man's freedom by their doctrine of a middle (mediate) knowledge; i.e., a contingent knowledge of the future; e.g., God knows what he is going to do IF David goes to Keilah, and also IF he does not go; etc.**

**(3) Roman Catholic theology accepts this mediate knowledge.**

**(4) Arminians and Lutherans are not hostile to it.**

**(5) Augustine and all Reformed theologians absolutely reject it.**

**(6) It is based on the Pelagian conception of the freedom of the will; it makes God dependent on man; it is not foreknowledge in any sense; for foreknowledge of a will which is entirely undetermined is impossible.**

Strictly speaking, foreknowledge cannot be ascribed to God for there is no "difference of time" with him. He calls the things that are not as if they were, and sees what is not as if it already existed. "For what is foreknowledge except knowledge of future events? But can anything be future to God, who is exalted above every measure of time? For if God's knowledge comprehends these very events (or objects), then they are not future but present to him; and for this reason we should not speak of God's foreknowledge but simply of God's knowledge." "Whatever is past and future to us is clearly present in his sight." "However much the times may roll along, with him is an eternal 'present.' " The division of God's omniscience into foreknowledge, knowledge of vision (i.e., of the present), and reminiscence is a totally human representation. Nevertheless, Scripture often speaks of God's omniscience as if it preceded the existence of things. And it is impossible for us to discuss God's omniscience apart from this representation. In theology, however, the question arose, "How can God's omniscience be harmonized with man's freedom?" If God knows all things beforehand, everything is settled from eternity, and it is very difficult to see how any room is left for free and contingent actions. Hence, Cicero maintained the freedom of the will and denied God's omniscience because he was unable to harmonize the two. Whereas God allowed man to fall into sin, Marcion denied not only God's goodness and omnipotence but also his omniscience. The Socinians in later times advocated the same idea. To be sure, God knows all things, but he knows all things according to their nature. Accordingly, he knows contingent and conditionally future events as contingent and conditional: he does not know them beforehand with absolute certainty, for in that case they would cease to be conditional; inasfar as future events depend on man they are not the objects of infallible foreknowledge. If the contrary were true, the freedom of the will would be lost, God would become the author of sin and the slave of necessity. Nevertheless, such a limitation of God's omniscience was not accepted by many; it was too unbiblical to receive favor. Christian theology usually looks for a solution of the problem in another direction. Two avenues of approach suggest themselves. On the one hand we have Origen who distinguishes between foreknowledge and predestination. God knows all beforehand, but this foreknowledge is not the cause of their happening; on the contrary, God knows them beforehand only because in time they are going to happen as a result of man's free determination: "for they do not happen because they were known, but they were known because they were going to happen." On the other side we have Augustine, who also wishes to maintain both foreknowledge and the freedom of the will. "But the religious mind chooses both, confesses both, and confirms both by the faith of piety." But he is aware of the fact that whenever God foreknows an act, its fruition is certain; otherwise the entire structure of divine foreknowledge would collapse like a house of cards. "If foreknowledge does not foreknow things that will certainly happen; it is nothing at all." Hence, he states that man's will together with its entire nature and all its decisions is included in, established, and maintained by God's foreknowledge, and is not destroyed by it. "For, since he foreknows our will, it follows that he foreknows whose will it is going to be. Therefore, there is going to be a will, because he has foreknown it." "Wherefore our wills have power to do all that God wanted them to do and foresaw they could do; and therefore, whatever power they have, they have most certainly; and whatever they are to do they themselves most certainly do, for he whose foreknowledge is infallible foreknew that they would have the power to do it and that they would do it." Scholasticism, although it made all kinds of fine distinctions agreed in principle with Augustine.

But the Jesuits brought about a change. In order to harmonize God's omniscience with human freedom they — in agreement with Semi-

Pelagianism—interposed a so-called "mediate or middle knowledge" between God's necessary knowledge and his free knowledge. By this middle knowledge they meant a divine knowledge concerning conditionally future events, a knowledge logically preceding God's purpose in regard to those events. The object of this knowledge is not the merely possible that will never become realized, nor that which as a result of God's decree will certainly happen, but all those possible events which depend for their futurition on certain conditions. In his government of the world God often suspends the realization of possible events upon the fulfilment of conditions, and he knows beforehand what he will do in case these conditions are or are not fulfilled by man. Accordingly, God is ready for whatever may happen. He foreknows and sees all possibilities, and he has made provision for all of them. He knows beforehand what he is going to do if Adam falls, and also if he does not; if David goes to Keilah, and also if he does not; if Tyre and Sidon are converted, and also if they are not; etc. Hence, the knowledge of "future contingent events" precedes the decree concerning "absolutely future events." At every moment man chooses with complete freedom and independence, but he is never able to surprise God or annul his plans, for God in his foreknowledge has taken into account every possibility. In order to bolster up their theory of a middle foreknowledge its advocates cited those passages of Scripture in which God is said to know what will happen in a given case if this or that condition attains or fails to attain fulfillment; e.g., Gen. 11:6; Ex. 3:19; 34:16; Deut. 7:3, 4; I Sam. 23:10-13; 25:29 ff.; II Sam. 12:8; I Kings 11:2; II Kings 2:10; 13:19; Ps. 81:13, 14; Jer. 26:2, 3; 38:17-20; Ezek. 2:5-7; 3:4-6; Matt. 11:21, 23; 24:22; 26:53; Luke 22:66-68; John 4:10; 6:15; Acts 22:18; Rom. 9:29; I Cor. 2:8.

It is true that this theory was challenged by the Thomists and Augustinians, e.g., by Bannetz, the Salmanticenses, and Billuart, but it was zealously defended by the Molinists and Congruists, Suaretz, Bellarminus, Lessius, etc. The doctrine of a "middle knowledge" profited by the Roman Catholic prejudice against Calvinism and Jansenism, and a more or less pronounced form of it gradually gained favor with nearly all Roman Catholic theologians. Thus the line of Augustine was surrendered and that of Origen taken up again. Greek theology had taken this position from the beginning; Roman (Catholic) theology now followed in its wake. Lutherans and Remonstrants were not unfavorably disposed toward the doctrine of a middle knowledge. Of late also others similarly teach that the universe is for God a means of knowledge; i.e., that God actually derives knowledge from the universe. He indeed foreknows future, contingent events as possible; nevertheless, he is dependent on the world for finding out whether or not they were realized. However, for every contingency he knows "an action that will exactly answer the action of the creature, whatever that may chance to be." He establishes with certainty the outline of the plan of the universe, but leaves the filling out of this outline to the creature. After the example of Augustine, Reformed theologians absolutely reject this "bare foreknowledge," this "middle knowledge."

Now in regard to this "middle knowledge" the question is not, of course, whether there does not exist a certain conditional connection between future events, a connection known and determined by God. We have no objection to middle knowledge thus interpreted; in fact Gomarus and Walaeus accept it in this sense. But something entirely different is usually meant by this doctrine; its purpose is to harmonize the Pelagian conception of the freedom of the will with God's omniscience. According to that conception the human will is by nature indifferent. It can do the one thing as well as the other. It is determined neither by its own nature nor by circumstances. Circumstances may perhaps exert their influence upon the will; in the end, however, the will is free and chooses according to its own desire. Of course, freedom of the will thus conceived cannot be harmonized with God's decree; it really consists in "freedom from dependence on God's decree." God has not determined that will, but allows it to assert itself without his interference. God could not determine that will without destroying it. Over against that will God assumes an attitude of patient watching and waiting. He watches to see what that will is going to do. However, by virtue of his omniscience God knows beforehand all possibilities, all conditionally future events, and also all absolutely future happenings. His decrees have been made in accordance with this foreknowledge: God has elected a man to everlasting life, provided that this individual under given conditions is going to accept God's grace; if not, he has been rejected. It is plainly evident that this doctrine differs in principle from that of Augustine and Thomas Aquinas. With them foreknowledge precedes the events, and nothing can happen except by God's will. "Nothing, therefore, happens but by the will of the Omnipotent." The medium whereby God knows all things is not the universe but the decree. Accordingly, free actions and contingent events are known in their relations with a certain and infallible knowledge. It is true that even scholasticism departed in certain instances from expressing itself after the manner of Augustine. Anselm, e.g., stated that "foreknowledge" did not imply an "internal and antecedent necessity" but merely an "external and consequent necessity"; and Thomas Aquinas asserted that God does indeed know future contingent events eternally and certainly, inasmuch as they are subject to the divine sight "in their presentiality"; but that they are, nevertheless, future contingent things in relation to their own causes. At the same time, however, as far as the "primary cause" was concerned these "future contingent events" were absolutely certain, and hence, not really contingent; and elsewhere Th. Aquinas definitely affirms, "whatever *is* was destined to *be* before it came into being, because it existed in its own cause in order that it might come into being."

But the doctrine of mediate knowledge represents future events as contingent and free even as far as God is concerned, with reference both to his "predestination" and to his "prescience," for, in agreement with Origen, things do not occur because God knows them, but God foreknows them because they are going to occur. Accordingly, the order of sequence is not "necessary knowledge, knowledge of vision, decree to create," etc., but "necessary knowledge, mediate knowledge, decree to create, etc., knowledge of vision." God does not derive his knowledge concerning the free actions of men from his own being, from his decree, but from man's will. Hence God becomes dependent upon the world; he derives from the world a knowledge which he could not have derived from his own being, and consequently, as far as his knowledge is concerned, God is no longer simple and independent; in other words, he ceases to be God. On the other hand, the creature in a large measure becomes independent of God; it has received existence and potentiality from God, but it has volition of itself. Man decides sovereignly, and he either performs an act or chooses not to perform it, apart from any preceding divine decree. Accordingly, entirely apart from God's will a thing can come to existence; the creature has become creator, autonomous, sovereign; and the entire history of the world is withdrawn from the controlling and directing power of God, and is made subject to the will of man. First, man makes a decision, and afterward God intervenes with whatever plan answers to that decision. Moreover, such decisions of greater or less importance occur not only once — e.g., in the case of Adam — or twice but thousands of times in the life of every human individual. What, therefore, must we think of a God who patiently awaits all these decisions, and makes all possible plans for all possible decisions? What is left of a scheme or outline for the history of the universe, of which the "filling-out" is left to man? And of what value is a government which makes the king the slave of his subjects? Mediate knowledge does indeed make God the slave of man. God is looking on while man decides. It is not God who makes a division among men, but men themselves bring about this division: grace is distributed according to merits, predestination becomes dependent upon good works; that which is everywhere rejected as false by Scripture and by Augustine — over against Pelagius — has been made the standard Roman Catholic doctrine by the Jesuits. The appeal to Scripture made by the advocates of mediate knowledge is without any justification. Scripture surely affirms the fact that God has placed events in all kinds of relations to each other, and that these relations are often conditional in character, so that one event must of necessity occur before another can happen — e.g., apart from faith there is no salvation, apart from work there will be no food, etc. — but all these passages cited by the Jesuits do not prove what was to be proved: they speak of condition and fulfillment, of obedience and promise, of presupposition and consequence, of what shall happen in this or that given case, but not any of them denies the fact that in all these cases God knew and determined beforehand what would certainly come to pass. This is true in spite of the anthropomorphisms in which these passages abound. Between that which is purely possible but will never become actual — present in God merely as an idea — and that which is certain and has been decreed by God, there is no sphere which can be controlled by the will of man. A thing belongs either to the one or to the other. If it is possible merely and will never become actual, it is the object of God's "necessary knowledge"; if it is going to become realized, it is the object of his "free knowledge." There is no middle ground between the two: there is no "middle knowledge."

Moreover, the advocates of the doctrine of mediate or middle knowledge miss their mark. Their purpose is to establish harmony between man's freedom, in the sense of indifference, and foreknowledge. Now it is claimed that this "prescience" taken in the sense of "middle knowledge" leaves room for freedom of human actions, and does not imply the necessity of these actions. Now this is correct, with this qualification, however, that this "prescience" ceases to be prescience. Real divine foreknowledge of a person's actions in any given case is only then possible when a man's motives determine his will in *one* definite direction, so that his will is, therefore, not indifferent. Conversely, if man's will were indifferent, foreknowledge would be utterly impossible, and a mere "subsequent knowledge" would result. God's "foreknowledge" and an arbitrary, undetermined will, exclude one another. "For if he knows it, it will certainly come to pass; but if it certainly comes to pass, there is no chance." Hence, with Augustine we must seek a solution of this problem in another direction. The freedom of the will does not exist in "indifference," in arbitrariness or chance, but in "reasonable self-determination." This "reasonable self-determination" instead of being in conflict with "God's prescience" is implied and required by it. The human will, together with its nature, its antecedents and motives, its decisions and their consequences, is included in the "order of causation which is certain to God and is embraced by his foreknowledge." In God's mind events stand in that relation to each other which is afterward realized. A foreknowledge (and a predestination) which intervenes now and then is not true to reality; on the contrary, every deed and action is motivated by that which precedes, and is thus included in "God's knowledge." According to their own divinely ordained order and nature contingent events and free actions have their proper place in the "order of causes" which in the course of history gradually become known to us.

**E. God's wisdom.** **Wisdom is knowledge from another point of view.**

(1) **Definition: choosing the best end and the best means for reaching that end.**

(2) **Knowledge and wisdom compared:**

(a) **the source of knowledge is study; of wisdom, discernment;**

(b) **knowledge is discursive; wisdom intuitive;**

(c) **knowledge is theoretical; wisdom practical: it is the art of right living; it is teleological;**

(d) **knowledge is a matter of the mind apart from the will; wisdom is a matter of the mind made subservient to the will;**

(e) **knowledge receives greatest emphasis in the West; wisdom is preeminent in the Orient.**

(3) **The wisdom of which we find mention in Scripture is not rooted in human knowledge, but in the fear of the Lord, and manifests itself in a God-glorifying life; it expresses itself in wisdom-literature, cf. the proverbs.**

(4) **Scripture ascribes wisdom to God, a wisdom which is manifest:**

(a) **in creation,**

(b) **in redemption (in the foolishness of the cross), and**

(c) **in God's providence over Israel and the Gentiles.**

Viewed from another angle God's knowledge is called wisdom. The distinction between the two is universally known. Nearly all languages have different words to indicate these different concepts. Everyone knows that knowledge, study, learnedness do not always accompany wisdom, and that the two have different meanings. The ordinary individual frequently surpasses in wisdom the man of learning. Wisdom and knowledge are rooted in different capacities of the soul. The source of *knowledge* is study; of *wisdom,* discernment. *Knowledge* is discursive; *wisdom* intuitive. *Knowledge* is theoretical; *wisdom* practical, teleological; it makes knowledge subservient to an end. *Knowledge* is a matter of the mind apart from the will; *wisdom* is a matter of the mind made subservient to the will. *Knowledge* is often very unpractical; i.e., not adapted to the common affairs of life, *wisdom* is adapted to life; it is ethical in character; it is the art of proper living; it characterizes the man who rightly employs his greater store of knowledge, and who chooses the best end and the best means for reaching that end. The etymology of the words (wisdom and knowledge) point out this distinction in meaning. *Sapiens* is derived from *sapere,* to taste; hence, it points in the direction of experience, and indicates that a person by means of experience has arrived at an independent judgment; the Greek word *sophos,* probably connected with *saphēs,* has the same meaning. Among oriental nations we also notice this distinction in meaning, but with a notable difference. While in the Occident *knowledge* is given the seat of honor, *wisdom* receives greatest emphasis in the Orient. Oriental people prefer contemplation to abstract thinking; they do not occupy themselves with abstract concepts but with the images of things; subjectively, their life is an expression of the heart rather than of the mind; objectively, they come closer to the immediate reality of life. Not the mind but the heart, the root of personality, is the place where subject and object meet each other, and either repel each other most violently, or attract each other most tenderly. Israel exhibits this oriental characteristic in an intensified degree. Naturally, also in Israel there arose a philosophy of wisdom. The Hebrew word *Chokmah* is derived from *hkm,* to be firm, sound, steadfast; subst., "sterling character." Divine revelation gave to Chokmah its distinct character. Accordingly, real, true wisdom is not rooted in the human mind, but in the fear of the Lord. It consists in that "sterling character" which has the law of God as its norm, and which manifests itself in a life of high moral conduct, Deut. 4:6-8; Ps. 19:8; 111:10; Job 28:28; Prov. 1:7; 9:10. When, in the course of history, men began to penetrate more deeply into God's revelation in nature and in "the law," a separate place was given to Chokmah, which soon developed its own literature and its own characteristic mode of expression: the proverbial. Not only mind and knowledge are now ascribed to God, but also wisdom. By means of the word God created the world, Gen. 1:3; Ps. 33:6; 107:20; 119:105; 147:15; 148:5; Is. 40:8; 48:13. At first this work of creation reveals to Israel especially God's *power and majesty.* Gradually, however, the soul of the Israelite, educated and nourished by the fear of Jehovah, begins to penetrate more deeply into the work of God in nature and in "the law," and admires the *wisdom* of God manifested in this work. Both creation and redemption are ascribed to God's wisdom, Job 9:4; 12:13, 17, 37, 38; Is. 40:28; Ps. 104:24; Deut. 4:6-8; Jer. 10:12; Ps. 19:8; while in Prov. 8:22 ff., and Job 28:23 ff., the wisdom by means of which God created all things is personified. In the N. T. we find the same idea; not only does it ascribe wisdom to God in several passages, Rom. 16:27; 1 Tim. 1:17; Jude 25; Rev. 5:12; 7:12; but it also declares that the world was created through the word, John 1:3; Heb. 11:3; and it magnifies the wisdom of God revealed in the foolishness of the cross, I Cor. 1:18; in Christ, I Cor. 1:24; in the church, Eph. 3:10; and in the work of God's providence in behalf of Israel and of the Gentiles, Rom. 11:33.

> **F. Philo and especially Augustine connected this Scriptural doctrine of wisdom with Plato's "ideas." The very fact that the work of creation is a realization of God's "ideas" indicates God's wisdom. The doctrine of ideas gradually disappeared from dogmatics because the word "idea" acquired a different meaning. Formerly an idea was considered to be the pattern of a thing in the creative mind of God, an archetype; now it is generally defined as the subjective conception of an object in the mind of a person. The word is used here in its former sense. God is not an unconscious Creator, but he created all things with a purpose, after a pattern, an "idea," hence, with wisdom. Creation is the realization of these ideas. God is the great Architect. His ideas are:**
>
> **(1) absolutely original,**
>
> **(2) eternal, unchangeable,**
>
> **(3) manifold yet unified, having as their ultimate purpose God's glorification.**
>
> **Because of the archetypal character of the divine ideas there is no idea of sin.**

It was especially Philo who connected this Scriptural doctrine concerning the divine word and wisdom with the "ideas." Thus the foundation was laid for the doctrine of the logos, which is more fully discussed in the chapter on the trinity. In later times Plato's ideology again exerted a powerful influence on Christian theology, this time by way of Neo-Platonism. In this way it was handed down to Augustine, who gave it a place in theology. But in order to do this he had to modify it considerably. In the first place, the ideas as viewed by Augustine do not constitute a world by themselves, a "totality of ideas" next to and apart from God, but they exist in God and form the contents of his thinking: "Moreover, these ideas *(rationes:* reasonable causes, active creative principles) must be viewed as existing only in the mind of the Creator." They are God's thoughts concerning all his creatures both before and after creation; hence, they are eternal and immutable, for in God there can be nothing which is not eternal and immutable, "For to affirm that God has a new plan is, to say the least, most absurd, if not wicked." Nevertheless, in God's mind the ideas are not identical with his self-knowledge nor with the Logos or the Son, as had been maintained by earlier church-fathers. Augustine maintains the essential distinction between God and the universe, and avoids pantheism. "For in one sense those things are present in him which were made by him; in another sense those things are present in him which he is himself." On the other hand, Augustine cannot conceive of creation except by assuming that God created everything according to ideas. Therein is his wisdom manifested. "Thus, the wisdom of God, by which all things have been made, contains everything according to design before it makes everything." "With reason all things were formed. For he has not made anything unwittingly. They were known to him; therefore—he made them; he did not learn to know things after they had been made." Creation is the realization of Divine ideas. Hence, between creation and the ideas there is a close connection. The ideas are the forms and patterns of things, "basic forms, reasonable causes, fixed and immutable" hence, not only of species but of individual objects. "Whereas the formation of all things rests upon a reasonable cause, therefore the creation of each individual object must rest upon particular reasonable causes (ideas)." Nevertheless, Augustine does not always adhere to this representation. At times his ideas appear as types and patterns which gradually receive embodiment, and are fully realized only in the new heaven and on the new earth. Moreover, the relation which according to Augustine exists between the ideas and created objects is not clear. The ideas are not only the divine patterns of objects, but also the active causes and principles immanent in the objects. Hence, Augustine preferred the word "reasonable causes" to Cicero's "forms" or "species" as the Latin equivalent of the Greek "ideas." The ideas are, as it were, given with the objects. Ideas and created objects do not stand alongside of or over against each other as examples and copies true and untrue, immutable and mutable, but the ideas are the soul and principle of the objects; movement pertains to the creature "by virtue of these innate reasonable causes." Yet the causality that pertains to the ideas is always mediated by the will of God; the latter is the real and final cause of the existence of things.

Many others besides Augustine teach this doctrine of ideas, also a few Reformed theologians. Later on it disappeared almost completely from Dogmatics. In the philosophy of the modern period the meaning of the word "idea" has undergone a change. Formerly an "idea" was considered to be the pattern of a thing in the creative mind of God, while a *conception* was the imprint of a thing upon the conscious mind. But in modern philosophy the word idea is used to indicate a concept that is independent of sensation and is the result of abstract thinking (Descartes); a conception of pure reason, the verification of which is beyond the sphere of experience and knowledge (Kant); an immediate object of intuition and reasoning (Jacobi). Nevertheless, the use of the word in common parlance, at least in the Dutch and German languages, serves as a reminder of its former meaning. Always—especially in the realm of art—it denotes an objective pattern, a paradigm, an ideal perfection. Accordingly, we speak of the idea of God, of freedom, of art, of science, of the true, the good, the beautiful, etc. Applied to God it refers to the fact that he has created all things with wisdom; that wisdom is the beginning of his way, the "beginning of creation," Prov. 8:2; Col. 1:15; Rev. 3:14. What is true of a human artificer is true in a higher degree of God. Just as the former expresses his idea in his masterpiece, so the latter creates all things in accordance with the ideas which he himself has formed. The universe is God's masterpiece. God is the Architect and Maker of the entire universe. He is not an unconscious Creator; on the contrary, in all his works he is guided by wisdom, by his ideas. Nevertheless, there are also differences between God and a human artificer. God's ideas are absolutely original; they arise out of his own being, and are eternal and immutable; indeed, they are one with his own being. The ideas in God themselves constitute the "essence of God" inasfar as this is the pattern of created things and can be expressed and reflected in finite creatures. Every creature is a revelation of the Deity, and partakes of God's being. The character of this participation is not such that a creature is a modification of God's being or that it has in reality received into itself the divine essence, but every creature has its own distinct essence because in its existence it is an ectype of the divine essence. Because of the multitude and abundance of the divine ideas realized in creation, God's wisdom is properly called "manifold," Eph. 3:10. Nevertheless, God's wisdom is one, and his idea of the universe is one, gradually unfolding itself in the course of the ages, and guiding reality onward toward the established goal. Because of this archetypal character of the divine ideas, there is no "idea" of sin as such; for sin is not a distinct being but an impairment of being, a deformation. To be sure, sin is an object of God's knowledge, and God's wisdom makes it subservient to his glory; yet, in itself it is never an idea of his wisdom, a ray of his light. Rather, the idea of goodness gives us a knowledge of the character of evil, for evil is the privation of goodness. But God's wisdom is manifest in the creation, ordering, guidance, and government of all things. It is and remains the "master workman," Prov. 8:30, the artificer of all things, Wisdom 7:21, creating and governing all things, and leading them onward toward their destination, i.e., toward the glorification of God's name.

**G. God's veracity.** The last mental attribute is God's veracity. It is an attribute of God's will as well as of his mind. It indicates both that God is the true God over against all false gods, and that he is faithful to his promises. Scripture everywhere teaches God's veracity.

The last mental attribute which requires our attention is God's veracity. The Hebrew word *'mth, 'munh,* adj. *'mn* is derived from

the verb *'mn,* to confirm, to support, intr. to be firm, hiph. to cling to,
to trust, to be assured of something, and signifies, subjectively: the act
of clinging to something, faith; and objectively: the firmness, fidelity,
and truthfulness of the person or cause in which one has put his trust.
In accordance with this two-fold meaning the LXX sometimes has
*pistis,* i.e., "faith" as the Greek equivalent of these Hebrew words,
while at other times it has *alētheia,* i.e., "truth"; similarly, the English
translations have both "faith" and "truth." Both words are necessary
in order to convey the comprehensive meaning of the original. It is
because of this twofold meaning of the original Hebrew word for
"veracity" that this attribute is not only an attribute of God's *mind* (a
mental attribute) but also of his *will* (a volitional attribute), so that to
be strictly correct we would have to discuss it twice; nevertheless,
because of the close organic connection existing between the two concepts, we shall not be able to separate them. The name Jehovah implies
God's veracity: a God of faithfulness, without iniquity and perversity,
Deut. 32:4; Jer. 10:10; Ps. 31:6; II Chron. 15:3. It implies (a) that
he is the real, the true God, over against the false gods, the idols, which
are "vanities," *habhālim,* Deut. 32:21, etc., and (b) that he will always
remain true to his words and promises: that he will establish them, so
that he is perfectly reliable, truthworthy. He is not a man, that he
should lie or repent, Num. 23:19; I Sam. 15:29. All his actions bear
the stamp of genuineness. Again and again mention is made of his
kindness, *hesedh,* and truth, Gen. 24:49; 47:29; Josh. 2:14; II Sam.
2:6; 15:20; Ps. 40:11; his lovingkindness and truth, Gen. 24:27; Ex.
34:6; Ps. 57:3; 61:7; 89:14; etc. His words, ordinances, paths,
works, commandments, and laws are all faithful, II Sam. 7:28; Ps.
19:9; 25:10; 33:4; 111:7; 119:86, 142, 151; Dan. 4:37. His truth
and faithfulness are so gloriously revealed upon the earth that they
reach unto the skies, Ps. 36:5; Ex. 34:6. To confirm his word he
swears by himself, Gen. 22:16; etc., Heb. 6:13. Hence, he is often called
a rock, in which, because of its unchangeable firmness, his people may
take refuge, Deut. 32:4, 15, 18, 30, 37; Num. 1:6, 10; 3:35; 34:28;
II Sam. 22:3, 32; Ps. 18:2, 31; 19:14; 28:1; 31:3; 71:3; 144:1; Is.
26:4. Being a God of truth and faithfulness, he keeps his covenant,
Deut. 4:31; 7:9; Ps. 40:11; Hos. 12:1; etc., and he is a perfectly
reliable refuge for all his people, Ps. 31:6; 36:5 ff.; 43:2, 3; 54:7;
57:3; 71:22; 96:13; 143:1; 146:6; etc. Accordingly, in the N. T. he
is called the "truth or very God" i.e., the God who has revealed himself in Christ is the only real and true God, John 17:3; I John 5:20.
Whatever he reveals is truth. He is found to be true, but every man a
liar; John 3:33; Rom. 3:4. His word is the truth, his gospel is the
truth, Christ is the truth, John 14:6; 17:17; Eph. 1:13. He is even

now what he has always been. The N. T. is the fulfilment and confirmation of the promises made in the days of the Old Covenant. God has remembered his oath and covenant, Luke 1 :68-73. His faithfulness is evident in this that he is and remains the God of the covenant, and that he grants complete salvation, I Cor. 1 :9; 10:13; I Thess. 5 :24; II Thess 3 :3; Heb. 10:23; 11 :11; I John 1 :9. He cannot deny himself, II Tim. 2:13. All the promises of God in Christ are yea, and in him Amen, II Cor. 1 :18, 20. Christ is the "faithful witness," Rev. 1 :5; 3 :14; 19 :11. For this reason he is and can be the unchangeable object of our "faith."

**H. We distinguish between:**
  **(a) metaphysical,**
  **(b) ethical, and**
  **(c) logical veracity.**
**By ascribing metaphysical veracity to God we mean that he is true over against all that which is false; by ethical veracity we mean that God's revelation corresponds to his being; while logical veracity indicates that God knows all things as they really are. These three are one in God.**

Scripture uses the word "truth" (veracity, truthfulness) in more than one sense. Philosophy also presents a threefold concept of truth: viz., "veracity in essence, i.e., in the objects; veracity in expression, i.e., in words; and veracity in knowledge, i.e., in the intellect"; or "metaphysical, ethical, and logical veracity." When we ascribe metaphysical *"truth"* to an object or person, we mean that that object or person is all that it is supposed to be. In that sense gold which is gold not only in appearance but in reality, is real, pure, "true" gold. Used in this sense the word "truth" has for its antonyms: falsehood, spuriousness, fictitiousness (cf. fiction), vanity, non-existence. In this sense truth is a property of all essence; it is one with the substance. Augustine often used the word in this sense. All essence, as such, is true, beautiful, and good. Though there is a rich variety in the degree of essence pertaining to creatures, nevertheless, every creature has received essence from God "after its own kind" and partakes of God's essence. Next Augustine discusses *God's* essence. Scripture calls God the *true* God, over against the idols, which are "vanities." Hence, Augustine calls God the true, simple, immutable, only and eternal essence. Compared to this essence the essence which pertains to creatures is to be considered non-essence. God is the "highest essence, the highest truth, the highest good." He is pure "essence." Truth does not merely pertain to him, but he is himself the truth. "O Thou Truth, who art really the Truth." Furthermore, God is truth also in the ethical sense. By "ethical truth of veracity" we understand the correspondence between a person's being and his revelation in word and deed. Whoever expresses himself differently from what he thinks, is untrue, a liar. Used in this sense the word "truth" is opposed to "lie." God's revelation corresponds exactly to his being, Num. 23:19; I Sam. 15:29; Tit. 1:2; Heb. 6:18. God cannot lie, nor can he deny himself. Finally, God is also called the truth in a logical sense. By truth in this sense is meant "correspondence between thought and reality." Our conceptions are true if they are an exact copy of reality. Taken in this sense "truth" is opposed to "error." God is truth also in this sense because he knows things as they really are. His knowledge is correct, immutable, adequate. Just as in his essence God is the metaphysical (ontological) truth, so in his knowledge he is the logical truth. God's knowledge is living absolute, adequate truth. It is not demonstrative or discursive, but essential in God and a priori. It is "essential truth." Accordingly, God's Word, Law, and Gospel are pure truth. They are just as they should be. Now these three meanings of the word "truth" are indeed distinct; nevertheless, they are also one. Common to all three is the fact that truth is always correspondence between thought and essence, between ideal and real essence. God is the truth in the metaphysical sense, for in him thought and essence are united. He is completely conscious of himself: he is *"very"* God, for there is a perfect correspondence between his being and the idea of God inherent in him. He is the truth in the ethical sense, for he reveals himself, speaks, and acts just as he really is and thinks. And he is the truth in the logical sense, for he thinks objects to be as they really are; or rather, things are as he thinks them to be. He is the truth in all its absolute fulness. Hence, he is the "original truth," the source of all truth, the truth in all truth; the ground of all truth, and of the true essence of all things, of their knowability and conceivability; the ideal and archetype of all truth, of all ethical reality, of all laws and regulations, the norm in accordance with which all things should be judged both as to their essence and as to their manner of manifestation; the source and fountain of all true knowledge in every sphere, the only light in which we can see light, the sun of spirits. "Thee I invoke, O God, the Truth, in whom and from whom and through whom all things are true which are true."

**III. Moral Attributes: Goodness, Holiness, Righteousness. God's Goodness Manifests Itself In Lovingkindness Toward His People, Compassion To Those In Misery, Longsuffering To Those Deserving Punishment, Grace Toward the Guilty, and Love, i.e., God's Goodness Revealed In Self-Communication. Holiness Means Separateness. It Implies Separation and Consecration. Applied To God Holiness Indicates that He is Exalted Above**

**That Which Is Sinful and Finite, i.e., It Expresses God's Majesty and Divinity, and It Implies that He Is the Sanctifier of His People. We Speak of Legislative Righteousness, Distributive Righteousness (Punitive or Retributive).**

A. Different interpretations of "goodness":

(1) According to Socrates, etc., "that is good which all strive to obtain." Cf. Nietzsche. The term "good" often has the meaning of "useful"; however, it is broader than this definition would indicate. We also speak of that which is good in and by itself.

(2) According to Scripture we can speak of the goodness of God in himself, i.e., of God's "perfection" or "perfectness," Matt. 5:48. We can also speak of God's goodness toward his creatures: God is the source of all blessings in the natural, moral, and spiritual realm. All creatures, though in varying degree, are objects of this goodness. Both creation and providence are ascribed to God's goodness, Ps. 8:36. This goodness is eternal; it should be the object of the praise of all creatures, I Cor. 16:34, Ps. 136:1, etc.

Among the ethical attributes first place should be assigned to God's goodness. Even the realm of nature reveals this attribute. Plato identified the idea of goodness with deity. But the term "good" is used in more than one sense. Its original and primary significance seems to indicate a *relation* of one thing to another rather than an inner *quality*. Socrates identifies goodness with usefulness, i.e., with that which is good, usable, useful for some purpose. According to this interpretation goodness in the absolute sense does not exist; it is always relative; usefulness and uselessness are the yardstick for measuring good and evil. On the whole, Greek ethics honored this conception and failed to go beyond it: the search for the highest good coincides with the quest for fortune; a "good" thing is that which every one desires. Hence, the ordinary definition: "That is good which all strive to obtain." Utilitarian and eudemonistic ethics clings to this meaning of the term and proclaims that the welfare of the individual or of society is the standard of goodness. In his "revaluation of all values" Nietzsche also proceeds from this meaning of the term. The word "good" originally meant as much as important, strong, mighty, beautiful; and "bad" was the adjective used to designate "the common, ordinary man." Now, it must be readily granted that the term "good" often has this meaning; e.g., when we speak of a good house, a good friend, etc., and use these expressions to indicate that a person or an object possesses certain attributes and is useful for some purpose. In that sense the term "good" does not have its own, independent, positive content, but is dependent for its meaning upon the purpose which the person or the object must serve; hence, its meaning varies with different peoples.

For the Greek goodness is "beauty"; for the Roman, noble birth and riches; for the German, that which is proper and "sterling or sound"; and in connection therewith the meaning of "virtue" also varies. In this very general sense the "good" comprises the useful, the agreeable, the esthetical and the ethical good. These synonyms all describe "the good" as something relative, as "that which all strive to obtain." However, the term "the good" is broader than this definition would indicate. We also speak of a "goodness in and by itself." When we take the term "the good" in the sense of "moral or honorable goodness" we have the transition. That which is good in the ethical sense is good in and by itself, regardless of advantages or disadvantages. It has absolute value.

According to Scripture God is the sum-total of all perfections. This is called "metaphysical goodness." All virtues are present in him in an absolute sense. Scripture seldom uses the term "good" in the absolute sense with reference to God. "None is good save one, even God," Mk. 10:18. Lk. 18:19; he is "perfect," Matt. 5:48. But no matter what virtue Scripture predicates of God, it always proceeds from the fact that that particular virtue pertains to God in an absolute sense. Knowledge, wisdom, power, love, justice, etc., pertain to him in a manner altogether unique and divine. His goodness is one with his absolute perfection. In him idea and reality are one. He is pure "idea," "purest actuality." He does not need to become anything, for whatever he is he is eternally. He does not have a purpose outside of himself but is "sufficient, all-sufficient, self-sufficient," Ps. 50:8 ff.; Is. 40:28 ff.; Hab. 2:20. He receives nothing; he only gives. Everything is dependent upon him, he is dependent upon nothing. He does everything with a view to himself, because he cannot rest in anything less than himself. As he is himself the absolutely good, the perfect one, he cannot and may not love anything else except with a view to himself. He cannot and may not be satisfied with anything less than absolute perfection. When he loves others, he loves himself in them: his own virtues, works, gifts. Hence, he is absolutely blessed in himself, the sum-total of all goodness, of all perfection. Aristotle already held that God was the blessed one because he was the unity of thinking and thought, completely transcendent above all desiring, striving, willing. And those who accepted the primacy of the intellect have expressed their agreement with Aristotle and have looked upon thinking, knowing, and contemplation as the seat of blessedness. Now this is correct to the extent in which absolute felicity is a condition of rest, irreconcilable with striving toward a goal, and to the extent in which it presupposes consciousness. Blessedness pertains to rational beings only. In the philosophy of von Hartmann *the unconscious* and in that of Schopenhauer *the will* is that kind of absolute blessedness which itself cries out for deliverance. Hence,

Drews declares in so many words that the attribute of perfection does not pertain to God; a perfect God would be "a complete abstraction" and would render the existence of the universe inexplicable; a God who has everything, who is perfectly blessed and self-sufficient, needs no change, no universe. But this very doctrine of God's absolute infelicity puts us on our guard against accepting the primacy of the will with respect to both God and man, as was done by Duns Scotus and by many others after him. Accordingly, the view of Bonaventura, who regarded the intellect and the will as together the seat of blessedness, is much better. Just as in the case of man blessedness includes soul and body and all his capacities, so in the case of God it does not merely consist in his perfect knowledge, but also in his perfect power, goodness, holiness, etc. "Blessedness is the perfect state of all blessings in their aggregation." But that which is good in itself is also good for others. And as the perfect and blessed one God is the highest good for his creatures, "the supreme good which all strive to obtain, the source of all blessings; the good of every good; the one necessary and all-sufficient good; the goal of all blessings," Ps. 4:7, 8; 73:25, 26. He alone is the "good which is to be enjoyed"; creatures are "good things which are to be used." More than any one else Augustine described God as "the supreme good." In him alone is everything which all creatures need and seek to obtain. He is "the supreme good" for all creatures, albeit in varying degree, depending upon the extent to which each creature shares the divine goodness and is able to enjoy God. He is the one unto whom all creatures strive to attain, whether consciously or unconsciously; he is the object of every one's desire. And the creature finds no rest except in God, in him alone. Thus Christian theologians have always ascribed the supreme good to God, and it did not even enter their minds to say that the seat of the highest good is the moral deed or the virtue of the creature, or duty (Kant), the kingdom of God (Ritschl), love (Drummond), or any other creature. However, as the "supreme good" God is also the source of all virtues. "Since God is perfectly good, he is perpetually beneficent." There is not any good in any creature except it be in and from God. He is the "efficient, exemplary, and final cause" of every good, no matter how it may vary in different creatures. All natural, moral, and spiritual good has its source in him. Scripture is a *Te Deum* in praise of the goodness of the Lord, from which it derives the work of creation and all life and blessing for man and beast, Ps. 8, 19, 36:5-7; 65:12; 147:9; Matt. 5:45; Acts 14:17; Jas. 1:17. Jehovah's goodness is over all his works, Ps. 145:9, and endureth forever, Ps. 136. Again and again all creatures are summoned to praise God's goodness, I Chron. 16:34; II Chron. 5:13; Ps. 34:9; 106:1; 107:1; 118:1; 136:1; Jer. 33:11, etc.

B. **God's goodness manifests itself in a variety of ways. We may distinguish:**

(1) **God's lovingkindness, which usually indicates God's peculiar favor toward his people.** (The Hebrew word is heṣedh, for which the Authorized Version has KINDNESS, LOVING KINDNESS, GOODNESS, MERCY, etc. The American Standard or Revised Version usually has LOVINGKINDNESS, sometimes KINDNESS; in Hos. 6:4 it has GOODNESS in the text and KINDNESS in the margin. Whereas the usual translation in the R. V. is lovingkindness we shall adopt that translation. The Greek word is chrēstotēs which is usually rendered GENTLENESS, KINDNESS; in Gal. 5:22 the R. V. has KINDNESS where the A. V. has GENTLENESS. The word LOVINGKINDNESS covers the meaning of both the Hebrew and the Greek words, as is clear from the foregoing. The Dutch word is GOEDERTIERENHEID —Translator's note).

(2) **God's compassion or pity.** By this is meant God's goodness toward those who are in misery. (The Hebrew word is rahamīn for which the A. V. usually has MERCIES, TENDER MERCES. The R. V. follows the A. V. The Greek words are SPLANCHNA, ELEOS, and OIKTIRMOS. For SPLANCHNA the A. V. has BOWELS or BOWELS OF COMPASSION eight times; the R. V. has COMPASSION, AFFECTION, TENDER MERCIES, HEART. For ELEOS both versions have MERCY. For OIKTIRMOS the A. V. has MERCY, MERCIES; the R. V. has mercies, compassion(s). From this it will be apparent that the translation COMPASSION, PITY, TENDER MERCY is preferred. The Dutch word is BARMHARTIGHEID. — Translator's note).

(3) **God's longsuffering:** his goodness manifested in patience toward those who are deserving of punishment.

(4) **God's grace:** his goodness toward the guilty.

(5) **God's love:** his goodness revealed in self-communication.

This goodness of God varies in accordance with its objects. It is very closely related to *lovingkindness, hesedh,* from *hsd,* stringere, to bind, *chrēstotēs,* in II Cor. 10:1 connected with *prautēs.* Sometimes it is used in a general sense, I Chron. 16:34, but it usually indicates God's special favor *toward his people,* his attachment to his people, to Joseph, Gen. 39:21, to Israel, Num. 14:19, to David, II Sam. 7:15, 22:51, Ps. 18:50, I Chron. 17:13, to the pious, Ps. 5:7. It stands in close relation to God's covenant, Neh. 1:5 ("Jehovah . . . that keepeth covenant and lovingkindness with them that love him and keep his commandments") ; it is the principle of forgiveness, Ps. 6:4, 31:17, 44:26, 109:26, Lam. 3:22; of grace, Ps. 51:1; of comfort, Ps. 119:76; it endureth forever, Is. 54:8, 10; and it is better than life, Ps. 63:3. In Christ it has been revealed in all its riches, Rom. 2:4, II Cor. 10:1, Eph. 2:7, Col. 3:12, Tit. 3:4; and it is imparted to believers, leading them to repentance, Rom. 2:4, 11:22, Gal. 5:22.

God's goodness *toward those who are in misery* is called *compassion* or *pity, rahamim, splanchna,* viscera, misericordia, N. T. eleos, oiktirmos. Again and again Scripture makes mention of God's compassion, Ex. 34:6, Deut. 4:31, II Chron. 30:9, Ps. 86:15, 103:8, 111:4, 112:4, 145:8, etc.; in contrast with man's attitude, II Sam. 24:14, Prov. 12:10, Dan. 9:9, 18. God's compassion is manifold, II Sam. 24:14, Ps. 119:156; great, Neh. 9:19, Ps. 51:12; it faileth not, Lam. 3:22; it is tender, "Like as a father pitieth his children, So Jehovah pitieth them that fear him," Ps. 103:13; it is shown to thousands, Ex. 20:6; and returns after chastisement, Is. 14:1, 49:13 ff., 54:8, 55:7, 60:10, Jer. 12:15, 30:18, 31:20, Hos. 2:22, Mic. 7:19, etc. In the N. T. God, the Father of compassion ("mercies"), II Cor. 1:3, revealed his compassion in Christ, Luke 1:50 ff., who is a compassionate ("merciful") high priest, Matt. 18:27, 20:34, etc., Heb. 2:17; and he furthermore reveals the riches of his compassion ("mercy"), Eph. 2:4, in the salvation of believers, Rom. 9:23, 11:30, I Cor. 7:25, II Cor. 4:1, I Tim. 1:13, Heb. 4:16, etc.

God's goodness manifested in patience *toward those who are deserving of punishment* is called *longsuffering, 'ōrekh appayim, makrothumia, anochē, chrēstotēs.* Scripture also often mentions this attribute, Ex. 34:6, Num. 14:18, Neh. 9:17, Ps. 86:15, 103:8, 145:8, John 4:2, Joel 2:13, Neh. 1:3. It was made manifest in the entire period before Christ's incarnation, Rom. 3:25, and even now it is often shown to sinners, in accordance with Christ's example, I Tim. 1:16, II Pet. 3:15, Rom. 2:4, 9:22, I Pet. 3:20.

More gloriously God's goodness is revealed when it is shown *to those who have deserved nothing but evil;* it is then called *grace, hēn, tehinnāh* from *hānan,* to bow down, to incline towards, *charis,* etc. This word also indicates the favor which one person finds in the sight of another, or the favor which one individual grants to another, Gen. 30:27, 33:8, 10, 47:29, 50:4, etc., Luke 2:52. Ascribed to God, however, its object is never creation in general or heathendom, but only his people. It is granted to Noah, Gen. 6:8; to Moses, Ex. 33:12, 17, 34:9, Job 8:5, 9:15, Dan. 1:9; to the lowly and to those in misery, Prov. 3:34, Dan. 4:27, especially to Israel as a people. The fact that God chose Israel, that he guided, delivered, and redeemed it, that he showered blessings upon it in distinction from other nations, is due to nothing else than God's grace, Ex. 15:13, 16, 19:4, 34:6, 7, Deut. 4:37, 7:8, 8:14, 17, 9:5, 27, 10:14 ff., 33:3, Is. 35:10, 42:21, 43:1, 15, 21, 54:5, 63:9, Jer. 3:4, 19, 31:9, 20, Ezek. 16, Hos. 8:14, 11:1, etc. The keynote of history and law, of the psalms and of the prophets is always: "Not unto us, O Jehovah, not unto us, but unto thy name give glory," Ps. 115:1. He does all things for his name's sake, Num. 14:13 ff., Is. 43:21, 25 ff., 48:9, 11, Ezek. 36:22, etc. Hence, again and again God's grace is extolled and magnified, Ex. 34:6, II Chron. 30:9, Neh.

9:17, Ps. 86:15, 103:8, 111:4, 116:5, Jon. 4:2, Joel 2:13, Zech. 12:10.
In the N. T. grace becomes even deeper and richer in content. Objectively, *charis* means beauty, charm, pardon, Luke 4:22, Col. 4:6, Eph. 4:29, and subjectively, it indicates favor or gracious inclination on the part of the bestower, and gratitude, devotion on the part of the recipient. Ascribed to God *grace is his voluntary, unrestrained, unmerited favor toward guilty* sinners, granting them justification and life instead of the penalty of death, which they deserved. As such it is a virtue and attribute of God, Rom. 5:15, I Pet. 5:10, which is made manifest in sending Christ, who is full of grace, John 1:14 ff., I Pet. 1:13, and in the bestowment of all manner of spiritual and natural blessings, all of which are the gifts of grace, and are themselves called "grace," Rom. 5:20, 6:1, Eph. 1:7, 2:5, 8, Phil. 1:2, Col. 1:2, Tit. 3:7, etc., thus excluding man's merits entirely, John 1:17; Rom. 4:4, 16; 6:14, 23; 11:5 ff.; Eph. 2:8; Gal. 5:3, 4.

Augustine was the first to develop the doctrine of grace, taken not in the sense of a divine attribute, but in the sense of the benefits which God through Christ grants to the church. Grace is usually not treated as one of God's attributes; however, as such it is not altogether wanting; e.g., Th. Aquinas speaks of God's "eternal delight, which is also called the 'grace of predestination,' because God gratuitously and not because of merits has predestinated and elected certain individuals," but the term "grace" is at once taken in a more comprehensive sense, in the sense in which it is treated in the doctrine of salvation, soteriology.

God's goodness revealed in self-communication is called *love*. In the O. T. love as a Divine attribute is not of very frequent occurrence; nevertheless, it is not altogether wanting, cf. Deut. 4:37; 7:8, 13; 10:15; 23:5; II Chron. 2:11; Is. 31:3; 43:4; 48:14; 63:9; Jer. 31:3; Hos. 11:1, 4; 14:5; Zeph. 3:17; Mal. 1:2; furthermore, it is vividly portrayed in God's election of, covenant with, and relation to Israel; it is the relation of a husband toward his wife, of a father toward his son, and of a mother toward her sucking child, Ps. 103:13; Is. 49:15; Hos. 2. Objects of love are not only virtues and attributes, e.g., justice and righteousness, Ps. 11:7; 33:5; 37:28; 45:7; but also persons, Ps. 78:68; 146:8; Prov. 3:12; Deut. 4:37; 7:8, 13; 23:5; II Chron. 2:11; Jer. 31:3; Mal. 1:2.

The N. T. reveals God's love far more gloriously. It describes to us how God gave himself in his beloved Son. The Hebrew word *'āhabhāh* was not rendered *erōs*, the usual term for physical affection, nor *philia* meaning love between relatives, but *agapē*, a word of which there is no trace in the writings of Philo and Josephus, and which indicates God's pure and perfect love far better than any other word could do, just as the Latin caritas (dilectio) is better suited to indicate this love than amor. The relation between Father and Son is described as one of love, John. 3:35; 5:20; 10:17; 14:31; 15:19; 17:24, 26. Moreover, through Christ, who himself loves, and who proved his love by laying down his life, John 15:13, love is bestowed not only upon the world or the church in general, John 3:16; Rom. 5:7; 8:37; I John 4:9, but also upon persons individually, John 14:23; 16:27; 17:23; Rom. 9:13; Gal. 2:20. Even more, God not only *loves,* but he *is* himself *love,* I John 4:8, and his love is the foundation, source, and pattern of our love, I John 4:10. Now it is indeed possible to speak of God's love to creatures or people in general, his love toward the creature, his philanthropy or love toward man, his love of benevolence as distinguished from his love of complacency; but to indicate this relation Scripture usually uses the word "goodness" while the word "love," like "grace" is generally used to indicate God's relation *to his chosen people or church,* love toward the elect, love of communion or friendship. Now the relation between love and the other attributes is not such that the center and core of God's being is love, and that the other attributes are its "modes," for all the attributes are equally God's being; in God there is no higher and lower, no greater and smaller; nevertheless, love is identical with God's being. It is independent, eternal, and immutable as is God himself. Love has its origin in God and via the creature it returns to him. Pseudodionysius, therefore, says that God's love is, "as it were, an eternal circle, moving around with constant revolution, on account of, out of, and with a view to the good, always proceeding from, remaining in, and returning to the same place."

C. **God's holiness.** It is generally admitted that the term "holiness" as used in Scripture indicates a relation of God to the world. The question remains: what kind of a relation? Notice the different answers:

(1) **Menken:** a relation of condescending goodness and grace.

(2) **Baudissin:** God's exaltation above the creature.

(3) **Schultz:** God's burning majesty, inapproachability and inviolability: the infinite distance between God and the creature.

(4) **Diestel and others:** the term does not indicate an essential quality at all; it is merely a Verhältnissbegriff.

Very closely related to God's goodness is his holiness. Formerly it was defined as "purity, free from every stain, wholly perfect and immaculate in every detail." It is not always treated separately next to "God's goodness, perfection, and beauty." Neither Lombard nor Thomas Aquinas discuss it. Protestant theologians defined God's holiness in terms similar to the definition just quoted; it was said to consist in "moral perfection, purity," and was discussed now in connection with

God's justice, then in connection with his goodness or with his veracity or wisdom. The study of the Biblical concept of holiness has gradually brought about a different view concerning the character of this attribute. At present all acknowledge the fact that the concept "holiness" in Old and New Testament indicates a relation of God to the world. But opinions are divided with respect to the exact character of that relation. With a view to passages like Hos. 11:9; Is. 57:15; Ezek. 20:9, ff.; Menken thought of God's condescending goodness or grace. Baudissin, however, was of the opinion that God's holiness was expressive rather of his absolute transcendence above and power over all creatures, and in this view he was supported by Ritschl and others, who appealed to Num. 20:3; Is. 5:16; Ezek. 20:41; 28:25; 36:20, 24; and to those passages in which the terms "glorious," "lofty" are used in connection with "holy," Is. 63:15; 64:11; Jer. 17:12; Ezek. 20:40; etc. Closely related to this is the opinion of Schultz, who, with an appeal to Ex. 15:11; I Sam. 2:2; 6:20; Is. 6:3; 8:14; 10:17, defines God's holiness as his consuming majesty, his inapproachability and inviolability, the infinite distance which separates him from every creature.

As, accordingly, there was the greatest difference of opinion with respect to the question which divine attribute might have been meant when the term "holiness" was used, others thought that this concept does not have an inner, essential quality, but indicates a *relation* (hence, this concept was called a Verhältnissbegriff). It was especially Diestel who defended this theory which was later accepted by many others. Moreover, also those who hold that holiness is more than a relation nevertheless proceed from this idea in their definition of this attribute.

> **D. Holiness means separateness. The term is used with reference to persons or things which have been separated, set apart (esp. for God's service). A twofold process was necessary to render a person or thing holy:**
>
> **(1) separation from other persons or things,**
>
> **(2) consecration to God by means of special laws and ordinances.**
>
> **Applied to God the term "holiness" as used in the O. T. indicates majesty and divinity; it describes God's relation to his people; in the N. T. it has especially a causative meaning: it is the principle of the sanctification of the church.**

The root *qdsh* is usually derived from the root *qd,* meaning to cut, to separate, hence it indicates apartness, separateness. The verb occurs in niph., pi., hiph., and hithp; the adjective is *qadhōsh,* the substantive *qōdhesh;* its antonym is *hōl* from *hillēl,* to make common, defile, profane, Lev. 10:10; I Sam. 21:5, 6; Ezek. 48:14, 15. It is related to *tāhôr* (antonym: *tāmē,* Lev. 10:10), from which it should also be distinguished, as there is a clear distinction in meaning. The word holy is used first of all with reference to all kinds of persons and things which have been separated from their ordinary sphere, and placed in a peculiar relation to God and to his service. Hence, mention is made of holy ground, Ex. 3:5; holy convocation Ex. 12:16; holy Sabbath, Ex. 16:23; holy nation, Ex. 19:6; holy place, Ex. 29:31; holy anointing oil, Ex. 30:25; holy linen coat, Lev. 16:4; holy jubilee, Lev. 25:12; holy house, Lev. 27:14; holy field, Lev. 27:21; holy tithe, Lev. 27:30; holy water, Num. 5:17; holy censers, Num. 16:37; holy firstlings, Num. 18:19; holy camp, Deut. 23:14; holy gold, Josh. 6:19; holy bread, I Sam. 21:4; holy ark, II Chron. 35:3; holy seed, Ez. 9:2; holy city, Neh. 11:1; holy covenant, Dan. 11:28; holy word, Ps. 105:42; the sanctuary, Ex. 15:17; with its Holy place and Holy of holies, holy ones (angels and children of Israel), Deut. 33:2, 3; Job 5:1; 15:15; Ps. 16:3, 10; 32: 6; 89:5, 7, 19; Prov. 9:10; 30:3; Dan. 4:17; 7:18, 22, 25, 27; 7:21; Hos. 12:1; Zech. 14:5. In all these cases the word holy does not yet signify an ethical attribute, but indicates that the persons and objects thus qualified are consecrated unto the Lord and to his service, and that they have been set apart (separated) from the common sphere. Of course the persons and things called holy do not sustain this peculiar relation to God of themselves. By nature God and the creature are separated from and opposed to each other. The entire universe is in itself *hol.* profane, not in a communion with God, unfit for his service; and that which is pure is not even as such holy. Neither are persons and things at all able to sanctify themselves, and to assume by their own power that peculiar relation to God which is expressed by the word holy. God alone sanctifies. It is he who sanctifies Israel, the priesthood, the temple, the altar, certain definite places, persons, and objects; it is he who chooses them in order that they may contribute to his service; it is he who separated them from that which is common. "I am Jehovah who sanctifieth you," Ex. 31:13; Lev. 20:8; 21:8, 15, 23; 22:9, 16, 32; Ezek. 20:12; 37:28. Now this process of sanctification consists of two elements: negatively, a people, person, place, day, or object is chosen, i.e., separated from all others; and positively, these persons or things are dedicated to God's service by means of certain definite regulations. God sanctified the sabbath not only by separating it from the other days of the week, but also by resting the seventh day and hallowing it, Gen. 2:2; Ex. 20:11; Deut. 5:12. He separated the people of Israel by choosing it out of all the nations of the earth, by entering into covenant-relations with it, and by giving it his laws, Ex. 19:4-6. Sanctification is the principle of the giving of the law, of the moral and ceremonial laws, and of God's special revelation to Israel in its entirety; for the purpose of this revelation is Israel's sanctification; Ex. 19:4-6; Lev. 11:44, 45; 19:2; 20:26. Israel is holy because

God makes Israel his own possession, because he comes to dwell among them, and because he is their God, Ex. 19:4-6; 29:43-46. Moreover, within the sphere of Israel God sanctifies the first-born by appropriating them to himself, Ex. 13:2; the people by letting them wash their garments in order to meet their God, Ex. 19:10, 14; the mountain by setting bounds to it, Ex. 19:23; the priests by anointing them, sprinkling them with blood, and putting upon them the garments of the priesthood, Ex. 28:3, 41; 29:1 ff., 21; the tabernacle and the altar by anointing them, Ex. 29:37; 40:9 ff.; Lev. 8:10, 11; Num. 7:1; the anointing oil by causing it to be prepared in a peculiar manner, Ex. 30:22; ff.; the Nazirites by causing them to live according to specific ordinances, Num. 6:2; etc.

Whatever is holy lives a peculiar life, bears a peculiar character, has been separated from the common sphere and from the common law, e.g., it may not be touched, Ex. 19:23, 24; it may not be eaten, Ex. 29:33; it may not be used, Ex. 30:32 ff.; it sanctifies whatsoever touches it, Ex. 30:29; Lev. 10:2 ff.; Num. 1,:51, 53; 3:10, 38; Is. 8:14. The positive act by means of which a thing is sanctified is not always expressed: at times sanctification seems to exist in separation only, Lev. 25:10; 27:14; Josh. 7:13; 20:7; Judg. 17:3; I Sam. 7:1; II Sam. 8:11; I Chron. 18:11; etc. Nevertheless, sanctification is something more than a setting apart; it means that by means of washing, anointing, sacrifice, sprinkling with blood, etc., a thing is made to lose its common character, and is made to bear a peculiar stamp, which it must reveal everywhere. Now the ceremonies necessary for sanctification indicate that also the impurity and sinfulness of the creature come into consideration and must be taken away in that manner. Washing, sacrifice, sprinkling with blood, and anointing served to take away the sinful character of a thing, and to consecrate it, Lev. 8:15; 16:16; Job 1:5; etc.; holy and pure are synonymous therefore, Ex. 30:35; Lev. 16:19; but this does not mean that purity covers the entire concept of holiness. Though the idea of purity is indeed included in that of holiness, nevertheless, the latter is not wholly expressed by the former. Holiness has a far broader meaning in the O. T., especially in the law. The distinction between outward and inward purity is not inherent in the Mosaic legislation as such, but has been introduced later on. Holy is whatever has been chosen and set apart by Jehovah, has been deprived of the character which it possessed in common with other things, and has by means of special ceremonies been given a distinctive character, so that it is now living in this new condition in accordance with those laws which have been prescribed for it. Israel is a holy nation because it has been chosen and set apart by God, has been accepted into the covenant, so that it must henceforth conduct itself in accordance with all God's laws, including the ceremonial. Holy is whatever is in harmony with those special laws which God has prescribed for it; holiness is perfection, not only in the sense of purity, but according to Israel's peculiar legislation, in the most comprehensive sense, as signifying religious, ethical, ceremonial, inward and outward perfection.

Now the idea of holiness becomes clear especially when we consider what it signifies when it is ascribed to God. Cremer correctly observed that holiness is not primarily a relation of the creature to the Creator, but vice versa, and that it pertains to God in the first place, and to the creature in a secondary sense. Creatures are not holy in themselves, neither are they able to sanctify themselves. All sanctification and holiness proceeds from God. Jehovah is holy; hence, he desires a holy nation, a holy priesthood, a holy dwelling, etc., Ex. 19:6; 29:43; Lev. 11:44, 45; 19:2; 20:26; 21:8; Deut. 28:9, 10. Holiness is often ascribed to Jehovah, Lev. 11:44, 45; 19:2; 20:26; 21:8; Josh. 24:19; I Sam. 2:2; 6:20; Ps. 22:3; 99:5, 9; Is. 5:16; 6:3; etc. Isaiah often uses the name "the Holy One of Israel," 29:23; 40:25; 43:15; 49:7; 62:12; cf. II Kings 19:22; Ezek. 39:7, Hab. 1:12; 3:3. Furthermore, mention is made of God's holy name, Lev. 20:3; 22:32; I Chron. 16:35; Ps. 99:3; 103:1; 111:9; etc.; of his holy arm, Is. 52:10; and of his holy majesty, II Chron. 20:21. Now when the word holy is ascribed to Jehovah, it does not signify one definite attribute. On the contrary, God is called holy in a very general sense: in connection with every revelation which impresses man with God's exalted majesty. Holiness is synonymous with divinity, Amos. 4:2. Jehovah is God, and not man, the Holy One in their midst, Hos. 11:9, the God or the Holy One of Israel. God's holiness is revealed in his entire relation to his people, in election, in the covenant, in his special revelation, in his dwelling among them, etc., Ex. 29:43-46; Lev. 11:44, 45; 20:26; Ps. 114:1, 2. This relation of God to Israel is rich in content. God himself has established it by means of the laws which he gave to Israel. Israel's entire legislation has for its principle Jehovah's holiness, and for its purpose the sanctification of the people. What this sanctification by Jehovah implies becomes evident in every part of the law: the people are holy when they live in harmony with that law. As the Holy One he gave himself to Israel, and dwells among them; furthermore, he abides faithful to his word and to his covenant, Ps. 89:34 ff.; and again and again delivers Israel. God is the Holy One of Israel, Israel's God, who is what his law reveals him to be. For Israel God's holiness means deliverance, Ps. 22:3, 4; 89:18; 98:1; 103:1; 105:3; 145:21; hearing of prayer, Ps. 3:4; 20:6; 28:2; comfort, Is. 5:16; Hab. 1:12; trust, Ps. 22:3, 4; 33:21; Is. 10:20. His holiness prevents Israel's destruction. As the Holy One he is Israel's Creator, Deliverer, and

King, Is. 43:14, 15; 49:7; 54:5; 62:12. Accordingly, his redeemed
people thank and praise him as the Holy One, Ps. 30:5; 71:22; 97:12;
I Chron. 16:10, 35. But God's holiness is also the principle of punishment and chastisement: when Israel breaks the covenant, desecrates
God's name, and transgresses his laws, it is God's holiness which
causes him to mete out punishment; his holiness demands that Israel
be holy, and sanctify him as the Holy One, Lev. 11:44, 45; 19:2;
20:7, 26; 21:8. In case of disobedience he chastens Israel, I Kings
9:3-7; II Chron. 7:16-20. The same holiness which is principle of
redemption and object of praise, is for the transgressors principle of
destruction and object of fear. In the latter case holy is synonymous
with jealous, Josh. 24:19; great and terrible, Ex. 15:11; Ps. 99:3;
111:9; high and lofty, Is. 6:3; 47:15. As the Holy One no one is like
unto him, Ex. 15:11; I Sam. 2:2; Is. 40:25. To sanctify him means
to fear him, Is. 8:13; 29:23. When men desecrate his name and his
covenant, he sanctifies himself by means of righteousness and judgment,
Is. 5:16; Ezek. 28:22. Even then, however, he does not forget his
people. For Israel his holiness remains the cause of their deliverance,
Is. 6:13; 10:20; 27:13; 29:23, 24; 43:15; 49:7; 52:10; etc.; Jer. 51:5;
Hos. 11:8, 9; and will finally reveal itself in this: that the Gentiles
will know that he is Jehovah, Jer. 50:29; Ezek. 36:23; 39:7; and that
he delivers Israel from all its iniquity, Ezek. 36:23; 39:7.

With this last idea God's holiness of which we find mention in the
N. T. is closely connected. Even the word chosen to represent the idea
is very significant. *Semnos* from *sebomai* indicates that which invites
reverence, Phil. 4:8; I Tim. 3:8, 11; Tit. 2:2; *hieros* merely indicates
a relation to the Deity, I Cor. 9:31; II Tim. 3:15; Heb. 8:2; 9:8, etc.;
*hagnos* means pure, chaste, II Cor. 11:2; Tit. 2:5, etc. These words
are never used with reference to God. In the N. T. God is called
*hosios,* Rev. 15:4; 16:5; cf. Heb. 7:26; and especially *hagios,* Luke
1:49; John 17:11; I John 2:20; I Pet. 1:15, 16; Rev. 4:8; 6:10. In
the O. T. God's holiness is not yet definitely distinguished from all the
other attributes, but indicates the entire relation in which Jehovah
stands to Israel, and Israel to Jehovah. Hence, Jehovah was called the
Holy One of Israel, who had given himself completely to Israel, and
who through various means keeps Israel as his possession. Hence
also, the people's sanctification is not only religious and ethical, but
also ceremonial, civil, and political in character. Just as holiness when
ascribed to God, was not as yet considered to be a distinct attribute to
be coördinated with the other attributes, even so when applied to
Israel it is very comprehensive in meaning, comprising all the various
phases of life. But when in the N. T. "the Holy One of God" appears
Mk. 1:24; Luke 4:34; Acts 3:14; 4:27; between whom and the world

there exists an absolute antithesis, John 15:18; and who devotes and consecrates himself to God in the most absolute sense, John 17:19; God's holiness ceases to be the principle of punishment and chastisement, and through the Holy Spirit—who is called by that name in only a few *O. T.* passages Ps. 51:13; Is. 63:10; but in the *N. T.* regularly—becomes the principle of sanctification of the church. From now on the church is the "holy nation," I Pet. 2:5, 9; Eph. 2:19; 5:27; consisting of "elect individuals, holy and without blemish," Eph. 1:1, 4; Col. 1:2, 22; 3:12; I Cor. 7:14; entirely freed and purified from sin, and eternally dedicated to God with soul and body. Holiness, which is the very foundation of Jehovah's peculiar relation to Israel, and which claims Israel's undivided service, finally culminates most gloriously in the fact that in Christ God gives himself to the church, which he redeems and purifies from all its iniquities.

**E. God's righteousness. God is called righteous because he rewards every man according to his work. In Scripture God's remunerative justice is much more prominent than his retributive justice. The Lord grants his righteousness to his people.**

There is a very close relation between the holiness and the righteousness of God. The words *çaddîq, çedheq, çedhāqāh* indicate the state of a person who adheres to the law. The primary meaning seems to be the forensic; *çaddîq* is the person who is righteous before the law, and must, therefore, be acquitted, *hiçedîq,* antonym of *hirshia',* Deut. 25:1. It also indicates the person who, in an argument, has the right on his side, Job 11:2; 33:12, 32; Is. 41:26; hence, the noun can also mean the justice or truth of an assertion or statement, Ps. 52:5; Prov. 16:13; Is. 45:23. Furthermore, it means, in general, that a person is in the right whether or not his case is passed upon by a court of justice; that he is on the side of right; that he is righteous and just, and that he is in harmony with the law, Gen. 30:33; 38:26; I Sam. 24:18; Ps. 15:2. In close connection with this is the meaning of the word in the religious sphere and its meaning when applied to God. The Pentateuch contains only two passages in which *çaddîq* is used with reference to God, Ex. 9:27; Deut. 32:4. God's righteousness is revealed first of all in history, in the government of the world, and in his providential guidance of Israel, and is, therefore, especially developed by the psalmists and prophets. God's righteousness is revealed everywhere, and is even spoken of with reference to his preservation of the beasts of the field, Ps. 36:6. God is the Judge of all the earth, Gen. 18:25. His righteousness consists in the fact that he grants every man according to his work, that he treats the righteous and the wicked distinctly, Gen. 18:25. It is worthy of special attention, however, that in Scripture God's remunerative justice is much more prominent than his retributive justice. Diestel called attention to this fact; others (cf. Ritschl) stated their agreement with him.

Scripture does indeed contain the idea of God's retributive justice (later on called jutitia vindicativa). God does not hold the guilty innocent, Ex. 20:7; Nah. 1:3. He does not spare, Ezek. 7:4, 9, 27; 8:18; 9:10. He does not regard persons, nor does he take a reward, Deut. 10: 17; his judgment is impartial, Job. 13:6-12; 22:2-4; 34:10-12; 35:6, 7. He is righteous and all his judgments are righteous judgments, Ps. 119:137; 129:4; the punishment of the wicked is often ascribed to God's righteousness, Ex. 6:5; 7:4; Ps. 7:12; 9:5-9; 28:4; 52:13, 73; 96:10, 13; II Chron. 12:5-7; Neh. 9:33; Lam. 1:18; Is. 5:16; 10:22; Dan. 9:14; Rom. 2:5; II Thess. 1:5-10. Nevertheless, it is true that the punishment of the wicked is usually derived from God's *wrath*, and that God's *righteousness* is by Scripture usually represented as the principle of the salvation of God's people. There are many Hebrew words which designate God's wrath or anger: *qeçeph, aph, etc.*, usually translated wrath, anger *hēmāh*, often translated fury; *ebhrāh*, usually translated wrath; the LXX and the N. T. have *thumos* for inward wrath, and *orgē* for wrath which manifests itself, cf. Rom. 2:8, where both are used. This wrath, which is indicated by words whose roots signify: to burn, and which, therefore, designates a strong and uncontrollable emotion, is often compared to a burning, Lev. 10:6; Deut. 32:22; Ps. 21:9; a fire, Deut. 32:22; II Kings 23:26; Ps. 2:12; Is. 30:27; Jer. 15:14; 17:4, and is, therefore, called fierce, Ps. 58:9; Deut. 13:17; II Chron. 28:11; Job 20:23; Is. 13:9, 13; and smoking, Deut. 29:30; Ps. 74:1. It is aroused by Israel's theocratic sins against God's covenant: as, perjury, Josh. 9:20; desecration of God's service, Lev. 10:6; Num. 1:53; 16:46; 18:5; idolatry, Deut. 9:19; the sin of Manasseh, II Kings 23:26; of David, I Chron. 27:24; and especially by the sins of the people, which merited various punishments, Is. 42:24, 25; Jer. 7:20; 21:5; 32:31; etc.; Lam. 2:2 ff.; 3:43; Ezek. 5:13 ff.; 7:3; 13:13; etc.; Zech. 7:12 ff. This anger is terrible, Ps. 76:7; and causes fear, Ps. 2:5; 90:7; anguish, Job 21:17; Ps. 102:10; punishment, Ps. 6:1; 38:1; Jer. 10:24; destruction, Jer. 42:18; II Chron. 29:8; etc.; cf. Job 9:5; Ps. 21:9; 56:7; 85:4. According to Deut. 6:15; 29:20; 32:21; Job 16:9; Nah. 1:2, Jehovah's anger, hatred, wrath, and jealousy are closely related. Usually this hatred has sinful deeds as its object, Deut. 16:22; Ps. 45:7; Prov. 6:16; Jer. 44:4; Hos. 9:15; Am. 5:12; Zech. 8:17; Rev. 2:6; exceptionally sinful persons are its object, Ps. 5:5; Mal. 1:3; Rom. 9:13. God's wrath, *ekdikēsis*, Nah. 1:2; I Thess. 4:6; Deut. 32:35; Rom. 12:19; Heb. 10:30; sometimes reveals itself in judgments, Num. 31:2, 3; Judg. 5:2; 11:36; 16:28; II Sam. 4:8; 22:48; Ps. 18:48; 99:8; but will not manifest itself in all its power until the day of wrath, Deut. 32:41, 42; Ps. 94:1; 149:7; Is. 34:8; 35:4; 59:17; 61:2, 4; Jer. 46:10; 50:15, 28; 51:11; Ezek. 25:14; Mic. 5:14. God's jealousy, *qināh, zēlos,* mentioned frequently, Ex. 20:9; 34:14; Deut. 4:24; 5:9; 6:15; Josh. 24:19; Nah. 1:2; results from the fact that Israel, Jehovah's bride, disregards the rights of her husband and bridegroom, Jehovah, by worshipping other gods, Deut. 32:16, 21; II Kings 14:22; Ps. 78:58; Ezek. 8:3, 5; and reveals itself in the fact that Jehovah, on his part, provokes Israel to jealousy by choosing another people, Deut. 32:21; Ps. 79:5; Ezek. 5:13; 16:38; 23:25; Rom. 10:19.

Next to all these virtues God's righteousness is usually taken "in a favorable sense" and described as that attribute by virtue of which God justifies the righteous, and exalts them to glory and honor. The manner in which the O. T. concept of righteousness developed can to a certain extent be traced. Even in the law every judge and also every individual Israelite is warned not to wrest the justice due to the poor, not to slay the righteous, not to take a bribe, and not to oppress the sojourner, the widow, and the orphan, Ex. 23:6-9. Righteousness (justice) consists especially in this: that persons are not respected in judgment; that the small and the great shall be heard alike; that the judges shall not be afraid of the face of man, for the judgment is God's, Deut. 1:16, 17; 16:19; Lev. 19:20. The righteous was to be justified, and the wicked was to be condemned, Deut. 25; this was to be the rule for kings, judges, and for every individual Israelite. The actual situation, however, was not at all in harmony with this rule: psalmists, prophets, writers of proverbs again and again complain about the terrible fact that there was no justice for the poor, for widows, orphans, strangers, for those in misery, even though the right was completely on their side, even though they are righteous and pious; hence, the truly pious were often unable to obtain justice; both in the courts of justice and in daily life they were evilly judged, suppressed, and neglected. Hence, they long for the future, for the Messiah, who will be the *righteous* Branch, Jer. 23:5, who will be righteous, Zech. 9:9; and who will not judge after the sight of the eyes, but with righteousness, Is. 11:3-5; and whose judgment, therefore, will consist in this: that "he will have pity on the poor and needy (who were now neglected and suppressed), and the souls of the needy he will save," Ps. 72:12-14. Hence, exercising righteousness would consist especially in delivering the needy; doing justice becomes with reference to these needy ones a deed of grace and compassion, as it were. All this is applied to God; rather, it is true first of all of God. Jehovah is the real Judge, he judges according to righteousness and not after the sight of the eyes; hence the judges must judge thus, Ex. 23:7; Deut. 1:17; and hence Messiah will once judge in that manner. God is perfect and righteous, and acts in accordance with justice. His righteousness consists especially in this: that he recognizes the justice of the righteous, and that he causes it to be brought to light and to triumph. He is righteous because he grants salvation to the pious, because he establishes them, Ps. 7:9; helps them, 31:1; answers them, 65:5. hears them, 143:1; delivers them, 143:11; revives them, 119:40; acquits them, 34:22; grants unto them the justice due unto them, 35:23; etc.; while the wicked do not come into his righteousness, 69:27, 28. Hence, Jehovah's righteousness is not contrasted with his lovingkindness, as is his anger, Ps. 69:24 ff.; but it is synonymous with lovingkindness, Ps. 22:31; 33:5; 35:28; 40:10; 51:15; 89:14; 145:7; Is. 45:21; Jer. 9:24; Hos. 2:18; Zech. 9:9. The manifestation of God's righteousness is at the same time the showing forth of his grace, Ps. 97:11, 12; 112:4; 116:5; 119:15-19. Even the forgiveness of sins is due to God's *righteousness,* Ps. 51:15; 103:17; I John 1:9. Hence, the revelations of that righteousness are deeds of redemption, deeds of salvation and deliverance, Judg. 5:11; I Sam. 12:7; Ps. 103:6; Is. 45:24, 25; Mic. 6:5. Especially Isaiah makes this soteriological character of God's righteousness very clear. Israel is, indeed, a sinful people and merits heavy punishments, 43:26; 48:1; 53:11; 57:12; 59:4; 64:5; nevertheless, over against the heathen nations Israel is in the right; in spite of all its transgressions, it favors a righteous cause; it is on the side of right. Hence, after sufficient chastisement God's righteousness will assert itself, and Israel's right will be acknowledged, and it will be delivered from all its misery, 40:1 ff.; 54:5, 7 ff.; 57:15 ff.; 61:1 ff.; etc. The same is true in regard to all God's children. Personally they are sinners, they are guilty of all manner of iniquity, and are a poor and needy people; but they favor a righteous cause, they trust in the Lord, and they expect that he will grant them justice, that he will fight their battle, and will give unto them the victory of salvation, Ps. 17:1 ff; 18:20, 21; 34:15: 103:6; 140:12. This salvation does not consist, exclusively, of outward blessings of prosperity and peace, but especially in this, that God grants unto his people forgiveness of sins, that he pours his Spirit into their hearts, that he grants unto them a new heart, and that he writes his law in their hearts, so that they walk perfectly before his countenance; briefly, salvation consists in this, that God will be their God in the fullest sense, and they in like manner will be his people, Is. 43:25; Is. 31:33, 34; 32:39, 40; 33:8; Ezek. 11:19; 36:25; Joel 2:28 ff. Moreover, this people, which confesses God's name and stands on the side of right is even now sinful and impure, Is. 43:26 ff.; 53:4-6; 59:2 ff., 12ff.; and no one else than Jehovah can deliver it from this sin; "only in Jehovah . . . is righteousness and strength," Is. 45:24; not only for

Israel but also for the nations, Is. 2:2 ff.; 45:22. Jehovah will grant his righteousness unto his people through the Messiah, who will bring forth justice to the Gentiles, Is. 42:1; and he will create a new heaven and a new earth, in which dwelleth righteousness, Is. 65:17 ff.; Jehovah's righteousness in relation to his people consists in this that he grants his righteousness unto them. Although in this manner righteousness and salvation are brought into very close relation to each other, it is nevertheless, incorrect to regard them as synonyms. Righteousness is not identical with favor, compassion, grace; neither does it mean covenant-faithfulness (Diestel, Ritschl, Kautzsch, and others); nor is salvation the negative side, and righteousness the positive, as Davidson would have it. Righteousness is always a forensic concept; but in the O. T. the most important task and the strongest evidence of righteousness is the protection of the oppressed, and the deliverance of the needy from the injustice and persecution to which they are subjected. That was the content of *God's* righteousness; hence, this execution of judgment in behalf of the needy became the primary task of the earthly king and judge. This idea of righteoussness is also found in the N. T. The "righteousness of God" through the Messiah brings righteousness to God's people, and in Christ it is a means of reconciliation by virtue of which he himself is proved to be righteous, and is able to justify the believer, and furthermore to grant forgiveness unto his own, I John 1:9; and also salvation, John 17:25; II Tim. 4:8. Finally, even God's anger and jealousy, hatred and wrath, become subservient to the salvation and redemption of his people. His anger is but for a moment, Ps. 30:5; 78:38; 85:3; 103:9; Is. 10:25; 48:9; 51:22; 54:8; Jer. 3:12 ff.; 32:37; Ezek. 43:7-9; Dan. 9:16; Hos. 14:5; Mic. 5:18; and his jealousy shall depart from Israel, Ezek. 16:42; 36:6 ff.; Zech. 8:2 ff. Then his anger, jealousy, and wrath shall be turned against the enemies of his people in the great day of anger and wrath, Deut. 32:41, 42; Is. 13:2 ff.; 26:11; 30:27; 34:8; 35:4; 42:11; 59:17; 61:2, 4; 63:3 ff.; Jer. 10:25; 46:10; 50:15, 28; 51:11; Lam. 3:66; Ezek. 25:14 ff.; 38:19; 39:25; Mic. 5:14; Nah. 1:2; Hab. 3:12; Zeph. 1:15 ff.; 2:2; etc., and thereby shall become a source of blessing and deliverance for Israel, II Kings 19:31; Is. 9:6; 37:32; Joel 2:18; Zech. 1:14; 8:2. And in the same manner the N. T. declares that although even now the wrath of God abideth on the wicked, John 3:36; Eph. 2:3; I Thess. 2:16, nevertheless, the manifestation of that wrath in all its terror is reserved for the future, Mt. 3:7; Luke 3:7; 21:23; Rom. 5:9; I Thess. 1:10; 5:9; Eph. 5:6; 3:6; Rev. 6:16, 17; 11:18; 14:10; 16:19; 19:15.

**F. Development of the concept "righteousness or justice" in theology:**

(1) In dogmatics the term "righteousness" has a broader meaning than in Scripture.

(2) According to the Gnostics and according to many people living to-day there is an antithesis between righteousness and grace.

(3) According to Scripture righteousness rests upon an ethical basis: although creatures have nothing whereby they can place God under obligation, God has given them certain rights. When these rights were forfeited through sin, God established a covenant of nature and a covenant of grace in order to restore them. Hence, our "rights" are not the result of a "social contract," neither are they "natural rights," but they proceed from God's gracious will.

(4) God's justice in determining the rights of his creatures is called "legislative justice." This legislative justice was not brought about by the entrance of sin; because of sin, however, justice must be maintained, if necessary, even by force. Hence, there must be "distributive justice" by which we mean the maintenance of legislative justice. This distributive justice is called "remunerative justice" when it manifests itself in rewarding obedience, and "retributive justice" when it asserts itself in punishing disobedience.

(5) Remunerative justice does not imply that man is ever able to merit anything, neither does retributive justice indicate that in the abstract, without punishment there can be no forgiveness; but God's covenant, his name, his honor demand that his people be saved and the wicked be punished.

In dogmatics the term "justice" was generally given a much more comprehensive connotation than in Scripture. Sometimes its meaning was so broad that it even included God's perfection or holiness; justice, thus defined, was virtue itself and the sum-total of all virtues; applied to God it was his perfect harmony with himself, "divine justice." Nevertheless, on the whole the term was given a more restricted meaning. Thus, in his Ethics, Aristotle had defined justice as "the virtue because of which each possesses what belongs to himself"; it is possible only in a society of individuals who can possess a greater or lesser quantity of goods; it does not pertain to the gods because there is no standard which determines how much they may possess, neither does it pertain to brutes for they cannot be said to possess anything. Accordingly, justice presupposes that there are certain rights established by the lawgiver; hence, we speak of "legislative justice"; furthermore, that by means of treaties and contracts these rights are respected; this we call "reciprocal or commutative justice"; and finally, that the rights which exist are maintained; this gives us "distributive justice." They are maintained either by means of rewarding obedience; hence, we speak of "remunerative justice," or by means of punishing disobedience; this is called "retributive or punitive justice." In every case justice is "the constant and perpetual desire to grant to every individual his due." All this was applied to God. Thus the term "justice" or "righteousness" was given a much broader meaning in dogmatics than in Scripture. Now against this use of the term in theology there is no decisive objection if the twofold sense in which the term is used be constantly kept in mind, for the ideas as such which are treated under this concept in dogmatics are all very clearly revealed in Holy Writ. The use of the term in its broader sense even has an advantage, namely, that it affords the opportunity to defend every aspect of God's justice against its assailants. The gnostics, especially Marcion, took great delight in contrasting the law with the Gospel, works with faith, flesh with spirit, thus also the God of anger, of wrath, of *justice,* who revealed himself in the O. T., with the God of love and grace who revealed himself in the N. T., particularly in Christ. But this error survived gnosticism and was proclaimed in this very sense at a much later date; the attack was directed especially against God's punitive justice which was considered to be in conflict with his love. Now it must certainly be admitted that in connection with God's justice many difficulties present themselves, e.g., there can be no law or standard which is higher than God so that he would be subject to it, for his will is the supreme law; mere creatures cannot establish any right, claim, or merit before God, for they have received everything as a gift out of his hands and have not given him anything in return; they have no claim to reward for even when they shall have done all the things that were commanded them, they are unprofitable bondservants. Furthermore, it would seem that there is nothing in God's nature that would make it necessary for him to deal out punishment; why would it be impossible for him, the Almighty One, to forgive without demanding satisfaction or exacting punishment? However, in order that we may not wander too far away from the Biblical concept of justice it may be better to discuss all these questions in connection with the doctrine of God's will and freedom. In Scripture justice is not a property of God's absolute Lordship but rests on an ethical foundation. Even though it is certainly true that a creature has no inherent rights and can never place God under obligation, Rom. 11:35; I Cor. 4:7, and although "commutative or reciprocal justice" is altogether out of the question, nevertheless, it is God himself, who, as it were, accords certain rights to his creatures. By virtue of creation every creature has received a certain distinct nature. Now, there are laws and ordinances for all created things; there are rights which are implied in the very existence and nature of all being. Especially have such rights been granted to rational creatures, and they apply respectively to every sphere of life: to mind and heart, soul and body, science and art, family and society, religion and morals. And when man forfeits these rights, then God establishes a "covenant of nature," revealed to Noah, and a covenant of grace with Abraham; and by means of these covenants he of pure grace again endows his creatures with all kinds of rights, and by means of an oath binds himself to maintain these rights. Thus, by the grace of God an order of justice was established both in the realm of nature and in the realm of grace, an order containing all kinds of instructions, ordinances, and laws which God himself establishes and maintains. However, in Scripture these institutions and rights are not derived from God's justice or righteousness—what kind of justice would it have to be to place him under obligation?—but from his holiness and grace. And, to be sure, this is a more accurate representation than the one which refers these rights, etc., to God's "legislative *justice*." Nevertheless, the latter way of speaking is not incorrect if we do not conceive of it in this sense, that, by virtue of some principle of *justice*, God granted and was morally obligated to grant these rights to his creatures. There is, however, an element of truth in the representation which we have criticised. It is this: God is, indeed, the supreme Lawgiver, and the entire judicial order with respect to every sphere is rooted in him. The final, deepest, and only ground of every right is not a "social contract or compact" nor an independent "natural right" nor the "verdict of history" but the *will of God,* viewed not as "absolute dominion" but as a good and gracious will. God's grace is the fountain of all rights.

Furthermore, God also *maintains* that judicial order in every sphere of life. He who is justice in person and the source of all rights is also the "arbiter and vindicator of justice." His "legislative justice" implies "judicial justice." Only when justice is maintained, if necessary by means of force and punishment, does it deserve the name *justice.* To be sure, the order of justice does not as such imply the means of execution. Had sin not entered, the order of justice would have existed just the same, but all creatures would have obeyed voluntarily, i.e., gladly and of their own accord. The fact that justice has "teeth," i.e., that it maintains itself by means of compulsion and force, though always in harmony with its own nature, is wholly due to the entrance of sin into the universe. Not the existence as such of the regime of justice but rather the compulsory character which it now bears is due to sin. But this compulsory character, far from being arbitrary or accidental, is so indispensable at the present time that apart from it we cannot even conceive of justice, a fact which is attested by our own conscience. The moral order, far from being opposed to the judicial, upholds, presupposes, and supports the latter. Justice constitutes a very important element in morality. By *righteousness* God maintains his grace and love and causes them to triumph. Those who follow Marcion and accept an antithesis between law and grace fail to do justice to the relation between the moral and the judicial order and do not understand the glorious character of righteousness. Accordingly, by reason of its very nature God's "justice or righteousness" must needs be "judicial justice"; hence, on the one hand, "remunerative," on the other hand, "retributive." Not that a creature would ever have any inherent claim to reward, nor that it would be wholly impossible as far as the creature is concerned to receive forgiveness apart from punishment; but because of his covenant, because of the order of justice which he himself has established once for all, and because of his name and honor, God is obliged to save his people and to punish the wicked. Thus only is justice able to reign and to triumph. The motto, "Let justice be done though the world perish," contains an element of truth. Nevertheless, Scripture emphasizes this much more beautiful thought: justice must be done that the world may be *saved*.

**IV. Volitional Attributes: God's Will and Omnipotence. According To Scripture God's Will Is the Final Ground of All Existence and of All That Ever Happens. Plato, Descartes, Hegel and the Mystics Are In Conflict With This Scriptural Position. God's Will Toward Himself Is Called His Necessary Will; His Will Toward the Creature Is His Free Will. God's Will Is Not Arbitrary But In Complete Harmony With His Goodness, Holiness, Etc. There Is A Distinction Between God's Will Which Prescribes What We Should Do, i.e., His Preceptive Will, and God's Will Which Declares What He Will Do, i.e., His Decretive Will. The Two Are Not Opposed To Each Other But In Complete Harmony. Scripture Teaches God's Omnipotence Everywhere. Over Against the Error of Nominalism Scripture Maintains that God Can Do Only That Which Is In Harmony With His Other Attributes. Over Against the Opposite Error of Pantheism Scripture Maintains that God Is Able To Do More Than He Actually Does.**

**A. God's will and sovereignty.** According to Scripture God's will is the final ground of all existence and of all that ever happens.

We shall now discuss those attributes which pertain to God as Sovereign. God is the Creator, and therefore the Proprietor, Owner, and Lord of all things; apart from him there is neither existence nor ownership; he alone has absolute authority; his will is decisive everywhere and always. Again and again Scripture makes mention of God's sovereign will, *hēpheç, raçôn, çebhû*, Dan. 4:35; 6:18; *thelēma, boulema*. That will is the final ground of all things and of their being what they are. Everything is derived from it: creation and preservation, Rev. 4:11; government, Prov. 21:1; Dan. 4:35; Eph. 1:11; Christ's suffering, Luke 22:42; election and reprobation, Rom. 9:15 ff.; regeneration, Jas. 1:18; sanctification, Phil. 2:13; the sufferings of believers, I Pet. 3:17; our life and destiny, Jas. 4:15; Acts 18:21; Rom. 15:32; and even the smallest and least significant things, Matt. 10:29; etc.

B. **Various views in regard to the "will" of God:**

(1) On the basis of Scripture Christian theology views the will of God as the final and deepest ground of all existence.

(2) Philosophy has sought a deeper ground: Plato tried to derive the universe from the "ideas"; according to Descartes and Hegel absolute "mind" is the final ground of existence. Hegel's "absolute mind" is a mere abstraction: actually it is nothing, potentially everything.

(3) According to Schelling the "will" is the ground of all existence. He proved the unsatisfactory character of rationalism. However, Schelling's "will" is an unconscious yearning, a blind force. Cf. also Schopenhauer and Von Hartmann.

(4) Mysticism advances the objection that, since all willing is a striving after something which one does not possess, therefore, willing implies imperfection; hence, God can have no will. Answer: to will does not always mean to strive after something not yet possessed; it also means to delight in the possession of an object.

(5) God's will is his delight in himself and his delight in his creatures for his own name's sake.

Now in accordance with this Scriptural representation Christian theology also rendered homage to God's will and viewed it as the final and deepest ground of all existence, the end of all contradiction. "The will of the Creator is the nature of every created object." Philosophy has never been satisfied with this and has ever been trying to find another and a deeper explanation of the universe. Plato tried to derive the visible world from the *ideas,* which he considered to be the real essence, but he failed. Aristotle conceived of godhood as pure "idea or form," as "intelligence of intelligence," to which all "production" and "action" are foreign, and although he viewed it as being also "first mover," he completely fails to explain the character of this motion and of God's relation to the universe. Among the Stoics this led to pantheism: God is the reason, the spirit, the soul of the universe; the universe is God's body, garment, manifestation. Modern philosophy indicates a return to this type of rationalism. Descartes regarded thought as the essence of spirit and the ground of being. By a process of logical reasoning this led to Hegel's philosophy of identity. The absolute· is absolute reason, pure thought, not, however, in the sense of a universe of ideas, as with Plato, nor in the sense of true reality; but it is thought *as such,* i.e., devoid of all content; it is not *being* but *becoming; actually* it is nothing; *potentially,* everything. And this theory, a mere philosophical abstraction, had to serve as a solution of the problem of the universe! It soon became evident that this "explanation" failed to explain anything. Hegel's "solution" does not bring us any farther than that of Plato and Aristotle. From this abstract oneness the manyness of the universe could not have come forth; thought, thus conceived, could not produce essence, being. The fact that this philosophy contained even a semblance of truth was due to a play upon words. Another name which Hegel gave to this "absolute thought" was "pure potentiality." However, dialectically this logical potentiality was changed into "real and absolute power" and thus it *seemed* to be able to produce all things. But this was merely a trick of dialectics, which was not able to give lasting satisfaction. Opposition to Hegel's philosophy arose from many sides. Rationalism had outlived its usefulness; idealism failed to explain essence; the primacy of the intellect suffered bankruptcy; it had become evident that existence, that a universe, could never be derived from "absolute thought." Hence, for a change, it was decided to try "the primacy of the will" as a possible explanation of the universe!

This attempt was made by Schelling in his second period. Via theosophy he returned to the cabala and neo-platonism. Plotinus had already taught that God was "his own cause," the product of his own will and power, and that the will was the deepest essence preceding even the intellect. And in accordance with this view Schelling declared the will to be the final principle of the existence both of infinite and of finite being. In his philosophical investigations concerning the essence of human freedom, published in the year 1809, he already took this position. He declared, "In the last and highest resort there is no essence whatever except willing." "Willing is original essence, and to it alone all the attributes of original essence are applicable: unfathomableness, eternity, freedom from dependence upon time, self-affirmation. The entire body of philosophy strives to attain to this highest expression." With respect to God and creatures one should distinguish between essence inasfar as it exists and essence inasfar as it is the ground of existence. God has the ground of his existence in himself, i.e., in a nature which is distinct from God himself. This nature is, as it were, "the ardent longing experienced by the eternal unity to produce itself." It is *will*, "but a will devoid of intellect, and for that very reason it is not an independent and complete will, since the intellect is the will in the willing. Nevertheless, it is a willing of the intellect, i.e., it is the longing and the ardent desire of the intellect, not a conscious but a foreboding will." Moreover, this is said to be the case with respect to all things. They differ from God but can have no existence apart from God. This paradox has only one explanation, "that things have their ground in that which in God is not God himself, i.e., in that which is the ground of his existence." Things have their ground in this dim, obscure nature, in this unconscious will of God. To be sure, the world, as we now know it, reveals order, regularity, and form, just as in God the light of spirituality and personality arose out of the darkness of his nature. "But the irregular is ever lying at the bottom, as if it would break through to the surface once more, and nowhere does it appear as if orderly arrangement and form were first but rather as if an original state of irregularity had been changed to a state of orderly arrangement." Schelling derives the whole process of the development of the universe from the opposition of nature and spirit, darkness and light, the real and the ideal principle, which coexist in God from all eternity.

This position enabled Schelling to deliver himself from the chain of Hegelian rationalism and to exert great influence upon modern philosophy. To be sure, the ideas which he had already expressed in his inquiry into the nature of human freedom were by him afterward brought to fuller and theistic development; but he adhered to his theory concerning the primacy of the will, and in that emphasis upon the will he was followed by Schopenhauer and Von Hartmann. Now it is true that with these philosophers the will is not will in the real sense of the term, but merely an unconscious desire, a blind urge, a dark force. But, to a certain extent, they themselves admit this. Schelling explicitly affirms that without the intellect the will is not independent and complete "seeing that the intellect is the will within the will." Schopenhauer did not exclude consciousness from the manifestation of the will and deemed the latter to be dependent on individuality and brains, but between the will and the phenomenal world he placed the ideas, which he regarded as the eternal forms and patterns of things. And Von Hartmann speaks of the unconscious as subject and as "overconscious." The will determines the existence of things; the intellect, their essence. But entirely aside from this admission, their philosophy is of the greatest significance for theism. It has indicated the intenable character of rationalistic and idealistic pantheism. God is inconceivable apart from will, freedom, and power. To be sure, the objection has been advanced that all willing is desiring and striving and is, accordingly, an indication of imperfection, of discontent, of unrest, which cannot be predicated of God. Accordingly, mystics have sung, "We pray: my Lord and God, thy will be done; and lo! he has no will; he is an eternal silence." But this objection is based upon an erroneous conception of the will. To be sure, willing often indicates a striving after something that one does not yet have in his possession, but when once the will has obtained the desired object and rests and delights in it, then also that resting and taking delight in something is, indeed, an activity of the will; it is even the highest and most powerful activity of the will. Now, *this* kind of will, namely, a will which rests in that which has come into one's possession, also pertains to creatures. It is simply another name for *love,* which embraces its object and therein is blessed. If such a resting or taking delight does not pertain to the will, then either: the creature can never attain unto blessedness, or if, after all, blessedness will at length be granted to the creature, this will imply the annihilation of the will, the stupefaction of consciousness, and the total submersion of personality. Accordingly, pantheistic mystics are of the opinion that only then is the soul truly blessed when it loses itself completely in God; true felicity is absorption into the divine, i.e., Nirvana. But this is not the teaching of Scripture and of Christian theology. True blessedness does not kill the will but raises it to the highest degree of activity, for love is the highest, the most powerful energy of the will. Thus also there is a will in God. His willing is not an attempt to obtain but an actual possession without which God would lack something and would not be truly blessed. For he is all-sufficient and truly blessed in himself. He is himself the supreme good for his creatures and also for himself. He can rest in nothing but himself. Because he is God he cannot be blessed except in and through himself. His love is self-love; hence, it is absolute, divine love. And that absolute love of self is nothing but a willing of oneself. It is the highest, absolute, divine will-energy. Accordingly, the object of God's will is God himself. Not, however, in the sense that he would be the product of his own will, as if he had brought himself into being and were "his own cause," for then we would again be guilty of the error of ascribing to God a process of becoming, of striving, hence, of imperfection. But thus: that God wills himself eternally with a "will of complacency," that he loves himself eternally with divine love, and that he is completely blessed in himself. His will is "his superlatively wise propensity toward his own self as the supreme good"; it is not merely a dim capacity or energy; rather, the subject, the activity, and the object of that will coincide with the very being of God.

However, Scripture also speaks of God's will with respect to creatures. Just as God's knowledge is twofold: necessary and free knowledge, so is also God's will; hence, we speak of his "propensity toward himself" and his "propensity toward his creatures." But just as God's "free knowledge" is not derived from the creature and does not make him dependent upon the creature, but is his from within, so also we should be on our guard against entertaining a dualistic view of the relation between God's will with respect to creatures and his will with respect to himself. Scripture clearly teaches that God wills "other things apart from himself" and constantly speaks of his will with respect to creatures, but, as it were in one and the same breath, it adds that God does not will these creatures because he needs them but only "for his own purpose," for his own name's sake, Prov. 16:4. Accordingly, we should not conceive of creation as something standing outside of or over against God, as something which he lacks and desires to possess or as something which he hopes to obtain in order that he may possess what was not his before. For of him and through him and also *to* him are all things. He does not realize himself in the creature but the creature realizes itself in him. "The things apart from himself which he wills, these are, in a certain sense, in God, in whom are all things." He wills creatures not because of some quality inherent in them but for his name's sake. He ever remains his own object. He never goes out to creatures *as such* but through them he goes out unto himself. Going beyond himself he returns unto himself. It is a "going out unto himself as the supreme goal and unto creatures as means through which he delights in himself." His self-love implies his love for creatures and through these returns unto himself. Hence, his willing, also with respect to creatures, is never "a striving to obtain something not yet possessed" nor, accordingly, is it a sign of imperfection or of infelicity, but his willing is ever absolute self-delight, perfect bliss, divine rest. This is true also with respect to that exercise of the will of which the creature may be said to be the object. In God rest and work are one; his self-sufficiency is also absolute actuosity.

**C. God's will toward himself is called his necessary will; that toward the creature is called his free will.**

Although, strictly speaking, God's will toward himself, and his will toward his creatures are one; nevertheless, it is necessary that we bear in mind that distinctions must be made. The reason for these distinctions is the fact that God's single will has different objects. Pantheism cannot recognize that distinction because it identifies God with the world. But according to Scripture, creatures have a distinct, not an independent, essence; hence, they cannot be objects of God's will in the same sense in which God himself is object of his will. God's will toward himself is his "propensity toward himself as the *goal*"; his will toward creatures is his "propensity toward his creatures as the *means*." The former is *necessary,* just like God's necessary knowledge, "knowledge of simple intelligence," God must needs love himself; he necessarily and eternally delights in himself. This will is, therefore, exalted above all arbitrariness; nevertheless, it is not bound or enslaved; freedom and necessity are perfectly congruous as far as God's will is concerned. God's will in relation to his creatures is not necessary, however. In the most absolute terms Scripture declares that God does whatsoever he pleases, Ps. 115:3; Prov. 21:1; Dan. 4:35. He does not need to give account to any one, Job 33:13. In his hand we are like clay in the hand of the potter, Job 10:9; 33:6; Is. 29:16; 30:14; 64:8; Jer. 8:1 ff.; "the nations are as a drop of a bucket, and are accounted as the small dust of the balance, all the nations are as nothing before him," Is. 40:15 ff. For a man to exalt himself against God is just as foolish as it is for an axe to boast itself against him that heweth therewith, and for a saw to magnify itself against him that wieldeth it, Is. 10:15: No man can ever stay the hand of God or say unto him, "What doest thou?" Shall the clay say to him that fashioned it, "What makest thou?" Job 9:2 ff.; 11:10; Is. 45:9. Therefore, let man be silent, and lay his hand upon his mouth, Job 40:4. God has the right to do whatsoever he desires with his own, Mt. 20:15. All things are absolutely dependent on God's will for their very existence, and for their being what they are, Rev. 4:11. God's will is the final ground of everything. Both mercy and hardening have their origin in God's will, Rom. 9:15-18. In the church the Holy Spirit "divides to each one severally even as he will," I Cor. 12:11. Man has no right to offer the least objection to God's free disposals, Mt. 20:13 ff.; Rom. 9:20, 21.

**D. The theological development of the doctrine of God's will:**

**(1)** According to Augustine the only answer to the question why God created the world, is: because he so willed; beyond that answer we cannot go.

**(2)** Duns Scotus and especially William of Occam define the will as "absolute indifference"; God could have granted salvation apart from regeneration; the Son could have assumed the nature of a stone. This nominalistic view was accepted by the Jesuits, Socinians, Arminians, the Cartesian theologians, etc. God's will, according to this conception, sustains no relation to the other attributes.

**(3)** This definition of the will was rejected by the Church. God's will is always in harmony with his other attributes. God has good reasons for willing as he does. We, however, can seldom determine why God wills one thing instead of another. Hence, for us the fact that God wills a thing should be the end of all argumentation.

Now just as God's knowledge of vision was called "free," in Christian theology, so upon grounds mentioned in the preceding paragraph, was also "God's will" which has the creature for its object. Augustine said that the will of God was the final and deepest ground of all things; a deeper ground does not exist. There is but one answer to the question why God created the world, namely, "because he so willed." He who inquires into the *cause* of this will "demands something that is greater than the will of God, but such a thing cannot be found"; this was the unanimous verdict of the Christian Church and of theology. All taught not that God could act "more" or "better" than he did, for he always acts in a divine and perfect manner, but that he could have made his creatures "more in number, greater and better" than he did make them. To be sure, there were those who maintained that the moral law was natural and eternal, that it was the very expression of God's being, but even here a distinction was made between that which was regarded as essential and that which was viewed as contingent, and it was held that exemption from the requirements of many of the commandments could be granted under special circumstances. Many regarded the incarnation and the atonement as not altogether necessary; if God had so willed he could have forgiven sin entirely apart from any atonement for he is not absolutely obligated to punish sin. This divine freedom was held to be even more clearly evident in the work of election and reprobation for which not a single ground or reason could be adduced and which rests upon the sovereign will of God alone. That the creature should possess any inherent right over against God was regarded altogether out of the question. There is no "commutative justice." And since the creature can have no merit in the sight of God, there is, in the real sense of the term, no "remunerative justice" either. Some even went so far as to say that, if God wanted to, he could punish the innocent either for time or for eternity, although he does not use this right. Thus, adopting as their starting-point God's absolute freedom, many theologians proceeded in the direction of medieval nominalism. Duns Scotus was the man who consistently applied to God the pelagian conception of the freedom of the will as absolute indifference. In his commentary on the *Sententiae* of Lombard he maintains, in opposition to Aristotle and Avicenna, that apart from God nothing is necessary. The universe as a whole and in all its parts is contingent; its existence is unnecessary as far as God is concerned. The question why God has willed this, and why he has willed one thing rather than another he answers by saying, "To demand the reasons and the exact proof for everything indicates lack of mental discipline. For, the principles of exact proof are not identical with exact proof. Moreover, that the will wills this thing is an immediate principle so that there is no intervening cause. Just as it is a self-evident truth that heat is heat-imparting, so also for this, namely, why the will willed this thing there is no reason except it be this one: because the will is will, even though the former is an illustration drawn from the realm of nature while the latter concerns freedom. Similarly, for this, namely, why heat is heat-imparting there is no reason except it be this one: because heat is heat, for there is no antecedent cause or reason." We should abide by this declaration, "The will of God wills this." There is no antecedent cause. Scotus remains true to this principle and applies it to all that takes place in time. If the entire universe is contingent, this characteristic can be maintained only when we agree that God, the first cause, contingently causes the universe. Now God causes the universe by his mind and will. But the contingent character of the universe does not find its explanation in the nature of God's mind as far as it antecedes his will, for this mind "perceives in a purely natural manner and by natural necessity." Hence, it must find its explanation in the nature of the will. This divine will "regards nothing else as necessarily preceding the object, except its own essence; it is contingently related to everything else, so that it is able to be in opposition." Now, Scotus does, indeed, admit that God's knowledge antecedes his will and that the ideas in God, although distinct from his "essence" antecede his decree. But it is the will that chooses from the total number of possible ideas and that determines which of these shall be realized. The will is the cause of all reality. And not until the will has decided does the mind know what will be realized. Accordingly, God has created the world with absolute freedom, even though it is true that his decree to create is from eternity. Naturally, Duns Scotus also conceived of the human will as being absolutely free. The will is free "with respect to opposite actions and opposite objects"; there is nothing that determines this human will; it is able to choose a lower as well as a higher good; in and by itself it is the complete cause of all actions; "moreover, it is not any goodness in the object which necessarily brings about the assent of the will, but the will assents freely, i.e., without any restriction, to any kind of good whatever, and thus without any restriction it assents to a greater or to a lesser good. The will alone is the complete cause of its own volition." The will even antecedes the intellect, for although it is true that the mind furnishes the will with the object of its striving, nevertheless it is the will which fixes the attention of the mind upon the object; and formally the will, not the mind, is the seat of blessedness. Furthermore, although Scotus recognizes the fact that love toward God, as prescribed in the first table of the law, is necessary and natural, he also maintains that the commandments of the second table are positive and might have been different than they are. With respect to the incarnation Scotus teaches that the Logos could have assumed a different nature than the human, e.g., that of a stone, had he so desired. He deems it probable that even apart from sin the incarnation would have taken place and that sin does not render it absolutely necessary; God could have redeemed in another way. The merits of Christ were not sufficient in themselves but God accepted them as such. In the abstract, as far as God's "absolute power" is concerned, God could have saved the sinner apart from the merits of Christ, and the sinner himself could have rendered satisfaction if only God had been willing to regard his works as satisfactory. Transubstantiation is possible "because *one* substance can wholly begin to exist and *another* one can wholly cease to exist." God can even cause a person or thing to cease to exist for "an intermediate time" without destroying his or its identity.

Nevertheless, Scotus did not go as far as certain Mohammedan theologians, who taught that by the will of God all things are created anew every moment, entirely apart from any connection with each other, from any laws of nature, substances or qualities. Scotus at least acknowledges that there are ideas in God which precede the will; he regards love toward God to be necessary and natural; teaches that there is a natural knowledge of God, a system of the universe, natural law; and even states that the incarnation and the atonement were necessary as regards "God's ordinate power." Nevertheless, he so exalts freedom and omnipotence that the *means,* at least, which must lead to the goal, are absolutely arbitrary. Others elaborated this theory of divine freedom and omnipotence. The theory of Occam was entirely in line with the ideas of Scotus. Occam taught that according to his "absolute power" God can grant salvation apart from regeneration and that he can damn the regenerate; that he can forgive without having received satisfaction and that he can consider the works of sinful man to be sufficient and satisfactory; that instead of the Son the Father could have become man, and that the Son might have assumed the nature of a stone or of an animal; that God by a dispensation can exempt a person from obligation to any or all of the commandments of the moral law, etc. Later on this nominalistic standpoint was accepted first of all by the Jesuits, then also by the Socinians, Remonstrants, Descartes, and Cartesian theologians, e.g., Burmann, and during the previous century, especially by Charles Secretan. This theory completely severs God's will from his being and from all his virtues; the will consists in absolute indifference or arbitrariness. All things could have been different; that applies to creation, incarnation, atonement, good and evil, true and untrue, reward and punishment. Nothing is natural, everything is positive.

But this very nominalistic position caused Christian theology to be on its guard. Even though with Augustine it maintained that the will of God is the final and deepest cause of all existence, nevertheless, it avoided the error of regarding that will as having no definite character and as being purely arbitrary and indifferent. First of all, in the doctrine of God Christian theology chose as its point of departure "God's *essence*" instead of his "will." The "knowledge of simple intelligence" logically preceded the "knowledge of vision," just as the "necessary will" preceded the "free will." Self-knowledge and self-love was absolutely necessary in God; moreover, the knowledge and the will which have the creature as their object do not stand in dualistic relation to but are very closely connected with the former. The "knowledge of vision" is dependent upon the "knowledge of simple intelligence" just as the "free will" is dependent upon the "necessary will." According to consistent nominalism not only the existence but also the essence of things is wholly fixed and determined by God's formal will; in reality there is in God no "knowledge of simple intelligence," which comprehends all possibilities; there is in him a "knowledge of vision" only, a knowledge which follows the will. But according to Christian theology the "knowledge of simple intelligence" was, as it were, the reservoir containing all possibilities. These were drawn from that source by the "knowledge of vision" and were actualized by the "will." Accordingly, the *existence* of objects is, indeed, dependent upon God's will, but their *essence* upon the mind. The theory of Leibnitz is based upon this foundation but he changed its meaning somewhat when he said that although God was indeed free to create the universe, man, the animals, the plants; nevertheless, having once determined to create them, he must needs make them according to the idea which had been conceived in his mind previous to and apart from the will. Given God's will to create, the world must be exactly what it is. Accordingly, the existing universe is the best possible universe, and all its parts are so closely related that "he who knows one well knows all." Further, it was the teaching of Scripture throughout that God had created and was preserving the world by his Word, by the Logos. Hence, the universe rested in the ideas of God. God did not act in an arbitrary or contingent manner but with supreme wisdom. Hence, even though we should not be able to discover the reasons for his actions, they would nevertheless be present in his consciousness. And Christian theology tried to find these reasons. Creation was said to rest in God's goodness or love; for the permission of sin all kinds of reasons were given. Incarnation and atonement were not absolutely necessary, perhaps; nevertheless, this way of salvation was deemed to be the best and most proper; and although many theologians hesitated to limit God's "absolute power," nevertheless, all acknowledged that he did not make use of this absolute right, and were in complete accord with one another in their doctrine of God's "ordinate power." Finally, certain concrete theories of nominalism were absolutely rejected: Christian theology maintained that the moral law cannot have any other content than it has; that sin must be punished; that the incarnation and the atonement are rooted in God's righteousness, and God's power was so defined that the notion that God can effect contradictions was definitely rejected. Thus Christian theology triumphed over nominalism: at least, it checked the latter and hindered its progress. When the "free will" was defined as "God's propensity toward his creatures as the *means* through which he delights in himself," that very definition implied the definite rejection of the idea that the divine will consists in absolute indifference or arbitrariness, for the end determines the character of the means. Hence, although Christian theology placed the will of God in the foreground and returned to it again and again, it nevertheless tried to discover the motive which induced the will. It was the aim of realism to conceive of the universe as being one harmonious whole, in which nothing was arbitrary; in which everything, even sin, had its proper place; and which in its entirety was subservient to the glorification of God's name. If the nature of a branch of knowledge consists in "learning the causes of things," theology cannot withdraw itself from a similar investigation. Only, it is absolutely necessary that the person who cultivates any branch of knowledge first of all and most of all study to be modest and humble. This applies especially to the theologian. He should not think of himself more highly than he ought to think. All knowledge is dependent upon its object; it has no right to falsify or to deny the phenomena which come under its observation, not even in order to satisfy a certain preconceived theory. Thus, theology is absolutely dependent upon the facts and evidences which God reveals in nature and Scripture. It must allow these to stand intact and unimpaired. If it cannot explain them, it must confess its ignorance. God's will, which expresses itself in facts, settles every argument as far as Christian theology is concerned. For, Christian theology rests in God's sovereignty. In that sense Augustine was right when he said, "The will of God is the nature of every creature." Christian theology permits itself to be deceived neither by pantheism, which conceives of the universe as necessary, for God and universe, necessary will and free will, are distinct; nor by deism, which views the universe as a result of chance, for the whole world reveals God's wisdom. Against both it maintains that the world was brought into being by an act of God's free, sovereign will, and that there were good and wise reasons which induced God to will thus. *We* regard something to be good, for the simple reason that God wills it; *God himself* can never will anything except it be good either in and by itself or with a view to something else. We can seldom discern why God willed one thing rather than another; hence, we are forced to say that God could have willed the one as well as the other. But in reality choosing is foreign to God inasmuch as it presupposes uncertainty, hesitation, deliberation. What God wills he knows eternally, definitely, immutably. Every inkling of indifference, arbitrariness, contingency or uncertainty is foreign to God's will, which is ever definite and immutable. Not God but the *creature* is contingent, and, be it said with all reverence, even God cannot rob the creature of this characteristic. In God alone existence and essence are one; by reason of its very nature every creature is of such a character that it might not have existed. But with an eternal and immutable will God willed that all creatures should be contingent. Hence, it is not possible nor even permissible for us to look for some deeper ground of things than the will of God, because all such attempts result in seeking a ground for the creature in the very essence of God, in robbing it of its creatural, i.e., contingent, character and making it necessary, eternal, and divine. In that sense it is true that God's will which has the creature as its object is free. But this freedom does not exclude the other divine attributes: wisdom, goodness, justice, etc. For, even among creatures the true freedom of the will does not presuppose a lengthy period of doubt, deliberation, and consideration; but that is the highest freedom which, at one stroke, "by a single intuition" establishes both the end and the means ordained to that end, and to which all hesitation and indecision is foreign. Now, that kind of freedom pertains also to God; a freedom which is neither limited by other divine attributes nor made independent of them in a nominalistic sense, but such a freedom that is free indeed and in the absolute sense because it is that of a wise, just, holy, merciful, and omnipotent God. Accordingly, when Augustine, Thomas Aquinas, Calvin, etc., asserted that there was no "reason" for the divine will, they meant that the will of God, as being one with his essence, is not dependent upon a higher or deeper cause. But they certainly did not mean to say that the divine will is irrational; that, in the sense of Schopenhauer's theory, the divine will would be blind, alogical. On the contrary, God's will is identical with his being, his wisdom, his goodness, and with all his attributes. And it is for this reason that man's heart and mind can rest in that will, for it is the will not of blind fate, incalculable fortune, or dark energy of nature, but of an omnipotent God and merciful Father. His sovereignty is a sovereignty of unlimited power, but it is also a sovereignty of wisdom and grace. He is King and Father at one and the same time.

> **E.  In our study of the doctrine of God's will we are confronted with the problem of evil. There is a difference between God's will which prescribes what WE should do, and his will which declares what HE will do.**

Still another difficulty in regard to the doctrine of God's will arises from the fact of creation. Just as God and the world are distinct, and we are therefore forced to distinguish between his "delight in himself" (propensio in se) and his "inclination toward his creatures," so there are all kinds of distinctions within the realm of creation. These distinctions are based upon the different relations which God's knowledge and will sustain toward individual creatures. God does not will everything in the same sense, in the same manner, and with the same energy of his being; otherwise, all diversity would be absent from creation, and the universe would be a monotonous uniformity. On the contrary, though God wills all creatures as means for his own sake, he wills some more than others because they are better adapted to promote his glory. God is a Father for all his creatures, but in a special sense he is a Father for his children. His love for creatures in general is not as great as is his love for the church; while his love for Christ, the Son of his good pleasure, is greatest of all. We speak of a general, special, and very special providence; in the same manner we also make distinctions in regard to God's will to creatures: God's "free will" is as rich in content as is the universe; it is not an indifferent potentiality or a blind force, but a rich and powerful, divine energy, the source of that abundant life which we see manifested in creation. A special difficulty, however, confronts us in the study of the doctrine of God's will; namely, the fact of evil, both "evil as guilt and evil as punishment." It may be ever so true that God controls evil; nevertheless, evil cannot be the object of God's will in the same sense and manner as is its opposite. Hence, with a view to these two entirely different and opposite objects, viz., the good and the evil, we must make a distinction in regard to the will of God. Scripture leads the way; according to it there is a great difference between God's will which prescribes *what we should do,* Mt. 7:21; 12:50; John 4:34; 7:17; Rom. 12:2; and his will which declares *what he will do,* Ps. 115:3; Dan. 4:17, 25, 32, 35; Rom. 9:18, 19; Eph. 1:5, 9, 11; Rev. 4:11. The *petition:* "Thy will be done," Mt. 6:10 has a meaning entirely different from the childlike *expression of resignation:* "The will of the Lord be done," Acts. 21:14; cf. Mt. 26:42. History is full of examples of the twofold aspect of God's will. God commands Abraham to sacrifice Isaac; but he prevents the execution of this act, Gen. 22. He tells Pharaoh: "Let my people go," but he hardens Pharaoh's heart, so that the latter refuses to let Israel go, Ex. 4:21. He informs Hezekiah that he will die; but, he nevertheless adds fifteen years unto his days, Is. 38:1, 5. He forbids the condemnation of the righteous; yet Jesus was delivered up by the determinate counsel and foreknowledge of God, Acts 2:23; 3:18; 4:28. God does not will sin, he is far from iniquity, he forbids it and punishes it severely; but sin nevertheless exists and is controlled by him, Ex. 4:21; Josh. 11:20; I Sam. 2:25; II Sam. 16:10; Acts 2:23; 4:28; Rom. 1:24, 26; II Thess. 2:11; etc. He wills the salvation of all, Ezek. 18:23, 32; 33:11;

I Tim. 2:4; II Pet. 3:9; nevertheless, "he hath mercy on whom he will, and whom he will he hardeneth," Rom. 9:18.

**F. Various distinctions with reference to God's will. Cf. under heading G:**

(1) the distinction between God's secret and his revealed will; decretive and preceptive, etc. This distinction is based on Scripture.

(2) the distinction between God's antecedent and subsequent will. This distinction may be used correctly. However, it is used incorrectly by Roman Catholics, Lutherans, Arminians: according to his antecedent will God wills the salvation of all men; hence, he offers grace to all. Then, after man has decided, God according to his subsequent will determines to grant salvation to those who believe, perdition to those who do not believe. This view robs God of his honor and makes man his own savior. Roman Catholics and others regard God's revealed will as the real will; Reformed theologians view God's secret will as the real will.

In theology the distinction between these two aspects of the divine will was soon recognized. Tertullian already speaks of a concealed or higher and a lower or lesser will. Augustine points out that God often fulfils his good will through the evil will of men. Later on this twofold character of God's will was indicated, on the one hand by the terms: "the will of God's good pleasure," "God's secret will," "the decreeing or decretive will"; and on the other by the terms: "the expressed or signified will," "the revealed will," "the preceptive will." The term "expressed or signified will" owes its origin to the fact that this will "expresses" or "signifies" what is pleasing to God and is our duty. It is made known to us by means of the five "signs" or "marks": "precept, prohibition, counsel, permission, and operation." Elaborated by scholasticism this view in regard to the distinctions in God's will was adopted by Roman Catholics in general and discussed with special predilection by Reformed theologians. Other distinctions besides this one were made with respect to the divine will; e.g., the distinction between "the antecedent and the consequent will," which distinction is already found in the works of Tertullian and of John of Damascus; that between "the absolute and the conditional, the efficacious and the inefficacious will of God," which already occurs in the writings of Augustine. Now what applies to other distinctions is true also with respect to these, namely, that they may be used correctly in *this* sense, that "antecedently" and "conditionally" God wills many things (e.g., the salvation of all men) which "consequently" and "absolutely" he does not will and therefore does not allow to happen. Zanchius, writing on this subject, says that all these distinctions may be reduced to one and the same thing. This is also the opinion of Hyperius, Walaeus,

Voetius, and others. But although in his book *De servo arbitrio* Luther had made a sharp distinction between "God concealed and God revealed," the Lutherans rejected this distinction between "the will of God's good pleasure" and "the expressed or signified will"; at least, they did not accept it in the Reformed sense. The Arminians followed the example of the Lutherans. And Roman Catholic theologians, although retaining the terms, explained them in this way that the will of God was always "the will of his good pleasure," and with respect to this will they distinguished between "antecedent" and "consequent" volition. They taught, moreover, that "the expressed or signified will" was nothing but a particular revelation of that "will of God's good pleasure." Thus it came about that the Roman Catholics and others retained one distinction only, namely that between "antecedent" and "consequent," "absolute" and "conditional" will; while the Reformed confined themselves to the distinction between "the will of God's good pleasure" and "the expressed or signified will," i.e., between decretive and preceptive, hidden and revealed will; for they rejected the (R. C.) distinction between the antecedent and consequent will. The difference may be stated thus: Roman Catholics, Lutherans, Remonstrants, etc., proceed from the "expressed or signified will"; they regard this as God's real will consisting in this: that God does not will sin but merely permits it; that he wills the salvation of all men; that he offers grace to all; etc.; then, after man has decided, God conforms himself to that decision and determines what he wills, namely, salvation for those who believe, perdition for those who do not believe. The "consequent will" follows man's decision and is not the real, essential will of God; it is the act of God which is occasioned by man's deportment. The Reformed, on the other hand, proceeded from "the will of God's good pleasure"; they regarded this as the real, the essential will of God. That will is always fulfilled; it always effects its object; it is eternal and immutable. The "expressed" or "signified" will, on the contrary, is God's precept revealed in the Law and in the Gospel; it is for us the rule of life.

**G. God's preceptive will seems to be in conflict with his decretive will:** it seems that according to the former God does not will sin, while according to the latter he does will it; that according to the former he wills the salvation of all men, while according to the latter he does not, etc. It should be observed however, that the idea of the two wills in God opposed to each other is erroneous:

(1) By the decretive will God has determined what he will do; by the preceptive will he reveals what we must do.

(2) Even according to the decretive will God does not delight in sin, and even according to the preceptive will he does not will the salvation of every man individually.

(3) The preceptive will, instead of being opposed to the decretive, is the means whereby the latter is carried out.

(4) Not only the preceptive will but also the decretive will is holy and wise and good.

(5) Those who reject God's preceptive will do injustice to God's holiness; those who deny God's decretive will come in conflict with God's omnipotence, wisdom, and sovereignty.

(6) For a proper understanding of this section it will be well to remember that the terms:

(a) God's secret will

(b) the will of God's good pleasure, and

(c) God's decretive will

all refer to the same thing, namely, God's eternal counsel or decree by which he has foreordained whatever comes to pass. Similarly, the terms:

(a) God's preceptive will,

(b) God's revealed will, and

(c) God's expressed or signified will

all refer to the same thing, namely, God's precept for our conduct.

Both in the O. T. and in the N. T., Scripture teaches that God's will is eternal, immutable, independent, and efficacious. This truth is not only expressed in a few passages, e.g., Ps. 33:11; 115:3; Dan. 4:25, 35; Is. 36:10; Mt. 11:26; Rom. 9:18; Eph. 1:4; Rev. 4:11; etc., but is either expressed or implied everywhere in Scripture, is demanded by all God's attributes, and is evidenced by the entire history of the church and of the world. Hence, the Christian church; especially since Augustine, taught that God's will is single (simple), eternal and immutable, identical with his being. God's antecedent will is not really a will; "it should rather be called a willingness than an absolute will." God's expressed or signified will is called God's will in a metaphorical sense, "just as when any one lays down a precept, it is sign that he wishes that precept obeyed." The real will in God is the "will of God's good pleasure," identical with God's being, immutable and efficacious. Pelagians abandoned this correct view, and raised a mere desire, an unfulfilled wish to the dignity of a will. By doing this it came into conflict with the very being of God, with all his attributes; for if God's real will be a mere "willingness," he is robbed of his omnipotence, wisdom, goodness, immutability, independence, etc; the universe ceases to be governed by his providence; an insoluble dualism is created between God's purpose and the actual result of the history of the world. This result will be an everlasting disappointment for God; his plan for the history of the world suffers shipwreck, and in the end Satan triumphs. Now Pelagianism maintains that it takes this position with a view to God's holiness, and that Paul and Augustine, Thomas Aquinas and Calvin fail to do justice to this attribute seeing that in their system God is made the Author of sin. But this is true in appearance only, not in reality. Pelagianism does not explain the problem of sin any better than does Calvinism (Augustine, Calvin, etc.); on the contrary, the latter does justice to God's holiness, for it is more in accordance with Scripture and with Christian faith in general to believe that for good reasons, unknown to us, God in a certain sense willed sin, than to think that God permits and tolerates sin though he did not in any sense will it. The *latter* position (Pelagianism) is in conflict with God's holiness and with his omnipotence, not the *former.*

In connection with this it should be born in mind that though Scripture, theologically, places the decretive will in the foreground, nevertheless by means of its doctrine of the signified or revealed will it makes clear in which sense God does not will sin. By means of the "signs" of prohibition, warning, admonition, chastisement, punishment, etc., God reveals himself to us, and tells us what he requires of us. Because man is a rational, moral being, God does not treat him as if he were a stone or a log but deals with him and addresses him in accordance with his nature. Just as a father forbids his child to touch a sharp knife though he himself uses it without injury or damage, so God forbids us to sin though he himself is able to use and does use sin as a means of self-glorification. The usual objection advanced against the decretive (secret) will and the preceptive (revealed) will, namely, that they are in conflict with each other, is not justifiable, for: the preceptive will is really not God's will but his precept for our conduct; by means of it God does not reveal to us what he will do; it is not a law for his conduct; but it tells us *what we must do;* it is a rule for our conduct, Deut. 29:29. It is called God's will in a metaphorical sense. The objection is advanced, however, that the preceptive or revealed will bears that name because it reveals what God really wills, and that it must, therefore, be in harmony with his decretive will. With this we agree: the preceptive will reveals what God wills that we should do. The decretive will and the preceptive will do not conflict in the sense that according to the first God takes pleasure in sin, but according to the second he does not; that according to the former he does not desire the salvation of every individual, but according to the latter he does, etc. Even according to the decretive will God takes no pleasure in sin: it is not an object of his delight, neither does he afflict willingly. And even according to the preceptive will God does not will the salvation of every individual. History very plainly gives the lie to the idea that God wills to save every individual: the word "all" in I Tim. 2:4 ("who would have all men to be saved . . .") is given a restricted meaning by every interpreter. God's revealed will instead of being opposed to the secret will is the means whereby the latter is carried out: by means of warnings and admonitions, prohibitions and threatenings, conditions and commandments, God's counsel is accomplished; while because of the decretive will man, when he transgresses God's commandment, does not for a moment become independent of God but in the very act of transgressing serves God's counsel, and becomes an instrument (however unwillingly) of God's glory. Not only God's revealed will but also his decretive will is holy, and wise, and good, and will become manifest as such in the way of righteousness and obedience to the law. Hence, the distinction between the two should be maintained. The problem of what is and what ought to be, of history and idea, of reality and morality, of what actually happens and what should happen, meets us here. Those who deny the revealed will do injustice to God's holiness, the majesty of the moral law, and the seriousness of sin; while those who reject the decretive will come in conflict with God's omnipotence, wisdom, and sovereignty. Thus one either falls into the error of superficial optimism, so that he does not see things as they really are, and calls things reasonable because they are real; or, accepting the other extreme position, he becomes a one-sided pessimist, begins to curse the day of his birth, and to despair of the universe and of destiny. Theism, however, does not seek the solution by canceling one of the terms of the problem, but accepts and maintains both; it knows that the problem of what is and what ought to be is met with in every instance of history; it refers both to God's sovereignty which it esteems very highly and which it regards as being fully able to effect the execution of God's wise decree in such a manner that his name is glorified even by means that are contrary to holiness and reasonableness. In this God's sovereignty shines forth most marvelously, namely, that in the foolishness of men his wisdom is exalted, in their weakness his strength, in their sin his righteousness.

**H. God's omnipotence. Scripture teaches God's omnipotence everywhere.**

Finally, God's sovereignty is revealed in his omnipotence, which with a view to what has already been said does not call for a long discussion. Scripture nowhere sets bounds to God's power. The idea of power is in the foreground in such names as El, Elohim, El-Shaddai, Adonai. Furthermore, God is called great and terrible, whose countenance no man can behold and live, Deut. 7:21 ff.; the Mighty One of Israel, Is. 1:24; the great, the mighty God, whose name is Jehovah of hosts, Jer. 32:18; mighty in strength, Job 9:4; cf. Job 36:5; strong and mighty, Ps. 24:8; Lord, Mt. 11:25; Rev. 1:8; 22:5; i.e., the Owner and Ruler, who possesses authority and majesty; The King, who

eternally rules over all things, Ex. 15:8; Ps. 29:10; 93-99; II Kings
29:15; Jer. 10:7, 10; etc., exercising kingship especially over Israel.
over which he reigns and which he protects and saves, Num. 23:21;
Deut. 33:5; Judg. 8:23; I Sam. 6:7; Ps. 10:16; 24:7; 48:3; 74:12;
Is. 33:22; 41:21; 43:15; etc., and in the N. T. he is called "the great
King," Matt. 5:35; I Tim. 1:17; "King of kings and Lord of lords"
I Tim. 6:15; cf. Rev. 19:16; "the Lord Almighty," II Cor. 6:18;
Rev. 1:8; 4:8; 11:17; "the only Potentate," I Tim. 6:15; who possesses both the "right, authority," Matt. 8:18; Rom. 9:21; and the
"ability and power to act," Matt. 6:13; Rom. 1:20. Furthermore, God's
omnipotence is evident in all his works. It becomes manifest in creation, providence, Israel's deliverance from Egypt, in the laws of nature,
and in the history of Israel with its many miracles. Psalmists and
prophets again and again refer to God's mighty deeds, in order that
the proud may be humbled and the believer may receive comfort. God
is strong in power, Is. 40:26; he creates heaven and earth, Gen. 1;
Is. 42:5; 44:24; 45:12, 18; 48:13; 51:13; Zech. 12:1; establishes them
by perpetual decrees, Jer. 5:22; 10:10; 14:22; 27:5; 31:35; causes
rain to descend and creates the wind; turns the shadow of death into
the morning and makes the day dark with night; makes peace and
creates evil, Am. 3:6; 4:13; 5:8; Is. 45:5-7; 54:16. He makes and
gives speech; he kills and makes alive; he delivers and destroys, Ex.
4:11; Deut. 32:39; I Sam. 2:6; II Kings 5:7; Ex. 15; Deut. 26:8;
29:2; 32:12; I Sam. 14:6; Hos. 13:14; Matt. 10:28; Luke 12:20.
He possesses absolute power in regard to everything so that nothing is
able to stay his hand, Ps. 8, 18, 19, 24, 29, 33, 104, etc. Job 5:9-27;
9:4 ff.; 12:14-21; 34:12-15; 36:37. Nothing is too hard for him, all
things are possible with him, Gen. 18:14; Zech. 8:6; Jer. 32:27; Matt.
19:26; Luke 1:37; 18:27; he is able of stones to raise up children
unto Abraham, Matt. 3:9. He does whatever he pleases, Ps. 115:3;
Is. 14:24, 27; 46:10; 55:10; and no one can appoint him a time (sum-
mon him, "hem dagvaarden") Jer. 49:19; 50:44. In a special measure
his power is evident in the work of redemption; in the resurrection of
Christ, Rom. 1:4; Eph. 1:20; in the giving and strengthening of faith,
Rom. 16:15; Eph. 1:19; in the distribution of grace above all that we
ask or think, Eph. 3:20; II Cor. 9:8; II Pet. 1:3; and in the resurrection of the last day, John 5:25; etc. Finally God's omnipotence is
the source of all power and authority, ability and strength, among
creatures: of man's dominion, Gen. 1:26; Ps. 8; of the rule of kings
Prov. 8:15; Rom. 13:1-16; of the strength of his people, Deut. 8:17,
18; Ps. 68:35; Is. 40:26 ff.; of the might of the horse, Job 39:22; of
the mighty voice of thunder, Ps. 29:4; 68:33; etc. In a word: power

belongeth unto Jehovah, Ps. 62:11; glory and strength are his possessions, Ps. 96:7; Rev. 4:11; 5:12; 7:12; 19:1.

I. God's absolute and his ordinate power:

(1) According to the nominalists God's "absolute power" signifies that he is able to do absolutely everything; e.g., to sin, to suffer, to die, to effect contradictions, etc. He is not only able to do all he wills but he is also able to will everything.

(2) On the other hand, according to Plato, Plotinus, Abelard, the Cartesian theologians, Spinoza, Schleiermacher, etc., God is able to do only that which he actually does.

(3) According to Scripture both of these extremes are to be avoided:

(a) In contradistinction to the view of the nominalists Scripture maintains that there are certain things which God cannot do: he cannot deny himself, etc.

(b) In opposition to the error of the pantheists Scripture defends the truth that God is able to do more than he actually does.

(4) In agreement with Scripture Christian theology defines God's absolute power as his ability to do whatever is in harmony with all his perfections, i.e., with his being; and God's ordinate power, as his ability to perform whatever he decrees.

Entirely in harmony with their doctrine concerning will and freedom the nominalists defined God's omnipotence as his power not only to do whatever he wills but also to will anything whatever. Distinguishing between "absolute and ordinate power" they taught that by virtue of the former God was able to sin, to go astray, to suffer, to die, to be changed into a stone or into an animal, to change bread into the body of Christ, to effect contradictions, to undo the past, to make false what was true and true what was false, etc. According to his "absolute power" God is pure indifference or arbitrariness, absolute potency, without content; he *is* nothing but may *become* anything. In principle this is the standpoint of all those who accept the primacy of the will; hence, we meet it again and again, not only in the *Christian* religion but also in others, especially in Mohammedanism. In contradistinction to this theory is the one which teaches that God can do only that which he wills and that he cannot do that which he does not will: the possible equals the actual. Whatever does not become reality is not possible either. God's power is exhausted in the universe. Plato and Plotinus already held this view; it was also accepted by some of the church-fathers, while during the middle ages it was especially Abelard who advocated this theory, "God is not able to do anything beyond that which he does." And this was the opinion of the Cartesian theologians: Burmann, Braun, Wittichius, and of Spinoza, Schleiermacher, Strauss, Schweitzer, Nitzsch, and others.

Now Scripture condemns the one position as well as the other. On the one hand, it clearly teaches that there are certain things which God cannot do: he cannot lie, he cannot repent, he cannot change, he cannot be tempted with evil, Num. 23:19; I Sam. 15:29; Heb. 6:18; Jas. 1:13, 17, "he cannot deny himself"; II Tim. 2:13; for his will is identical with his being, and the view with respect to God's "absolute power" which separates this attribute from the others is nothing but a vain and unwarranted abstraction.    On the other hand, Scripture declares in language equally clear that that which is possible to the power of God extends much farther than that which is actually realized, Gen. 18:14; Jer. 32:27; Zech. 8:6; Matt. 3:9; 19:26; Lk. 1:37; 18:27. And Christian theology was in accord with this position. On the one hand, Augustine states that God's will and power are not distinct from his essence. "With man it is one thing *to be,* another, *to be able* . . . . With God, however, it is not so, that his substance is one thing so that he is, and his power another thing so that he is able; but whatever is his, and whatever he is, is consubstantial with him because he is God: it is not so that in one way he *is,* and in another way he *is able*: he has being (*to be*) and ability (*to be able*) together because he has the will (*to will*) and the deed (*to do*) together." To be sure, God's omnipotence consists in this, that he can do whatever he wants to do "for certainly for no other reason is he called omnipotent except because he is able to do whatever he wills." But God cannot will everything. He cannot deny himself. "And since he does not will it, he is not able to do it because he is not even able to will it. For righteousness cannot will to do that which is unjust, or wisdom that which is foolish, or truth that which is false. Whence we are reminded that the omnipotent God not only cannot deny himself, as says the apostle, but that there are many things which he cannot do . . . the omnipotent God cannot die, he cannot be changed, he cannot be deceived, he cannot be created, he cannot be vanquished." Augustine further shows that far from being lack of power this is, in reality, absolute omnipotence. If God could go astray, if he could sin, etc., this, indeed, would be an indication of impotence.    Augustine makes this very clear when he answers the objection which is often advanced against the doctrine of God's omnipotence, namely, that God cannot undo what has been done. He shows that this statement is ambiguous. It may mean that God undoes the event that has occurred; but this does not yield any sense, for an event that has occurred does not exist any more; hence, it cannot and need not be undone. But it may also mean that God might undo the event as regards man's consciousness, so that a man may now begin to think that it has never occurred. Neither, however, does this yield any sense, for in that case God, who is the truth, would have to make untrue that which is true. Other theologians have spoken about God's omnipotence in a similar manner and have but repeated what Augustine had said.

Reformed theologians, in particular, were careful to state that their approval of the distinction between "God's absolute power" and his "ordinate power" was not unqualified. Nominalists had made misuse of this distinction so that they had even taught that with reference to the former God was able to do everything, even that which was not in harmony with his nature. They used this argument to prove the doctrine of trans-substantiation. Calvin rebelled against this notion and branded as profane this "fiction of absolute power." Roman Catholics, accordingly, accused Calvin of limiting and thereby denying God's omnipotence. Calvin, however, did not deny the fact that God can do more than he actually does, but he assailed the notion of an "absolute power" apart from God's being, a power that would enable him to effect all kinds of contradictions. In the sense in which Augustine and Thomas Aquinas defined the distinction it was accepted by Reformed theologians in general. And, understood in that sense, it is correct. Pantheism, indeed, declares that God and world are correlates and that God does not have essence and life, consciousness and will, in distinction from the world; but this theory jumbles everything and is hopelessly confusing. God and the world, eternity and time, the infinite and the finite, being and becoming, the possible and the actual, the necessary and the contingent, etc., are not terms of identical content and meaning. The world is of such a character that our thinking is not able to rob it of its contingent character. The idea of the non-existence of the universe does not imply any self-contradiction. It is possible that there were motives which induced God to bring the world into being; it is possible that in its entirety and in every one of its parts the cosmos is the embodiment of divine ideas. All this, we say, is, indeed, possible. But it is *impossible* to give a logical explanation of the existence of the world apart from belief in an omnipotent God. Hence, the *actual* does not completely cover the *possible*. God does not exhaust himself in the universe; eternity does not empty itself in time; infinitude is not identical with the sum-total of all finite existence; and omniscience does not coincide with the thought-content embodied in creation. So also God's omnipotence infinitely transcends the unlimited power which is revealed in the universe.

**V. Attributes Which Reveal God's Absolute Blessedness: Perfection, Blessedness, Glory. God's Perfection Is That Attribute Which Describes God As the Sum-Total of All Excellencies. God's Blessedness Indicates that God Delights In His Perfection. God's Glory Indicates the Splendor and Brilliancy that is Inseparably Connected with His Self-Revelation in Nature and in Grace.**

**A. God's Perfection:** God's perfection is that attribute which describes God as the sum-total of all excellencies, as the One than whom no greater, higher, and better can exist either in thought or in reality. It indicates that all those perfections which we observe in creation (whether present in God characteristically, e.g., eternity; preeminently, e.g. knowledge; or virtually, e.g. physical sight) pertain to God in an absolute manner, and that he is exalted above all shortcomings and limitations.

God's "highest perfection" is the sum and substance of all the attributes which have been discussed so far. Accordingly, when we speak of God's perfection, we do not refer exclusively to his moral excellence, whether "goodness or holiness," but we mean that God is the sum-total of all excellencies, the One than whom no greater, higher, better can exist either in thought or in reality. In other words, God answers fully to the idea of God. *That* creature is perfect in a creaturely, finite manner which fully answers to its norm. So also God is perfect because the idea of God is in full accord with his being. Of course, this is the case *humanly speaking;* it must not be misinterpreted. We should remember that God posits the norm for the creature; hence, this norm is authoritative for the creature: the creature is morally bound to live up to it. In that sense we cannot speak of any idea or norm with reference to God. There is no norm which is authoritative for God and to which he must answer. But the idea of God is derived from the being of God himself. In him being and self-consciousness are one; he *is* that which he *knows* himself to be, and he *knows* himself to be that which he is. But not only does God have (perfect) knowledge of himself, he has also imprinted an idea of himself in the heart of man. This idea is men's common heritage; we associate with it every conceivable kind of perfection. It is perfectly true that our idea and consciousness of God has been darkened, true also that our conceptions of God vary widely; nevertheless, when a man allows himself to be instructed by Holy Scripture, and when his mind and heart receive the illumination of the Holy Spirit, his conception of God becomes clarified; he learns to know God as he is in truth, and he gladly acknowledges all of God's perfections. Every attribute of God becomes dear to the believer: he cannot do without even a single one of them; he is satisfied with no other God than the only true God, who has revealed himself in Christ, and he exalts all his virtues. The Christian is filled with admiration, love, thanksgiving, and adoration not only because his God is a God of grace and love but also because he is a God of holiness and righteousness, not only because he is benevolent but also because he is omnipotent, not only because of his communicable but also because of his incommunicable attributes. Now when we ascribe the highest perfection to God, we acknowledge thereby that all those perfections which we perceive either positively or negatively through the things that are made, pertain to God in an absolute and preëminent manner, i.e., in the highest degree. This implies that they are not all his in the same sense. Some attributes pertain to God *"characteristically"*; as eternity and simplicity, etc., for they do not pertain to the creature. Others pertain to him *"preëminently"*; as, knowledge and volition, for of these there is a faint reflex in the creature. Still others are ascribed to God figuratively or *"virtually"*; as physical sight and hearing, for these attributes do not pertain to God literally, (i.e., as they pertain to creatures), but they are present in him in a divine manner. But although there is a difference in the manner in which we must ascribe this or that attribute to God, he is nevertheless the sum-total of all conceivable excellencies; he is the highest perfection, exalted infinitely above all shortcomings and limitations.

**B. Blessedness. When applied to God "blessedness" comprises three elements:**
(1) that God is absolute perfection, absolute life;
(2) that this perfection is the object of God's knowledge and love; and
(3) that God delights in himself in an absolute sense; that he rests in himself; that he is perfectly self-sufficient.

According to Scripture God's absolute perfection implies his blessedness. In the O. T. a person's state of blessedness is expressed by the exclamation *'ashrēy*, construct, plural meaning, "O the blessedness (of) . . . !" It is derived from the verb *'shr* meaning: to go straight, Hiph.: to lead the way, also to bless a person, to wish one joy, to congratulate somebody. The N. T. equivalent is *makarios* (according to Cremer more emphatic than *eudaimōn*), Lat. beatus, Eng. blessed, D. zalig. The word "zalig" does not mean "full," so that "rampzalig" would mean "full" of misery, and "gelukzalig" would be equivalent to "full" of blessedness, but is derived from the Gothic word "sels," meaning good, virtuous. "Zalig" is that person who is virtuous, who is whole, sound, who is what he ought to be. In Scripture the words *'ashrēy, makarios,* blessed ("zalig") usually have a religious meaning; they indicate the man who has communion with God, is the recipient of God's special benefits, particularly of the blessing of forgiveness, Ps. 32:1; Rom. 4:8. In the

N. T. God is called blessed, *makarios* in two passages: I Tim. 1:11 and I Tim. 6:15.

Now blessedness when ascribed to God comprises three elements: In the first place it expresses the fact that God is absolute perfection, for blessedness is the property of every being that is perfect or complete: that has life, and is free from disturbance, whether inwardly or outwardly. Moreover, the degree of blessedness corresponds to the measure of perfection that pertains to a being. Because of the fact that God is absolute perfection, the sum-total of all virtues, the highest essence, the supreme of goodness and truth, in other words, because he is absolute life, the fountain of all life, he is the God of absolute blessedness. The concepts life and blessedness are very closely related in Scripture: life without blessedness is not worthy of the name life, and for the child of God life means blessedness. Secondly, the word blessedness when applied to God implies that this absolute perfection is the object of God's knowledge and love. Scholasticism debated the question whether blessedness on the part of God or man pertains chiefly to the mind or to the heart, whether it is primarily a matter of knowledge or of love. Now apart from knowledge or consciousness there can be no blessedness; hence, for pantheism God is needy and unhappy; he is pure potentiality: really nothing; potentially everything; if he will ever become happy or blessed, the creature must make him so. Nevertheless, although it is perfectly true that one must needs be conscious in order to be truly blessed, love also is indispensable to blessedness. God knows himself with a knowledge that is absolute, and he loves himself with a love that is absolute; love without knowledge is inconceivable; in like manner knowledge without love is inconceivable, neither does the one take precedence over the other. Hence, the word blessedness when applied to God implies, thirdly, that God delights in himself in an absolute sense, that he rests in himself, that he is perfectly self-sufficient. His life is not a continual development, a mere striving and becoming, as is taught by pantheism, but an uninterrupted rest, an eternal peace. Moreover God's delight in his creatures is a corollary of his delight in himself. "God is his own blessedness. Blessedness and God are the same. By means of his intellect he is fully conscious of his own perfection, and by means of his will he supremely loves it, i.e., he regards it with calm delight; and from this delight inward joy springs forth: the joy with which God delights in himself as the highest good."

**C. Glory.**  God's glory indicates the splendor and brilliancy that is inseparably connected with all of God's virtues and with his self-revelation in nature and grace. Threefold aspect of this glory:

(1) As an object of the ADORATION of the creature it is called GREATNESS.

**(2)  As an object of our GRATITUDE it is called GLORY.**
**(3)  As an object of our REVERENCE it is called MAJESTY.**

Because God is perfect, he is inwardly blessed and outwardly glorious. The Biblical words for glory are *kābhōdh* and *doxa;* the O. T. word *kābhōdh*, from *kbd*, means heavy, weighty, significant. The word *hōdh*, which is used in connection with *kābhōdh*, indicates the glorious appearance of him whose name is known, while *hādār* signifies the splendor and beauty of this appearance. The LXX and the N. T. use the word *doxa* which indicates subjectively the recognition to which a person is entitled, the honor or glory he receives or is entitled to receive (synonyms: *timē,* honor; and *eulogia,* blessing, Rev. 5:12; antonym, *atimia* dishonor, II Cor. 6:8); objectively, the appearance, figure, semblance, splendor, luster, glory pertaining to a person or thing as it becomes manifest. It also indicates the person or thing itself in glorious manifestation. In this sense it is related to *eidos,* appearance; *eikōn* image, form, Is. 53:2; I Cor. 11:7. The "glory of the Lord" *kābhōdh Yhwh, doxa tou theou,* indicates the splendor and brilliancy that is inseparably connected with all of God's virtues and with his self-revelation in nature and grace, the luster of his manifestation to creatures. God's glory and majesty is revealed in all of creation and especially in the realm of grace, I Chron. 16:27; Ps. 29:4; 96:6; 104:1; 111:4; 113:4; Ps. 8; Is. 6:3. It was manifested to Israel, Ex. 16:7, 10; 24:16; 33:18 ff.; Lev. 9:6, 23; Num. 14:10; 16:19, etc.; Deut. 5:24. It filled the tabernacle and the temple, Ex. 40:34; I Kings 8:11; and was imparted to all the people, Ex. 29:43; Ezek. 16:14; etc. This glory is especially manifest in Christ the only begotten Son, John 1:14; and through him in the church, Rom. 15:7; II Cor. 3:18; which is looking for the blessed hope and appearing of the glory of our great God and Saviour Jesus Christ, Tit. 2:13. (R. V. margin, this translation is better than "the great God and our Savior Jesus Christ"—Translator's note). God's glory is often associated with his holiness, Ex. 29:43; Is. 6:3; and therefore also described as a cloud, I Kings 8:10, 11; Is. 6:4; or as a devouring fire, Ex. 24:17; Lev. 9:24.

Undoubtedly this cloud and fire indicate the visible, creaturely forms by means of which God manifested his presence. However, when the word "light" serves to indicate God's glory, it should be taken symbolically, as indicative of God's veracity, holiness, and blessedness, Ps. 43:3; Is. 10:17; Ps. 97:11. This mode of comparison is so simple and natural that in order to understand it one does not need to suppose that Jehovah was originally a sun-god, no more than one needs to conclude that the appellation "rock" indicates that Jehovah was originally a stone-deity. The light of the sun and the fire of heaven furnish the Israelite with the material for the description of Jehovah's virtues; but the O. T. believer is clearly conscious of the fact that whenever he describes God as a "light" he is using a metaphor. Just as the thunder is the voice of the Lord, Ps. 104:7; Am. 1:2; Is. 30:30; so the light of nature is his garment, Ps. 104:2. God is in the spiritual realm what light is in the natural sphere, namely, the source of knowledge, purity and joy. By the believer God is called "my light," Ps. 27:1; God's children walk in the light of God's word and of his countenance, Ps. 44:3; 89:15; 110:105; in his light they see light, Ps. 36:9. God himself is light, and in him is no darkness at all; he is the Father of lights, I John 1:5; I Tim. 6:16; Jas. 1:17; and according to the promise, Is. 9:1; 60:1, 19, 20; Mic. 7:8; he was revealed in Christ as light, Matt. 4:16; Luke 2:32; John 1:4; 3:19; 8:12; I John 2:20; so that the church is light in him, Matt. 5:14; Eph. 5:8; I Thess. 5:5; and will by and by receive the inheritance of the fulness of light, Rev. 21:23 ff.; 22:5; Col. 1:12. To the expression "glory of the Lord" the Jews afterward gave the connotation: created, visible luster, by means of which God made known his presence in creation; they even conceived of it as the personal subject of the Shekinah. Theosophy borrowed this conception from Jewish theology. Böhme describes the "glory of the Lord" as a "spiritual body," as a "kingdom of the glory of God, the eternal kingdom of heaven, in which the power of God is real, tinged with the luster and the energy of fire and of light." Early Lutheran theologians already debated the question whether God is called light in a real or in a figurative sense. The former was held by Dannhauer and Chemnitz; the latter, by Musaeus and others. In the year 1431 the council of Constantinople of the Greek Orthodox Church approved of the doctrine of an uncreated, divine light, distinct from the being of God.

Nevertheless, this idea is erroneous. Scripture very plainly teaches God's spirituality and invisibility. These divine attributes cannot be maintained when one interprets the expression *"temūnāh, eidos, morphē,"* "glory of the Lord" as indicating a place (*māqōm*), a form, a face (*pānim*) a body, a kingdom, a heaven, which, although uncreated would be distinct from God's being. The "glory of the Lord" so interpreted is also in conflict with God's simplicity. When Scripture speaks of God's countenance, glory and majesty, it employs figurative language. God's glory is not physical, but in creation there is a dim reflection of God's ineffable splendor and majesty. Just as a study of the creature directs our mind upward to God and causes us to speak of God's eternity and omnipresence, of his justice and grace, in like manner this study of the creature gives us a glimpse of God's glory. Nevertheless, God's glory should not be identified with its reflection in creation; there is analogy, there is no identity. Ordinary speech points out the difference: we employ the words pretty, lovely, beautiful, when we refer to creatures, but with reference to God we speak of glorious. The expression "beauty of the Lord," used by the church-fathers, scholastics, and the R. C. theologians, is not deserving of commendation. Augustine already employed this term. He started with the thesis, "Whatever exists, inasfar as it has being, is true, good, and beautiful." He proceeds as follows: in the realm of being as also in the sphere of the true, the good, and the beautiful, there is diversity, gradation, progression. A greater measure of truth, goodness and beauty pertains to an object in proportion as it has a greater degree of reality. Everything is beautiful after its kind. "A laudable proportion, number, and arrangement after their own kind, whatever kind, that is, is discernible in the individual works of God." "For every object has a natural beauty of its own." Accordingly, all creatures contribute to the beauty of the whole. But all creaturely beauty is transient and mutable; a creature is not beautiful in itself, but it participates in a higher, absolute beauty. When creatures are interrogated, "in answer to thy question they all reply, 'Behold, see, we are beautiful!' Their beauty is their confession." That supreme of beauty, to which all creatures refer, is God. He is the "highest essence" the "supreme truth," the "supreme goodness" and also the supreme immutable beauty. "Who has made these objects endowed with changeable beauty, unless it be the unchangeably Beautiful One?" God is the supreme of beauty because his being is characterized by absolute unity, harmony, and order. In God there is neither superfluity nor lack of anything. From this idea of Augustine it appears that he was influenced by Neo-Platonism. Neo-Platonism also regarded God as the supreme of beauty and as the cause of all beauty. As presented by Augustine this idea was accepted by many scholastic and Roman Catholic theologians. Protestant theologians, on the other hand, preferred to speak of God's majesty and glory. In God's glory his greatness and transcendence are reflected. Psalmists and prophets often picture these attributes, cf. Ps. 104; Is. 40; Hab. 3. We may distinguish a threefold aspect of God's glory: As an object of the admiration and adoration of the creature it is called *greatness*. As an object of our gratitude and praise it is called *glory*. As an object of our reverence, it is called *majesty;* as such it is connected with God's absolute dignity, demanding the subjection of every creature.

# THE HOLY TRINITY

CHAPTER VI

# The Holy Trinity

**I. The O. T. Contains the Adumbration, the Nucleus of the Doctrine of the Trinity. In the Apocryphal Literature and in Philo the Truth of this Doctrine Is Buried Beneath a Load of Heathen Speculation. In the N. T. This Doctrine Is Clearly Revealed. Scripture Reveals To Us the Relations Between Father, Son, and Holy Spirit.**

    A. The doctrine of the trinity in the O. T.:
        (1) In the O. T. we have a foreshadowing of the N. T. Doctrine.
        (2) This O. T. nucleus of the doctrine of the trinity is evident from:

        (a) passages in which the Word or Wisdom of God is personified, Ps. 33:6, 9; Job 28:23, 28; Prov. 8:22 ff.;
        (b) passages in which the Spirit of God is spoken of as a distinct person, Gen. 1:2; Ps. 33:6; 139:7; Job 26:13; 33:4; Is. 63:10 etc.;
        (c) a few (not all) of those passages which mention the MAL'AKH YHWH, Gen. 16:6-13; 21:17-20; Gen. 18, 19, 22, 24:7, 40; Gen. 28:13-17; 31:11-13; 32:24-30; etc.;
        (d) the three-fold blessing of Numbers, 6:24-26;
        (e) passages that indicate distinctions within the Divine Being, Gen. 19:24; Ps. 45:7; 110:1; Hos. 1:7; and
        (f) passages in which mention is made of more than one, sometimes even three persons, Ps. 33:6; Is. 61:1; 63:9-12; Hag. 2:5, 6.

When Scripture makes known to us not only God's proper names but also his personal names, which indicate the distinctions existing within the unity of the divine essence, a certain progress in revelation becomes very evident. This revelation in regard to the trinity begins in the O. T. To be sure we do not find a complete trinitarian revelation in the O. T., as was erroneously maintained by the church-fathers and by some of the later theologians, who disregarded the historical character of divine revelation. When, however, the Socinians, Arminians, and afterward, Semler, Herder, Doederlein, Bretschneider, Hofmann, etc., taught that the doctrine of the trinity was entirely absent from the O. T., they also were mistaken. The O. T. gives a vague idea of God's trinitarian existence: it is the first instalment of progressively revealed teaching concerning the trinity. However, not only in a few separate passages but especially in the entire organism of its revelation the O. T. contains elements which are of the highest importance for the doctrine of God's tri-personality. The fact that the name Elohim is plural in form to be sure does not prove the trinity; nevertheless, the additional fact that the advocates of monotheism never objected to the use of this name proves that the latter is not to be explained as a reminiscence of polytheism, but that it indicates the richness and fulness of the Divine Being. The God of revelation is not an abstract monad but is the living and true God, who contains the highest distinctions within the one divine essence, infinite in fulness. This is already evident in the work of creation. Elohim creates by means of Word and Spirit. The Word spoken by God is not a mere sound but a power so great that the universe is thereby created and upheld; Jehovah utters his voice and it comes to pass, Gen. 1:3; Ps. 33:6, 9; 147:18; 148:8; Joel 2:11. That Word, which is spoken by God, proceeds from him, and is therefore distinct from him, is later on personified as Wisdom, Job 28:23-27; Prov. 8:22 ff.; cf. Prov. 3:19; Jer. 10:12; 51:15. From everlasting Jehovah possessed, set up, and searched this wisdom. It was God's master workman, through whom he created and still maintains everything.

But the work of creation and providence is established not only through the agency of the Word and of Wisdom, but also by means of the Spirit of God, Gen. 1:2; Ps. 33:6; 104:33; 139:7; Job 26:13; 27:3; 32:8; 33:4; Is. 40:7, 13; 59:19. Whereas God calls everything into being by means of the Word, as Mediator, he is immanent in all creation through the Spirit, who gives life and adornment to all things. Hence a threefold cause of the origin and preservation of all things is already evident in the O. T. doctrine of creation. Elohim (God) and the cosmos (the universe) do not stand over against one another in dualistic fashion; but the world, created by God has his Word for its objective, and his Spirit for its subjective principle. God first thought the universe; hence, the latter is called into being by means of God's omnipotent Word; once realized, it does not have a separate existence, i. e., apart from God or opposed to him, but it rests in his Spirit.

This threefold cause of which mention is made in the O. T. becomes still more evident in the sphere of special revelation, in the work of redemption. Then it is no more Elohim alone but Jehovah, who reveals himself as the God of the covenant and of the oath, of revelation and of history. But even so he does not reveal himself without a mediator, Ex. 33:20. Through his Word he makes himself known, and delivers his people, Ps. 107:20. This revelation of redemption is entrusted to the *Mal'akh Yhwh*, the Messenger of the Covenant. The expression

*Mal'akh Yhwh* or *Mal'akh Elohim* does not always indicate the Un-created Angel as Hengstenberg erroneously assumed. In the following passages an ordinary angel is meant: II Sam. 24:16 ff.; I Kings 19:5-7; II Kings 19:35; Dan. 3:25, 28; 6:23; 10:13; cf. Matt. 1:20, 28; Luke 1:11; 2:9; Acts 5:19; 8:26; 10:3; 12:7, 23; 27:23, Jude 9; Rev. 12:7. Other passages leave room for doubt; as, Num. 22:22 ff.; Josh. 5:13, 14; Judg. 2:1-14; 6:11-24; 13:2-23. But in Gen. 16:6-13; 21:17-20; Gen. 18; 22:11-19; 24:7, 40; 28:13-17; 31:11-13; 32:24-30; cf. Hos. 12:4; Gen. 48:15, 16; Ex. 3:2 ff.; 13:21; 14:19; 23:2-23; 32:34; 33:2 ff.; cf. Num. 20:16; Is. 63:8, 9; Zech. 1:8-12; 3; Mal. 3:1, the subject which speaks through the angel of Jehovah far surpasses a created angel. The church-fathers before Augustine were unanimous in explaining this Angel of Jehovah as a theophany of the Logos. This opinion was often closely connected with the idea that the Father is really invisible, inapproachable, ineffable, but that the Son can reveal himself and that he is the principle of all revelation. This view was held by Justin Martyr, Theophilus, Irenaeus, and Tertullian. But this separation and contrast between the Father and the Son was rejected by the later church-fathers: Athanasius, and the three Cappadocians. They pointed out that the Son was very God, hence equally invisible as the Father. This gave rise to the opinion of Augustine, who held that the O. T. theophanies were always mediated by created angels. This same view was later on adopted by the scholastic and R. C. theologians. Luther and Calvin interpreted the expression *Mal'akh Yhwh* as referring in some passages to a created angel, in others to the uncreated Angel. Later Protestant theologians saw the Logos in all these passages. The Socinians, Arminians, Rationalists, Hofmann, Baumgarten, Delitzsch, and Cremer understood them to refer to angelophanies only. The older view was defended by Stier, Hengstenberg, Keil, Kurtz, Ebrard, Philippi, and others. The difference between the two views is not as great as it may seem. On the one hand, those who favor the interpretation of the ancient church will have to admit that the Logos appeared in human form, and on the other hand, Augustine and those who agree with him will have to grant that in that created angel the Logos manifested himself in a very special manner. Also, not all the passages in which the angel of Jehovah is mentioned can be interpreted similarly. So much is clear: that in the *Mal'akh Yhwh* who is pre-eminently worthy of that name, God (esp. his Word) is present in a very special sense. This is very evident from the fact that though distinct from Jehovah this Angel of Jehovah bears the same name, has the same power, effects the same deliverance, dispenses the same blessings, and is the object of the same adoration. This exegesis is supported by the entire Old and New Testament, Job 33:23; Ps. 34:7; 35:5; Prov. 8:22 ff.; 30:4; Is. 9:5; Hos. 12:6; Mic. 5:6; Zech. 1:8-14; 3:1 ff.; 12:8; Mal. 3:1; John 8:56, 58; cf., John 1:1-5; I Cor. 10:4, 9; while Acts 7:30, 35, 38; Gal. 3:19; and Heb. 2:2 are not in conflict with this view. Moreover, just as in the work of redemption Jehovah reveals himself objectively through his Word in the *Mal'akh Yhwh,* so he manifests himself subjectively in and through his Spirit. God's Spirit is the principle of all blessings and comfort, gifts and talents within the sphere of revelation; it is the source of courage, Judg. 3:10; 6:34; 11:29; 13:25; I Sam. 11:6; of bodily strength, Judg. 14:6; 15:14; of skill, Ex. 28:3; 31:3-5; 35:31-35; I Chron. 28:12; of government, Num. 11:17, 25; I Sam. 16:13; of knowledge and wisdom, Job 32:8; Is. 11:2; of holiness and sanctification, Ps. 51:12; Is. 63:10; cf. Gen. 6:3; Neh. 9:20; I Sam. 10:6, 9; of prophecy and prediction, Num. 11:25, 29; 24:2, 3; Mic. 3:8; etc. In a special manner the Spirit will rest on the Messiah, Is. 11:2; 42:1; 61:1; but afterward he will be poured out upon all flesh, Joel 2:28, 29; Is. 32:15; 44:3; Ezek. 36:26, 27.

This threefold, divine principle, which is the basis of the work of creation and of the work of redemption, and upon which rests the entire economy of the O. T. revelation, is sometimes referred to in one and the same passage. Such a threefold revelation we should not read into the threefold repetition of Dan. 9:19; Zech. 1:3; Is. 6:3; 33:22; but we do find it in the high-priestly blessing of Num. 6:24-26; after which the apostolic blessing was patterned, II Cor. 13:13. The plural forms found in Gen. 1:26, 27; 3:22; Is. 6:8; etc., lack sufficient force to prove the trinity, inasmuch as they can be explained in the same manner as the plural Elohim.

Of greater importance are such passages as Gen. 19:24; Ps. 45:7; 110:1; Hos. 1:7; which indicate a distinction within the Divine Being.

The clearest threefold distinction within the Divine Being is found in Ps. 33:6; Is. 61:1; 63:9-12; and Hag. 2:5, 6. Many have interpreted the story of the three men who appeared to Abraham as a revelation of the trinity, Gen. 18. Others held that one of the three was the Logos and that the other two were ordinary angels; so, e.g., Calvin and the authors of the marginal explanation of the Dutch Authorized Version (Kantt. Statenvertaling). We prefer, however, the exegesis given by Augustine, namely that the three men were three created angels in whom Jehovah revealed himself in a special manner.

**B. In THE WISDOM OF SOLOMON, Philo, and Jewish theology these trinitarian ideas receive further development. However, the differences between what we find here and what is found in Scripture (both Old and New Testament) is very great:**

(1) **The root or origin of the doctrine is different:** the doctrine of mediating entities as we find it in Philo, etc., is derived from the idea of an absolute metaphysical contrast between God and the world. The O. T. offers no traces of this dualism.

(2) **The mediating entities of Philo, etc., are different in character** from the "word" and "wisdom" of the O. T.: in Philo the logos is primarily a mere attribute immanent in God. In the O. T. the "word" is more than an attribute, and "wisdom" is definitely personal.

(3) **The mediating entities of Philo, etc., have no soteriological significance.** The O. T. indicates a close relation between the "word" and the Messiah.

(4) **Philo's doctrine of mediating entities knows no boundary;** it is a dualism with a vengeance; it does not establish contact between God and the world; it neglects the significance of the Holy Spirit.

(5) **The similarity between Philo's doctrine of the logos and the N. T. doctrine of the logos is merely verbal:** the same words "logos," "image," etc., are used by both. The meaning is totally different.

These ideas which we find in the O. T. have been fruitful in many directions. In the first place they were adopted and developed by the authors of apocryphal literature. In *Ecclesiasticus* (*The Wisdom of Jesus, the Son of Sirach*) wisdom is given a prominent place. We are told that she has her origin in God and that he created her from the beginning before the world, and that to the end she will not fail. She is revealed in all the works of God but finds her resting place especially in Zion and in the law, ch. 1:1-30; ch. 24; cf. Baruch, ch. 3:9-4:4. In *The Wisdom of Solomon* this thought receives further development, Ch. 6:22—ch. 9. Wisdom is personified in such a manner that divine attributes and works are ascribed to her. She is described as distinct in existence from God, for she is called the breath of God's power, a clear effluence of the glory of the Almighty, an effulgence from everlasting light, 7:25, 26. Nevertheless, she is described as existing in intimate union with God, as living with him, having been initiated into his knowledge, and as choosing his works for him, 8:3, 4. She is "the one who sits with God in his throne," knows all his works, and was present when God made the world, 9:4, 9. Even more: she is herself the one who creates, rules over, and renews all things, 7:27; 8:1, 5. She is identical with God's Word, 9:1, 2; cf. 16:12; 18:15, 16; and with his Spirit, 1:4-7; 9:17; 12:1. Even in this work the influence of Greek philosophy is noticeable, especially in chapter 7:22 ff.; but this is true much more emphatically in Philo.

Philo already tried to determine the relation of God to the universe. He held that just as natural objects are the objective causes of our sense-perceptions, so eternal and immutable "ideas" are the objective causes of our notions. These ideas, though in themselves merely general concepts, were by Plato elevated to the rank of metaphysical principles, distinct substances, a kind of intermediate beings after which the "demiurge" had patterned the universe. Accordingly they were viewed as the "patterns" (paradigms) and "causes" of natural objects. Although Aristotle subjected Plato's doctrine of ideas to a severe criticism, nevertheless, the belief that an intelligent, spiritual principle underlies all things never disappeared from Greek philosophy. The Stoics especially emphasized the thought that a divine, rational principle is the ground of all phenomena. They called this principle "the seminal word" because whatever exists and lives germinates from that logos as from a seed. They sometimes used the plural and spoke of "seminal words" in order to indicate not only the unity but also the diversity that pertains to the all-creating power of nature. Even the distinction which later on became so important, between the "immanent and the emitted word" was borrowed from the Stoics. Now even before the time of Philo this Greek doctrine of ideas, of the mind, and of the logos had been connected with the O. T. teaching concerning "word" and "wisdom." But it was especially Philo who fused these different elements—Platonic doctrine, of ideas, Stoic doctrine of the logos, O. T. teaching concerning wisdom, etc.,—into *one* system. His starting-point was the absolute metaphysical contrast between God and the world. God is "absolutely bare of quality"; we can merely say *that* he is, not *what* he is. Between God and matter there can be no direct contact. Before God created the sensible world, he made a plan and conceived the "totality of ideas" or "patterns and energies" of all things. In Philo these ideas are the forces through whose mediation an active relation of God to the world is brought about. Employing a varying degree of metaphorical language and personification he describes these ideas as servants, governors, ambassadors, inter-mediaries, "operative ideas" and energies, joints and pillars. He identifies his "ideas" with the "angels" of Moses and with the "daemons" of the Greeks; they are thoughts that are immanent in the mind of God, uncreated and eternal as is God himself. These ideas are many in number but they are all comprehended in one highest Logos or Reason, Idea, or Force—the unity of the individual ideas—the "world (or totality) of ideas." And this Logos is described now as a divine attribute, namely, God's wisdom, then again as a being distinct from God: Philo's description of Reason is characterized by the same kind of amphiboly that marks his theory of the divine ideas. Reason is, as it were, an hypostasis standing between God and the world and partaking of the nature of both. He is not uncreated in the sense in which God is uncreated, neither created in the sense in which finite objects are created; he is the vicar, ambassador interpreter, vice-gerent, angel, tool, image, and shadow of God, his first-born son even, his oldest son in comparison with the world which is his youngest son. Philo even calls him God; i.e., a "second God." Zeller very clearly indicates that "Reason" in the philosophy of Philo bears and must bear this double character. He is an intermediate being, hence a double being, a divine attribute and a person, identical neither with God nor with the world, an idea immanent in the mind of God and a force immanent in the world, pendulating between an impersonal attribute and a distinct hypostasis, and for that very reason viewed as a suitable mediator between God and the world.

In Jewish theology this doctrine of mediating entities received further development. Whereas God is absolutely transcendent, direct contact between God and the world is impossible. Mediators are necessary in order to establish the required contact. When God wishes merely to guide the powers present in the realm of mankind and nature, he avails himself of the service of angels. But when he wishes to carry out his work of creation or redemption, there appear on the scene hypostases, who, although creatures, yet possess divine attributes because they are God's representatives. Such hypostases are Metraton, God's "throne-sharer"; Memra, the word of God; Shekinah, the presence of God's glory; Bath Kol, the oracular voice of God, a means of divine revelation; Ruach hakkōdesh, the spirit that proceeds from God and imparts a higher knowledge.

Although *Ecclesiasticus* bears close resemblance to canonical literature, by contrast the Wisdom of Solomon, Philo, and Jewish theology give clear evidence of the influence of philosophy upon religion and consequently of an increasing departure from the teachings of the O. T.

There is first of all a difference in principle. The doctrine of mediating entities as we find it in Philo and in later Jewish theology is derived from the Platonic dualism between God and the material universe. The O. T. offers no trace of this dualism. In the O. T. "word" and "wisdom" are not viewed as intermediaries between God and the world, but stand wholly in the side of divinity. They pertain to God, and are the originating causes of the created universe. In Philo the mediating entities are self-contradictory. They are neither divine nor human, neither persons nor attributes, neither independent substances nor energies, but they partake of the nature of both. They indicate that the boundary-line which in the O. T. always separates the creature from the Creator has been erased, and pave the way for the philosophy of Gnosticism and for the the cabala.

Secondly, there is a difference equally great between the character of the "word" and "wisdom" of Scripture on the one hand, and of Philo's mediating entities on the other. In Philo "Reason" is *primarily* merely an attribute: God's reason, thought, mind; hence, as such, Reason is immanent in God. The meaning "Word that proceeds from God and mediates between God and the world" is secondary in Philo. In the O. T., on the contrary, the primary significance of "word" is not God's reason or intellection, even less an ideal image or plan of the universe, a "totality of ideas," but the spoken word by means of which God creates and preserves all things. Similarly, "wisdom" in Job and Proverbs is not pictured as a divine attribute, but as a person possessed and ordained by God from eternity, searched and consulted in connection with the creation of the world.

Thirdly, the mediating entities in Philo and Jewish theology have no soteriological significance. They impart light and knowledge but there is no connection between them and the Messiah. They even relegate to the background the doctrine of the Messiah as Revealer of the truth and as Savior. Now it must be admitted that even the O. T. does not clearly reveal the relation between word and wisdom, servant of God and Messiah, "Angel of Jehovah" (*Mal'akh Yhwh*) and Son of David. Nevertheless, the lines do not run parallel but are gradually converging. Elohim and Jehovah indicate the same God. He who creates and cares for the world as Elohim through the Word and the Spirit is the same person as the Jehovah who guides Israel through his Angel, the same as the One who will save his people through the Servant of Jehovah, the same as the One who will reign forever through the Messiah of the house of David, and the same as the One who will renew and sanctify all his children through his Spirit. And these lines of thought which gradually approach one another in the O. T. have as their common focus the One who is the Logos, the Prophet, Priest, and King, in whom God condescends to his people to dwell with them forever. To Philo an incarnation of "Reason" would have seemed absurd; in the N. T. the incarnation of the "Word" is God's highest revelation. (The Greek *logos* means both "Reason" and "Word"— translator's note.)

Finally, it may be added that Philo's doctrine of mediating entities is not fully rounded. It knows no boundary. Philo brings about a certain amount of unity by comprehending the divine ideas in the one "Reason" but he describes Reason in terms similar to those which he uses to describe the ideas. Jewish theology offers an ever increasing number of mediating entities. It is an emanation comparable to that of the eons (or aeons) of Gnosticism. It is dualism with a vengeance. Inasmuch as these mediating entities are really neither divine nor human, the dualism between God and the world remains. The antithesis between God and the universe remains unchanged; the world remains something entirely separate from God. The significance of

God's Spirit is not understood. In the O. T. this doctrine of the Spirit is very prominent. In apocryphal literature, in Philo, and in Jewish theology it is hardly mentioned. At best it is a spirit of prediction granted to some, but it is not the Spirit of the O. T. who rounds out and consummates the work of creation and of redemption.

For all these reasons there is a fundamental difference between the manner in which the trinitarian thoughts which we find in the O. T. are developed in apocryphal literature, Philo, and Jewish theology, and the manner in which these ideas are developed in the N. T. The N. T. and Philo, etc., may have some words in common, e.g., both speak of Christ as "Reason or Word," (*logos*) "image," "effulgence or reflected brightness," "Son," "God," etc., but that is where the similarity ends. That there is this verbal similarity is due to the fact that the N. T. was written in Greek, in "the common language of the people," the language which existed at that time and was spoken everywhere. The N. T. did not create a new vocabulary. The thoughts of God were clothed in the humble and earthly garb of human language. But God invested these words with new meaning. Hence, there is correspondence in form, but difference in content. Philo and John have merely the *name* Logos in common. Gradually scholars are beginning to recognize and understand this fact.

    C. **The doctrine of the trinity in the N. T.:**

        (1) The N. T. contains the true development of the O. T. teaching concerning the trinity.

        (2) The N. T. does not give us an abstract doctrine; instead the idea of the trinity is presupposed and implied everywhere.

        (3) The N. T. teaching is based upon the trinitarian ideas that are found in the O. T.: the Father, Son, and Spirit of the N. T. are the same as those in the O. T.

        (4) The real N. T. equivalent for Yhwh is Father. In the incarnation of the Son of God and in the effusion of the Holy Spirit we have the fulfilment of the O. T. prophecies and the basis for the N. T. doctrine of the trinity.

        (5) In the N. T., however, the revelation concerning the trinity is much more explicit than in the O. T. The entire N. T. is trinitarian. The trinity is manifested:

           (a) in connection with the facts of Christ's life on earth, Matt. 1:18 ff.; Matt. 3:16 ff.; etc.;

           (b) in the teaching of Jesus, esp. Matt. 28:19;

           (c) in the teaching of the apostles, esp. I Cor. 8:6, 12; II Cor. 13:14; II Thess. 2:13, 14; Eph. 4:4-6; I Peter 1:2; I John 5:4-6. (I John 5:7, "For there are three that bear record in heaven the Father, the Word, and the Holy Ghost: and these three are one," is probably not genuine.)

    The N. T. contains the true development of the O. T. trinitarian ideas. This N. T. revelation, however, is much clearer: it does not

consist in abstract reasoning concerning the being of God, but God
manifests himself in the incarnation, in word and in deed. As in the
O. T. so also in the N. T. God's unity is emphasized. The word *God,*
Elohim, *theos* can properly be applied to one being only, John 17:3;
I Cor. 8:4; but this one God reveals himself as Father, Son, and Spirit;
as such he becomes manifest especially in the incarnation of the Son
and in the outpouring of the Spirit.

These N. T. facts do not give us something which is absolutely new.
The N. T. principles involved in the doctrine of the trinity are contained in the O. T. teaching concerning creation, and in fact in the
entire O. T. economy. The Father, who bears this name especially in
relation to the Son and to his children, is the Creator of the universe.
In the sense of Creator he may also be called Father, Matt. 7:11; Luke
3:38; John 4:21; Acts 17:28; I Cor. 8:6; Heb. 12:9. Of him are all
things, I Cor. 8:6.    The Son, who bears this name because of his
peculiar relation to God, is the Logos through whom the Father created
all things, John 1:3; I Cor. 8:6; Col. 1:15-17; Heb. 1:3. And the Holy
Spirit, called thus with a view to his work in the church, is the Spirit
who together with the Father and the Son adorns and finishes the
work of creation, Matt. 1:18; 4:1; Mark 1:12; Luke 1:35; 4:1, 14;
Rom. 1:4. The Father, Son, and Holy Spirit are the same in both dispensations: already in the O. T. dispensation they revealed themselves
to the fathers in word and deed, in prophecy and miracle.

In the N. T. Jehovah is called "Father," (*patēr*) richer in meaning
than "Lord" (*kyrios*). In the incarnate Son of God all the O. T.
prophecies and shadows of prophet and king, of priesthood and sacrifice,
of Servant of Jehovah and Son of David, of Angel of Jehovah and
Wisdom, reach their fulfilment. And the outpouring of the Holy
Spirit is the realization of the O. T. promise, Acts. 2:16 ff.

But the N. T. revelation concerning the trinity not only links itself
to the O. T. but surpasses it. The fact that the God of the covenant is
triune becomes very clear now: it becomes evident that he *must needs
be* triune, and that salvation itself rests upon a threefold principle.
This trinitarian revelation is not limited to a few texts; the entire N. T.
is trinitarian in character. God: Father, Son, and Holy Spirit, is the
source of all blessing, comfort, and salvation. Christ's birth and baptism
reveal the trinity, Matt. 1:18 ff.; Luke 1:35; Matt. 3:16, 17; Mark
1:10, 11; Luke 3:21, 22. Christ's teaching is trinitarian throughout.
He declares unto us the Father, whom he describes as a Spirit who
has life in himself, John 4:24; 5:26; and who is in a very special sense
*his* Father, Matt. 11:27; John 2:16; 5:17. Though Christ and the
Father are distinct, nevertheless, the former is the only begotten and
beloved Son of the Father, Matt. 11:27; 21:37-39; John 3:16; etc.,

equal to him in glory, life, and power, John 1:14; 5:26; 10:30. And the Holy Spirit who leads Christ and qualifies him for his task, Mark 1:12; Luke 4:1, 14; John 3:34; is called another Comforter (Paraclete) whom the Son will send from the Father, John 15:26; and who will convict, teach, guide into all the truth, and remain forever, John 16:7 ff.; 14:16. Before Christ departs from this earth he sums up his trinitarian teaching in that beautiful phrase: "the name of the Father, and of the Son, and of the Holy Spirit." It is the single Name in which, nevertheless, three distinct subjects (notice the purposeful repetition of the article) are revealed. The apostles continue and augment this teaching: they all recognize and glory in a threefold, divine cause of salvation. The good pleasure, foreknowledge, election, power, love, and kingdom pertain to the Father, Matt. 6:13; 11:26; John 3:16; Rom. 8:29; Eph. 1:9; I Pet. 1:2. Reconciliation, mediatorship, redemption, grace, wisdom, and righteousness pertain to the Son, Matt. 1:21; I Cor. 1:30; Eph. 1:10; I Tim. 2:5; I Pet. 1:2; I John 2:2; etc. Regeneration rejuvenation, sanctification, and communion pertain to the Holy Spirit, John 3:5; John 14:16; Rom. 5:5; 8:15; 14:17; II Cor. 1:21, 22; I Pet. 1:2; I John 5:6; etc. Moreover, just as Christ sums up his teaching on the trinity in the phrase: "the name of the Father, and of the Son, and of the Holy Spirit," in the same manner the apostles again and again mention these three together, giving equal prominence to each, I Cor. 8:6; 12:4-6; II Cor. 13:14; II Thess. 2:13, 14; Eph. 4:4-6; I Pet. 1:2; I John 5:4-6; Rev. 1:4-6. The genuine character of the text of I John 5:7 remains doubtful. It is not found in any of the Greek codices except in a few dating from the sixteenth century, nor in any of the Latin codices that antedate the eighth century, and it is absent from nearly every version. Furthermore, it is never quoted by the Greek fathers, not even during the period of the Arian controversy, nor by the Latin patres: Hilary, Ambrose, Jerome, Augustine, etc. *If* quoted or presupposed by Tertullian, it must have been in existence since about the year 190; and *if* cited by Cyprian, it must have been known about the year 220. *If* the African Version contained this text — as is maintained by one manuscript dating from the fifth and by one dating from the seventh century — we can go back still further, for the African Version dates from about the year 160 and was brought to Italy circa 250. With certainty we can state that this text occurred in the writings of Vigilius toward the close of the fifth century. In the sixteenth century it was included in the Complutensian Greek N. T., by Erasmus in the third edition of his work, by Robert Estienne (Stephanus), by Theodore Beza, and in the Textus Receptus. It is not definitely required by the context, and it would be very difficult to account for its omission and subsequent disappearance. There are still some who defend this passage as genuine, and in 1897 the question whether I John 5:7 may safely be rejected or at least omitted as being doubtful was answered negatively by the congregation of the holy office at Rome, a decision which was ratified by the pope. But apparently this verdict did not settle the question of the authenticity of I John 5:7, or otherwise there may have been a secret repeal. At any rate even after this official declaration many Roman Catholic theologians have defended with many arguments the unauthenticity of I John 5:7; e.g., Künstle maintains that this passage is not genuine, and that it was derived from a sentence in an apology of Priscillian, dating from the year 380.

> D. **Relations existing between the three persons:**
> (1) **The Father:**
>  a. The name "Father" means God as Creator, Num. 16:22; God as Father of Israel, Deut. 32:6; God as Father of believers, Matt. 6:4; or the first person of the trinity, i.e., the Father of the Son, Luke 22:29.
>  b. The Father is pre-eminent in the works of creation and redemption; he represents the trinity; hence, he is often called God, even by Christ. Nevertheless, the Son and the Holy Spirit are also God.
> (2) **The Son is the Logos** through whom God reveals himself, John 1:13, 14; he is called the Son of God by nature and from eternity. Matt. 3:17; and the image of God, Gal. 1:15.
> (3) **The Holy Spirit:**
>  a. He is called Spirit because he is the life-giving principle immanent in creation; he is called Holy because he is the Spirit of GOD, Job 33:4; Ps. 33:6; he is the Spirit of the Father and the Spirit of the Son for he proceeds from both, John 15:26.
>  b. His personal and divine character becomes very evident in the N. T.:
>  1. The Holy Spirit is a person, John 15:26; 16:13, 14; I John 2:1; I Cor. 2:10, 11; etc.
>  2. The Holy Spirit is God, for the terms Spirit and God are used interchangeably; divine attributes, works and honor are ascribed to him, etc.

But Scripture gives us more than these data; it also furnishes us with some knowledge regarding the relations that exist between the three distinct subjects, Father, Son, and Holy Spirit. Accordingly, let us first consider the name "Father." In its most general sense this name indicates God as Creator of all things, especially of man, Num. 16:22; Matt. 7:11; Luke 3:38; John 4:21; Acts 17:28; I Cor. 8:6; Eph. 3:15; Heb. 12:9. In the O. T. this name receives theocratic significance; God is *Israel's* Father, having created and preserved it by means of his wondrous power, Deut. 32:6; Is. 63:16; 64:8; Mal. 1:6; 2:10; Jer. 3:19; 31:9; Ps. 103:13; Rom. 9:4; in the N. T. the name receives an ethical meaning, according to which God is the Father of his spiritual children, Matt. 6:4, 8, 9; Rom. 8:15, etc. But in a very special metaphysical sense God is the Father of the Son. Jesus always makes an essential distinction between the relation in which he himself stands over against the Father, and the relation of others (the Jews, the disciples, etc.) to the Father, Matt. 11:25-27; Luke 22:29; John 2:16; 5:17; 20:17; etc. He called God his *"own* Father," John 5:18. Scripture points out very clearly that the name "Father" does not primarily indicate the relation in which God stands to Israel and to believers, but that in its original significance it indicates the relation of the Father toward the Son, John 14:6-13; 17:26. God is essentially and primarily Father of the Son, he loves the Son, John 5:19 ff.; 10:17; 17:24, 26; and this love proceeds from the Father through the Son to others, John 16:27; 17:26. This relation of the Father toward the Son did not originate in time, but is from eternity, John 1:14; 8:38; 17:5, 24. Hence, again and again God is called in a special sense the Father of our Lord Jesus Christ, Rom. 15:6; I Cor. 15:24; II Cor. 1:3; Gal. 1:1; Eph. 1:3; etc. Paternity with reference to the Son is the distinctive, personal property of the Father. The Father is the first in the order of existence, John 5:26; hence, both with reference to the work of creation and to the work of redemption he is the Father, of whom are all things, I Cor. 8:6. Both in the Old and in the New Testament the Father occupies the first position. The purpose, Acts 4:28; Eph. 1:11, the good pleasure, Matt. 11:26; Eph. 1:9; the initiative in the work of creation and of redemption, Ps. 33:6; John 3:16; the "authority" and "power," Matt. 6:13; Rom. 1:20; Eph. 1:19; righteousness, Gen. 18:25; Deut. 32:4; John 17:25; Rom. 3:26; II Tim. 4:8; goodness, wisdom, immortality, and light unapproachable, Matt. 19:17; Rom. 16:27; I Tim. 6:16, pertain to him. Accordingly, he is often in a special sense called God. He is Elohim, Jehovah Elohim, El Elyon, El Shaddai, "the only true God," John 17:3, "the one God," I Cor. 8:6; I Tim. 2:5; called God and Father in conjunction with the Lord Jesus Christ and the Holy Spirit, I Cor. 12:6; II Cor. 13:13; I Thess. 1:3; Rev. 1:6. Even Christ himself calls him not only his Father but also his God, Matt. 27:46; John 20:17; Heb. 1:9; 2:17; 5:1; 10:7, 9; and Jesus is called the Christ of God, Luke 9:20; I Cor. 3:23; Rev. 12:10. From this fact the Arians — both early and later — have without just grounds derived the conclusion that the Father alone is God, and that the Son and the Holy Spirit are not divine in essence, though they are closely related to God. But Scripture ascribes divine names, attributes, works, and honor not only to the Father but also to the Son and to the Spirit. Furthermore, it should be observed that Scripture nowhere maintains that the *Father only* is the true God, but it does maintain that the Father is *the only true God,* a fact which is fully recognized in the doctrine of the church. Then also, it should be noted that the passages cited do not establish an antithesis between the Father on the one hand and the Son and the Spirit on the other hand; but between the Father, as the only true God, on the one hand, and the gods of heathendom on the other. Moreover, to conclude from passages in which the Father is called the only true God, who only hath wisdom, immortality, etc., that the Son and the Spirit do not partake of the same divine essence, wisdom, immortality, etc., would be just as illogical as it would be to conclude from I Cor. 8:6 that God is not our Lord, through whom are all things and we unto him, but that this distinction pertains only to Christ. Finally, to describe the Father as only wise, good, etc., is proper because all things are *of him*; he is "Fountain of Deity," whereas the Son and the Spirit have the same being and the same attributes by communication. Whenever the name "God" is in a special sense applied to the Father, it indicates that in the divine economy he is first; it is as it were an official title, indicative of order and rank, just as among men there are distinctions of social standing and honor though all share the same human nature.

The names ascribed to the Son give us more light in regard to the immanent relations between the three persons. Because most of these names refer to Christ's earthly manifestation, and are therefore discussed under Christology, we shall discuss only those which pertain to him entirely apart from the incarnation. There is first the name "Logos." Many explanations have been given of this name. It has been translated Reason, Speech, Word, both internal and external. Undoubtedly, however, the real reason why Christ bears this name is the doctrine found everywhere in Scripture, namely, that in the work both of creation and of redemption God reveals himself through the Word. By means of the Word God creates, preserves, and reigns over all things, and through the Word he also transforms the universe. Accordingly, the Gospel is called the "Word of God." John calls Christ the Logos, because in him and through him God reveals himself both in creation and in redemption, John 1:3, 14. In the O. T. God reveals himself through the Word in creation. The personal and eternal existence of that Word is not expressed. In Prov. 8 Wisdom is represented as eternal and personal, and it is closely connected with the work of creation; with a view to creation it was formed, (R. V. "possessed") set up, and searched, vv. 22, 23. From the word *qānānî,* he formed me, of verse 22, LXX *ektise me,* Syr. Trg. *berā'ni,* cf. Sirach 1:4, 9; 24:8, the Arians concluded that the Son was not generated from eternity but created before all things. The church-fathers, on the other hand, maintained that *qānāni* should be translated *ektēsato*: he possessed me, Aq.

Symm; or possedit, Jerome; or that this word did not refer to the essence of the Son but to his office and dignity with a view to creation and redemption. The latter is doubtless the truth. Eternal generation is not referred to here; all we are told is that God formed, *qānānî*, wisdom and established it, *nissakti;* that it was brought forth *hōlati,* before and with a view to creation. The N. T., however, is much more explicit. John not only tells us that he through whom God reveals himself is a person, but states in so many words that the Logos (the Word) *was* "in the beginning." He did not *become* Logos; he was not formed and established as Logos at the time of creation; he *was* Logos; as a person and by nature, Logos from eternity. Furthermore, he himself was "God"; "he was in the beginning with God," verse 2; "in the bosom of the Father," verse 18; the object of his eternal love and self-communication, 5:26; 17:24. Hence, he was able to reveal the Father completely, because the Logos possessed the divine nature, life, love, etc., from all eternity.. Because God communicated himself to the Logos, therefore the latter is able to impart himself to us. The Logos is the absolute revelation of God, for from eternity God has imparted himself in all his fulness to the Logos.

Another name which Christ bears is *Son of God.* In the O. T. this name is usually theocratic in meaning. Israel is called God's son because it was chosen, called, and adopted by God, Ex. 4:22; 19:5; Deut. 1:31; 8:5; 14:1; 32:6, 18; Is. 63:8; Jer. 31:9, 20; Hos. 11:1; Mal. 1:6; 2:10. In the N. T. the church takes the place of Israel. It consists of "sons of God" by adoption, or "children of God" by birth. The title "son of God" is often an official title, used to indicate judges, Ps. 82:6; angels, Job 38:7; and especially the king, II Sam. 7:11-14; Ps. 89:26, 27. In Psalm 2:7 Jehovah says to Zion's anointed king, "My son (art) thou, I to-day have begotten thee"; LXX: *gegennēka se;* Vulg. genui te: on the day in which the Lord anointed him and appointed him as king he begat him as Son, and gave unto him authority to rule the world. With a view to David this refers to the decree of God of which mention is made in II Sam. 7, and with a view to the Messiah — of whom David is a type — Heb. 1:5; 5:5 interprets it as referring to eternity, in which Christ as the Son was generated by the Father, that is, in which he was brought forth as the effulgence of God's glory and the very image of his substance. Moreover, according to Acts 13:33; Rom. 1:3, the second person of the trinity was declared to be the Son of God with power, by the resurrection from the dead. In Micah 5:2, we find a similar thought. The Ruler of Israel, who shall come forth out of Bethlehem, is from everlasting. His goings forth are from of old, from everlasting. From eternity he was Ruler; he has revealed this in Israel's history, and as such he shall visibly appear, coming forth out of Bethlehem. The name Son of God, when applied to the Messiah, is undoubtedly based on the theocratic significance of this expression in the O. T. Very likely the full meaning of this name was not grasped by the demoniacs, Matt. 8:29; cf. 4:3; by the Jews, Matt. 27:40; by the high priest, Matt. 26:63; and by the disciples in their first period, John 1:50; 11:27; Matt. 16:16. It is true that Christ is sometimes called God's Son in the sense of King or Mediator, Luke 1:35. Even then, however, the view of the Adoptionists, namely, that according to his divine nature Christ is Son by generation, and according to his human nature by adoption, as was later on also held by the Socinians and the Arminians, is contrary to Scripture. But the name Son of God when ascribed to Christ has a far deeper meaning than the theocratic: he was not a mere king of Israel who in time became an adopted Son of God; neither was he called Son of God because of his supernatural birth, as the Socinians and Hofmann held; neither is he Son of God merely in an ethical sense, as others suppose; neither did he receive the title Son of God as a new name in connection with his atoning work and resurrection, an interpretation in support of which John 10:34-36; Acts 13:32, 33; and Rom. 1:4 are cited; but he is Son of God in a metaphysical sense: by nature and from eternity. He is exalted high above angels and prophets, Matt. 13:32; 21:27; 22:2; and sustains a very special relation to God, Matt. 11:7. He is the beloved Son in whom the Father is well pleased, Matt. 3:17; 17:5; Mark 1:11; 9:7; Luke 3:22; 9:35; the only begotten Son, John 1:18; 3:16; I John 4:9 ff.; God's *own* Son, Rom. 8:32; the eternal Son, John 17:5, 24; Heb. 1:5; 5:5; to whom the Father gave "to have life in himself," John 5:26; equal to the Father in knowledge, Matt. 11:27; in honor, John 5:23; in creative and redemptive power, John 1:3; 5:21, 27; in work, John 10:30; and in dominion, Matt. 11:27; Luke 10:22; 22:29; John 16:15; 17:10; and because of this Sonship he was condemned to death, John 10:33; Matt. 26:63 ff.

Thirdly, we should consider the name Image of God. By way of analogy, this name can be ascribed to man in general, but in an absolute sense it pertains to Christ. Before the incarnation, as Logos and Son, Rom. 1:3, 4; 8:3; Gal 4:4, he existed in the form of God, Phil. 2:6; was rich, II Cor. 8:9; clothed with majesty, John 17:5; and by means of his resurrection and ascension he returned to that state of glory. Hence, he was and is even now "the image of the invisible God," Col. 1:15; II Cor. 4:4, "the effulgence of his (God's) glory and the very image (impress) of his substance," Heb. 1:3. Notice that the original does not have *apaugasmos*: the effulgence itself, but *apaugasma*: the image resulting from the effulgence or reflection of God's glory, and the imprint of the Father's substance or being. As such he is the "firstborn of all creation," Col. 1:15; Rev. 1:16, "born before any creature"; first-*born*, not first-formed or first-created, in whom all things were created. Moreover, he is the "beginning, the firstborn from the dead, having the preëminence in all things," Col. 1:18; the "first-born among many brethren," Rom. 8:29; into whose image the believers are transformed, II Cor. 3:18; Phil. 3:21. The expression "first-born" does not *in*clude Christ in the realm of the creatures, but *ex*cludes him from that realm. Being the firstborn and only begotten Son and Logos, and the adequate image of God, he from eternity sustained a very unique relation to the Father. And although as Mediator Christ is represented as dependent upon and subordinate to the Father, so that he is the servant sent to complete the Father's work, obedient unto death, and delivering his kingdom unto the Father; in essence and being he remains, nevertheless, co-equal with the Father. Accordingly, when in John 14:28 Jesus says that his going to the Father is for the disciples an occasion for rejoicing, "for the Father is greater than I," he does not mean that the Father is greater in power — for John 10:28-30 teaches differently — but he refers to himself in his *humiliation*. The Father in his glory is greater than the Son in his humiliation. But when Jesus goes to the Father, this inferiority will end. Hence, the disciples ought to rejoice when their Master returns to the Father. Though while on earth Christ is lower than the Father in position and in office, he is co-equal with the Father in essence and nature. He is not a creature, but he was and is and remains God, who is over all, blessed for ever, John 1:1; 20:28; Rom. 9:5; Heb. 1:8, 9; II Pet. 3:18; I John 5:20; Rev. 1:8, 11; perhaps also II Thess. 1:2; Tit. 2:13; II Pet. 1:1. Under Christology we shall discuss the attempt made by the Socinians, Ritschl, Schultz, Kaftan, etc., to interpret the word "God" when applied to Christ as referring not to his being but to his office. At this place we wish merely to remark that the title "God" (*theos*) cannot be properly applied to Christ if the latter does not partake of the divine nature.

Finally, by means of the name *the Holy Spirit* Scripture sheds some light on the immanent relations within the trinity. It must be remarked at the very outset that the doctrine of the Holy Spirit is the same throughout the various books of both the Old and the New Testament. Though in the N. T. this doctrine comes to clearer expression, it is found already in the O. T. The N. T. itself testifies that its teaching concerning the Holy Spirit is not different from that which we find in the O. T.: the Holy Spirit which aforetime spoke through the prophets, Matt. 22:43; Mk. 12:36; Acts 1:16; 28:25; Heb. 3:7; 10:15; I Pet. 1:11; II Pet. 1:21; testified in the days of Noah, I Pet. 3:19; was resisted by Israel, Acts 7:51; and wrought faith. II Cor. 4:13, is the same Spirit which descended upon the Messiah and dwells in the church, as was prophesied, Matt. 12:18; Luke 4:18, 19; Acts 2:16. Although the word "Spirit" is applied to the Divine Being as such, John 4:24, nevertheless, the term "Holy Spirit" indicates a distinct person, distinguishable from the Father and the Son. The name "Holy Spirit" owes its origin to the mode of subsistence peculiar to the third person of the trinity. Spirit really means wind, breath. The Holy Spirit is the breath of the Almighty, Job 33:4; the breath of his mouth, Ps. 33:6; compared by Jesus to the wind, John 3:8; and breathed upon the disciples, John 20:22; cf. II Thess. 2:18. The Spirit is God as the immanent principle of life in all creation. He is called "Holy" (Spirit) because he himself bears a peculiar relation to God, and because he determines the distinctive relation between God and all existing objects. He is not the Spirit of man or of any other creature, but he is the Spirit of *God,* the *Holy* Spirit, Ps. 51:12; Is. 63:10, 11. As breath proceeds from our mouth, so the Spirit proceeds from God and preserves every creature. Hence, he is called the Spirit of God, the Spirit of the Lord, the Spirit of the Father, Gen. 1:2; Is. 11:2; Matt. 10:20; and also the Spirit of Christ, the Spirit of the Son, Rom. 8:2, 9; I Cor. 2:6; II Cor. 3:17, 18; Phil. 1:19; Gal. 3:2; 4:6; I Pet. 1:11; standing before the throne of God and of the Lamb, Rev. 1:4; 3:1; 4:5; 5:6. This procession of the Holy Spirit is indicated by means of various expressions in Scripture. Usually the Spirit is represented as being given by God or by Christ, Num. 11:29; Neh. 9:20; Is. 42:1; Ezek. 36:27; John 3:34; I John 3:24; 4:13; sent or sent forth, Ps. 104:30; John 14:26; 15:26; 16:7; Gal. 4:6; Rev. 5:6; poured out or poured forth, Is. 32:15; 44:3; Joel 2:28; Zech. 12:10; Acts 2:17, 18; as descending from God, Matt. 3:16; put in the midst of Israel, Is. 63:11; Hag. 2:6; put upon any one, Matt. 12:18; breathed on a person, John 20:22; etc. But we are also told that the Holy Spirit "proceedeth from the Father," John 15:26. In a special sense this occurred on the day of Pentecost. Hence, the personality of the Holy Spirit now becomes very clear. In the O. T. there is, indeed, a distinction between God and the Spirit, but the nature of that distinction is still obscure, "for the Spirit was not yet given because Jesus was not yet glorified," John 7:39. But he is now spoken of as a person. The personal pronoun is used with reference to him, John 15:26; 16:13, 14. He is called "Paraclete," John 15:26; cf. I John 2:1; "another Paraclete." John 14:16; who speaks of himself in the first person, Acts 13:2; to whom all kinds of personal actions and works are ascribed; viz., searching, I Cor. 2:10, 11; judging, Acts 15:28; hearing, John 16:13; speaking Acts 13:2; Rev. 2:7, etc.; 14:13; 22:17; wishing, I Cor. 12:11; teaching, John 14:26; interceding, Rom. 8:27; witnessing, John 15:26; etc.;

and who stands in a co-ordinate relation to Father and Son, Matt. 28:19; I Cor. 12:4-6; II Cor. 13:13; Rev. 1:4. All this is impossible except he be very God.

Not only the personality but also the divinity of the Holy Spirit first becomes clear in the N. T. This divinity is evident first of all from the fact that although God and his Spirit are distinct, it nevertheless amounts to the same thing whether God or the Holy Spirit speaks to us, dwells in us, or is resisted by us, Is. 6:9; cf. Acts 28:25; Jer. 31:31; cf. Heb. 10:15; Ps. 95:7, 8; cf. Heb. 3:7-9; Acts 5:3, 4; Rom. 8:9, 10; I Cor. 3:16; cf. 6:19; Eph. 3:22. This can be true only when personal distinction and essential equality go together. Furthermore, all kinds of divine attributes are ascribed to God's Spirit as well as to God, viz., eternity, Heb. 9:14; omnipresence, Ps. 139:7; omniscience, I Cor. 2:10, 11; omnipotence, I Cor. 12:4-6. This also pre-supposes the fact that the Spirit and God are one in essence. The divinity of the Holy Spirit becomes especially apparent in the divine works of creation, Gen. 1:2; Ps. 33:6; Job 33:4; Ps. 104:30; and of redemption: in the anointing of Christ (qualifying him for his office) Is. 11:2; 61:1; Luke 4:18; Is. 42:1; Matt. 12:18; Luke 1:35; Matt. 3:16; 4:1; John 3:34; Matt. 12:28; Heb. 9:14; Rom. 1:4; in the preparation of the apostles for their specific work, Matt. 10:20; Luke 12:12; 21:15; 24:49; John 14:16 ff.; 15:26; 16:13 ff.; etc.; in the distribution of gifts and talents among believers, I Cor. 12:4-11; and in the spiritual immanence of the fulness of Christ in the church. The Holy Spirit sustains the same relation to Christ as does Christ to the Father. Just as the Son has nothing and does nothing and speaks nothing of himself, but receives everything from the Father, John 5:26, 30; 16:15; in the same manner the Holy Spirit takes everything from Christ, John 16:13, 14. As the Son declares and glorifies the Father, John 1:18; 17:4, 6, so the Holy Spirit declares and glorifies the Son, 15:26; 16:14. Just as no one comes to the Father than through the Son, Matt. 11:27; John 14:6; in the same manner no one can say "Jesus is Lord," than in the Holy Spirit, I Cor. 12:3. Apart from the Holy Spirit communion with God is impossible. But that Spirit does indeed grant all the blessings which were merited by Christ; viz., regeneration, John 3:3; conviction of sin, John 16:8-11; adoption, Rom. 8:15; renewing, Tit. 3:5; God's love, Rom. 5:5; all kinds of spiritual fruits, Gal. 5:22; sealing, Rom. 8:23; II Cor. 1:22; 5:5; Eph. 1:13; 4:30; and resurrection, Rom. 8:10. Through the Spirit we even have communion with the Son himself and with the Father himself; and this communion is direct and immediate. The Holy Spirit is God himself in us, John 14:23 ff.; I Cor. 3:16; 6:19; II Cor. 6:16; Gal. 2:20; Col. 3:11; Eph. 3:17; Phil. 1:8, 21. Who is able to grant us all these blessings? Who can cause God to dwell in our hearts? Who can do all these things if it be not God himself? Accordingly, divine honor is ascribed to the Holy Spirit. In co-ordination with the Father and the Son he is the source of all blessing, Matt. 28:19; I Cor. 12:4-6; II Cor. 13:13; Rev. 1:4. In his name we are baptized, Matt. 28:19. All life and energy is of him. He is the Author of our prayers, Zech. 12:10; Rom. 8:15, 16. The church, accordingly, receives the admonition not to grieve the Holy Spirit. Is. 63:10; Eph. 4:30; and the blasphemy against the Holy Spirit is unforgivable, Matt. 12:31, 32.

**II. History of the Development of the Doctrine of the Trinity: Scripture Does Not Give Us A Fully Formulated Doctrine of the Trinity, But Contains All the Elements Out Of Which Theology Has Constructed This Doctrine. The Apostolic Fathers Simply Quote Scripture. They Avoid Both the Ebionitic and the Docetic Errors. In the Second Century as a Result of the Rise of Gnosticism the Doctrine of the Trinity Begins To Have Dogmatic Significance. The Apologists Are Not Free From the Error of Subordinationism and Are Under the Influence of Gnostic Dualism. After the Apologists and Before the Council of Nicea, Irenaeus, Tertullian, and Origen Made Their Specific Contributions To the Development Of This Doctrine: Irenaeus Defends the Consubstantiality of the Persons, Their Essential Unity; Tertullian Complements Irenaeus and Emphasizes the Distinctions In the Persons, Which He Derives From the Being Of God. He Also Supplies the Terms that are Necessary To Convey the True Meaning of the Trinitarian Dogma. Origen Sets Forth the Eternal Character of the Interpersonal Relations. The Church Rejected Origen's Subordinationism and at Nicea (325 A. D.) Officially Confessed the Consubstantiality of the Three Distinct Persons. During the Fourth Century and the Beginning of the Fifth the Doctrine of the Trinity Was Defended By Athanasius (Who Devoted His Life To the Defense of This Doctrine and Pointed Out Its Indispensability Unto Salvation), the Three Cappadocians (Basil, Gregory of Nyssa, and Gregory Nazienzen), and Augustine. The Western Church Follows Augustine. No New Elements Have Been Added.**

**A. Scripture does not offer us an elaborate, fully formulated trinitarian doctrine but it contains the essential elements out of which this doctrine has been constructed.**

Now we must not suppose that Scripture by means of these various elements of divine revelation gives us a fully defined trinitarian dogma. It does, indeed, teach us that the one name of God is fully explicated in that of Father, Son, and Holy Spirit. The Bible very plainly declares that God's outgoing works, both creation and redemption, have a threefold cause. It also positively affirms that this threefold cause indicates three distinct subjects and that these subjects sustain a personal relation to one another. Thus Scripture contains all the elements out of which theology has constructed the trinitarian dogma. Not a single essential element is lacking. Hence, philosophy does not need to add anything: even the logos-doctrine is found in the New Testament. All is ready and waiting for the time when the powers of Christian reason will be sufficiently developed to penetrate into the mystery that is presented to it by Scripture.

**B. The apostolic fathers simply quote Scripture. They clearly confess the exalted character of the Son. They do not make frequent mention of the Holy Spirit. They avoid both the Ebionitic and the Docetic errors.**

During the time of the apostolic fathers that moment had not yet arrived. They merely imitate the language of Scripture but do not grasp the depth of the truths under study nor their interrelation, and they use expressions which would have been indefensible in a later period. Nevertheless, their writings are of the greatest significance for the doctrine of the trinity inasmuch as they avoid both the Ebionitic and the Docetic errors and confess the exalted, supra-angelic nature of Christ. From the very beginning it is clear that the trinitarian dogma was not born of philosophic reasoning concerning the being of God, but of earnest meditation upon the facts of revelation. upon the person and work of Christ. It was concerned from the beginning with the deity of Christ, the truth of God's revelation, the true redemption from sin, and the absolute certainty of salvation. Now the apostolic fathers ascribe to Christ an altogether unique position and they assign to him attributes that do not pertain to any creature. He is called Son, only Son, only begotten Son of God, Clement, *I Cor.* 36; Ignatius *Rom.* 1; *Eph.* 20; *Smyrn.* 1; Diognetus. 9, 10; Barnabas, 7, 12; effulgence and scepter of God's majesty. Clement, 1 Cor. 16:36; Lord of the earth to whom everything has been subjected; Creator of all things, Judge of the living and of the dead, Barn. 7, 12; Diog. 7 *Did.*, Apost. 16; Polyc. *Phil.* 1, 2, 6, 12; holy, incomprehensible Logos, who was sent to the earth "as God" Diogn. 7; and who may properly be called "God"; Clement *II Cor.* 1; Ign. *Rom.* 3; *Smyrn.* 1, 10; *Eph.* 1, 18, 19. Moreover, Father (God), Son (Christ) and Spirit are mentioned in one breath, Clement, I Cor. 46; Ign. *Eph.* 9; *Mag.* 13. The apostolic fathers do not make frequent mention of the Holy Spirit. Nevertheless, they distinguish him from — and place him on an equality with — the Father and the Son. Only in regard to the *Pastor* of Hermas is there a difference of opinion on the question whether or not he identifies the Holy Spirit with the Son, Sim. V, 5, 6.

**C. In the second century as a result of the rise of Gnosticism the doctrine of the trinity begins to have dogmatic significance. The apologetes defend this doctrine but they are somewhat under the influence of Gnostic and subordinationistic errors.**

With the rise of Gnosticism in the second century Christian thought awakens from its slumber. The deity of Christ begins to have dogmatic significance and is expressed in clearer terms. Justin Martyr often calls Christ "God"; he even calls him "God" with the definite article prefixed to the term, *ho theos, c. Tryph.* 34, 56, 58, 113, 126, etc., and ascribes divers exalted attributes to him. He is the firstborn of creation, the chief of another race, equipped not with one single charisma but with all the gifts of the Spirit, possessing not only a "seed" of the logos but "the entire logos," able to exalt mankind to the divine level, and therefore himself God, *c. Tr.* 87, 138; *Apol.* II, 10, 12. Furthermore, he very clearly teaches Christ's preëxistence, not only as a power but as a person, *c. Tr.* 128. Whereas the Father is hidden, ineffable, exalted above the limitations of space and time, *c. Tr.* 127; *Apol.* II, 6, all the revelations in the O. T. and in the heathen realm are manifestations of the Logos, *c. Tr.* 127; *Apol.* I, 46, 61, 63; *Apol.* II, 10, 13. Christ existed before creation, and the words contained in Gen. 1:26 were spoken to him, *Tr.* 62. But the immanent relation existing between Father and Son is not yet clear from the writings of Justin. It seems that the Logos, who is distinct from the Father "in number but not in mind" was generated by the Father with a view to and for the sake of creation, and although he was not begotten by abscission, he was nevertheless generated "by the power and will" of the Father: as one fire is kindled from another and as the word proceeds out of our mouth, *Apol.* II, 6; *c. Tr.* 61, 100, 128. Accordingly, he is called "first-begotten and first-born of God," *Apol.* I, 46, 58. This generation is called a "bringing forth" but more often a "begetting," *c. Tr.* 62, 76, 129; *Apol.* I, 23, 26, whence the Logos is called "offspring" or "work," *c Tr.* 62, 114, 129. Justin tries to maintain God's unity by asserting that the Son is distinct from the Father "in number but not in mind," *c. Tr.* 56, and that he is subordinate to the Father. The Son is "the first power after the Father," *Apol.* I, 32; he holds the "second place," *Apol.* I, 13: he has received everything from the Father, *c. Tr.* 86; is God and Lord according to the will of the Father, *c. Tr.* 127; and "was made subject to the will of the Father and Lord," *c. Tr.* 126. Accordingly, Justin's conception of the trinity is faulty in more than one respect. He represents the Father as hidden, in opposition to the Son; he teaches the generation of the Son by the will of the Father and with a view to creation; and he represents the Son as subordinate to the Father. The church later on rejected these errors. Because of these faults some have called Justin an Arian. This, however, is unjust. For, in the first place, this question did not yet exist in Justin's time, and furthermore, in many respects the views of Justin are diametrically opposed to those of Arius. Justin clearly and unequivocally teaches that the Son is God. He states that the Son was not created but generated, and he explains this by using the illustrations of one fire kindled by another and of the word that proceeds out of one's mouth. Moreover, he has a clear conception of the meaning which Christ's deity has for the entire work of redemption and for the truth of the Christian religion. Hence, he often mentions Father, Son and Spirit together as the object of our prayers, *Apol.* I, 6, 13, 60, 61, 65, 67; and although it is true that he assigns to the Son the "second place" and to the Spirit the "third rank," nevertheless in these very statements he plainly confesses the distinct existence and personality of the latter. To be sure, some have tried to deny this on the ground of *Apol.* I, 33, but this passage merely means that Justin interprets the expression "the Spirit" in Luke 1:35 as indicating not the Holy Spirit but the Logos, an interpretation favored also by other expositors. Moreover, we may also state with certainty that Justin does not view the Holy Spirit as an angel or ordinary creature. Nevertheless, he says very little about the divine nature of the Holy Spirit and of his ontological relation to the Father and to the Son. The religious significance of the doctrine of the Holy Spirit was not yet sufficiently appreciated. The Spirit was still viewed as being merely the Spirit of prophecy, who inspired the prophets and apostles and qualified Christ for his task. But Justin has no idea of the necessity of the constant activity of the Holy Spirit in the church. It was clearly seen that God's objective revelation in the Logos was necessary unto salvation, but that the subjective illumination of the Holy Spirit is equally necessary was not yet understood. Finally, from the writings of Justin we are able to gain a true conception of the specific character of the influence of Greek philosophy upon Christian theology. No one denies the fact that there has been this influence upon Christian theology, especially in the case of Justin. But that influence is especially noticeable in those ideas of Justin which have later on been rejected by the church; e.g., the distinction which he makes between the "immanent and the emitted word," his representation of the Son as the "second God," his doctrine concerning the hidden God, and the fact that he assigns to the Son a place outside of the divine essence. The remaining elements of his teaching Justin has consciously derived and proved from the Word of God; e.g., the Logos-nature of Christ, his preëxistence, generation, the creation of all things through the Logos, Christ's Sonship and his Godhood.

The apologists that followed Justin, namely, Theophilus, Tatian, and Athenagoras, did not avoid his errors. Tatian does indeed state that inasfar as God is the necessary ground of all being all things exist in him ideally, i.e., as Logos; but this Logos is begotten by the will of God and is the "first-begotten work of the Father, by participation, not by abscission." *Or. c. Gr.* 5. Theophilus, indeed, presents the Logos as having been before creation the internal Word, the "Word immanent in God" seeing that he is the "mind and wisdom of God," but he nevertheless views this Logos as having been generated by the Father to be the "Word emitted" in behalf of creation, *Ad Autol.* II, 10, 22. Athenagoras, *Leg. pro. Chr.* 10, also teaches that although the Logos existed from eternity inasmuch as God is eternal "mind," he is nevertheless the first "offspring" of the Father, because he is the idea and energy that proceeds from the Father. Just as Theophilus was the first to speak of a "triad" in God, so also Athenagoras mentions as the one object of the adoration of the Christian: God the Father, God the Son, and the Holy Spirit, who influenced the prophets and is an effluence of God, proceeding from him and returning to him like a beam of the sun. Nevertheless, while maintaining the distinctness of the three persons, their unity is not sufficiently emphasized. The Father is represented as the one, unbegotten, eternal, invisible God; the Son and the Spirit are viewed as one with him not in being but in spirit and power, *Ib.* ch. 24.

> **D. The development of the doctrine of the trinity by Irenaeus, Tertullian, and Origen.**
>
> **Irenaeus defends the consubstantiality of the persons: their essential unity.**
>
> **Tertullian complements the teaching of Irenaeus and emphasizes the distinctions in the persons. He derives the trinity of the persons from the being of God instead of from the person of the Father. He also supplies the terms that are necessary to convey to the mind the true meaning of the trinitarian dogma.**
>
> **Origen sets forth the eternal character of the interpersonal relations. However, he falls into the error of subordinationism.**

The immediately following development of the doctrine of the trinity, consisting especially in the elimination of philosophical elements, must be ascribed to three men each of whom made his specific contribution. Irenaeus is the ardent opponent of the Gnostic conception of the Deity and of the theory that makes the Logos the rational principle in the universe. Now and then it would seem that even he has not completely put aside the old representation, e.g., he still calls the Father the invisible and hidden God, in opposition to the Son, *Adv. Haer.* IV, 20, 10. Nevertheless, he emphatically rejects the conception of God as the "depth" and that of the emanation of the aeons, and he maintains the

Scriptural distinction between Creator and creature. The Logos is, as it were, divested of his dual nature, and is definitely placed on the side of God. The Logos is not a creature but a hypostatic, i.e., distinctly personal, Word, III, 8, preëxistent, II, 6; IV, 12; very God, IV, 10, 14, etc. The distinction between the "Logos immanent in God and the Logos emitted" is also to be rejected II, 17, 18. For, not only does this distinction violate the personality of the Logos and his generation, by connecting the latter with a creative act, but it also erroneously assumes the Logos to be the mind and reason of God. God is simple, all spirit, all mind, all thought, all logos, II, 16, so that both the Son and the Father are very God. The unity of the Father, Son, and Spirit is very clearly expressed by Irenaeus; their divine nature is expressly maintained; and they are repeatedly mentioned together, IV, 6, 20, 33. The generation of the Son did not take place in time; the Son had no beginning; he existed from eternity with God, II, 18; III, 22; IV, 37.

But Irenaeus does not fully indicate how the trinity exists in the unity, and how Father, Son, and Spirit, though possessing one and the same divine nature, are nevertheless distinct. Here Tertullian complements and corrects the teaching of Irenaeus. To be sure, in gaining the victory over Gnostic dualism Irenaeus surpasses Tertullian. The latter distinguishes between the Father and the Son as between God invisible and unseen and God visible and seen *Adv. Prax.* 14, 15. In every way and by every kind of argumentation he tries to maintain that distinction: by referring to the name Logos, to the incarnation, to the theophanies, etc. He even goes so far as to argue that the Logos attains the full realization of his Sonship and distinct personality only as the result of God's speaking, generation, and incarnation, *Adv. Pr.* 6, 7, so that there was a time when the Son did not exist, *Adv. Hermog.* 3. But although it is true, on the one hand, that his zeal in defending against the Patripassianists the distinctions in the persons carries him beyond the proper bounds, it is also true, on the other hand that for that very reason he tries all the more to maintain the unity within the trinity and the trinity within the unity. The three persons are "of one substance, of one condition, and of one power; they are the one God." They are distinct as far as their order and economy are concerned. "The mystery of the economy distributes the unity into a trinity." They are three "not in condition but in degree" yet, they are "the one God, from whom these degrees and forms and aspects are reckoned under the name of the Father, and of the Son, and of the Holy Spirit." As a ray of the sun is also sun, so there are divers "aspects, forms, images, and modulations" in the one and undivided substance. The three persons are "one but not identical." The Son is distinct from the Father, and the Spirit is distinct from both, but they have the name

God and Lord in common. They are "one God," not to be separated. Just as the trunk and the branch, the fountain and the river, the sun and the sunbeam cannot be separated, so also the Father and the Son cannot be separated. The trinity does not obliterate the unity. The Son differs from the Father, but not by division or separation. There is "distinction, distribution, but not diversity and division." It is a "unity which derives the trinity out of its own self" *Adv. Prax.* 2 ff. So Tertullian moulds the cumbersome Latin tongue in order equally to maintain God's unity and his trinity. Both formally and materially he has been of great significance for the doctrine of the trinity. In spite of the fact that he does not always overcome subordinationism and does not sufficiently distinguish between the ontological, cosmological, and soteriological elements in the doctrine of the trinity, he is nevertheless the one who furnished the concepts and the terms that are necessary to express the true meaning of the trinitarian dogma.    For the Logos speculation he substituted the filiation, and thereby once for all freed the doctrine of the ontological trinity from the entanglement of cosmological speculation. Finally, he was the first to derive the trinity of the persons from the being of God, and not from the person of the Father.

But whereas Tertullian still failed to eliminate from the doctrine of the ontological trinity the idea of a cosmological and soteriological process, it was Origen who conceived of the generation of the Son as an eternal process immanent in the being of God. The "generation" of the Son is "eternal," *De Princ.* I, 2, 4. Just as it is in the very nature of light to shine so that it cannot exist without shining, so the Father cannot exist apart from the Son, *Ib.* I, 2, 4; *c. Cels.* VIII, 12. The Father is not Father before the existence of the Son but he is Father because of the existence of the Son, *De Princ.* I, 2, 10. There is no separation: "the Father does not exist apart from the Son," *c. Cels.* IV, 14, 16. The Father and the Son have all the divine attributes in common: the Son and the Father are one. It is not true that besides God we also worship the Son, but in God we worship the Son, *c. Cels.* VIII, 12, 13. The Son has "the same wisdom, truth, and reason as the Father," *c. Cels.* V, 41. But in order that, while affirming this unity and equality, he might at the same time maintain the distinctions in the persons, Origen falls back upon subordinationism, and, going back in his teaching beyond Tertullian, derives the trinity from the person of the Father instead of from the being of God. Consequently, Origen represented the Father as "God" with the definite article prefixed to the term (*ho theos*), and the Son as God with the article omitted (*theos*), the Father as "being of himself God, the fountain or root of divinity, the greatest God above all," "superior" to the Son, the one complete Godhead, exalted above all being, invisible, incomprehensible; the Son, as "other than the Father in substance," by so much inferior to the Father as the universe is inferior to the Son.

**E. The doctrine of the trinity as defined by the Council of Nicea. Origen's subordinationism is rejected by the church. The full divinity of the Son is confessed and formulated. Before Nicea the main difficulty was to derive the trinity from the unity. After Nicea the opposite difficulty presented itself.**

Nevertheless, the church did not follow Origen. It rejected his subordinationism, and at Nicea it confessed the full, true divinity of Christ. This confession was entirely religious in character: it vindicated the soteriological principle of Christianity. Henceforth, a new meaning attached to the doctrine of the trinity. Nicea maintained the personal distinctions in the being of God and confessed that the Father and the Son (and the Spirit) were God. From now on, one had to be on his guard against allowing his belief in the personal distinctions to obliterate the truth respecting God's unity. *Before* Nicea the main difficulty was to derive the trinity from the unity; *after* Nicea the opposite difficulty presented itself. The trinitarian dogma now receives its own, distinctive, and independent value and theological significance.

**F. The development of the doctrine of the trinity by Athanasius, the three Cappadocians, and Augustine.**
**Athanasius devoted his life to the defense of this doctrine; he pointed out its soteriological significance.**
**The three Cappadocians agree with Athanasius and use many illustrations.**
**Augustine made the following contribution to the development of this doctrine:**
**(1) He expounded the doctrine more profoundly than any one before him, cf. his fifteen books DE TRINITATE.**
**(2) He gave a summary of all that had been written about this subject by the earlier fathers. Besides this he presented his own ideas.**
**(3) He placed greater emphasis upon the absolute unity of the three persons than had ever been done before.**
**(4) Consequently, he banished all subordinationism: the Son is just as invisible, etc., as the Father.**
**(5) He made a more extensive use of illustrations than any church-father before him.**

The credit for thus elaborating the doctrine of the trinity and bringing it to complete development belongs to Athanasius, the three Cappadocians, and Augustine. Athanasius understood better than any of his contemporaries that Christianity stands or falls with the confession of the deity of Christ and of the trinity. He devoted his entire life and all his energies to the defense of this doctrine. He was not fighting in behalf of a philosophical problem but in behalf of the Christian religion itself, in behalf of the revelation of God, the teaching of the apostles, the faith and confession of the church. The doctrine of the trinity is the very heart of Christianity, differentiating it in principle from Judaism, which denies the distinctions within the Divine Being, and from heathenism which rejects God's unity, *Ad Serap.* I, 28. Accordingly, Athanasius completely avoids the philosophical intermingling of ontology and cosmology. He rejects the Gnostic and Arian dualism between God and the world together with all its intermediate beings, *c. Ar.* II, 26. Athanasius maintains that the trinity is devoid of all foreign elements; that it is not a union of the Creator and the creature, but entirely and perfectly divine in character, *Ibid.* Accordingly, the trinity is eternal. In God there are no non-essential elements. God does not *become* anything; he *is* everything eternally. Just as the trinity is *from* eternity so it is *to* eternity; hence, Father, Son, and Spirit are from eternity to eternity, *Ad. Serap.* III, 7; *c. Ar.* 1, 18. The Father was always Father. Fatherhood pertains to his very nature. The same cannot be said in regard to men, *De Decr. Nic. Syn.* 12. Just as one cannot conceive of the sun apart from its light, nor of the fountain apart from its water, so one is not able to conceive of the Father apart from the Son. God is not "incommunicative"; on the contrary, he is always speaking. He who denies the trinity reduces God to a lifeless principle or arrives at the doctrine of the eternal existence of the universe, *c. Ar.* I, 14. But inasmuch as God is never a lifeless principle, the generation of the Son is eternal. Neither for the Father nor for the Son was there a time when he did not exist, *c. Ar.,* the entire section I. The Son of God cannot be a creature and was not begotten by the will of God but is generated out of the being (essence) of God, *c. Ar.* I, 25. The same is true in regard to the Holy Spirit, although Athanasius does not make such frequent mention of the latter, *Ad. Serap.* I, 20, 21. These three persons are really distinct: they are not three parts of one whole nor three names for one and the same object. The Father alone is Father, the Son alone is Son, the Spirit alone is Spirit, *c. Ar.* III, 4; IV, 1; *Ad. Serap.* IV, 4, 6, 7. Nevertheless, Athanasius maintains their unity by teaching that the three are "the same in essence," in "substance" (*hypostasis* still synonymous with *ousia* in the writings of Athanasius), and in attributes, *c. Ar.* III, 3, 4; *De Decr. Nic. Syn.* 19-25; that the Father is the "first principle" and the "fountain" "of the Godhead" *c. Ar.* IV, 1; that the three persons exist in and through each other, *Ad. Serap.* I, 14; III, 6; c. Ar. III, 6; and that they are one in activity, *Ad. Serap.* I, 28.

This trinitarian teaching of Athanasius is also presented by Basil, with this difference that the latter uses more names, illustrations, and comparisons, cf. his *Libri V. c. Eunomium; De Spiritu Sancte,* and many of his letters and homilies; by Gregory of Nyssa, cf. his *Libri XII c. Eunomium* and *Oratio Catecnetica;* and by Gregory Nazienzen, cf. his five *Orationes Theologicae.* John of Damascus summarizes their conclusions and follows especially Gregory Nazienzen. The entire Greek Church has accepted this doctrine as embodied in the decisions of the ecumenical councils of which this church recognizes the first seven, and it differs from the Western view only with reference to the expression "and from the Son" (filioque).

In the West after Tertullian and Cyprian it was especially Hilary who vigorously defended the doctrine of the trinity. He proved it from Scripture in his twelve books which bear the title *De Trinitate* but contain very little material about the Holy Spirit and therefore lend support to the view that their original title was: *De Fide contra Arionos.* Even more profoundly and philosophically Augustine expounded the doctrine of the trinity in his fifteen books *De Trinitate,* which comprise the most learned discourse on this dogma that was ever written. He not only summarizes what had been said by earlier fathers but also treats it independently and introduces important modifications. In the first place Augustine's starting-point is not the person of the Father but the one, simple, uncompounded "essence" of God. Accordingly, he places greater emphasis upon the absolute unity of the three persons than was ever done before him. Every person is as great as the entire trinity *De Trin.* VIII, 1, 2. In every person the same, entire Divine Being is present, so that there are not three Gods, three Almighties, etc., but only one God, one Almighty, etc., *Ib.* V. 8. Consequently, the distinction between the persons does not consist in accidents or attributes pertaining to one person and not to another but in the interpersonal relations. The first person is called Father because he sustains a peculiar relation to the Son and to the Holy Spirit, etc., *Ib.* V. 5; just as the appellation Lord, Creator, etc., indicates the relation of God to creatures although it does not bring about any change in his being, *Ib* 16, 17. Secondly and consequently, Augustine rejected all the earlier theories that posited a dualism between the Father and the Son. The Son, being himself very God, is not less invisible than the Father and is perfectly equal to the Father. All subordinationism is banished. Augustine insists even more strongly upon the Son's equality with the Father than did Athanasius. In the writings of the latter a few remnants of subordinationism may still be found, *c. Ar.* I, 59, but Augustine has completely abandoned every trace of the idea that the Father is the real, the original God. He proceeds from the idea of God's essence dwelling equally in all three persons. Although he still calls the Father the fountain or beginning of the Godhead, *De Trin.* IV, 20, nevertheless he gives to this term a different meaning. It does not indicate that the Godhead logically exists first in the Father, and that he imparted it to the Son and to the Spirit, but that the Father may be thus spoken of only in this sense: that not as God but as person he is Father of the Son. In that sense Augustine also explains the Nicean phrase "very God of very God," *De Trin.* VII, 2, 3. For this reason Augustine also arrived at a different conception of the O. T. theophanies. Formerly these had always been interpreted as revelations of the Logos inasmuch as the Father was hidden, but Augustine ascribes them as well to the Father and to the Spirit, who as well as the Son are able to reveal themselves and whose manifestations cannot be separated from those of the Son, *De Trin.* II, and III. Finally, more than any church-father before him Augustine searched for illustrations, analogies, and "vestiges of the trinity," and thus he brought to light the relation between the doctrine of God and the doctrine of the whole universe. *De Trin.* IX — XV. Thus Augustine completed what Tertullian began.

**G. History of the development of the doctrine of the trinity after Augustine. Augustine's ideas received further development but no new elements were added to his trinitarian view. The Eastern Church differs from the Western Church in this respect, that the latter confesses the procession of the Holy Spirit from the Father and from the Son while the former denies his procession from the Son. The Athanasian Creed.**

In spite of all similarity the West differs from the East in its conception of the doctrine of the trinity. While the Eastern Church believes that both the Son and the Spirit proceed from the Father but do not sustain a definite relationship to one another, the Western Church understands that the procession of the Holy Spirit from the Father "and from the Son" (filioque) of necessity follows both from the substantial equality of the persons and from their interpersonal relations. The Western Church followed Augustine, and although it brought to further development certain aspects of his trinitarian doctrine, it did not introduce any modifications or new elements. The Athanasian Creed, which did not come into existence until after the year 400 and was erroneously ascribed to Athanasius, breathes the spirit of Augustine, and was therefore welcomed in the West but not in the East. The Reformers also expressed their agreement with this Creed. The Lutheran and Reformed Confessions are in harmony with the three ecumenical symbols: in the ninth article of the Belgic Confession the Athanasian Creed is expressly mentioned and in the Anglican Church it even received a place in the liturgy. Nevertheless, of late a strong opposition to this use has arisen. And in general there is an important difference between Roman Catholics and Protestants in their respective attitude toward the Athanasian Creed, for the Reformation has brought to light that not the mere historical belief in the doctrine of the trinity, no matter how pure, is sufficient unto salvation, but only the true heart-born confidence that rests in God himself, who in Christ has revealed himself as the triune God.

**III. Historical Review of the Erroneous Views With Respect To the Doctrine of the Trinity. On the One Hand There Is the Error of Stressing the Trinity Of the Persons At the Expense Of the Unity Of the Essence; e.g., Arianism; On the Other Hand, the Fallacy Of Emphasizing the Unity Of the Essence At the Expense Of the Trinity Of the Persons; e.g., Sabellianism. Both Errors Appear Historically In Many Degrees and Variations.**

A. Arianism: the teaching of Arius, pupil of Lucian:

(1) Its precursors: Ebionitism, the Alogi, Theodotus, Artemon, and Paul of Samosata.

(2) Its doctrine: God is unbegotten, the Son is begotten; hence, the Son does not partake of the divine nature; i.e., he is not consubstantial with the Father. There was a time when he was not. He was a perfect creature who of his own accord chose the right, and therefore, became, as it were, God (in a modified sense).

(3) Arguments upon which it is based:

a. Passages from Scripture which emphasize God's unity, the Son's subordination to the Father, etc;

b. Quotations from several earlier church-fathers;

c. Arguments derived from Aristotelian philosophy, stressing God's agennesia; and

d. Seeming self-contradictions in the Nicean Christology.

Nevertheless, this doctrine has always had ardent opponents. Not only have there been enemies without the gate, namely the Jews and the Mohammedans, against whose attacks the Christians defended the trinitarian truth, but even within the pale of Christendom many foes have arisen in order to dispute this doctrine. This was not only the case before the doctrine in question had been officially accepted and formulated by the church, but also afterward. Now in the confession of the trinity throbs the heart of the Christian religion: every error results from, or upon deeper reflection may be traced to, a wrong view of this doctrine. The belief in the trinity is such an integral element in the Christian faith that even the Unitarian is unable wholly to divest himself of it. All those who pride themselves in the name *"Christian"* continue to speak of Father, Son, and Spirit. Nevertheless, so much the greater has been opposition to and manifold misrepresentation of the ecclesiastical formulation of this doctrine. Yet, the history of this dogma clearly indicates that the ecclesiastical formulation given to it is the only one that is able to do justice to the truth with which we are concerned. Now the problem which this dogma presents to us is this: so to present this truth that the unity of the essence does not obliterate the trinity of the persons and that the trinity of the persons does not abolish the unity of the essence, for there is always a danger of deviating from the correct position in either direction and of falling into the error of Sabellianism or of Arianism.

The precursors of the Arians in the second and third centuries. A. D. were the Ebionites, the Alogi, Theodotus, Artemon, Paul of Samosata. etc., who held that Christ was a man born in a supernatural manner, at his baptism anointed by the Holy Spirit and qualified for his task, and exalted as Lord, but denied his preëxistence and divine nature. They accepted an adoptionistic Christology. In the fourth century this belief was advocated by Lucian and by his pupil Arius, and further by Aetius and Eunomius. According to a work entitled *The Banquet* of which a few fragments were preserved by Athanasius, cf. *c. Ar.* I, Arius taught that inasmuch as God is "unbegotten" and without beginning, he is absolutely unique. He is ineffable, incomprehensible, unable to enter into direct communion with that which is finite, unable to impart his being, the very essence of which is agennesia. All that exists outside of his being came into existence and was created by his will. He is not Father from eternity but Father by virtue of creation: he is the Father of his creatures. But before God began his creative activity, he brought into existence a kind of intermediate being to act as a medium through whom he created all things, a distinct "hypostasis," or "essence," called in Scripture wisdom, son, logos, image of God, etc.; and he also called into existence a third and lower hypostasis, namely, the Holy Spirit. This Logos is not generated out of the essence of God neither is he consubstantial with the Father, for in that case there would be two Gods, but he was born or created "out of nothing"; he is a "creature or work" of God, brought into existence "by his will and counsel." Accordingly, "there was a time when he was not" even though it is true that he was created "before the time periods and aeons," i.e., before "the universe." Hence, this Logos is not "consubstantial" (same in essence) with the Father, but entirely separate from him. He is not immutable like the Father, and he is able to choose the evil as well as the good. Nevertheless, he was "a perfect creature." He chose the good and thereby attained to immutability and, as it were, to divinity. This Logos also became man, proclaimed the truth, wrought our redemption, and is worthy of our honor but not of our worship.

Arianism exerted great influence and gained many adherents, especially among those who for various reasons had become nominal Christians after the conversion of Constantine. Moreover, from the works of Athanasius we learn that the Arians used very formidable weapons. First of all they appealed to a number of Scriptural passages which emphasize God's unity, Deut. 6:4; 32:39; John 17:3; I Cor. 8:6; the Son's birth or coming into existence, Prov. 8:22; Col. 1:15; his subordination to the Father, John 14:28; I Cor. 15:28; Heb. 3:2; the limited character of his knowledge, Mark 13:32; John 11:34; of his power, Matt. 28:18; and of his goodness, Luke 18:19; his increase in wisdom, Luke 2:52; his suffering, John 12:27; 13:21; Matt. 26:39; 27:46; and his exaltation to the dignity of Lord and Christ, Acts 2:36; Phil. 2:9; Heb. 1:4; etc. Furthermore, they proved on the basis of several quotations that many of the earlier church-fathers agreed with their position. Then, they derived divers arguments from Aristotelian philosophy, nominalistically conceived, and thereby proved God's unity and "agennesia." Finally, they pointed out certain flaws and self-contradictions which, as they saw it, adhered to the Nicean Christology; especially: that if the Son were begotten, then that very fact indicates that he differs essentially from God, "the unbegotten One" and that he came into existence in time.

**B. Sabellianism, monarchianism, patripassianism, modalism: the denial of a trinity of essence for which a trinity of successive revelation is substituted.**

(1) Its precursors: **Noetus, Praxeus, Epigonus, Cleomenes**

(2) Arguments upon which it is based: **Deut. 6:4; Ex. 20:3; Is. 44:6; John 10:38.**

The precursors of Sabellianism in the second and third centuries A. D. were Noetus, Praxeus, Epigonus, and Cleomenes, who taught that in Christ, the Father himself was born, suffered, and died; that the names Father and Son indicate one and the same person in different relations; namely, before and during the period of his incarnation *per se* and in his historical manifestations; or that Christ's divine nature is the Father and that his human nature is the Son. In the third century this monarchianism, patripassianism, or modalism was advocated and developed by Sabellius. Father, Son, and Spirit are three names for one and the same God, one and the same being. He calls this being *"Huiopatōr,"* and applies this name successively to its three consecutive energies or modes. God existed first in the person, manifestation, or mode of the Father, as Creator and Lawgiver; then in the person or prosopon of the Son, as Redeemer, from the time of the incarnation to the moment of the ascension; finally, in the person or prosopon of the Holy Spirit as Giver of Life. In order to prove this theory, Sabellius appealed especially to Deut. 6:4; Ex. 20:3; Is. 44:6: John 10:38. Sabellius included the Holy Spirit in the Divine essence and placed the Son and the Holy Spirit in a position of complete equality with the Father. He believed, moreover, that there is in God a process of becoming and that there is a historical succession in the revelation of his being.

**C. The historical development of Arianism.** The essence of Arianism is that it denies the Son's consubstantiality with the Father and that it assigns to him a position somewhere between God and man. Thus a very wide margin for speculation is allowed: some represent the Son as almost equal to God, others as merely a great man; still others assign to him a position somewhere between these two extremes. Historically the Son was more and more robbed of his divine character until at length nothing of his divinity remained. Notice, therefore, the order in which the following modifications or forms of Arianism are mentioned:

(1) Subordinationism: the Son is eternal and divine.

(2) Arianism proper: the Son is not eternal, merely pre-existent; he becomes divine.

(3) Socinianism: the Son is neither eternal nor pre-existent; he becomes a recipient of divine grace.

(4) Unitarianism: the Son is a mere man. The divinity and personality of the Holy Spirit are denied.

The doctrine of the trinity as established by the church and the deviating tendencies summarized in the preceding have existed side by side throughout the centuries. The essence of Arianism is that it denies the Son's consubstantiality with the Father; in other words, that it affirms that in the absolute sense of the word the Father alone is God. It follows, of course, that the Son is a being of inferior rank: that he does not share the divine nature. Arianism places the Son somewhere between God and the creaturely universe but allows a wide margin of interpretation in regard to the exact place which he occupies. The distance between God and the world is infinite and at every point in this distance a place may be assigned to the Son, from the place on the throne next to God, down to the position next to creatures, angels, or men. This accounts for the fact that Arianism has appeared in various forms.

First, there is subordinationism. According to its representation the Son is indeed eternal, generated out of the essence of the Father: he is not a creature and was not brought into being out of nothing; nevertheless, he is inferior and subordinate to the Father. The Father alone is "God" with the definite article prefixed to the term (*ho theos*); he alone is the "fountain of divinity," the Son is God with the article omitted (*theos*) and is viewed as having received his nature from the Father by communication. This was the teaching of Justin Martyr,

Tertullian, Clement, Origen, etc., and also of the Semi-Arians, Eusebius of Caesarea and Eusebius of Nicomedia, who assigned to the Son a place "outside of the Father" and called him *"similar, not same,* in essence to the Father." In a later period the Remonstrants (Arminians) supernaturalists, and many of the more recent theologians have advocated similar views.

Secondly, there is Arianism proper. This ancient form of the error with which we are dealing found favor with many post-Reformation theologians, especially in England. Milton, e. g., taught that the Son and the Holy Spirit, who existed before the creation of the world, owed their creation to the Father's free will, and that it was only because of their office that they were called God, just as even the O. T. judges and magistrates were called gods. Slightly modified, this was also the opinion of W. Whiston, whose Arianism occasioned the writing of many polemical treatises, and of S. Clarke, P. Maty, Dan. Whitby, Hardwood, many Remonstrants in the Netherlands, and at a later time the Groningen theologians.

Socinianism was the third form in which Arianism presented itself. The Father is the only true God. The Son was a holy man, whom God created by means of a direct and supernatural conception, prior to which he did not exist. He was created in order to proclaim a new law to mankind. Having completed this task he ascended to heaven where he became a partaker of divine grace. The Holy Spirit is merely a divine energy or power. From Poland, Socinianism spread to Germany, The Netherlands, England, and America. In the two countries last named it was advocated by John Biddle, Nathanael Lardner, Theoph. Lindsey, Joseph Priestly the founder of the Unitarian Society, etc.

From Socinianism to Unitarianism was but a step. Socinianism was not able to retain those supernatural elements which it had accepted at the beginning: Jesus came to be looked upon as a mere man, albeit an example of virtue and piety. Christianity was separated from its person: the Christ. This was also done by rationalism and by liberal theology. Neither of these leaves any room for the trinity of Father, Son, and Spirit. God is one. Jesus was an ordinary human being although, to be sure, he was a great man. Even Ritschl offered nothing else than a new form of Socinianism. Jesus was a man qualified by God to establish the kingdom of heaven on earth and was afterward exalted to the position of God and Lord of the church. It is easily seen that this rationalistic representation of the doctrine of the trinity leaves no room for divine grace, the necessity of which is not felt; consequently, the Holy Spirit is hardly mentioned; his divinity is denied and so is, as a rule, his personality.

**D. The historical development of Sabellianism.** Arianism and Sabellianism both deny the trinity: Arianism by denying the divinity of the Son and of the Spirit, Sabellianism by affirming the divinity of Father, Son and Spirit and viewing them as three successive revelations of one and the same person-being. Forms of Sabellianism:

(1) **Patripassianism:** the belief that the suffering of the Son can be predicated of the Father, i.e., that Father, Son, and Spirit are three names for the same being. Leader: Praxeus.

(2) **The theory of Marcellus of Ancyra and Photinus of Sirmium:** the Son and the Spirit are divine attributes which for a time become personal with a view to creation and redemption.

(3) **Sabellianism proper:** modalistic monarchianism. Sabellius, mediaeval pantheism, anabaptism, Servetus.

(4) **Böhme:** the trinity, the result of a process; **Zinzendorf:** the trinity, a family; **Swedenborg:** the trinity, analogous to soul, body and energy proceeding from both; **Kant:** the three persons represent God as Lawgiver, Ruler, Judge; **Schelling and Hegel:** philosophical construction.

(5) In many other ways the modal trinity of philosophic speculation has been substituted for the ontological trinity of Scripture.

Sabellianism also appears in different forms. Now Arianism and Sabellianism are alike in this respect that both deny the trinity. To arrive at this conclusion, however, Arianism denies the divinity of the Son and of the Spirit while Sabellianism follows the opposite course: it retains the divinity of the Son and of the Spirit but in such a manner that all distinctions between the three persons disappear. Now according to the doctrine of the trinity as established by the church, the personal properties, especially generation and spiration, constitute that which enables us to distinguish the three persons. When these personal properties are denied, the three persons are separated from one another and tritheism results. In ancient times the monophysites John of Ascusnages and John Philopon were charged with this error, in the middle ages Roscellin. Later on a similar accusation was advanced against Th. Sherlock, who taught that in God there are three infinite spirits; against Roëll, because he denied generation and against Lampe and Sibel, because they objected to the formulation "through communication of essence." When in addition to this God is conceived of in a Platonic-realistic sense, tritheism changes into tetratheism, the error of which Damian of Alexandria was accused. But whereas it is impossible to reconcile such a trinity of individual and separate persons, "divided beings," "individual natures," with God's unity, the latter can also be maintained by asserting that Father, Son, and Spirit are one and the same person-being. This patripassianism was taught by Praxeus in the second century. Marcellus of Ancyra and Photinus of Sirmium offer still another representation: they regard the Son and the

Spirit as divine attributes which, in order to accomplish the works of creation and redemption, come forth from God and become self-existent and personal. The Logos was indeed eternal as "reason immanent in God"; the Father never was without Logos, he was the "Logos-Father"; but not before the beginning of time was this Logos "emitted" as Son. In course of time God unfolds himself into Son and Spirit but afterward this triad is again resolved into a monad: God has returned unto himself. This construction of itself gave rise to modalistic monarchianism, which teaches that the three persons are merely three rôles (three modes of revelation) which the one Godhead successively assumes.

This in reality was the doctrine of Sabellius, which reappears in later times. The trinitarian speculations of Erigena and of Abelard were modalistic although not to such a degree as were the theories held by the pantheistic sects of the middle ages and by Joachim of Floris, Almarik of Bena, and David of Dinant, who distinguished a dispensation of the Father, of the Son, and of the Spirit, and regarded the latter as at hand. In the Reformation era anabaptism opposed the doctrine of the trinity as established by the church. The triune God is the God in us: he is the real Christ; and the Word or the Spirit in us is the true God. David Joris taught that God is one and that he successively reveals himself as Father, Son, and Spirit in the three periods respectively, of faith (beginning with Moses), hope (beginning with Christ), and love (beginning with David Joris himself). But it was especially Michael Servetus who concentrated all the power of his intellect upon this dogma. In three writings he *negatively* subjected the doctrine of the trinity as established by the church to a rigid criticism, and *positively* tried to present his own construction. He vilified the doctrine of the trinity as formulated by the church. In his eyes this doctrine is tritheistic, atheistic, a "three-headed monster," a "three-headed Cerberus," a "God divided into three parts." Over against this his basic thesis is that God cannot be divided, and that in order to maintain the divinity of Christ and of the Holy Spirit one must not speak of persons but only of dispositions, manifestations, divine modes. The Father is the entire Divine Being, the only God. But through the Logos, existing before Christ though not as a person but as word, reason, thought, God reveals himself in creation and in the O. T., and in Christ he becomes man. The Logos did not assume the human nature in Christ but became flesh in him. Accordingly, the man Christ is the true Son of God: God fully dwells in him. Similarly, the Holy Spirit, who is not self-existent and distinct from the Logos but immanent in the Logos, is the mode of God's self-impartation, for through the Holy

Spirit God dwells in and imparts his life to all creatures. At the end of the process the trinity ceases to exist.

These Gnostic and theosophic elements that present themselves in the teaching of Servetus reappear with double emphasis in the trinitarian theories of Böhme, Zinzendorf, and Swedenborg. Böhme's trinity is the result of a process in the Godhead, which has as its factors and constitutive elements mysterious (lit. dark) nature, the torch of reason (lit. the light of the idea), and the will. Zinzendorf called himself "a most fervent believer in the trinity," but he really proceeded from a Gnostic conception of God. God as he exists "in himself" is unapproachable, hidden, inscrutable, but he reveals himself in Christ. The latter is the real Creator of all things, the Jehovah of the O. T., who became flesh and who is the object of our invocation. In Christ the trinity also is revealed. Nevertheless, this trinity as manifested in Christ is not one of immanent relations, e.g., generation and spiration, but is a holy family. The first person is the Father; the Holy Spirit is the Mother; Christ is the Son; and the individual believer or also the church as a whole is received into this family as the Son's bride, who in a thoroughly realistic manner is created from the side and blood of Christ just like Eve was created from the side of Adam. Swedenborg took a still more radical stand against the doctrine of the trinity. For him as for Servetus this doctrine was tritheism pure and simple. God is one, but in Christ he was revealed as Father, Son, and Spirit, who are related to one another as soul, body, and the activity that proceeds from both. This theosophy paved the way for the trinitarian theories accepted by modern philosophy. Now in the philosophy of Spinoza, which teaches that there can be only one immutable substance, there is still no room for a trinity. In the philosophy of Immanuel Kant three qualities take the place of three persons: true religion is faith in God as holy Lawgiver, good Ruler, and righteous Judge. Schleiermacher subjected the trinitarian dogma to a severe criticism and recognized only one true element in it, namely, that through Christ and through "the one Spirit that pervades the church" a union has been effected between God and man. According to Schelling and Hegel an important philosophical truth is imbedded in the doctrine of the trinity, a truth which they interpreted as follows: God is spirit, thought, reason. Accordingly, it pertains to his very nature to form a conception of himself, to behold or to think himself, to objectify himself. However, that object-self cannot be a mere idea as with men but must have actual existence. Hence, while God thinks himself, he begets or objectifies himself in the world of nature, which is the real Son of God, and out of this state of "self-objectivation" he then in the Spirit returns to himself through the consciousness of mankind. Strauss, to be sure, saw the great difference between this speculation and the doctrine of the trinity as accepted by the church. Nevertheless, similar philosophic constructions are still favored by many. Others content themselves with distinguishing three potencies, moments or energies in a unipersonal God and so arrive at a trinity of revelation: God manifested in nature (creation), in history (Christ), and in the conscience (the church). Filled with aversion to metaphysics, which they regard as detrimental to the exercise of faith, they refuse to deduce the immanent and ontological trinity from God's self-revelation in Christ and from his self-impartation through the Holy Spirit. They reject the theological elements that are contained not only in the doctrine of the church but in Scripture itself and look upon these as vain speculation.

**E. The Reaction of the Church to the errors of Arianism and Sabellianism.**

**(1) The Church clearly perceived that Christianity was based upon the ontological trinity. Accordingly, as soon as the data of Scripture with reference to the trinity became the object of theological reflection it became necessary to use various descriptive and defining terms that do not occur in the Bible. The use of these terms is justified by:**

**(a) the example of Jesus and the apostles**

**(b) the believer's right of independent reflection upon revealed truth.**

**(c) their purpose: to defend the truth of Scripture against all errors.**

**(2) The meaning of the terms, although at first undetermined, gradually became established:**

**(a) Terms used to indicate the essence or being. In the East the word OUSIA was used; in the West SUBSTANTIA sounded more familiar to Latin ears than ESSENTIA. Nevertheless, Augustine objected to the use of the word SUBSTANTIA in this sense because it indicates the being viewed as bearer of the attributes, but in God being and attribute are one.**

**(b) Terms used to indicate the persons. In the East it was necessary over against the error of Sabellianism to emphasize the self-existent character of the persons; hence, the term HYPOSTASIS was used. In the West it was necessary in view of Arianism to speak of three persons rather than of three SUBSTANTIAE. The scholastics have worked out this terminology in detail.**

From the beginning the Christian Church followed a different course. It viewed the doctrine of the trinity as the outstanding dogma, the religious mystery par excellence. The church clearly perceived that Christianity is based upon the foundation and principle of the doctrine of the ontological trinity and that the essence of Christianity, namely, God's absolute self-revelation in the person of Christ and his absolute self-impartation through the Holy Spirit, can be maintained only upon this basis. As soon therefore, as the data of Scripture became the object of theological reflection, it became necessary to use various phrases which do not occur in Scripture but are, nevertheless, indispensable for the twofold purpose of giving expression, albeit imperfectly, to the trinitarian truth and of defending it against misrepresentation and error. It is true that this use of terms not found in Scripture was condemned by the Arians and by the advocates of various other religious tendencies; e.g., Socinians, Anabaptists, Arminians, and representatives of Biblical theology. Nevertheless, Christian theology has always defended it as proper and valuable. This attitude on the part of Christian theology is entirely correct, for Scripture was not given to us in order that we should merely repeat its exact words in parrot-like fashion but in order that we should digest it in our own minds and express it in our own words. That use was made of Scripture by Jesus and the apostles, who not only quoted the exact words of Scripture but also by a process of reasoning arrived at inferences and conclusions based upon these words. The Bible is neither a statute-book nor a dogmatics-text but it is the source of theology. As Word of God not only its exact words have binding authority but so have also all conclusions that are properly derived from it. Furthermore, neither study of Scripture nor theological activity is at all possible unless one uses terms that do not occur in the Bible. Not only are such terms used in connection with the doctrine of the trinity but in connection with every doctrine. Every phase of theological thinking requires them. The Christian's right of independent reflection upon the truth of Scripture and theology's right of existence are involved in this use of terms that do not occur in the Bible. Finally, such terms are not used in order to serve as means for the introduction of new dogmas that are foreign or even contrary to Scripture but in order to achieve the very opposite result: in order to defend the truth of Scripture against all error. Consequently, they have a negative rather than a positive function. They indicate the boundary lines of the sphere of Christian thought, beyond which it is not safe to venture forth lest one should sacrifice revealed truth. While pretending close adherence to Scripture Biblical theology has drifted farther and farther away from the Bible; while the orthodox, ecclesiastical formulation of doctrine with its employment of terms that do not occur in the Bible has been fully justified in its claim of being scriptural.

Accordingly, also in connection with the doctrine of the trinity, descriptive terms not found in the Bible have established themselves, such as, "homo-ousios," "ousia," "hyparxis," "hypostasis," "prosopon," "gennan," "triad," "unity," "trinity," "substance," "persons," "names," "positions," "species," "forms," "properties," etc. At first the meaning of these terms was far from definite. The "ousia" was usually employed in the sense of "being," to indicate the one divine being, but in the works of Origen, Athanasius, and Gregory of Nyssa it often referred to the three persons in that being. Athanasius expressly defended his position over against Sabellius by stating that the Son is not "mono-ousios" but "homoöusios" with the Father. So also the term hypostasis was sometimes used to indicate the one being, then again, to denote the three persons, so that at one time it was stated that there was only one hypostasis in God, then again that there were three hypostases. But Sabellianism viewed the persons as being merely the revelatory modes of the one essence. Over against that error the church was forced to emphasize the fact that the three persons are self-existent and really distinct in character: that there is a trinity of essence. To indicate this fact the name hypostasis, which thus becomes equivalent to person, was used. Basil in his letter entitled *Concerning Ousia and Hypostasis* brought about a greater degree of uniformity in the use of these words by employing the term "ousia" for God's essence or being and the word "hypostasis" or "prosōpon" for the three persons. Accordingly, every "hypostasis" has his "own subsistence" and is distinguished from the other persons by "peculiar traits, properties, distinctive features, tokens, marks, characteristics, forms." A similar terminology is used by the two Gregories, by John of Damascus, and by Greek theology and the Greek church in general.

In the West confusion was not so great. Tertullian had definitely established the use of the terms essentia and substantia for God's essence or being, and the words persona and subsistentia for the persons. This terminology was used in the confessions and accepted by the ministers and teachers. Hilary in his work, *De Trinitate,* constantly speaks of one essentia, substantia, natura, genus, and of three personae, distinguished from each other by their personal "properties." Augustine found fault with the word substantia as a translation of the Greek "hypostasis." The Latin words substantia and essentia do not bear the same relation to each other as the Greek words "hypostasis and ousia." In Latin one cannot properly speak of one essentia and three substantiae. "Substantia" rather than "essentia" was viewed as the Latin equivalent of the Greek "ousia." The word "essentia" sounded more or less unfamiliar to Latin ears. As a result the expression "one substance" (una substantia) and "three persons" (tres personae) was retained in Latin. Nevertheless, as a rule, Augustine tried to avoid the word substantia altogether; i.e., he used it neither for the being nor for the person. The reason for this was that the Latin word substantia indicates that which exists in itself and is the bearer of the attributes, the unchanging subject in which the accidents inhere. But inasmuch as in

God being and attributes are one, Augustine preferred to use the word essentia for God's being. Furthermore, just as in the East it was necessary, in view of Sabellianism, to emphasize the self-existent character of the three persons, hence, to use the term "hypostasis" for person, so in the West it was necessary, over against Arianism, to speak of the three persons as three personae rather than three substantiae. Scholasticism added more terms to those already given: it prepared a definite scheme that was afterward adopted by theologians in general, also by those of the Reformation. According to that scheme there is in God one being, "one essence," "unity of nature," and there are in him "three persons, a trinity of persons." Within that being these three persons are one, "consubstantial," "coessential," and exist in and through each other, a relation indicated by the words "coinherence or intercomprehension," "circumincession of persons." But they are distinct. For in God there are "two emanations: a natural and a volitional"; "three hypostases or persons: Father, Son, and Holy Spirit"; "four relations; paternity or fatherhood, filiation or sonship, active spiration and passive spiration"; "five notions: innascibility, paternity, filiation, active spiration and passive spiration; and three personal properties: the Father, who is unbegotten; the Son, who is begotten; and the Holy Spirit, who proceeds.

**IV. The Doctrine Of the Trinity Teaches that Within the Divine Essence There Are Three Distinct Subjects, Not Existing Alongside of One Another, But In, Through, and Unto Each Other, In Such a Manner that the Divine Essence In All Its Fulness Is Possessed By Each and By All. The Persons Differ From Each Other In Their Personal Attributes: Paternity, Filiation, and Procession. The View Of the Orthodox Eastern Church: That the Holy Spirit Proceeds From the Father Only, May Be Traced To Subordinationism and Results In False Mysticism. The Economic Trinity Reflects the Ontological. Illustrations Do Not Prove the Trinity, But Have Their Value. This Truth Is of Great Significance For Other Doctrines and For Practical Religion.**

A. **The doctrine of the trinity in general.** For a right understanding of this doctrine three questions must be answered:

(1) What is meant by the term "being," "essence"? Answer: The word "essence," "being," indicates the divine nature (considered apart from its modes of subsistence) possessed alike and equally by all the three persons, essentially distinct from all creaturely existence, and possessing all the divine attributes (discussed in a former chapter).

(2) What does the word "person" signify? Answer: The word "person" indicates the existence within the divine essence of a threefold self-distinction; i.e, of three distinct modes of

**subsistence, not existing alongside of and separate from one another as human individualities do, but in, through, and unto each other, in such a manner that the divine essence in all its fulness is possessed by each and by all.**

**(3) What is the relation between essence (being) and person, and between the three persons? Answer: The persons are not merely modes of manifestation, but modes of EXISTENCE, within the divine essence. The persons differ from each other with respect to their eternal, immanent relations; i.e., with respect to their personal properties: paternity, filiation, and procession.**

For a proper understanding of the doctrine of the trinity three questions must be answered: What is the meaning of the term "essence," "being"? What is indicated by the word "person"? What is the relation between essence and person, and between the persons severally? Aristotle defined "ousia" as "that which is neither predicated of any substrate nor is in any; as 'a certain man' or 'a certain horse.'" This was the sense originally given to the word in theology. Hence, the term was applied to the three persons as well as to the one Divine Being. Gradually, however, the word "ousia" was given a different interpretation, and was used to indicate the "essence" or "nature" of any object. *"Ousia"* came to be used as a synonym for "nature" (*physis*). Some object to the use of the word *"physis"* as an indication of the being of God, because it is derived from *phynai*: to come into being, just as "natura" is derived from "nasci." But this word gained currency in the sphere of theology as did the word "natura," and was supported by II Pet. 1:4. "Ousia," "physis," "substance," "essence," "nature" was the constant term used to indicate the one divine essence, the Godhead in general, considered apart from its "subsistence" and from its "modes of subsistence"; hence, it indicated the divine nature common to all the three persons. There is one simple divine essence, essentially distinct from all creaturely existence, and possessing all the attributes discussed in a former chapter. Of the distinction between this divine essence and the three persons we find an analogy in the realm of creatures. Paul, John and Peter all partake of the same human nature, but as individual persons they are distinct from each other and from human nature itself. But here we must guard ourselves against two errors. According to nominalism "being" (i.e., that which is common or universal) is a mere name or concept; accordingly, in the doctrine we are discussing this leads to tritheism. Excessive realism, on the other hand, regards the essence of a thing to consist in a separate substance existing behind and above the persons. This results in tetratheism and Sabellianism. Even Gregory of Nyssa was to a certain extent an exponent of extreme realism. In order to prove that God is *one*, and that it is incorrect to speak of three Gods, he asserted that it was even wrong to speak of *men* in the plural, forasmuch as they partake of *one* nature. But thus the essential distinction between God and man is lost sight of. To be sure, there is an analogy between the divine and the human nature. Accordingly, we have the right to speak of God's *nature*. But that analogy is at the same time suggestive of a very important distinction. The concept "human nature" is a universal concept. It is not, indeed, a *mere* term; it is real and present *in* each individual human being (not, of course, apart from the individual), but it is *differently* and *finitely* present in each individual. It is never fully and infinitely present in any single man. Just as the gods of polytheism are "similar in nature" but not "same in nature or one in nature," so also human individuals are not only "distinct but also separate." The same cannot be affirmed with reference to God. The divine nature is not a mere general concept, neither is it something that exists separate from, above, and next to the persons; on the contrary, not only is it present *in* the persons, but in each of these it is "totally and numerically the same." Hence, the persons of the trinity are "distinct" but not "separate." They are "the same in essence, one in essence, consubstantial." Neither space nor time nor anything else separates them. They all partake of the same divine nature and attributes. One and the same divine nature is present in each person individually and in all collectively. Hence, in God there is one eternal, omnipotent, omniscient nature. There is in God *one* mind, *one* will, *one* energy. The term "being" or "essence" indicates God's unity, emphasized throughout Scripture, maintained by monotheism, and defended also by unitarianism. No matter what distinctions are present within the Divine Being, the unity of God's essence can never be abrogated, for in God that unity is not imperfect and finite but complete and absolute. Among creatures distinctions necessarily indicate manyness, division, separateness. Creatures exist side by side; they follow one another in space and time. But eternity, omnipresence, omnipotence, goodness, etc., do not admit of partition and distribution. God is absolute unity and simplicity, without any composition or division; and that unity is not contractual or ethical as among men, but absolute; it is not accidental but essential to God's being.

Now the glory of the doctrine of the trinity consists in this that God's absolute unity does not exclude but demands diversity. The being of God is not an abstract unity; it is not an abstract idea but a fulness of essence, an infinite abundance of life, whose diversity unfolds the highest unity. The self-distinctions within the Divine Being, which in Scripture are designated by the terms "Father," "Son," and "Holy Spirit" are called "persons" in theology. In the East the word "prosopon" was first used to indicate "person." It was the Greek equivalent

of the Hebrew *pānīm,* face, outward appearance, rôle. But this word
was ambiguous. Sabellius interpreted it in the sense of "manifestation," and declared that the one divine *ousia* or *hypostasis* assumed
various *prosopa* or faces. In opposition to this view the church-fathers
contended that the three *prosopa* were not to be regarded as mere
manifestations or modes of revelation but as "hypostatical prosopa."
Consequently, the term "hypostasis" was substituted for "prosopon."
The word *hypostasis* means foundation, substructure, firmness; further,
that which exists in reality and not merely in appearance, or also that
which has existence in itself in contradistinction to "accidents" which
inhere in something else. In the West the Latin word *persona* was
used, meaning mask, hence, the rôle of an actor in a play; from this in
turn the meaning "condition, quality, capacity in which a person functions" was derived and in jurisprudence it indicated "a being having
legal rights and obligations." Accordingly, the meaning of this word
was rather indefinite, and was made even more indefinite by Tertullian,
who uses it as a synonym of "name, species, form, degree, and thing."
Nevertheless, the term was retained in Latin even after the East had
substituted *hypostasis* for *prosopon,* for the simple reason that in Latin
there was no word which could be considered an adequate translation
of the Greek *hypostasis.* The word substantia would not do because
this term was already used to indicate God's being or essence. But this
difference of expression led to much misunderstanding between the
East and the West. The Greeks interpreted the Latin *persona* in the
sense of *prosopon* while the Latins in turn understood *hypostasis* to
mean substantia. Each charged the other with poverty of expression;
nevertheless, in reality both taught the same thing, namely, that the
three persons are not merely modes but distinct or self-subsistent individualities. Accordingly, in the language of the church the meaning self-
existence, "hypostasis," "subsistence," "subsisting individuality," "sup-
positum" became the essential characteristic of the term "prosopon" or
"person." In the time of Athanasius and the three Cappadocians the
term still has this meaning. But afterward the word "person" (persona)
acquired an additional characteristic: if "person" (persona) merely indicated self-existence, in contradistinction to accident (accidens), it
could even be used to indicate *things.* In the Christological struggle
against Nestorianism and Monophysitism the church was forced to
come forward with a clearer definition of *nature* and *person;* hence
arose the definition of "person" as "the individual substance of a rational nature." Cf. the work *de duabus naturis et una persona Christi,*
the authorship of which is ascribed to Boëthius. According to this
definition the word "person" indicates two things: self-existence and
rationality or self-consciousness. This is the meaning of the word in the

works of scholastics and of the older Roman Catholic, Lutheran, and Reformed dogmaticians.

In modern philosophy and psychology an entirely different conception of personality has arisen: (1) Personality has been considered incompatible wth infinitude; hence, God's personality, self-consciousness, and self-determination were denied. If God exists, he is merely the omnipotent, omnipresent, unconscious energy and force present in all things. (2) In psychology the idea arose that even human personality does not imply self-existence: the ego, the soul, is not a substance but merely the nominalistic sum-total of psychical phenomena, and personality so-called is merely the temporal and passing mode of existence, pertaining to the individual being called man. (3) This in turn gave rise to the idea that personality, viewed as the flower and highest stage of the development of a human being, was to be regarded as man's final goal, the highest good which for a time he is able to attain. "Personality is the chief happiness of earthlings," according to Goethe. (4) This naturally led to a heroization and deification of those individuals who had reached that high stage of development and had attained personality. In the minds of some the idea has arisen that such individuals who by dint of great effort reached this peak of development become immortal (doctrine of conditional immortality).

Now this idea of personality, even when we consider *human* personality, is erroneous because personality or egoity is something else and something more than the sum-total of psychical phenomena. But it is even less applicable to the doctrine of the trinity. Here the term "personality" has its own distinct meaning. Even the definition of Boëthius belongs to the doctrine of Christ rather than to that of the trinity. The most eminent theologians have always felt this.    Richard of St. Victor rejected this definition because it speaks of "individual substance" and he described a person as the "incommunicable existence of the divine nature." Calvin merely spoke of "a subsistence in the divine essence." All admitted the truth of the word of Augustine, "We speak of three persons, not in order thereby completely to express it, but in order that it may not be left wholly unexpressed." In the doctrine of the trinity the word "person" simply expresses the truth that the three persons in the Deity are not modes  of manifestation merely, but have distinct and actual existence. The elements of rationality and self-consciousness do not at all receive emphasis; these are given in the fact that the three persons partake of the same *being,* hence of the same attributes, therefore also of wisdom and of knowledge. What *is* expressed by the term "person" is that the one Divine Being unfolds a threefold existence. It is a "unity which derives the trinity out of its own self." The three persons are not three modes of manifestation of the one divine personality, but the Divine Being is tripersonal because *divine,* *absolute* personality requires this. In man we have but a faint analogy of divine personality. Personality in man results from the fact that we have a subject which has itself for an object, and effects a union of the two (subject and object) in the act of self-consciousness. Hence three moments constitute the essence of human personality; we say: three *moments;* in God, however, these three are not merely moments or constituents—for he is not subject to space or time, to extension or division—but "hypostases," modes of existence pertaining to one and the same divine essence. But this comparison of divine personality to human personality is deficient in still another respect. Human nature is, as such, too rich in content to be embodied in one single individual: it reaches its full expression and unfoldment not in a single human being but in the human race, not in man but in mankind. Now the divine nature also unfolds its fulness in three persons, but the point of difference is this: in God these three persons are not three individuals alongside of and separated from one another but they are the threefold self-distinction within the Divine Being which results from the unfolding of the divine nature into personality causing the latter to be tripersonal in character. Of the *human* nature there is a dual unfolding: in the individual, human nature unfolds itself into personality; in the race human nature unfolds itself into many individuals, which in turn together constitute a unity, a personality, just as Christ and the church constitute *one* full-grown man, I Cor. 12:12; Eph. 4:13. Now this unfoldment which in man is double is single in God: the unfoldment of his being into personality coincides with the unfoldment of his being into three persons: the three persons are the *one* divine personality brought to complete self-unfoldment, a self-unfoldment which arises out of and takes place by means of and within the divine essence.

From this the answer to the third question may be derived; namely, "What is the relation between 'being' (essence) and person and of the persons to one another?" Tertullian describes the three persons as "of one substance, of one condition, of one power, but the one God"; they are three "not in condition but in degree"; they are "one but not identical"; they are "the one God from whom these degrees and forms and aspects are reckoned under the name of the Father, and of the Son, and of the Holy Spirit." There is distinction and distribution, but not diversity and division. Athanasius and the three Cappadocians define the "hypostases" as "modes of subsistence," by which they meant that although the persons are one in being or essence, they differ in manner of existence. Accordingly, the distinction between "being" (essence) and "person" and between the persons among themselves was regarded as consisting in their "reciprocal relation"; in the fact of their being

Father, Son or Spirit; in the personal properties: "paternity or agen-nesia, lit. unbegottenness," "sonship or passive generation," and "sanc-tification or procession." This idea was developed by Augustine. He does not derive the trinity from the Father but from the unity of the divine essence: from the "godhead," neither does he conceive of it as accidental but as essential to the being of God. According to him the trinitarian mode of existence pertains to God's very essence. In that respect personality is identical with God's being itself. "For to God it is not one thing to be, another to be a person, but it is absolutely the same thing." For if essence pertain to God in an absolute sense, but personality only in a relative sense, then the three persons could not constitute one being. Hence, every person is identical with the entire being, and equal to the other two persons taken together, or to all the three. With creatures this is different. One person does not equal three, "but in God it is not so; for the Father, the Son, and the Holy Spirit together are not a greater essence than the Father alone or the Son alone; but these three substances or persons, if they must be so termed, together are equal to each singly." "In the highest trinity one is as much as the three together, nor are two anything more than one; moreover they are infinite in themselves. So both each is in each, and all are in each, and each is in all, and all are in all, and all are one." "The trinity itself is as great as each several person therein." Accordingly, the distinction between being and person and between the persons severally, is not one of substance but one of mutual rela-tionship. "Whatever, therefore, is spoken of God in respect to himself is both spoken singly of each person, that is, of the Father, and of the Son, and of the Holy Spirit; and together of the trinity itself, not plurally but in the singular." "However, whereas in the same trinity some things severally are particularly predicated, these things are not at all predicated about themselves, but they are predicated in mutual reference or in respect to the creature; hence, it is clear that such things are predicated relatively, not in the way of substance." Similar-ly, later theologians asserted that being and person did not differ es-sentially or materially (in the thing) but "in reason"; not, however, "in subjective reason, rationally, nominally" as held by Sabellius, but "in objective reason." The distinction was held to be one of relation, and not one of substance; nevertheless, this distinction was considered real and objective, based on divine revelation. Being and person were held to differ not "in the thing, i.e., materially," but "really"; the dif-ference refers to a "mode of subsistence"; however, it is a *real* differ-ence. The persons are modes of existence within the being; accordingly, the persons differ among themselves as the one mode of existence differs from the other, and — using a common illustration — as the open palm differs from the closed fist.

If we must express this distinction between being and person, and between the persons among themselves, in a single phrase, what has been said so far in this paragraph is about all that can be said. Nevertheless, this distinction becomes even clearer when we consider the relation within the divine essence by means of which it is brought about. Although Scripture is very monotheistic, nevertheless, it ascribes divine nature and perfections to the Son, and the Spirit, and co-ordinates them with the Father. Accordingly, Father, Son, and Spirit are distinct subjects in the one divine essence. As such they bear different names, they have distinct personal properties, and they always appear in a certain definite order, both in their "internal" and "external" relationships. Hence the distinctness of the persons is completely expressed by the so-called "personal attributes or properties"; viz. (a) "paternity or fatherhood, innascibility or unbegottenness, active generation, active spiration; (b) filiation or sonship, passive generation, active spiration; and (c) procession or passive spiration." Of course, these personal attributes do not *add* anything to the being. When a person becomes father, his being does not change; he merely assumes a different relation than hitherto. So also the being of God does not differ essentially or substantially from the first person, the second person, or the third person. It differs "in reason, in relationship." One and the same being is and is called Father when viewed in his relation to that same being in the person of the Son. And the persons severally differ only in this respect that the one is Father, the other Son, and the third Spirit. In the realm of mankind we find only a dim reflection of this; nevertheless, it may make the point a little clearer. Among men fatherhood and sonship is also only a relation. Nevertheless, it presupposes a personal, individual subject, which, though it sustains that specific relation, has existence in abundance entirely apart from it. Fatherhood is not essential to manhood: some never attain to fatherhood; those who did, attained to it in later years, and gradually lose it again, etc. Accordingly, manhood and fatherhood are not co-terminous: the latter does not cover the former. In God, however, this is different. In him Godhead and personality coincide completely. "Just as to him to be is the same as to be God, or as to be great, or as to be good, so to him it is the same thing to be as to be a person." Expressing it in concrete language we could say that in the case of each of the three persons the divine essence is completely contained in the state of being Father, Son, or Spirit. Paternity, filiation, and procession are not to be viewed as accidental properties of God's being; but as the eternal modes of existence of, and the eternal, immanent relations

within that being. Of *human* nature there is a multiplex unfoldment;
in the individual, human nature is unfolded into personality; in the
human race, into individuality; furthermore, there is an unfoldment of
human nature along the lines of sex and of blood-relationship. Now
every one of these unfoldments brings into view a new phase of human
nature. This triple unfoldment of human nature differs with respect to
space and time. There is a real development here: each distinct unfoldment shows us a new phase of human nature. But in God there is
neither separation nor division. The unfoldment of his being into personality instantaneously, absolutely, and completely coincides with and
includes the unfoldment of his being into persons, and also the unfoldment of his immanent relations expressed in the names Father, Son,
and Spirit. Thus God is man's arche-type: that which in the realm of
mankind we find separate and alongside of each other, diffused in space
and extended in time, is simple, undivided, and eternal in God. The
processions within the essence simultaneously bring about God's absolute personality, his trinitarian existence, and his immanent relations.
They are the absolute arche-types of all the processions by means of
which human nature comes to complete unfoldment in man, in the
family, and in the human race. Hence, of the three persons each is
"distinct but not different from the other"; the trinity exists in, through,
and unto the unity; the unfoldment of the being takes place within the
being; hence, the latter's unity and simplicity remain unimpaired. Furthermore, although the three persons are not, indeed, different in
essence, they are three distinct subjects, "hypostases or subsistences."
For that very reason they bring about within the being of God the complete unfoldment of that being. Finally, among themselves the three
persons are related to one another in an absolute manner, by means of
generation and spiration; their personal distinctness coincides completely with their immanent relationships. The Father is *Father* only
and eternally, the Son is *Son* only and eternally, the Spirit is *Spirit*
only and eternally. And because each is himself in an eternal, simple,
and absolute manner; hence, the Father is God; the Son is God; and
the Holy Spirit is God. The Father is God in his character of Father,
the Son as Son, and the Holy Spirit as Holy Spirit. And inasmuch as
all three are God, they all partake of one divine nature. Hence, there
is one God: Father, Son, and Holy Spirit, worthy of eternal praise!

**B. The three persons discussed separately.**
   **(1) The Father:**
      **(a) Personal attribute of the Father: negatively, it is agen-
nesia; positively, it is paternity or Fatherhood. Agennesia
literally means unbegottenness, i.e., the state of being ingenerate or unbegotten; it should not be confused with agenesia
(with one n), which indicates the state of being without be-**

ginning. **Agennesia is a personal attribute and as such pertains to the Father whereas agenesia pertains to all three persons equally.**

**(b) Meaning of the Father's paternity or fatherhood:**

1. **It is the arche-type of fatherhood among men, not vice versa: when we call God our Father, we are not using a mere metaphor; i.e., the truth is not that fatherhood is a primary attribute of man while it pertains to God merely in a secondary or derived sense; on the contrary, the relation is reversed: God is Father in the real and complete sense of the term. As such:**

2. **It differs from fatherhood among men in the following respects:**

   **a. It is EFFICIENT, i.e., of and by himself alone the Father generates the Son.**

   **b. It is ABSOLUTE AND UNQUALIFIED: in God the Father is not also Son.**

   **c. It is ETERNAL: God is Father everlastingly: God's fatherhood is not a temporal, passing relation.**

   **d. It is ESSENTIAL: fatherhood pertains to the very essence of God.**

**(2) The Son:**

**(a) Personal attribute of the Son: filiation or sonship, passive generation**

**(b) Meaning of the Son's filiation or sonship:**

1. **It is SPIRITUAL; hence, it does not imply any separation or division in the divine essence.**

2. **It is a generation out of the BEING of the Father, out of the divine ESSENCE: The generation of the Son, though completely in harmony with the Father's will, is not determined by the will of the Father; i.e., the Son is not a creature.**

3. **It is ETERNAL: timeless, without beginning or end.**

**(3) The Holy Spirit:**

**(a) The personality of the Holy Spirit must be maintained.**

**(b) Personal attribute of the Holy Spirit: procession, spiration.**

**(c) Meaning of the Holy Spirit's procession or spiration:**

1. **In order, it follows procession**

2. **It is the work of both Father and Son.**

Having set forth the doctrine of the trinity in general, we shall now discuss each of the three persons separately. The first person is the Father, and his personal attribute is "paternity or *agennesia.*" The word agennesia figured prominently in the Arian controversy. It was borrowed from the Greek vernacular. Plato called his "ideas," "ingenerate"; Aristotle applied this word to matter; the Gnostics called God "ingenerate depth." From the latter this term was copied by Paul of Samosata and by the Arians, by Aetius and Eunomius, in order thereby to combat the theory that the Son and the Spirit are co-essential with the Father. They maintained that the term "agennesia'" is expressive of God's essential nature, and that it differentiates him from the creature. Further that, whereas the Son is not ingenerate or unbegotten but generate or begotten — as is taught by Scripture and admitted by the church, both of which ascribe the term "only-begotten" to him — hence, it cannot be true that the Son is God; he must needs be a creature; it would be illogical to posit two ingenerate beings, i.e., "two gods." Over against this, however, we should be careful to observe that in the Greek there are two words spelled nearly alike. One is *gennētos* from the verb *gennan,* gignere, generare; the other is *genētos* from the verb *gignesthai,* fieri; of the two the latter is by far the broader term, and denotes whatever has beginning, whether it results from creation, generation or propagation. Now the distinction between these two words was not always clearly understood. It was simply pointed out that the word agennētos or agenētos could be used in a twofold sense and that in one sense the word was applicable to the Son, and in the other not. Gradually, however, the two words were distinguished. In contradistinction to every creature the term agenetos (without beginning or increate) could be applied to every one of the three persons, as not any of the three was brought forth after the manner of the creature, and not any of the three had a beginning in time. *Agenesia* is an attribute of God's *being,* common to all three persons. It must not be confused with *agennesia,* which is an attribute of the Father alone. The Son is *gennetos* (i.e., begotten) not because he was brought forth in time like a creature, but because he is eternally generated out of the essence of the Father. The church-fathers were careful to state that *agennesia* is a property pertaining to the person and not to the being. God's being is one and the same in each of the three persons, but the agennesia is a relation within the being. Just as Adam, Eve, and Abel partake of the same human nature or essence, though each obtained it in a different manner than the other two, so also there is in God one essence, although this subsists in a threefold manner. In addition to this it should be noted that the term *agennesia* is negative and merely expresses the fact that the Father transcends generation, but it tells us nothing positive with reference to God's nature; in reality it does not tell us anything about the person of the Father, for *agennesia* and paternity differ widely. Hence, the name *Father* is to be preferred above the adjective "agennetos." The Scriptural name Father is a much better indication of the personal attribute of the first person than the term *agennetos.* Fatherhood (paternity) implies a positive relation toward the second person. The name Father is even more proper as an indication of the deity than the name God, for the latter is a common name indicating dignity, but the name Father in the New Testament as well as the name Jehovah in the Old Testament is a "proper name," an indication of a personal property of God. He who refuses to honor God as Father shows even greater disrespect than the person who fails to acknowledge him as Creator. Accordingly, we do not ascribe the name Father to God in a merely metaphorical sense as if it primarily indicated an attribute of man. Exactly the opposite is the truth: fatherhood on earth is but a dim reflection, a faint shadow of *God's* fatherhood, Eph. 3:15: "from whom every fatherhood in heaven and on earth is named." God is Father in the true and complete sense of the term. Among men a father is also some one else's son, and a son in turn is father. Again, among men a father is not able of and by himself alone to bring forth a son; also, fatherhood is a temporal and in a certain sense an accidental relation, i.e., it is not an *essential* attribute of manhood: it is a relation which becomes a reality rather late in life; it also ceases again when a person dies, or perhaps even before that time. In God, however, this is different. He is Father only and completely; he is Father alone; he is Father by nature: he is Father from eternity, without beginning or end. Hence, the generation of the Son is eternal, and the Son is as eternal as the Father; for if the Son were not eternal, neither could the Father be. The *eternal* character of the divine fatherhood implies the eternal character of the divine sonship: addressing God as Father implies belief in the Son. Because of this relation of the Father to the Son, and also because of the Father's relation to the Spirit ,the first person has often been called "self-born, self-produced, uncreated, without beginning, self-originated, the ground of his own substance, self-caused"; also, "the Beginning, Cause, Root, Fountain, Origin, Head," etc., of the Son and of the Spirit and of the Godhead as a whole.

The personal attribute of the Son is filiation. In Scripture the second person receives various names indicating his relation to the Father; such as Word, Wisdom, Logos, Son, firstborn, only-begotten, only Son. Image of God, "Image, Substance, Expression." The doctrine of "eternal generation" termed thus by Origen, was based upon these names and upon a few texts which have already been mentioned. Of course, when we discuss the relation between Father and Son, we must needs express ourselves in human and therefore imperfect language; mindful of this we shall use all caution. Nevertheless, it is proper for us to speak of the Son's generation. For, just as we speak symbolically of God's ear, eye, and mouth, in the same manner human generation is an analogy and reflection of that divine act by means of which the Father "giveth unto the Son to have life in himself." Of course, whatever in the relation as it exists among men implies imperfection or physical condition must be eliminated. Among men generation is incomplete and imperfect: a man needs a woman in order to bring forth a son. No man is able fully to reflect his own image in a child, not even in several children. A man becomes father in course of time; afterward he ceases to be father, and the child soon becomes entirely independent of the father. But with God this is not the case. To be sure, God generates. The beautiful idea of the divine fecundity is emphasized and repeated over and over by the church-fathers. He is not an abstract, "distinctionless unity." In him is fulness of life. His nature is a "generative, fruitful essence"; it is capable of unfoldment and communication. Whoever denies that divine fecundity does not figure with the truth that God is infinite, blessed life. All such a person has left is an abstract, deistic idea of God. In order to supply the deficiency thus brought about he now in pantheistic fashion incorporates into the being of God the life of the universe. Apart from the idea of the trinity the act of creation becomes inconceivable: if God is absolutely incommunicable, he is a darkened light, a dry spring; how then would it be possible for him to impart himself to creatures?

Nevertheless, it should be remembered that this generation is a *divine* act. Hence, it is in the first place *spiritual*. The Arians offered especially this objection, that generation means "separation, division," also "passion and emanation." This would be true if we were speaking of bodily, physical, creaturely generation. But in *God* generation is spiritual and simple, and does not involve any division or separation; it takes place "without emanation or division." It gives rise to "distinction" and "distribution," but it does not bring about any "diversity" and "division" within the divine essence. Athanasius states, "But whereas God is simple or uncompounded, it follows that the Father of the Son is indivisible and without passion, for although in the realm of man we can speak of efflux and afflux, we cannot predicate these of anything which is incorporeal" Thought and speech offer the best analogy of divine generation, and Scripture itself fixes our attention on this by calling the Son "Logos" (Word). As the human soul objectifies itself by means of speech (lit. "by means of the word") so also God comes to complete expression in the Logos. Also with reference to this comparison, however, we should discriminate carefully. Man needs many words in order to express his thoughts. These words are sounds; hence, they are physical and material; and they have no existence of and by themselves. But whenever God speaks, he completely expresses himself in the one divine Logos (Word), unto whom he giveth to have life in himself. Secondly, therefore, divine generation implies that the Father begets the Son "of the essence of the Father, God of God,

Light of Light, very God of very God, begotten, not made, being of one substance with the Father" as the Nicean Symbol has it. The Arians taught that by the will of the Father the Son was begotten out of nothing. This, however, would not be generation but creation, as John of Damascus points out: "Creation refers to the fact that the thing created or made is not produced from the substance of the Creator and Maker but arises from without and is wholly different in substance, but generation refers to procession of that which is begotten out of the substance of the Begetter so that it is similar in substance." The Son is not a creature, but he is God blessed forever, Rom. 9:5. Accordingly, he was not brought forth by the will of the Father, out of nothing, and in time. But he is generated out of the essence of the Father, in eternity. Hence, instead of viewing generation as a real work or *"energy"* (*energeia*) of the Father, we should rather ascribe a "generative nature" to the Father. Of course, this does not mean that generation is contrary to the Father's will, neither does it imply that generation is an unconscious emanation that stands in no relation to the Father's will or power. All that is meant is that it does not result from a previous "decree of God's determining will" as is true of the work of creation, but that it is so natural to the Father that his "concomitant will" takes perfect delight in it. It is a revelation of "that which is genuine to his nature and proper to his essence," hence also of his knowledge, will, and power, and of all his attributes. Thirdly, therefore, the church confesses to believe in the *eternal* character of this generation. With reference to the Son the Arians held that "there was a time when he was not," appealed especially to Proverbs 8:22 (*ektise,* creavit), and pointed out that if the Son were "eternal," he could not have been "begotten." But if the designations Father and Son are to be taken in a metaphysical sense, as Scripture abundantly teaches, it follows that generation must needs be eternal. If the Son is not eternal, neither can God be Father eternally. In that case God became Father in course of time. Hence, disbelief in the doctrine of eternal generation involves a denial not only of the divinity of the Son but also of the divinity of the Father, of his immutability, divine nature, and eternal fatherhood; while it leaves unexplained how God can be truly and justly called Father in time if this fatherhood is not eternally rooted in his nature. Accordingly, we must conceive of divine generation as eternal in the true sense of that word. It is not to be regarded as having been completed once for all in the past, but it is an act eternal and immutable, eternally finished, yet continuing forevermore. As it is natural for the sun to give light and for the fountain to pour forth water, so it is natural for the Father to generate the Son. The Father is not nor ever was without generating. He begets everlastingly. "We must not think that the Father by a single act in the past generated the Son and that he then severed him from his origin, but we must hold that the Father eternally generates the Son." God's begetting is speaking and his speaking is eternal. "Everlasting is God's generation."

The third person is called the Holy Spirit, and his personal property is "procession or spiration." The doctrine of the Holy Spirit has always been treated in theology as a necessary implication of the doctrine of the Son. While in regard to the Son the point of controversy was his deity—in general his personality was left unchallenged—the Spirit's *personality* was the butt of argumentation. It was held that to accept the Spirit's personality would mean to believe in his deity; along with the Son's deity the deity of the Spirit had to be accepted. However, Pneumatomachians of earlier and later date raised all manner of objections against the personality and divinity of the Holy Spirit. They claimed that the name God is never in Scripture applied to the Holy Spirit, that he is nowhere spoken of as being worshipped or adored as God, that he always appears as a power and gift of God, and that those few passages which speak of him as a person should be interpreted as personifications. According to Gregory Nazienzen the controversy carried on in his time concerning the Holy Spirit is to be interpreted in the light of the fact that while the O. T. clearly revealed the Father and less clearly the Son, the New Testament sheds the clear light of day upon the deity of the Son but furnishes a merely vague conception of the Spirit's deity. At present, however, the Holy Spirit dwells among us, fully revealing himself to us. There is an undeniable element of truth in this statement. The personality and deity of the Holy Spirit does not present itself to us with such outward and objective clearness as that of the Father and of the Son. The term "Spirit" does not express this personality as plainly as do the terms "Father" and "Son." The specific work of the Holy Spirit, namely sanctification, does not stand out in such bold relief before our consciousness as do the works of creation, incarnation, and redemption. We ourselves are living in the dispensation of the Holy Spirit: the Holy Spirit dwells in us and among us; hence, our prayers are directed to the Father and to the Mediator rather than to the Spirit. The latter is more properly called the author than the object of prayer. Hence, in the church controversy raged for a long time with respect to the deity and personality of the Holy Spirit. The religious significance of the doctrine was not fully realized at first. Generally, the personality of the Holy Spirit was indeed admitted, but his activity in the past, illumining the prophets and apostles and anointing Christ for his task, received all the attention. The necessity of "internal grace" was not yet clearly perceived; the need of the work of God's omnipotent grace in the heart was not yet definitely felt; there was as yet no fathoming of the depth of the mystic union between God and man; God's objective revelation in Christ was held to be sufficient, and the need of a subjective illumination was not yet realized. As soon, however, as the church began to reflect and meditate upon its own source of life, and to account for the subjective as well as for the objective principles of salvation, it confessed with joy the personality and deity of the Holy Spirit. Thus it has always been, throughout the centuries. The denial of the personal existence and divine nature of the Holy Spirit can always be traced to (conscious or unconscious) rationalism, pelagianism, and deism; it is intimately connected with Arianism, Socinianism, Arminianism, etc.

From this it becomes clear that belief in the personality and divinity of the Holy Spirit is not a product, of philosophy, but proceeds from the heart of the Christian religion itself, from the faith of the church: the Christian religion itself is bound up with the confession, just as it is bound up with the belief in the divinity of the Son. Scripture established beyond any degree of doubt the fact that the Holy Spirit is the subjective principle of all salvation: of regeneration, faith, conversion, sanctification, etc.; i.e., that there is no communion with the Father and with the Son than in and through the Holy Spirit. Now either one must be true: the Holy Spirit is a creature—whether a power, gift, or person—or else he is God. But if he is a creature, he cannot truly impart unto us God himself, the Father and the Son, together with all the benefits bestowed by them; in that case he cannot be the principle of new life in the church and in the individual believer; and in that case there is no real communion between God and man; God remains at a distance from us; he then exists above and outside of us, and it cannot be true that he has made his abode among men in whom he dwells as in his temple. But the Holy Spirit is not and cannot be a creature, for he sustains the same relation to the Son as does the latter to the Father, and he imparts unto us the Father and the Son. He is as closely related to the Son as the latter is to the Father. He is in the Son, and the Son is in him. He is "in substance the same as the Son." He is the Spirit of wisdom and of truth, of power and glory, the Spirit by means of whom Christ sanctifies the church, and imparts unto it himself together with all his benefits, "the divine nature," "the adoption as sons," and "the mystic union." He who imparts God unto us must himself be very God.

Having discussed the soteriological significance of this doctrine let us now look into its theological meaning. Apart from belief in the personality and deity of the Holy Spirit a true oneness of the Father and the Son will never result; he who denies the deity of the Son cannot maintain the deity of the Spirit. The trinity is not complete apart from the

person of the Holy Spirit considered as truly God; thus only is established the trinity of the persons in the unity of the essence and the
unity of the essence in the trinity of the persons. The entire dogma of
the trinity, the mystery of Christianity, the heart of religion, stands or
falls with the deity of the Spirit. This was understood by the church-
fathers. Hence, together with the deity of the Son they also confessed
the deity of the Spirit. The Niceno-Constantinopolitan Creed confessed
belief "in the Holy Spirit, the Lord and Giver of Life; who proceedeth
from the Father: who with the Father and the Son together is worshiped and glorified; who spake by the prophets." And since that time
all of Christendom confesses its belief in "the consubstantial trinity."

The relation which the third person sustains to the Father and to
the Son is to some extent expressed by his very name "the Holy Spirit"
and also by means of many verbs; such as, *given, sent, poured out,
breathed, proceeded,* and *descended.* Christian theology called this relation a "projection, procession, outgoing, spiration, emission, outpouring," etc. It was usually viewed as a "spiration." This was based upon
the fact that in Scripture the Spirit is called *ruah,* and that it is often
compared to breath and wind, Ps. 33:6; Job 33:4; John 3:8; 20:22;
Acts 2:2; etc. For the rest, however, theology was very careful in its
description of spiration. As was true of generation so it was also held
that spiration is an eternal act of self-communication taking place within
the divine essence. It was differentiated from generation in this respect
that while the latter gives unto *the Son* to have life in himself, spiration
does the same with reference to the Spirit, but the difficulty of going
into further details was generally felt. Said Augustine, "However, in
speaking of that transcendently excellent nature, who is able to set forth
what is the difference between 'being born' and 'proceeding'? Not
everything that proceeds is born although everything that is born proceeds, just as not every biped is a human being though every human
being is a biped. So much I know. But I do not know, I cannot give,
and I am insufficient for the task of pointing out the distinction between generation on the one hand and procession on the other." To be
sure, theologians tried to discover a certain kind of distinction. The one
usually given is: 1) that the Son proceeds only from the Father, whereas the Holy Spirit proceeds from both Father and Son; or 2) that the
Holy Spirit proceeds from the Father and from the Son "as *given* by
both, not as *born* of both." It was especially pointed out that the Holy
Spirit could not be the Son of the Son because in that case the "triad"
would become an "unlimited quantity" with an infinite number of inter-
personal relations within the divine essence. "The Holy Spirit by means
of himself fully completes the trinity, blessed and honored with many
hymns." The trinity is not capable of being augmented or decreased,

it is "complete." To be sure, in answer to the objection of the Arians that the Father is more powerful than the Son if the former is the only person of the three who is able to beget a Son through whom all things are created, Augustine states, "But it be far from any one to suppose, as you do, that the Father is stronger than the Son because the Father brought forth the Creator whereas the Son did not bring forth the Creator; for the reason for this is not that it was im*possible* but rather that it was im*proper* for the Son to do so"; but he immediately explains this statement by the following: "For divine generation would be unbounded if the generated Son would in turn bring forth a grandson to the Father . . . and the chain of generation would not be completed if each in turn would bring forth another, and if *one* would not be sufficient neither would any number ever be able to complete the series." "But within that essence of the trinity in no way can any other person whatever exist out of the same essence." Finally, especially Thomas Aquinas, c.s., thus described the distinction between generation and spiration that the former took place "after the manner of the intellect," the latter "after the manner of the will." Comparing generation to thought and speech and describing the Holy Spirit as love uniting the Father and the Son paved the way for thus stating the distinction. The mediaeval and Roman Catholic theologians followed Thomas Aquinas. The Protestant theologians, however, though accepting a distinction between generation and spiration, and between Son and Spirit, and acknowledging to a certain extent the correctness of the traditional distinctions, expressed themselves more carefully. On the whole they regarded the distinction given by Thomas Aquinas as lacking in Scriptural support.

C. **The difference between the Eastern and the Western Church regarding the procession of the Holy Spirit:**

(1) Athanasius and the three Cappadocians accept a close relation between Son and Spirit but do not expressly teach a procession of the Spirit from the Son.

(2) In the East, John of Damascus definitely denied the procession of the Holy Spirit from the Son; his view remains the view of the Eastern Church.

(3) The Western Church teaches the procession from both Father and Son. Tertullian and Hilary approached this doctrine. Augustine clearly taught it. The symbol of the third synod of Toledo added the words "and from the Son" to the text of the Constantinopolitan Creed.

(4) The Reformers followed Augustine.

(5) The Eastern Church does not deny the Holy Spirit's procession THROUGH the Son, but holds that belief in the double procession implies the acceptance of two originating causes in God. This very objection results from the error of subordina-

**tionism:** the Son and the Spirit are subordinate to the Father, from whose person the trinity is derived.

**(6) Practical results of this error:** two more or less independent revelations of the Father, one by means of the Son causing us to KNOW God, giving us something for our MIND, namely, DOCTRINE (cf. the Son's name: Logos); the other by means of the Holy Spirit, causing us to DELIGHT in God, supplying the needs of the HEART, giving us LIFE AND SPIRITUAL JOY. Thus doctrine and life are separated, and free reins are given to false mysticism.

Nevertheless, between the Eastern and the Western Church an important difference of opinion in regard to the doctrine of the trinity gradually developed. During the second century the ontological procession of the Son from the Father was viewed as an eternal generation implying a similar procession on the part of the Holy Spirit. The time had arrived for the determination of the relation of the Holy Spirit to the Father and the Son. Athanasius pointed out that the Holy Spirit is called both the Spirit of the Father and the Spirit of the Son or of Christ, and that he sustains the same "characteristic relation, order, and nature" with reference to the Son as does the Son with reference to the Father. He is said "to proceed" from the Father because he is sent and given "by the Logos" who is of the Father. As the "One who proceeds" from the Father the Holy Spirit can never be separated from and is always in the hands of the Father who sends him and of the Son who sustains him. He is not the brother or the son of the Son, but he is the Spirit of the Father just as the Logos is the Son of the Father. But although he is not called Son, nevertheless he does not exist "apart from the Son," for he is called the Spirit of wisdom and of adoption; whoever possesses the Spirit possesses the Son, and vice versa. Just why the one is called Son and the other Spirit is incomprehensible, but Scripture speaks thus. The Spirit is the "image of the Son"; the Spirit and the Son are united just as are the Son and the Father. Accordingly, Athanasius clearly teaches the Holy Spirit's dependence on the Son, but he does not say in so many words that the Holy Spirit proceeds from the Father *and from the Son.* The three Cappadocians express themselves similarly. They plainly teach that the Holy Spirit sustains the same relation to the Son as does the Son to the Father, that the Holy Spirit follows the Son in order, that the Spirit gives us the Father and the Son, that he proceeds from the Father and is thought of in subsequent relation to and in connection with the Son, that he is of the Father and "through the Son," and that the three distinct names given to the three persons result from "their relation to each other"; but the Spirit's procession from the Son was neither expressly taught nor denied by any of them: that question simply did not exist for them. Accordingly, in the works of Gregory of Nyssa, Epiphanius, Dydimus, Cyril, and others, expressions occur which seem to teach the procession of the Holy Spirit from the Son. They use the prepositions "from" and "out of," teach that the Holy Spirit takes everything from Christ, and that Christ is the fountain-head of the Holy Spirit, John 7:38; they state that he is out of the essence of the Father and of the Son and that possessing "the very essence of the Son" he is the image, the mouth, the breath of the Son; they recognize him as the third person, in order following the Son, and they hold that he receives all things from the Father through the Son, etc.

But the difference between the Eastern and the Western Church is apparent in the twofold development of the doctrine of the trinity. In opposition to Nestorius, who reversed the order of the persons by making Christ dependent upon the Holy Spirit, Cyril was in perfect agreement with the Greek fathers, who maintain that the Holy Spirit proceeds from the Father "through the Son." Similarly, John of Damascus states that the Spirit is also the Spirit of the Son who gives and reveals him; that he proceeds "from" (or "out of") the Father "through the Son," but he definitely rejects the idea that the Spirit is from (out of) the Son and has his existence from (out of) the Son, and he refers the Son and the Spirit "to one originating cause." This has remained the doctrine of the Greek Church. The East did not make any advance upon the teaching of the fathers. The West did. Tertullian already taught that the trinity should not be derived from the person of the Father but from the being of God, and he already expressed himself thus: "I believe that the Spirit proceeds from no other source than from the father through the Son." Hilary maintains that the same relation exists between the Spirit and the Son as between the Son and the Father, and says that the Spirit proceeds from the Father, is sent and given by the Son, and even has the Son for his "Author." But it was especially Augustine who made an advance upon the Greek fathers. He views the three persons as relations in the one indivisible Godhead, and was thereby forced to relate the Spirit not only to the Father but also to the Son. Hence ,Augustine plainly teaches that the Holy Spirit must be referred to both Father and Son, that he is "a certain unutterable communion of the Father and the Son." To be sure, the names Father and Son reveal only the mutual relations existing between the first and the second persons and not the relation in which they stand to the Holy Spirit, for that relation cannot be properly expressed in human language. Nevertheless, the Spirit is called a gift of the Father and of the

Son. Not only the Father but also the Son is the originating cause or principium of the Holy Spirit; "it is clear that the Father and the Son constitute the principium of the Holy Spirit." But these are not two principia any more than Father, Son, and Spirit are three principia of the work of creation. But the Father and the Son are the *one* principium of the Spirit. The Son has also received this from the Father; that he causes the Spirit to proceed from himself as well as from the Father, for the Son cannot differ in anything from the Father except only in this respect, namely, that he is the Son.

After Augustine this doctrine of the procession of the Holy Spirit is found in the symbol of the synod of Toledo 400, in the epistle of Leo I to Turribius, in the Athanasian Creed, article 23, and in the confession of the third synod of Toledo, 589, which inserted the words "and from the Son" (filioque) in the text of the Constantinopolitan Creed. The Church and the theology of the West followed Augustine and repeatedly defended the phrase, "and from the Son" (filioque) over against the East, and the Reformers accepted this position. But the East in spite of all efforts to reach an agreement—an effort was put forth as late as 1875 when the Old Catholics held a conference at Bonn—maintained their ancient position. The fruitlessness of all these efforts is all the more remarkable in view of the fact that the difference seems to be so trivial. The Eastern Church does not expressly teach subordinationism; it fully recognizes the equality of the three persons; it also accepts a certain relation between the Holy Spirit and Christ who sends and imparts the Spirit; and it does not object to the statement that the Spirit proceeds from the Father "through the Son." The Western Church in turn has declared that the procession of the Holy Spirit from the Father and the Son should not be understood as a procession from two principia or originating causes neither as consisting of two "spirations," but should be viewed as a procession "from one principium and by a single spiration." Pope Leo admitted that the insertion of the phrase "and from the Son" (filioque) in the ancient symbol was formally unjustifiable; moreover, the Western Church did not object to the expression "out of the Father through the Son." Nevertheless, no agreement was reached.

The great objection which the Eastern Church advances against the expression "and from the Son" (filioque) is this, that accepting a procession of the Holy Spirit from the Father and from the Son implies the belief in two originating causes or principia (Grk. *aitiai*). Now this very objection points back to a different doctrine of God and a different type of religion. It points back to a last remnant of subordinationism. However much Father and Son are viewed as one and equal, that unity and equality in the thinking of the Eastern Church is always derived from the Father. The Father is viewed as "Fountain-head and Origin of the God head." Hence, after this manner of reasoning, if the Holy Spirit proceeds also from the Son, the latter is coördinated with the Father, the principle of unity is sacrificed, and a kind of ditheism is introduced. The Greeks derived the unity of God's essence and the trinity of the persons not from the divine nature as such but from the person of the Father. He is the only "originating cause." The three persons are not viewed as three relations within the one essence, the self-unfoldment of the Godhead, but the father is viewed as the One who imparts his being to the Son and to the Spirit. As a result, the Son and the Spirit are so coördinated that both in the same manner have their "originating cause" in the Father. In both the Father reveals himself. The Son causes us to know God: the Spirit causes us to delight in him. The Son does not reveal the Father in and through the Spirit, neither does the Spirit lead us to the Father through the Son. The two are more or less independent of each other; each leads to the Father in his own peculiar way. Thus, orthodoxy and mysticism, mind and will, are placed in antithetic relation to one another. And this peculiar relation between orthodoxy and mysticism characterizes the religious attitude prevailing in the Eastern Church. Doctrine and life are separated: doctrine is for the mind only: it is a fit object of theological speculation. Next to it and apart from it there is another fountain of life, namely the mysticism of the Spirit. This fountain does not have knowledge as its source but has its own distinct origin and nourishes the heart. Thus a false relation is established between mind and heart: ideas and emotions are separated, and the link that should bind the two in ethical union is lacking.

**D. These distinctions interior to the divine essence are also revealed outwardly. To be sure, outgoing works are works of the Divine Being as a whole. Nevertheless, some of these works are more particularly ascribed to one person, and others more especially to another; creation to the Father, redemption to the Son, sanctification to the Holy Spirit. Similarly, in the order of revelation the Father is first, the Son second, the Holy Spirit third. Thus the order of subsistence in the ontological trinity is beautifully reflected in the order of manifestation in the economical trinity.**

Now these inter-personal relations existing within the divine essence are also revealed outwardly. To be sure, outgoing works always pertain to the Divine Being as a whole. "God's outgoing works are indivisible although the order and distinction of the persons is preserved." One and the same God reveals himself in creation and in redemption. But in this unity the order of subsistence within the divine essence is preserved. The ontological trinity is reflected in the economical trinity.

Hence, certain attributes and works are ascribed particularly — though not exclusively, as was held by Abelard — to one person, others especially to another, in such a manner that the order of subsistence pertaining to the ontological trinity is revealed in this outward manifestation. Hence, these attributes are not "proper" but "appropriate" to the persons. With an appeal to Scripture: Matthew 28:19 and I Cor. 8:6, Hilary maintains that the Father is the Author *of* (out of) whom are all things; the Son, the Only-begotten, *through* whom are all things; and the Holy Spirit, a gift *in* all. Accordingly, there is *one* power, *one* Son, *one* gift. Nothing is lacking to this perfection. "Eternity" pertains to the Father; "form in the Image" to the Son; "use in the Gift" to the Spirit. This is evident from the fact that the Father is the originating cause, himself without principium; the Son, the image of the Father, gloriously revealing the latter; and the Holy Spirit, a gift of Father and Son, by means of which we are made partakers of the communion with the Father and the Son. So reasons Hilary. Augustine offers certain objections to this view, and distinguishes somewhat differently: "In the Father is unity, in the Son equality, in the Holy Spirit the harmony of unity and equality; and these three attributes are all *one* because of the Father, all *equal* because of the Son, and all *coherent* because of the Holy Spirit." This distinction is developed in detail in *De trinitate*. In this work, Augustine ascribes to the Father the attribute of power; to the Son, wisdom; and to the Holy Spirit, benevolence or love. This does not mean, however, that the Father is dependent upon the Son for wisdom, and that apart from the Holy Spirit he has no love; for Father, Son, and Spirit all partake of the same divine nature and attributes. Nevertheless, with reference to the economy of the trinity it is proper to ascribe these distinct attributes to the three persons. All later theologians accepted this view.

With reference to the "outgoing works" a corresponding economic distinction must be maintained. Although all of these "outgoing works" pertain to the being of God as a whole, nevertheless to each person that particular work is assigned which corresponds to the order of his existence within the divine essence. The Father works *of* himself, *through* the Son, *in* the Spirit. Scripture clearly points out this distinction by means of the so-called distinguishing prepositions: "of" or "out of," "through" or "by means of," and "in," I Cor. 8:6; John 1:3, 14. Col. 1:16, presents no *real* obstacle to this view. Rom. 11:36, often referred to in behalf of this distinction, is not trinitarian. This Scriptural distinction between the three persons was already noticed and pointed out by the early church-fathers. Athanasius often appeals to Eph. 4:6, and states that in the person of the Father, God is *over* all; in the person of the Son, *through* all; and in the person of the Holy Spirit, *in* all; and that the Father carries out the works of creation and redemption through the Son and the Spirit. Basil was accused because sometimes he would in his prayers address the Father *"with the Son together with the Holy Spirit,"* and at other times *"through the Son in the Holy Spirit."* In his work *De Spiritu Sancto* he defends the first expression on the ground that the Son and the Spirit are one in essence with the Father, and therefore worthy of the same honor; and he discusses in detail the distinction between the prepositions. In opposition to the views of the Arians he maintains that the difference in the use of the prepositions does not prove the inequality of the persons, but that it points to a definite order of subsistence and of outward manifestation. The Father is the "principle of origination," the Son is the "principle of operation," the Spirit is the "principle of consummation." Later theologians make the same distinction.

All "outgoing works" have *one* Author, namely God; but they are produced by means of the co-operation of the *three* persons; and in the works of creation, redemption, and sanctification, a definite place and order is assigned to each of these three. All things are originated by the Father, are carried out through the Son, and are brought to completion by the Holy Spirit. To a certain extent it is true that the "outgoing works" are distributed among the persons. According to Gregory Nazienzen the controversy concerning the Holy Spirit as it was carried on in his time is to be interpreted in the light of the fact that the third person did not become clearly revealed until he took up his abode in the church. Pantheism has often misinterpreted this truth. From the time of Montanus to that of Hegel the view has been defended that the three persons represent three successive periods in the history of the church. In this manner the economical trinity was torn loose from its metaphysical basis; the attribute of "becoming" was ascribed to God, and cosmogony was changed into theogony. The fathers have struggled hard in order to eliminate from theology this paganistic, pantheistic doctrine, to make clear that only such existence should be ascribed to God as is raised above all evolutionistic becoming, and to establish the truth that the trinity is an eternal and vital relation within the divine essence itself. Gregory Nazienzen does not mean by his statement that the Son and the Holy Spirit become God in course of time: on the contrary, he appeals to Scripture to prove the deity of both. What he means is this: in his self-revelation God figured with the finite character of man's capacity to receive truth; it would have been unwise to reveal the deity of the Son as long as the deity of the Father was not yet acknowledged, and to teach the deity of the Holy Spirit as long as the Son was not yet confessed as God. Our Lord did not wish to overload us with food; he did not desire in a single moment to dazzle our eyes by means of the full light of the sun. All "outgoing works" pertain to the trinity as a whole. This is true with reference to creation, providence, government, incarnation, redemption, regeneration, sanctification, etc. Nevertheless, in the economic sense the work of creation is ascribed more particularly to the *Father,* the work of redemption to the *Son,* and the work of sanctification to the *Holy Spirit.* As in the ontological trinity the Father is first in the order of subsistence, the Son second, and the Holy Spirit third; so also in the history of revelation the Father preceded the Son, and the Son preceded the Holy Spirit. The economy of the Father pertains in a special sense to the Old Testament, Heb. 1:1; the economy of the Son began with the incarnation; and the economy of the Holy Spirit commenced at Pentecost, John 7:39; 14:15. The Father comes without having been sent; the Son is sent by the Father, Matt. 10:40; Mark 9:37; Luke 9:48; John 3:16, 5:23, 30, 37; 6:8 ff.; and the Holy Spirit is sent by both Father and Son, John 14:26; 16:7.

But this procession in time is a reflection of the immanent relation existing between the three persons in the ontological trinity, and is based upon generation and spiration. The generation of the Son is the eternal arche-type of the incarnation of the Logos, and the procession from the Father and the Son is the proto-type of the outpouring of the Holy Spirit. Hence, the church-fathers derived the knowledge concerning the eternal and immanent relations existing between the persons of the trinity from what was revealed concerning those relations in time. In this they were correct. Says Augustine, "For the Son is not called 'Sent' because he became flesh, but he is and is called 'Sent' in order that he might become flesh." The truth is not that the Father in the course of history uttered a command that the eternal Son should be sent. "But it was in that Word of God himself who was in the beginning with God and was God, i. e., it was in the wisdom itself of God, apart from time, at what time that wisdom must needs appear in the flesh. Accordingly, whereas without any commencement of time, the Word was in the beginning and the Word was God, it was in the Word himself, without any time, at what time the Word was to be made flesh and dwell among us. And when this fulness of time had come, God sent forth his Son, made of a woman, i. e., made in time, that the incarnate Word might appear to men; while it was in that Word himself, apart from time, at what time this was to be done; for certainly the order of times is in the eternal wisdom of God without time. Since then the appearance of the Son in the flesh was wrought by both the Father and the Son, it is fitly said that he who appeared in that flesh was sent, and that he who did not appear in it sent him; because those things which are transacted outwardly before our physical eyes have their existence from the inner constitution of the spiritual nature, and for that reason they are fitly said to be sent." And the same is true with reference to the procession of the Holy Spirit. "For in due time a certain outward appearance of the creature was wrought, wherein the Holy Spirit might be visibly shown . . . This operation, visibly exhibited and presented to mortal eyes, is called the sending of the Holy Spirit; not that his very substance appeared, in which he himself also is invisible and immutable like the Father and the Son, but that the hearts of men, moved by things seen outwardly, might be turned from his manifestation in time and arrive at his hidden eternity as ever present." The Holy Spirit was a gift before he was given to any one. "Because he so proceeded that he was capable of being given, he was already a gift even before there was one to whom he might be given. For one thing is meant by 'a gift,' another by 'that which has been given.' For a gift may exist even before it is given, but it can in no way be called a thing which has been given unless it has been given." Accordingly, the temporal procession is closely related to the eternal procession within the being of God. And this manifestation of the Son and of the Spirit which was visible in the incarnation and in the outpouring is brought to completion by means of this invisible entrance into the hearts of all believers, into the church of Jesus Christ, and into the temple of the Holy Spirit. There has been an eternal procession of the Son and of the Spirit from the Father in order that through and in them he himself might draw near unto his people, and that at length God might be all in all. See Augustine, *De trin.*, II, 5; V, 15.

E. **Attempts to illustrate the trinity:**

(1) **Illustrations taken from Scripture: three patriarchs, three divisions of the tabernacle, three beloved disciples, three witnesses, etc.**

(2) **Analogies taken from the realm of heathendom: the Trimurti of the Indians, etc.**

(3) **Similitudes in nature: fountain, rivulet, and stream; root, trunk, and branches, etc.**

(4) **Resemblances in the sphere of logic, grammar: first, second, and third person, etc.**

(5) **Approximations in the processes of our mind: memory, understanding, and will, etc.**

(6) **Various philosophical reconstructions of the doctrine of the trinity have been attempted.**

(7) **Criticism: the analogies taken from the realm of heathendom are without any value; as to the illustrations in general: in all of them we have a certain trinity but no tripersonality in unity of substance; not any of these analogies nor all of them**

**together can prove the divine trinity; for that doctrine we are
dependent wholly on Scripture. Nevertheless, these illustrations
serve to prove that belief in the divine trinity is not absurd or
unreasonable.**

The doctrine of the trinity is so difficult to grasp that from the time
when it was first formulated attempts have been made to elucidate it
by means of illustrations or to prove it by means of argumentation. In
the first place it was considered a remarkable fact that the number three
is so prominent in Scripture. Mention is made of the division of the
universe into heaven, earth, and the region under the earth. Mankind is divided among the three sons of Noah into three racial groups.
There are three dispensations of the covenant of grace: before, under,
and after the law; also three patriarchs. The tabernacle has three
divisions. There are three great feasts. The O. T. is divided into three
parts. Christ's public ministry lasted three years. Further, mention is
made of the three offices, the three days in the grave, three crosses on
Golgotha, the fact that the superscription over the cross was written
in three languages, the three beloved disciples, the three witnesses of
I John 5:8, the three Christian virtues, three kinds of lust, I John 2:16,
three woes, Rev. 8:13, the threefold blessing, the three elements in
salutations and benedictions, the three fasts, the three periods of prayer,
etc.

But even outside of Scripture the number three is prominent. Not
only the mediating entities of Jewish theology and the Sephiroth of
the cabalistic system: the Crown, Wisdom, and Understanding (Kether,
Chokmah, and Binah) furnished analogies for the Christian doctrine
of the trinity but indications and vestiges of the trinity were also found
in the realm of heathendom: the Trimurti of the Indians: Brahma,
Vishnu, and the Siva; the three forms of the Chinese Tao; the three
chief gods of the Germans: Odin, Thor, and Loki; and in various
Chaldean, Egyptian, and Grecian ideas concerning the gods. A passage
in the Hermetic Books was quoted with predeliction and reference was
made to the three principles accepted by Plato in his explanation of the
universe: the highest "mind" (that which exists, the good), the universe
of ideas, and "matter." But inasmuch as all these analogies are polytheistic it is difficult to connect them with the Christian doctrine of the
trinity.

The physical analogies taken from the realm of nature are of greater
value. Philo, and afterward Justin Martyr, used the illustration of the
flame that kindles another but remains the same. Tertullian said that
God brings forth the Logos "just as the root produces the fruit, just
as the fountain produces the river and just as the sun produces the sunbeam," and he spoke of the fountain, the rivulet, and the stream; root,

trunk, and branches, etc. Later church-fathers repeat these illustrations and enlarge on them. In their endeavor to penetrate to the inner essence of things they more and more began to see the tripartite nature of all existing objects. As similitudes of the Christian trinity, the following were called into service: the three dimensions of space; the three measurements of time; the three kingdoms of nature: matter, spirit, and the union of the two in man; the solid, fluid, and gaseous state; the power of attraction, repulsion, and equilibrium; the three functions of the human soul: reasoning, feeling, and desiring; the three capacities of the soul: mind, will, and moral nature; the three factors that constitute a family: husband, wife and child; the three classes in society: teachers, soldiery, and peasantry (Lehr-Wehr-und Nährstand); the three ideals: the good, the true, and the beautiful; the three tones in music: key-tone, tierce-tone, and quint-tone; the rainbow and its many colors; the sun with its quickening, illumining, and warming energy; the three basic colors: yellow, red, and blue, etc.

Of greater value are the resemblances which have been discovered in the realm of logic. Augustine repeatedly refers to the fact that every object has first of all essence, unity, measure; secondly, it differs from other things because it has a form of its own: it is a distinct species; and finally, between that which it has in common with other objects and that which distinguishes it from other objects there is a certain relation, correspondence, order. Matter, form or beauty, and the harmony existing between the two, or love, are the constituent elements of all existence. "Whatever has existence has that in which it consists, that which distinguishes it from other objects, and that in which it corresponds with other objects." Medieval theologians elaborated a system of resemblances and tried to find a triad everywhere. Accordingly, they looked upon the following as similitudes of the trinity: the trivium of grammar, logic, and rhetoric; the three philosophical branches: logic, physics, ethics; the first, second, and third person of grammar; the active, passive, and middle voice; the singular, plural, and dual number; the three primary vocal sounds and the triliteral roots in the Hebrew language; the disposition, style, and delivery of rhetoric; the definition, division, and argumentation of dialectics; the three forms of poetry: epic, lyric, and dramatic; the three phases of mysticism: cogitation, meditation, and contemplation; or faith, reason, and contemplation; or purification, illumination and ecstatic union; etc. Dionysius the Areopagite gives a trinal division of the celestial hierarchy, and Dante's Divine Comedy is arranged on the same plan. In modern philosophy the formal trinal arrangement is preponderant. According to Hegel, Kant rediscovered triplicity as if by instinct and in accordance with it he schematized the organs of knowledge, the faculties of the soul, the categories, the ideas, etc. But this triplicity does not become a dialectical method until we come to the idealistic philosophy of Fichte, Schelling, and Hegel, who derived it from Kant. Idealism tries to view objects as products of consciousness, as the unfoldment of an idea. Accordingly, ideas are regarded as living, moving, and producing. This is possible only when there is a continual contradiction between the idea itself and that which it produces, and this antithesis is dissolved and synthesized into a third principle. The law of antithesis is the essence of thought. Thus the idea in its unfoldment and development is continually moving forward by means of the activities of affirmation, negation, limitation; by means of thesis, antithesis, synthesis; "in itself, for itself, in and for itself" (subject, object; subject-object). The entire universe develops itself in accordance with "the order of triunities." *Logic,* with its doctrine of being, essence, and notion, views thought (mind) *in itself; the Philosophy of Nature* in the three forms of mechanics, physics, and organics, deals with thought *for itself* (objectified), considered as the other, in its self-alienation; the *Philosophy of Mind,* with its subjective mind (the individual), objective mind (society), and absolute mind, has to do with thought *in and for itself* (subject-object), returning into itself, becoming conscious of itself. Through the influence of this philosophy triplicity became the foundation of many philosophical and theological systems.

But some were not satisfied with attempts to illustrate the trinity; they tried to furnish positive proof for this doctrine and to establish it as a necessary corollary of the essence of thought or of love. The logos-doctrine, both in Scripture and Greek philosophy, naturally suggested the idea that in human thought and speech we have an analogy of the trinitarian process in God. This comparison is already employed by Justin Martyr, Tatian, Tertullian, Lactantius, etc. Athanasius and the Cappadocians constantly described generation as God's vision of himself in his image, an eternal speaking of a word. Father and Son were related to one another as "mind" and "word" (logos). But it was especially Augustine who discovered clear evidences of the trinity in human consciousness and reason. By various methods he discovered various resemblances. In the first place he discovered the trinity of existing, knowing, and willing; essence, cognition, and love; mind, knowledge, and love. In the second place he saw vestiges of the trinity in the activities of the soul, particularly in sense-perception brought about by "the object itself" which we see, the picture of that object in our eye, and the "attention of the mind" which directs our sense of sight to the object; and this trinity remains even when the object disappears, for then an image of it is stored away in memory, inner vision takes the place of sense-perception, and the will remains the connecting-link between the two. But Augustine finds the closest resemblance to the trinity in the self-consciousness of the human soul with its "mind, knowledge, and love (delight)"; or "memory, intelligence, and will." First the soul is memory, i.e., consciousness both of other things and of itself, for there is a consciousness, a kind of awareness that does not yet amount to real knowledge; in the human soul viewed as memory many notions lie hidden including those concerning itself: a person is able to know something even though he does not think of it just at that moment. But now "intelligence" springs from the soul viewed as memory, i.e., from the impressions which are stored up in memory. The mediating agent which causes the soul viewed as memory to produce intelligence is cogitation, the activity of thinking. In that intelligence the soul forms an adequate image of itself; it comprehends, knows, and sees itself. "Accordingly, when the mind beholds itself in thought, it knows and recognizes itself." And this self-knowledge and self-contemplation is generative in character, for "it begets this its own understanding and cognition." Now these two are united by the will or by love. "And these two, the begetter and the begotten, are united by love, as by a third, which is nothing else than will, seeking or holding fast the enjoyment of something" (*De trin.* XIV, 6). Thus, Augustine is deeply convinced that all creatures as works of the triune God reveal "vestiges or evidences of the trinity" (*De trin.* VI, 10, XV, 2). Above all he seeks an image of the trinity in man, who was created in the image of the triune God (*ib.* and *De. civ.* XI, 26). Augustine regards the entire created universe as a mirror of God. Hence, in every possible way he tries to indicate the resemblances which he sees between the trinity in creation, especially in man, and the trinity in the Divine Being. In the case of both, the triad consists in this, that the three are one and equal, that each of the three exists in the other two and that these two exist in the one, hence, that "all are in all" (*De trin.* IX, 5; X, 11). Nevertheless, he frankly admits that all these comparisons are merely illustrations and analogies, and that side by side with the resemblances there are important differences. Thus, the trinity in man is not man himself but something in man or belonging to man, while in God the trinity is God himself and the three persons are the one God. "Memory, understanding, and love" are merely energies in man but the three persons in the divine trinity are three subjects. In man these three energies are not always equal: they often serve to complement each other, but in God there is complete unity and equality of persons (*De trin.* XV, 7, 17, 20 ff.) Accordingly, Augustine did not use these illustrations, and analogies in order, in an a priori fashion, to prove the trinity. Rather, his *starting-point* is faith in the trinity on the basis of Scripture; but upon that basis he now by a posteriori reasoning wishes to point out the evidences of the trinity in the entire universe and to present them clearly to the mind (*De vera relig.* 7, *De trin.* I, 1, V, 1, IX, 1). Hence in the first seven books of his work "On the *Trinity*" (*De trinitate*) Augustine's main purpose is to establish the doctrine of the trinity upon the basis of Scripure; it is only in the last eight books that he tries to furnish evidences from the realm of nature and mankind. And he finally added that although every one is able to notice this trinity in the human soul, it is only the believer who is able to recognize it as the image of God's trinitarian existence. Now trinitarian existence is indeed an essential characteristic of the human soul, an attribute that has not been destroyed by sin; nevertheless, it has been darkened by sin and it is renewed by faith when man again learns "to remember, to understand, and to love" God. And only then do we completely become God's image when we shall see him face to face (*De trin.* XIV, 12 ff). "There our being will have no death, there our knowledge will have no error, there our love will have no stumbling block" (*De civ.* XI, 28). This method of argumentation in defense of the trinity, based on the activities of the mind, was adopted by many. But in close connection with this type of reasoning derived from the realm of thought Augustine employs another, derived from the realm of love. He proceeds from the Biblical passage: *God is love,* and indicates that there is always a trinity in love: "he who loves, that which is loved, and love itself." In love there is always a subject, an object, and that which links the two. "Verily, thou seest the trinity when thou seest love" (*De trin.* VIII, 8, IX, 1, 2). This speculative idea was also adopted by many, especially by Richard of St. Victor. The fulness of divine love, just like the fulness of divine goodness, requires an object, and this object must be equal to the one who loves. But this love is not complete until both he who loves and he who is loved welcomes a third person into their love by whom in turn they are loved. Bonaventura and many later theologians employ the same method of reasoning.

Aside from these general trinitarian speculations derived from the mind and will of God other constructions of the trinity have been attempted. The most remarkable one is that offered by theosophy, which was revived through the influence of Neo-Platonism, Gnosticism, and cabalistic literature; was advocated on the eve of the Reformation by Pico of Mirandola, Reuchlin, Nettesheim, and Paracelsus; found its real philosopher in the person of Jacob Böhme; and was favored in the nineteenth century by Schelling and Baader. Schelling's point of departure is that the first principle of all being is not thought or reason. The "what" (or quality) of an object may be derived from reason, the "that" (fact *that* it exists) cannot be thus explained. The *essence* of a thing and its *existence* point back to different principles. Hence, both deism and pantheism must be rejected. God is not the abstract unity of the Eleatic school. He is an "all-unity," a "plurality" in which the oneness or unity of deism and the allness or totality of pantheism are merged. Even the concept "God" contains three elements: first, ability to exist, the subject, the will; next, pure essence, the object, the idea; finally, the identity of both, the subject-object. In these three the concept of the Absolute has been completed and has become Spirit, perfect Spirit, personal and self-conscious, an "individual being." But even though in our thinking these three moments serve as necessary stepping-stones by means of which we arrive at the idea of the perfect Spirit, that Spirit is not himself the product of these three. On the contrary, the Spirit is first, and contains within himself these three moments as "immanent destinations." Accordingly, the perfect and absolute Spirit is the Spirit as he exists "in himself, for himself, and with himself." But all future existence is concealed in that Spirit. He is the free Spirit and is able to reveal himself outwardly. These three destinations which inhere in the Spirit explain the possibility of a universe distinct from God: they are the powers that account for the existence of such a universe. Schelling derives the entire created universe, mythology, and revelation from the separation and union of these three powers; they are the forms of all potentialities, the principles of all existence. With Schelling, however, this cosmogony is at the same time a theogony. As the universe develops, these powers immanent in the Divine Being ascend to higher and higher levels; as God reveals himself to his creatures, he also becomes revealed to himself. The three "destinations" inherent in the absolute Spirit, the three powers in the creation of the universe and in mythology causes us to view the one and only God as existing in these persons. The absolute Spirit becomes Father, Son, and Spirit in the progressive development of revelation. God—not merely a certain aspect of God but God in all his fullness, the absolute personality—may be called Father, not only in the sense of "Originator" of all things, but also because (and inasfar as) by means of the first power of his being he causes the second power to attain to self-realization. However, he is not really Father at the beginning and continuation of this process but only at the completion of it. The second form is the Son, whose generation is not eternal, but has reference to the existence of the Son distinct from the Father. Accordingly, this generation begins at the moment of creation. Hence, the Son is Son only at the end or completion of the process. And the same is true with reference to the third power. Finally, the entire Godhead has been realized in three persons distinct from each other. These three persons are neither three separate Gods nor are they merely three different names.

By means of this speculation modern philosophy revived the doctrine of the trinity. All kinds of attempts were made to construct a trinity especially upon the basis of the essence of the mind, of self-consciousness, or of personality. Günther even rejected the distinction between "the pure and the mixed articles," as Raymond of Sabunde, Raymond Lullus, and a few other rationalists had done before him, and viewed the doctrine of the trinity as merely derived from reason and as demonstrable on the basis of the character of self-consciousness.

The church and theology assumed a very reserved attitude toward these philosophical constructions of the doctrine of the trinity. At best they were willing to grant after-consideration to proofs for the trinity, that they might use these proofs in order to render this dogma easier to understand, but even then many warned against an appeal to reason for support of this doctrine. More than any other dogma the dogma of the trinity was considered a mystery exalted above the sphere of reason and of nature and known only from special revelation. Thomas Aquinas was willing to accept the existence of "vestiges of the trinity" in the realm of creation — as Augustine had done before him — and he tried to explain them by a posteriori reasoning, but he expressly declared that reason in itself is not able to arrive at the trinity, for the universe is the work not of one single person but of all three: hence, it reveals the unity of God's essence but not the distinction of the persons. "Moreover, he who tries to prove the trinity of the persons from natural reason deals a double blow to faith"; first by disparaging the unique importance of faith, which has only invisible things as its objects, and secondly, by hindering others from becoming Christians when they see that our faith rests on such feeble grounds. Calvin expressed his doubts about the value and propriety of seeking resemblances of the trinity in the realm of nature and mankind. And many Reformed and Lutheran theologians have expressed themselves similarly.

In opposition to the stand of all those who try to rest the doctrine of the trinity upon rational grounds it must be emphasized that we owe our knowledge of this doctrine entirely to God's special revelation. Scripture is the only and final ground of our belief in the doctrine of the trinity. After it has been accepted by faith, the most reason can do is to present it somewhat more clearly to our consciousness. Nevertheless, the arguments which have been advanced in order to throw light upon the doctrine of the trinity are not without value. In the first place, Scripture itself gives us the right to use these arguments when it tells us that the entire universe and especially man is the work of the triune God. To be sure, God's outgoing works are all undivided and common to the three persons, so that the unity of the essence rather than the distinction of the persons is emphasized; nevertheless, in that unity the diversity is apparent. Scripture itself teaches us that all creatures reveal "traces of the trinity" and that man is the "image of the trinity." Hence, however much, objectively, God's revelation, and subjectively, our minds have been darkened by sin, the fact that the mind illumined by God's revelation, is able to find in the realm of nature traces of that God whom it learned to know from Scripture as being triune in his existence and works cannot be summarily denied. Furthermore, although not any of these arguments can prove the doctrine of the trinity and although not any of them should ever become a ground of our faith — for in that case we would be surrendering the truth to the ridicule of our opponents if we would accept it on the basis of such feeble grounds as our reason is able to advance — nevertheless, these arguments are valuable as answers to various objections that have been advanced against this dogma. They indicate that the truth revealed to us in Scripture is neither impossible nor absurd, and that the belief of the opponents is insufficient and contrary to reason itself. The doctrine of the trinity is by no means as absurd as it appears to superficial rationalism either ancient or modern. It cannot be refuted by the simple observation that *one* cannot be *three* and that *three* cannot be *one*. Philosophy has again and again returned to a belief in the doctrine of the trinity — it has done so even in the present century — and has to a certain extent recognized the rich meaning and great significance of this doctrine. Finally, by means of these illustrations and arguments the relation that exists between nature and grace, between creation and redemption, is brought to light. The God who created us and provides for us is the God who renews us after his own image. Grace indeed triumphs over nature but it is not in conflict with nature. While repairing the injuries inflicted upon nature by sin, it also illumines and perfects what remains of God's revelation in nature. The thoughtful person places the doctrine of the trinity in the very center of the full-orbed life of nature and mankind. The confession of the Christian is not an island in mid-ocean but a mountain-top overlooking the entire creation. And it is the task of the Christian theologian to set forth clearly the great significance of God's revelation for (and the relation of that revelation to) the whole realm of existence. The mind of the Christian is not satisfied until every form of existence has been referred to the triune God and until the confession of the trinity has received the place of prominence in our thought and life. Accordingly, though the analogies and proofs which we have discussed can never demonstrate the dogma of the trinity, they indicate the manifold usefulness and the rich significance of this confession for our thought and life. In the final analysis they owe their origin not to a craving for useless speculation and vain curiosity but to a real religious need. If God is triune, this fact must be of the greatest importance, for all things are of him and through him and unto him.

F. **Significance of the doctrine of the trinity:**

(1) **For the doctrine of the divine nature and attributes. Deism rejects the idea that God is FULNESS of essence; pantheism denies God's DISTINCT essence and existence; over against both of these errors the church maintains in its doctrine of the trinity that God is distinct in essence from the creature, but that he nevertheless enjoys a glorious fulness of life. The doctrine of the trinity makes clear to us how God can be perfect in love, knowledge, etc., apart from the universe.**

(2) **For the doctrine of creation. The doctrine of the trinity is the foundation of the doctrine of creation: if there can be no divine self-communication within the divine essence, neither can there be a communication of God to the creature.**

(3) **For practical religion. Belief in the trinity is the heart and essence of true religion; it is indispensable unto salvation.**

In the first place, the doctrine of the trinity reveals God to us as the truly *Living One*. The church-fathers already observed that this doctrine rejects what is false and embraces whatever elements of truth there are in deism and pantheism, in monism and polytheism. Deism creates a great gulf between God and the creature, denies the relationship existing between both, and reduces God to an abstract distinctionless entity, to pure, unvarying, monotonous existence. It satisfies neither the mind nor the heart, and stifles all true worship. Pantheism brings God nearer, but it identifies him with the creature, denies his distinct existence, and undermines religion. But the doctrine of the trinity maintains God's distinct existence, on the one hand, and his glorious fulness of essence, on the other. God is fulness of being, "ocean of essence." He is not "unproductive" (incommunicative). He is absolute essence, indeed; the Eternal One, who is and was and is to come; nevertheless, he is not a merely abstract existence, but the Ever-Living-and-Producing One. Attempts have been made to derive the trinity from God's thought or volition, from his love, goodness, perfection, etc. Intended as philosophical constructions of the doctrine of the trinity these attempts are wholly inadequate. The derivation from thought does not result in tri-personality, and leaves unexplained the procession of the Holy Spirit, which is referred to divine volition. The derivation of the trinity from love is open to the same objections. Nevertheless, it is true that God's trinitarian existence is necessary in order to give life and reality to the attributes of love and knowledge, as well as to all the others. Apart from the trinity these attributes are mere names, sounds without connotation, empty concepts. Ascribed to the triune God they have meaning for our heart and mind. Once we have accepted the trinity we begin to understand that even apart from the universe and entirely in and by himself God is the independent, eternal, omniscient, and all-benevolent One, love, holiness, and glory. The doctrine of the trinity reveals God to us as fulness of essence, genuine life, eternal glory. Also in *him* there is unity in variety, and variety in unity. Even more: this order and harmony is present in him in an absolute manner. Of this we find but a dim analogy among crea-tures. In their case unity and variety are not in perfect equilibrium, neither are they ideal in character: space and time pertain to creatures, bringing about division and separation. If there be any unity, it results from attraction, from volition and inclination; it is a moral oneness, unstable and prone to destruction; while physical unity, as between the different capacities of the same substance, reveals a total lack of in-dependent existence on the part of these capacities so that all variety is lost in unity. But in God both are present: absolute unity and also absolute variety. One and the same being exists in three supposita. This results in the most perfect kind of unity, for the three partake of the same essence; also in the most beautiful variety, for Father, Son, and Holy Spirit are distinct persons. Accordingly, if God is triune, the only adequate conception in regard to the persons is that they are "consubstantial." Arianism of every description fails to satisfy the mind, for it does not attain to a proper conception of the being of God. If there are distinctions *in* God, these distinctions or distinct persons must be equal in essence. *In* God there can be nothing which is other than or less than God. Between Creator and creature there is no transition or half-way station. Either, Father, Son, and Spirit are all equal in essence and very God, or else they are creatures. From the Christian point of view there is no third possibility. But the same line of reasoning also condemns Sabellianism's modal trinity. For, the homoöusia or consubstantiality of the three persons is intelligible only when these three are truly and really distinct from one another: distinct bearers of the same essence (lit. substance). The variety of the sub-jects, which appear separately in God's revelation in creation and redemption, results from the variety of the persons in the being of God. If there were no variety inwardly, there could be no variety outwardly.

Secondly, the doctrine of the trinity is full of significance for that of creation. Creation presupposes a triune God. Only upon the basis of this confession are we able to maintain over against deism the rela-tion, and over against pantheism the distinction, between God and the universe. Mere chance does not produce a universe, neither is the work of creation a manifestation of the self-developing God. Creation must be rooted in God; nevertheless, it cannot be an element in the inner processes of his becoming. How can both of these truths be maintained except on the basis of belief in the trinity? God is the Living One; this divine life is rich in essence, active, and productive. Accordingly, the doctrine of the trinity teaches the Son's generation and the Holy Spirit's procession. To be sure, both of these acts are essentially distinct from God's creative activity; they are immanent relations, while creation is an "outgoing work"; the former are self-sufficient, while God does not need the latter: even apart from the universe he is life, blessedness, and glory. Nevertheless, there is the closest relation between God's fecundity and the work of creation. Athanasius already stated that if God is not productive and is unable to communicate himself inwardly, neither can he impart himself outwardly, in revelation and creation. The doctrine of God's incommunicability and the consequent denial of the Son's generation and of the Holy Spirit's procession results in the idea that the universe is separate from, outside of, and opposed to God. God becomes absolutely concealed, hidden "depth," "silence," the unconscious, the groundless One; the universe does not reveal him; knowledge of God is impossible. Over against this view the doctrine of the trinity teaches that God is able to impart himself: in an absolute sense, to the Son and to the Spirit; in a relative sense, also to the creature. For, according to the idea of Augustine, the divine self-communication within the essence of God is the archetype of God's work in creation. Scripture repeatedly indicates that there is a very close connection between the Son and the Spirit on the one hand, and the work of creation, on the other. The appellatives Father, Son (Word, Wisdom), and Spirit most certainly indicate immanent relationships, but they are also reflected in the inter-personal relations revealed in God's "*outgoing* works." All things are of the Father; the "ideas" of all things are in the Son; the first principles of all life are in the Spirit. Generation and procession within the being of God are the immanent deeds of God, which render possible an outward work of creation and revelation. Thus is to be interpreted the fact that sufficient knowledge concerning the "outgoing works" is gained only then when their trinitarian existence is recognized. To be sure, of the illustrations mentioned under E. some are artificial and of doubtful value, while all are merely analogies; nevertheless, consciously or unconsciously, philosophy from Plato to Von Hartmann has always endeavored to reduce the universe — as a whole and in its component elements — to three "first principles." The statement that the universe everywhere displays "vestiges of the trinity" gives expression to an important truth. And because in man these reveal themselves most clearly, so that he may be called "the image of the trinity," hence there is in him an immanent urge and desire to search the universe for these traces. Only the *triad* give adequate expression to the symmetry of the creature, the completeness of the system, and the harmony of beauty. The higher the order pertaining to an object in the range of creation, the more it resembles the triad. This fact is even apparent from the contents of deviating religious systems. Schelling's attempt to interpret mythology along trinitarian lines was more than a mere phantasy.

Thirdly, the doctrine of the trinity is of the utmost importance for practical religon. Whenever any one rejects God's tri-unity, he destroys the very foundation of Christian belief, and casts aside all of special revelation. The doctrine of the trinity is the sum and substance of Christian faith, the root of all dogmas, the essence of the new covenant. The development of the truth of the trinity as an ecclesiastical doctrine arose from this practical and religious need. The church was not interested in a mere philosophical speculation or in a metaphysical problem, but it was concerned about the very core and essence of the Christian religion. That this is felt and admitted by everyone is clear from the fact that whoever calls himself a Christian has a certain kind of faith in the triune God. The deepest question in every Christian confession and dogmatics is this: How can God be one and, nevertheless, three? The degree of purity with which the other truths are presented depends upon the degree of accuracy with which this question is answered. The doctrine of the trinity is the heart of God's entire revelation of redemption. While the Old Testament is not without some foregleams of this doctrine and thus prepares the way for its complete unfoldment, it becomes perfectly and clearly manifest only in Christ. Religion cannot afford to be satisfied with anything less than God. In Christ God himself comes to us, and in the Holy Spirit he imparts himself to us. The work of redemption is thoroughly trinitarian in character. Of God, and through God, and in God are all things. It is one divine act from beginning to end. Nevertheless, it reveals a threefold distinction: it is summarized in the love of the Father, the grace of the Son, and the communion of the Holy Spirit. The Christian's faith points back to these three principles, just as article nine of our Confession of Faith tells us that we know the doctrine of the trinity as well from the testimonies of Holy Writ as from the operations of the three persons, and chiefly from those that we feel in ourselves. We know ourselves as children of the Father, redeemed by the Son, and having communion with both through the Holy Spirit. The *triune* God is the source of every blessing we receive. He is the mainspring of our entire salvation. In his name we are baptized; that name is the summary of our confession: that name is the source of all blessings that descend upon us; that name is and remains eternally the object of our praise and adoration; in that name we find rest for our soul, and peace for our conscience. Above, before, and within him the Christian has a God. Connected with the doctrine of the trinity is our salvation in this life and in the life to come, true though it be that of the knowledge of this mystery we cannot ascertain the exact degree which would be necessary for genuine faith.

# GOD'S COUNSEL

# CHAPTER VII

# God's Counsel

## I. Among the Works of God We Distinguish Between Personal (Or Distinctly Immanent) Works: Generation and Spiration; Works Immanent Until They Are Outwardly Realized: The Decrees; and Outgoing Works: Creation, Providence, Redemption. According To the O. T. the Eternal Counsel, Decree, Or Plan of God Is the Ground Of the Existence Of all Things and the Foundation Of All Events Both In the History Of the World In General and In That Of Israel In Particular. The N. T. Sheds Even More Light On This Divine Decree. It Employs Various Terms To Characterize It.

A. Among the works of God we distinguish between:

(1) personal or interpersonal works, i.e., distinctly immanent works: those activities of the Supreme Being which take place within the divine essence and are confined to it, internal works: generation and spiration; and

(2) those divine works by means of which a relation is established between God and the creature. This group is subdivided into:

(a) works immanent until they are outwardly realized: the decrees, and

(b) outgoing works or emanant acts, i.e., acts that go beyond the divine essence: creation, providence, redemption. We have discussed the distinctly immanent works; we shall now discuss the works immanent until they are outwardly realized: the decrees. Thus the relation between this and the former chapter becomes evident.

Thus far we have dealt with God's being as it exists in itself. Not in this sense, however, that we conceived of God and spoke of him apart from what he has revealed concerning himself in nature and Scripture. It is altogether impossible for us to think or to speak of God except on the basis of his revelaton; whenever we make bold to take his name upon our lips, we speak of him as Christians, taught by God himself and instructed by his Word. Nevertheless, in the foregoing we dealt with God as, according to his revelation, he exists in himself. We learned to know him as the Eternal Being, who is at one and the same time the highest existence and the highest life; as "supreme existence," pure "essence," and also as "veriest energy," "purest activity," "the wholly active One." Scripture throughout describes God as the living and acting God. Creation, preservation, and government are works established by God, Gen. 2:3; Deut. 11:7; Job 34:19; Ps. 102:25; Is. 64:8; John 9:3, 4; Heb. 1:10; and all these works are perfect, Deut. 32:4; done in faithfulness, Ps. 33:4; truth and justice, Ps. 111:7; 145:17; Dan. 9:14; great, terrible, and wonderful, Ps. 66:3; 92:5; 104:24; 111:2; 139:14; Rev. 15:3; so that Jehovah himself rejoices in his works, Ps. 104:31. He neither slumbers nor sleeps, Ps. 121:3, 4; he fainteth not, neither is weary, Is. 40:28. Activity is an attribute of his being: he must needs work, he ever works, John 5:17.

Accordingly, the work of creation does not mark the beginning of God's activity, for he works from everlasting to everlasting. The personal properties, which we studied in the foregoing chapter, are eternal and immanent *works* of God. Eternally the Father gives to the Son, and with the Son to the Spirit, to have life in himself, John 5:26. Furthermore, the communion of essence, existing between the three persons, is a life of absolute activity; the Father knows and loves the Son eternally, from before the foundation of the world, Matt. 11:27; John 17:24; and the Spirit searcheth all things, yea, the deep things of God, I Cor. 2:10. All *these* divine works are immanent; they do not bear any relation to anything that has existence distinct from God; they pertain to the inner essence of the Divine Being, and they indicate the relations existing between the three persons. Nevertheless, they are of great importance to us, for they make God known unto us as a being independent and fully self-sufficient, who is "not served by men's hands as though he needed anything, seeing he himself giveth to all life, and breath, and all things," Acts 17:25. God does not need the universe in order to be perfect; he does not need to create and to preserve in order not to be idle; in himself he is absolute activity.

From these purely immanent works of God we differentiate those which have reference to creatures which were to come into existence outside of God's essence. Those works of God by means of which a relation is established between God and the creature are subdivided into "internal works" and "external works." The name "decrees" or "the eternal counsel of God" is usually applied to the "internal works." These decrees establish a relationship between the distinctly immanent works of God and the transeunt or outgoing works of creation and redemption. As such they bear three characteristics: in the first place, all the ideas contained in the divine decrees and thereby designed for realization outside of the divine essence are derived from the fulness of knowledge eternally immanent in God. The possible and the actual do not coincide: creation does not exhaust God's wisdom and knowledge: the entire universe in its length and breadth will never be able to give us a comprehensive view of God's infinite being. That which is taken up in the decrees is but an epitome, a summary, of the depth of the riches both of the wisdom and of the knowledge of God; with God all things are *possible,* Matt. 19:26; but they are not all *actual.* Secondly, all decrees are based upon God's absolute sovereignty; God is entirely self-sufficient: he does not need to bring any of his ideas into outward realization by means of the work of creation. He is entirely free in his choice; it is only and entirely because of his will that all things are, and were created, Rev. 4:11. Accordingly, even though the decrees of God are eternal, because in God there is no before or after, and even though to that extent the "decrees" coincide with the "God who decrees," nevertheless we must differentiate between God's knowledge of himself and his knowledge of the universe, between the infinite being of God and the object of his decrees. Thirdly, the idea of "decrees" implies their realization in time. Though the all and self-sufficient God does not need a created universe, nevertheless, the decree makes creation and providence necessary. Scriptural theism views the counsel of God as the link that connects God and the world; thus it maintains both God's absolute sovereignty and the complete dependence of the creature, and avoids the error of pantheism as well as that of deism. "What is seen hath not been made out of things which appear," Heb. 11:3; but has its cause in God's thought, in his will, in his decrees.

**B. Scripture, as such, does not give us an abstract description of the divine decrees, but presents them to us in their historical realization. This is true especially of the Old Testament.**

Scripture, as such, does not give us an abstract description of these decrees, but presents them to us in their historical realization. God is Lord of the entire universe, and he shows this every day in the work of creating, preserving, and governing all things. The same is true also with reference to election and reprobation. The O. T. does not describe these as eternal decrees but on every page it presents to us election and reprobation as facts of history. From the very beginning the human family is divided into two groups: the Godfearing line of Seth, Gen. 4:25, 26; 5:1-32; and the godless line of Cain, increasing in wickedness right along, Gen. 4:17-24. When these two intermarry so that iniquity is added to iniquity, Noah alone finds favor in the eyes of the Lord, Gen. 6. After the flood the blessing is pronounced upon Shem and Japheth, the curse upon Canaan, Gen. 9:25-27. Of the children of Shem, Abraham is chosen, Gen. 12. Not Ishmael but Isaac is the son of promise, Gen. 17:19-21; 21:12, 13. Of the sons of Isaac, Esau is hated. Jacob loved, Gen. 25:23; Mal. 1:2; Rom. 9:11, 12. To each of the sons of Jacob a certain definite task and rank is assigned, but Judah receives the primacy, Gen. 49. While all the other peoples are temporarily passed by and allowed to walk in their own ways, Israel alone is by God chosen to be a people for his own possession. This election, Hos. 13:5; Am. 3:2, *bhr, ydh'*, is not based upon Israel's worth (or meritoriousness) but only upon God's condescending love, Deut. 4:37; 7:6-8; 8:17; 9:4-6; 10:15; Ezek. 16: 1 ff.; Am. 9:7; and this love is from everlasting, Jer. 31:3. The object of this love was Israel as a people and as a nation, although thousands broke the covenant, so that we must differentiate between Israel according to the flesh and Israel according to the promise, Rom. 2:28, 29; Rom. 9:11. And its purpose was to make Israel a people for God's own possession, walking before the countenance of Jehovah in holiness, Ex. 19:5; Deut. 7:6; 14:2; 26:18; Ps. 135:4; Mal. 3:17. Within the sphere of the people of Israel mention is made of a particular election with a view to a certain definite position of honor or service. Accordingly, Jerusalem and Zion are chosen to be a dwelling of Jehovah, Deut. 12:5; 14:23; I Kings 11:30; II Kings 21:7; Ps. 78:68, 70; Moses is chosen to be the Mediator of the Old Covenant, Ex. 3: Levi is chosen to the office of the priesthood, Deut. 18:5; 21:5; Saul and David to the office of kingship, I Sam. 10:24; II Sam. 6:21; Isaiah, Jeremiah, Ezekiel, Amos, etc., to the prophetic office, I Sam. 3: Is. 6: Jer. 1: Ezek. 1-3; Am. 3:7, 8; 7:15; the Messiah is chosen to be the Redeemer of his people; he is in a very special sense the Israel, the Servant, of Jehovah, Is. 41:8; 42:1; 44:1; 45:4; etc.

Now although in the O. T. this fact of divine election is usually presented to us in its historical realization, and therefore coincides with the "calling" to a certain task or office, nevertheless it is based upon God's foreknowledge and foreordination. In general, the O. T. teaches that God creates, preserves, and governs all things by means of the word and with wisdom, Ps. 33:6; 104:24; Job 38; Prov. 8; etc., so that everything is based upon God's thought. But we are expressly told that God knows and declares beforehand what shall happen, Is. 41:22, 23; 42:9; 43:9-12; 44:7; 46:10; 48:3 ff.; Am. 3:7. By means of prophecy he reveals to us future events and their manner of occurrence, Gen. 3:14 ff.; 6:13; 9:25 ff.; 12:2 ff.; 15:13 ff.; 25:23 ff.; 49:8 ff.; etc. Man's days are ordained; they are written in God's book, when as yet there is none of them, Ps. 139:16:

> "Thine eyes did see mine unformed substance;
> And in thy book they were all written,
> Even the days that were ordained for me,
> When as yet there was none of them."

Ps. 31:15:

> "My times are in thy hand";

Ps. 39:5; Job 14:5:

> "Seeing his days are determined,
> The number of his months is with thee,
> And thou has appointed his bounds that he cannot pass."

The righteous are written in a book of life, just as the names of the inhabitants of a city or of the citizens of a nation are recorded in a book. Thus the righteous have the assurance that they shall be partakers of the life in communion with God in Israel's theocracy, Ex. 32:32; Ps. 87:6; Ezek. 13:9; Jer. 17:13; Ps. 69:29. According to Is. 4:3 and Dan. 12:1 those whose names are written in the book of life will partake of the theocratic salvation of the future. We have here a beginning of the New Testament idea that the book of life contains the names of those who will inherit eternal life. Furthermore, all things happen in accordance with God's counsel. With him is wisdom and power, counsel, *ēçāh*, and understanding. Job 12:13; Prov. 8:14; Is. 9:5; 11:2; 28:29; Jer. 32:19. Because of this he ever chooses the best means in order to realize his purpose; he needs no one's advice; he is great and exalted infinitely high above the counsel of the saints and of all those who surround him, Is. 40:13; Jer. 23:18, 22; Ps. 89:7. God's decree is his definite purpose with reference to all things, Is. 14:24-27; Dan. 4:24. That counsel or decree is secret indeed, Job 15:8; nevertheless, it is realized in history; for all things happen in accordance with that eternal and irresistible decree, Is. 14:24-27: " . . . that is the purpose that is purposed upon the whole earth; and this is the hand that is stretched out upon all the nations. For Jehovah of hosts hath purposed, and who shall annul it? and his hand is stretched out, and who shall turn it back?" Is. 46:10: "declaring the end from the beginning, and from ancient times things that are not yet done: saying, My counsel shall stand, and I will do all my pleasure;"

Ps. 33:11:

> "The counsel of Jehovah standeth fast forever,
> The thoughts of his heart to all generations";

Prov. 19:21: "There are many devices in a man's heart: But the counsel of Jehovah shall stand": while, on the other hand, the counsel of the enemy is brought to nought. Neh. 4:15; Ps. 33:10; Prov. 21:30; Jer. 19:7.

**C. The N. T. sheds even more light upon the divine decree. It emphasizes the eternal nature, individual and personal bearing, and final purpose of the decree. It employs the following names:**

(1) "boule," plan, counsel, Eph. 1:11

(2) "thelema," (God's) will as such, Eph. 1:11

(3) "eudokia," good pleasure, delight, Luke 2:14; Eph. 1:5, 9; Phil. 2:13; II Thess. 1:11

(4) "prothesis," purpose, Rom. 8:28; 9:11; Eph. 1:11

(5) "prognosis," prescience or fore-knowledge, Rom. 8:28; I Pet. 1:2

(6) "ekloge," election, a choosing out of, Mk. 13:20; Acts 9:15; Rom. 9:11; Eph. 1:4; etc.; and

(7) "pro-orismos," predetermination or fore-ordination, Eph. 3:11; II Tim. 1:9; Eph. 1:4.

The N. T. places this divine decree in an even clearer light. Not only are all God's works known unto him from the beginning of the world, Acts 15:18 (cf. the various readings, however), but all things occur according to the definite decree and foreknowledge of God. The N. T. word "boule," indicates the will of God as based upon counsel and deliberation; it differs from "thelema," which indicates God's will as such, cf. Eph. 1:11; "counsel of his will." All events are included in that counsel, even the sinful deeds of man, Eph. 1:11: "in whom also we were made a heritage, having been foreordained according to the purpose of him who worketh all things after the counsel of his will"; Acts 2:23: "him being delivered up by the determined counsel and foreknowledge of God, ye, by the hand of lawless men, did crucify and slay," 4:28; cf. Luke 22:22: "For the Son of man indeed goeth as it hath been determined, but woe unto that man through whom he is betrayed." God "determined the appointed seasons of each nation, and also the bounds of the habitation of every people," Acts 17:26. God's will is revealed also in the perdition of Judas, John 17:12; in the fact that the heathen were given up in the lusts of their hearts unto uncleanness, Rom. 1:24; in the rejection of Esau, Rom. 9:13; in the hardening of the wicked, Rom. 9:18; in the raising up of Pharaoh, Rom. 9:17; in the endurance of the vessels of wrath fitted unto destruction, Rom. 9:22; in the setting of Christ not only for a rising but also for the falling, Luke 2:34; for judgment (crisis), John 3:19-21; for a stone of stumbling, and a rock of offence, I Pet. 2:7, 8; cf. I Thess. 5:9; Jude 4. But in a special sense "counsel of God" has reference to the work of redemption, Luke 7:30; Acts 13:36; 20:27; Heb. 6:17. The N. T. has many words which give us a more detailed description of God's counsel. The word "eudokia" is used, meaning good pleasure, delight, Matt. 11:26; Luke 2:14; 10:21; Eph. 1:5, 9; Phil. 2:13; II Thess. 1:11; furthermore "prothesis," meaning purpose, Rom. 8:28;

9:11; Eph. 1:11; 3:11; II Tim. 1:9; "prognosis," foreknowledge, Rom. 8:29; 11:2; I Pet. 1:2; "ekloge," election, Mark 13:20; Acts 9:15; 13:17; 15:7; Rom. 9:11; 11:5, 28; I Cor. 1:27, 28; Eph. 1:4; I Thess. 1:4; II Pet. 1:10; Jas. 2:5; "pro-orismos," foreordination, Rom. 8:29; I Cor. 2:7; Eph. 1:5, 11; cf. also Acts 13:48, where we read, "as many as were ordained to eternal life believed," i.e., not; as many as had prepared themselves or as many as were subjectively predisposed, but as many as were predestinated to eternal life; and also Eph. 2:10, where we read that God afore prepared the good works done by believers. We differentiate as follows: "prothesis" indicates that in the work of redemption God does not act arbitrarily, but according to a fixed and definite plan, an immutable purpose; "ekloge" shows that this purpose of redemption does not include all men, but is a "purpose according to election," Rom. 9:11; so that not all but many are saved; "prognosis" reveals the fact that in this purpose according to election the persons are not the objects of God's "bare foreknowledge" but of his "active delight"; while "pro-orismos" refers to the means used by God to bring his "known ones" to their appointed destiny. "The term 'prothesis' indicates the certitude of the events; 'prognosis' directs attention to the singleness of the persons; while 'pro-orismos' points out the order (or succession) of the means." Although the eternal character of this purpose is not necessarily expressed by the prefix "pro" used in the composition of these words, it is nevertheless, clearly indicated in Eph. 3:11; II Tim. 1:9; cf. Matt. 25:34; I Cor. 2:7; and Eph. 1:4.

To be sure, some have tried to maintain that Paul in Rom. 9 does not deal with God's sovereignty and with his eternal decree but merely with "a divine conduct whose causes as well as operations belong to this temporal order." But Rom. 9 is a refutation of this idea, for the "purpose according to election" very clearly *precedes* the facts of history; history serves to cause the already-existing purpose to stand, Rom. 9:11. A long time before the birth of Isaac, the son of the promise was promised to Sarah, verse 9, and even before Isaac's children were born God had declared that the elder would serve the younger, verse 11. The verses 15-18 indicate that not works, but the will of him who calls is the cause of election. To be sure, Rom. 9 speaks of God's activity and his deeds in time, but the cause back of these divine operations lies not in time but in God's eternal will and good pleasure. Moreover, in other passages the "ground of election" is very clearly indicated to be God's grace, love, and good pleasure, and nothing else. Matt. 11:25; Luke 12:32; Eph. 1:5, 9, 11; II Tim. 1:9, 10. We find the same thought in Rom. 9:21, which according to supralapsarianism refers exclusively to the "uncorrupted mass," and according to

Augustine and infralapsarianism exclusively to the "corrupt mass," but which simply means that God has the absolute right to lead his creatures to whatever destination seems best to himself, cf. Is. 10:15; Jer. 18; Matt. 20:14. In the passage referred to (Rom. 9:21) Paul does not have in mind the distinction between the "uncorrupted mass" and the "corrupted mass," but he wishes to make clear that from the standpoint of absolute right a creature can never have anything to say against the Creator. Paul does not try to prove the fairness of the decree of election, but he silences all objectors by means of an appeal to God's absolute sovereignty.

The New Testament not only sets forth in clearer light the eternal nature of election, but also its individual and personal character. While the object of election is in the O. T. the people of Israel, in the N. T. the objects are certain definite individuals, chosen in Christ, constituting his body, and called "elect," Matt. 24:31; Luke 18:7; Acts 13:48; Rom. 8:33; Eph. 1:4; Tit. 1:1; II Tim. 2:10; I Pet. 1:1, 2, 9; etc. In the book of life are recorded the names of those who shall inherit eternal life, Luke 10:20; Heb. 12:23; Phil. 4:3; Rev. 3:5; 13:8; 20:12; 21:27; 22:19. Finally, it is the plain teaching of the N. T. that the purpose of election is not an earthly life in Canaan, nor a place of eminence in the kingdom of God, but very definitely the heavenly blessedness. To be sure, within the sphere of the church some are elected to a certain office or service, e.g., the apostles, etc., Luke 6:13; John 6:70; etc., but election proper has for its purpose sanctification, Eph. 1:4, the adoption as sons, Eph. 1:5; blessedness, II Thess. 2:13; eternal life, Acts 13:48; conformity to the image of Christ, Rom. 8:29; John 17:24; the glory of God, Eph. 1:6, 12. Also in Rom. 9 Paul is not discussing a higher or lower position in the kingdom of God, but within the sphere of Israel he differentiates between children according to the flesh and children according to the promise. He speaks indeed of "vessels unto honor" and "vessels unto dishonor." He places the manifestation of mercy and the hardening over against one another, and in the verses 14 and 19 he introduces objections which, taken seriously, themselves presuppose the doctrine of God's sovereign election.

**II. The History Of the Development of the Doctrine Of God's Decree: Philosophy, Jewish Theology, and Mohammedanism Do Not Do Justice To the Doctrine Of Predestination. Pelagianism and Semi-Pelagianism Teach A Predestination Dependent Upon Foreknowledge. Augustine Teaches An Unconditional Predestination. The Roman Catholic Church Accepts Semi-Pelagianism. The Lutheran Church Was Augustinian At First, But Became Semi-Pelagian (Arminian). Partly Through the Influence**

## Of Calvin, the Reformed Churches Have Remained Faithful To the Doctrine Of Unconditional Predestination.

A. Philosophy, Jewish Theology, Mohammedanism:

(1) Philosophy usually teaches either a pantheistic determinism or a deistic freedom of the will.

(2) According to Jewish theology sinful man has a free will.

(3) Mohammedanism usually conceives of God as an absolute despot over against whom man is completely passive.

Also outside of the sphere of Christian religion predestination and the freedom of the will have been subjects of manifold controversy. Philosophy usually pendulates between pantheistic determinism and a deistic doctrine of free will. Jewish theology ascribes freedom of the will to man even in his sinful condition. Within the bosom of Mohammedanism there has been a controversy about predestination and the freedom of the will that in many respects resembled the controversy carried on in the church. In Islam God is the absolutely omnipotent Despot over against whom man is completely passive. But in the second century after the hegira the Motazilites objected to this view. They defended the freedom of the will, rejected foreordination, and held the Divine justice instead of omnipotence constitutes God's essence.

B. The Early Church, Pelagianism, Semi-Pelagianism, Augustinianism.

(1) In the early church the doctrine of predestination was not developed to a great extent because of the necessary emphasis with which human responsibility had to be defended over against heathen fatalism and gnostic naturalism.

(2) Pelagius taught man's natural goodness, the non-hereditary character of sinful traits, the auxiliary nature of saving grace, and a predestination based on foreknowledge.

(3) According to Semi-Pelagianism man is by nature neither healthy nor dead but sick: he cannot merit but he can accept God's grace. The decree is based on foreknowledge.

(4) Augustine taught an unconditional predestination: an election not because of but unto faith, a predestination based on God's sovereignty. Reprobation and election are not strictly co-ordinate.

The early church was not able to do justice to the doctrine of God's counsel because of the necessary emphasis with which man's moral nature, freedom and responsibility had to be defended over against heathen fatalism and gnostic naturalism. Man was indeed more or less injured by the fall, nevertheless he remained free and was able to accept the grace offered to him by God. An absolute predestination and an irresistible grace were not taught; God's counsel consisted in his foreknowledge plus the determination of reward and punishment which was demanded by this foreknowledge. God gives up unto unbelief those whose persistent unbelief he foresees, and he elects those whose merits he foresees. In essence this remained the position of the Greek church. Sin weakened man and made him mortal. Nevertheless, he is able to choose natural good and to accept or reject the grace offered to him (prevenient grace). If he accepts it, it will cooperate with him (co-operating grace), but he must persevere to the end. Those who do so have been foreknown and foreordained unto salvation. The rest God leaves in their fallen condition and predestines them unto perdition, although "by an antecedent decree" he wills the salvation of all.

In manner of expression Pelagius followed in the footsteps of the early church, but his rationalism and ascetic moralism caused him to tamper with certain points of doctrine which formerly had been recognized and accepted by every one, e.g., the doctrine of original sin and of death as a punishment for sin, etc. Thus he arrived at a set of ideas which were irreconcilable with Christian theology, and which were carried to their logical consequences and systematized by his followers Coelestius, and Julian, bishop of Eclanum. The starting-point of the theology of Pelagius was that God is good and just; consequently, that every creature that owes its existence to him must be good by nature. Now if this is the case, that good nature can never be changed into an evil and wicked nature. Especially is this true in regard to free will, God's greatest gift to man, the real image of God in man. By virtue of this will man has the glorious and inalienable freedom to do the right and also to do the wrong. This *ability* he has received from God, but the willing and the doing are completely in his own power. And even though he commits evil, his will remains the same in nature, i.e., he still has the ability and the power to do good. "Free will" in the sense of the "ability to do right or wrong" is an inalienable "blessing of nature." Sin is always an act of the free will; it can never become a natural disposition or a condition, and it leaves unimpaired man's nature and free will.

It follows first of all that Adam's fall has no significance for his posterity. All men are born in the same moral condition in which Adam was created. There is no original sin; death is not a punishment for sin but something common and natural; the enormous dissemination of sin is the result of the imitation of evil example; moreover, sin is not absolutely universal, for some of the O. T. saints lived without sin, and Christians are able to remain free from every kind of sin. Furthermore, according to this view grace can only consist in this, that in creation God granted unto man "natural power" and in the moral law and the example and teaching of Jesus a "divine help" ever "according to merits," i.e., offered to those who use their free will to good advan-

tage. Finally, on this basis predestation is reduced to a divine pre-
vision of man's free deeds and merits plus a corresponding predetermination of punishment and reward. In reality, therefore, there is no
predestination on God's part at all, neither unto grace nor unto salvation;
for predestination is entirely dependent upon foreknowledge of man's
good deeds.

Yet in infant baptism — requiring no merit on the part of the recipient — Pelagius encountered a real difficulty which he was unable to
overcome except by resorting to every kind of subterfuge and incoherent
argumentation.

The teachings of Pelagius were presented in milder form by John
Cassianus, abbott of the cloister at Marseille, pupil of Chrysostom, and
well versed in the Greek fathers. The name *Semi-Pelagianism* was
given to this modified doctrine during the middle ages. According to
Cassianus human nature has indeed been vitiated by sin. Nevertheless,
man is not dead but merely ill. He resembles a sick person who is
unable to cure himself but is able to take medicine and to long for
recovery; he is like a man who fell into a well and is unable to bring
himself to safety but is able to seize the rope thrown out to rescue him.
Accordingly, sinful man cannot merit grace but he can accept it, and
aided by it he is able to persevere. Moreover, God grants that grace
to those persons, children, and nations, whose faith and perseverance
he has foreseen. On the other hand, he withholds his grace from those
whose adverse conduct he has foreseen. Predestination and reprobation
have no deeper meaning than this; they are dependent upon "God's
foreknowledge" in regard to man's attitude toward the grace that is
offered to him. "To will is in our power, to make perfect is in God's
power."

Even long before the Pelagian controversy Augustine taught the
doctrine of predestination. He arrived at it by means of his study of
the epistle to the Romans and intended to present nothing beyond the
teaching of the Scripture (*De dono pers. c.* 19). In his *Quaestiones
ad Simplicianum,* written in the year 397, he already presents this truth,
and he developed it further in his writings, *De correptione et gratia,*
427, *De praedestinatione sanctorum* and *De dono perseverantiae,* 428
or 429. Augustine differentiates between "foreknowledge and foreordination." The former is wider in scope than the latter. "To have
predestinated is to have foreknown what he (God) himself should do,"
*De dono persev.* 18; *De praed. sanct.* 10, 19. Predestination is nothing
else than "the foreknowledge and the preparation of God's kindnesses,
whereby they are most certainly delivered whoever are delivered" (*De
dono pers.* 14). This predestination is not according to merit or worth,
but is purely of grace; it is not because of faith, but unto faith. "They

are not elected because they have believed but they are elected in ordei
that they may believe" (*De praed. sanct.* 17). Are not all men equal, a
"doomed mass" (*De civ. XIV,* 26; *De praed. sanct. i; De nat. et
gr.* 4, 8), *etc.* This is especially apparent in the predestination of little
children, of whom some perish without having been baptized while
others are saved by means of baptism (*De praed. sanct.* 12; *Enchir.*
98). God's sovereign will, his absolute authority, is the only cause
of predestination. God owes no man anything, and can with justice
condemn all, but in his good pleasure he makes one vessel unto honor
and another unto dishonor (*De praed. sanct.* 8). Accordingly, predestination implies reprobation. Augustine often subsumes reprobation
under predestination. He speaks of "a predestination unto eternal
death," (*De an. et ejus orig. IV,* 10; *De civ. XXII,* 24), of "those
who were predestined unto everlasting destruction" (*John Ev. Tract.*
48), of "The world predestined unto condemnation" (*Ib., III*), of
Judas as "predestinated unto perdition" (*Ib.,* 107), etc. According to
Augustine the expression "all men" of I Tim. 2:4 does not mean every
single individual. He gives more than one interpretation of this passage
(*Enchir.* 103; *De corr. et gr.* 14). As a rule, however, Augustine uses
the word predestination in the sense of foreordination unto salvation.
In connection with goodness (virtue) predestination is necessary, in
connection with evil, foreknowledge—not merely passive but active—is
sufficient. For God does not foreordain unto perdition and the means
thereto, namely, sins, in the same sense in which he foreordains unto
salvation and the means thereto. With Augustine predestination
is ever "adequate," i.e., unto grace. Among the predestinate are
those who as yet do not believe and even those who are not yet born.
But the number of predestinate is fixed and immutable. In time they
come to Christ, receive baptism, faith, and above all the "gift of perseverance." This gift is granted only to the predestinate. One can
know whether he is a predestinate only from this: whether he perseveres unto the end. For God has allowed some to enter the church
whom he did not choose and who do not persevere, in order that those
who were really predestinated would not exalt themselves and be satisfied with a false peace (*De corr. et gr.* 13). Just why God saves some
and leaves others to perish is a mystery. It is not unjust, for God owes
no man anything. Reprobation is an act of God's justice just as predestination is an act of his grace. In both God manifests his virtues
(*De civ. XIV,* 26).

**C. The Development of the Doctrine of Predestination from Augus-
tine to the Reformation:**

    **(1) The Council of Ephesus, 431, condemned Pelagianism.**

(2) The controversy was continued between the followers of Augustine and the Semi-Pelagians.

(3) After about one hundred years this controversy was brought to a close by the decision of the Synod of Orange, 529, which failed to take a definite stand.

(4) As a result of this failure Semi-Pelagianism subsequently triumphed at the Synod of Chiersy, 853; which condemned Gottschalk. Hincmar, Rabanus Maurus, Scotus Erigena opposed Gottschalk. Prudentius, Remigius, Ratramnus, Lupus, etc. Two-fold predestination.

(5) The Synod of Valence, 855, endorsed Augustinianism.

(6) Nominalism, the rejection of the Reformation, and Jesuitism combined their influence against the doctrine of predestination with the result that the Roman Catholic Church drifted farther and farther away from the truth.

(7) Consequently, the Council of Trent, 1563, rejected the doctrines of irresistible grace, perseverance, and absolute predestination.

At the council of Ephesus, 431, Pelagianism was condemned along with Nestorianism. The controversy between the followers of Augustine, Prosper, Hilary, the anonymous author of *De vocatione omnium gentium,* Lucidus, Fulgentius, and others, on the one hand, and the Semi-Pelagians, Cassianus, Faustus (bishop of Rhegium), the unnamed author of the much discussed work *Praedestinatus* that originated during the fifth century and was published by the Jesuit Sirmond in 1643, Gennadius, Vincent of Lerins, and others, on the other hand, was finally brought to a decision at the Synod of Orange held in the year 529. On the one hand the Synod clearly stated that the sin of Adam has corrupted the entire man, can. 1, 2; that man has of himself nothing but untruth and sin, can. 22; and that he owes both the beginning and the growth of faith not to any natural power within himself, e.g., to free will, but to God's grace operating in his heart, i.e., to the infusion, operation, inspiration, and illumination of the Holy Spirit, who bends the will so that it changes from unbelief to faith, can. 3-8. On the other hand, however, it is merely stated that man's free will was "weakened and attenuated" by sin, can. 8, 13, 25; further, that by means of baptismal grace and with Christ's help and cooperation all baptized persons are able and under obligation to perform that which is necessary unto salvation, "if they will only labor faithfully," can. 13, 25; moreover, not a word is said about unconditional predestination nor about irresistible and particular grace. This failure to take a definite stand had evil results as is clear from the predestinarian controversy in the time of Gottschalk. By that time either the Semi-Pelagian or the Pelagian view had already been accepted by many, e.g., by Hincmar, Rabanus, Maurus, and Scotus

Erigena, and it gained the victory at the synod of Chiersy, 853. Nevertheless, many learned nen disagreed with the condemnation of Gottschalk and the decisions of Chiersy; e.g., Prudentius, Remigius, Ratramnus, Lupus, and others. They defended a "twofold predestination" · (1) a "predestination unto glory" which is not conditioned on "foreseen faith or merits" but is the cause of "predestination unto grace, faith, merits," etc., and (2) a "predestination unto damnation" which does not in the same manner involve a "predestination unto sins" but is at least in its character of "positive reprobation" dependent on the "foreknowledge" and "permission" of sin. Hence, the expression "all men" of I Tim. 2:4 was still interpreted in the restricted sense as indicating many or all classes of people, not every single person without exception. Moreover, in this connection it was considered absurd to suppose that Christ had actually made atonement for all people: also for the heathen who never hear of him and even for the man of sin, antichrist. This was also the view of the Synod of Valence, 855, and later on of scholasticism. "Predestination unto death" was usually not called by that name because it was apt to be misconstrued as if it involved "predestination unto sins" as a means thereto. It is usually treated under the term "reprobation." At times a distinction is made between negative and positive reprobation; the former logically precedes foreseen merits and is an act of God's sovereignty; the latter is dependent upon and logically follows foreknowledge and the decree to permit sin. Accordingly, the restricted interpretation is still given to I Tim. 2:4, and a universal benevolence and a general atonement are not yet taught.

But nominalism, the rejection of the Reformation, and Jesuitism cooperated in combating the doctrine of predestination, and as a result the Roman Catholic Church and R. C. theology drifted farther and farther away from the teachings of Augustine and Paul. Rome was not able with impunity to make light of the demand for reform, and at Trent it established the following dogma:

(1) By means of sin "free will" is indeed "attenuated in its power and bent down," but it is not "lost and extinguished" (*Trid.*, sess. 6, ch. 1 and can. 5); before justification man is able in the natural sphere to perform many deeds that are not at all sinful but really good (*Ib.*, *can. 7*).

(2)) Nevertheless, bereft of "super-added gifts" (dona superaddita) because of original sin, natural man is unable to attain to supernatural good, namely, to faith, hope, and love, to justification, and to life eternal. In order to attain to these he needs more than the "teaching of human nature or of the law," namely, divine grace, the prevenient inspiration of the Holy Spirit (*Ib., can. 1-3*).

(3) This divine grace is granted to children of believers in baptism, and in the case of adults it consists in this, that God calls them objectively through the Gospel and that he touches their hearts subjectively through the illumination of the Holy Spirit. This grace is unmerited and prevenient; it is a "grace bestowed gratuitously," (*Ib., ch.* 5).

(4) This grace excites, assists, and moves man, and enables him to convert himself to his own justification and to assent freely to that said grace. Nevertheless, it is not irresistible, and man is able both "to accept and to reject" the inspiration of the Holy Spirit (*Ib. ch.* 5). If he accepts this grace, and moved and excited by it cooperates with God, and by means of seven steps "disposes and prepares" himself for justification, then he receives this justification in baptism, by grace, and merely in accordance with what scholastics called a "merit of congruity" (*Ib. ch.* 6 and 8, *can.* 4.)

(5) The infused grace of justification remains such that it can be resisted and lost; but when man accepts it and perseveres in it, it enables him to perform good works and by means of a "merit of condignity" to obtain eternal life (*Ib., ch.* 9-16).

(6) In harmony with this teaching Rome has absolutely rejected Augustine's doctrine of unconditional predestination. Nevertheless, in connection with this rejected doctrine it has always avoided the mention of Augustine by name. Moreover, whenever Augustine's views of predestination reappear in the works of his followers the church of Rome has pronounced upon these men the sentence of condemnation, and has caricatured their teachings. The aforementioned book *Praedestinatus* pictures the quasi-existence during the fifth century of a sect of ultra-predestinationists living in Gaul and it describes Augustinianism by means of a number of paradoxes which no follower of Augustine has ever taught. And in the same manner the genuine Augustinianism of Gottschalk, Bradwardine, Wyclif, Huss, Bajus, Jansen, and Quesnel has been condemned under a false name.

The Council of Trent expressed itself very cautiously on the subject of predestination. On the one hand it seems to teach a kind of election, for it declares that no person has the right to determine in this life that he "is surely included in the number of the predestinate," for except by means of a special divine revelation it cannot be known "whom God has elected unto himself." (*VI,* 12 *and can.* 15, 16). But on the other hand it plainly states that Christ was sent in order that "all men might receive the adoption of sons," i.e., that he made atonement for all (*VI. ch.* 2 *and* 3); that man is able to accept or reject, to retain or lose God's grace; and it anathematizes those who hold that "only those who have been predestinated unto eternal life are able to attain unto the grace of justification, and that all others who are called are called indeed, but receive no grace, as being by the divine power predestinated unto evil" (*Ib., can.* 17), as if any one really taught what is contained in the last clause! The church has never made an attempt to reconcile those two groups of expressions, but theology is continually making all kinds of attempts to harmonize them. In the first place, nearly all Roman Catholic theologians teach that "by an antecedent decree" God desires the salvation of all, and therefore caused Christ to die for all; this antecedent decree embraced even those children that died unbaptized, and even the heathen. But by a "consequent decree," which takes into account the good or evil use man makes of his freedom or grace, God does not desire the salvation of all. Thus at the very outset "predestination" is suspended on "foreknowledge." In the second place, a distinction between "predestination in the full sense" and "predestination in the restricted sense" has generally been accepted by them. The former has been called "adequate"; the latter, "inadequate predestination." By the first is meant a "predestination both unto grace and unto glory"; by the second, a predestination unto one of these only. This distinction is made in order to indicate that the predestination unto grace and the predestination unto glory are not inseparable: one may be an object of predestination unto grace, and may have received the grace of faith and justification, and yet lose all this, and have no part in the predestination unto glory. This distinction was unknown to the theologians of the middle ages: Anselm, Lombard, Thomas Aquinas, etc., is still opposed by some, but in general is gaining favor increasingly.

As concerns "predestination unto initial grace," all agree, in opposition to Pelagianism, that this is unmerited, Rom. 9:16; John 6:44; it is not "a result of foreseen merits." Also, in opposition to Semi-Pelagianism, it precedes the will of man; it is a "prevenient, preceding grace." Now inasmuch as predestination unto initial grace is the beginning of complete or adequate predestination, we can say that predestination is entirely of grace and unmerited: it is "gratuitous in its cause," and according to the Thomists it is "gratuitous in itself." Nevertheless, predestination unto initial grace and unto every subsequent grace follows a certain order. According to Molina God foresaw, by virtue of his "mediate (fore-) knowledge," that some men would make good use of the grace that is offered repeatedly, and in accordance with that foreknowledge God determined to bestow his grace. Moreover, God has also foreseen that by means of prayer or "merit of congruity" the saints would obtain grace to benefit others, and he accordingly decided to grant it to those others. A person is not able to merit for himself predestination unto initial grace, but the saints can merit it for others, and Christ above all is the "cause of our predestination." According to the Augustinians and Thomists (Sylvius, Thoma, the Salmanticenses, Gonet, Gotti, Billuart, Alvarez, Lemos, Goudin, etc.) and according to Bellarmino and Suarez, predestination unto glory is absolute, i.e., God first decided to grant salvation to some previous to and entirely apart from all merits, and afterward decided so to influence their hearts with his grace that they would be able to merit this salvation by their works; but according to the Molinists: Molina, Valentia, Vasquez, Tanner, Lessius, Becanus, Petavius, Lapide, etc., "predestination unto glory is dependent upon foreseen merits." Finally, in regard to reprobation, the opinions of Augustinians and Thomists are divided: some agree entirely with Augustine, are infralapsarian, and make the decree of reprobation follow original sin and only that, so that reprobation is "a righteous abandonment in the same mass" (Gonet, Gotti, Gazzaniga); others distinguish between a negative yet absolute decree not to grant salvation to some, and another decree to withhold grace, to permit sin, and to punish it (Alvarez, Estius, Sylvius, the Salmanticenses); still others view the decree of reprobation merely as the will of God to allow some to perish because of their own guilt (Billuart, Goudin). They are opposed by the Molinists, who completely reject the so-called negative reprobation, i.e., an absolute, sovereign decree preceding sin, teach that "by an antecedent decree" God desires the salvation of all, and furthermore accept a "positive reprobation" only, i.e., a decree of God to punish eternally those whose sin and unbelief he has foreseen. Accordingly, reprobation is in every respect "based on foreseen merits"; and according to Hincmar it is even then merely a foreordination of punishment for the wicked, not a foreordination of the wicked unto punishment.

**D. The Development of the Doctrine of Predestination in the Lutheran Church:**

    **(1) The Reformers: Luther, Zwingli, and Calvin taught God's sovereign decree.**

    **(2) Because of the anthropological and soteriological basis of Luther's doctrine of predestination and because of the gradual change in the views of Melanchton, the Lutheran Church soon surrendered its former position. It sided with the Remonstrants, whose views were condemned by the Synod of Dort, 1618, 1619.**

The Reformation returned to Paul and Augustine, and in the confession of God's sovereign election it discovered a power that would enable it to offer opposition to Roman Catholic Pelagianism. Luther at first defended the doctrine of predestination, as did Zwingli and Calvin; and although in opposition to the Anabaptists he afterward laid greater stress on God's revelation in the Word and the sacraments, he never retracted his statements in regard to predestination. At first Melanchton was in thorough accord with Luther's teachings, cf. *Loci communes rerum theoligicarum,* ed. 1521, the chapter on the power of man and free will, and also his commentary on Romans 9; but from the year 1527 on he departed step by step from the doctrine of predestination, and finally openly confessed synergism; cf. the later editions of the *Loci,* 1535 and following years, and the *Conf. Aug. variata* of 1540. This synergism was definitely rejected by the strenuous Lutherans: Flacius, Wigand, Amsdorf, Hasshusius, and others, as was also Sam. Huber's universalism. Moreover, the Formula of Concord stated in the most positive terms that man is by nature unable to perform any spiritual good, and that faith is completely a gift of God. This should have led to the acceptance of the doctrine of absolute predestination. But the spirit that dwelt in Luther differed from the very beginning from that dwelling in Zwingli and Calvin. Luther's doctrine of predestination rested merely on an anthropological basis: on the deep corruption of sin and on man's impotence. To him it seemed to be sufficient to point out clearly that man has no merit and that he is completely dependent on grace. Accordingly, Luther more and more evaded the speculative doctrine of predestination, the "will of God's good pleasure," the hidden God, attended to the grace-imparting administration of the Word and sacraments, and placed in the forefront more and more God's desire to save all: his "expressed (revealed) will." He quietly noticed Melanchton's gradually changing view with respect to predestination, and confined himself to the defense of the doctrine of justification by faith. Predestination did not have a distinct, theological significance; it was of secondary importance. The synthetic method of approach to this doctrine was frowned upon, while the analytical method, which derives predestination from man's lost condition instead of from the doctrine of God, gained favor.

Hence, although some continued to oppose Melanchton's synergism, the doctrine of predestination itself was gradually set aside. Hesshusius in the years 1560, 1561, already advanced the objection that the doctrine of Calvin and Beza was fatalistic and made God the author of sin. In Strassburg, Marback in the year 1561 opposed Zanchius. Andreae indeed taught a decree of election whose sole cause was God's grace. but for the rest he confined himself to the preaching of the Gospel, and did not wish to go beyond faith and unbelief as secondary causes. The Formula of Concord unreservedly teaches the slavery of the human will, but says nothing about an absolute and particular decree of predestination, and confines itself to God's universal and earnest will revealed in the Gospel. Nevertheless, it does not deny election, neither does it call in the help of foreknowledge, and it still agrees with the Augsburg Confession: that the Holy Spirit works faith "where and when it pleases God." Election is unconditional and has as its sole cause the will of God. But election and predestination are identified, and reprobation is made dependent upon foreknowledge. Moreover, after teaching election, the Formula at once adds, for fear of possible danger or misuse, that one should not attempt to theorize with respect to that secret counsel, but that it should be studied in the light of the revelation furnished by Christ and the Gospel with its universal and earnest proclamation, and that the sole cause of perdition is man's own unbelief. God would have all men to be saved; he does not will any one's sin nor any one's death. After the Formula of Concord, especially during the controversy with the universalist Huber, some of the Lutherans, e.g., Gerlach, Hunnius, and Lyser, began to advocate the theory that God "by an antecedent act of the will" desires the salvation of all men, but that "by a consequent act of the will" he desires the salvation of those whose faith and salvation he has foreseen. Toward the close of the sixteenth century the distinction between foreknowledge and foreordination began to be emphasized more and more, predestination was identified with election, and while election was looked upon as depending upon the merits of Christ, reprobation was viewed as having man's sin as its sole cause. This is clear from the *Saxon Visitation Articles* of 1592, prepared by Aegidius Hunnius, and from other writings by the same author, viz., *De providentia Dei et aeterna praedestinatione*, 1597, and *De libero arbitrio*, 1598. The solution was sought in the direction of the earnest use which natural man is able to make of the means of grace.

But the Lutherans were not able to stop at this point, and when the Remonstrants were condemned at the Synod of Dort, the former felt themselves attracted to the latter more and more. They held that their own doctrinal position had been condemned by the Synod of Dort, although the Reformed were always careful to distinguish between Lutherans and Remonstrants. The Lutheran theologians of the seventeenth century approached the Remonstrant confession. First, they taught an "antecedent will" by virtue of which Christ died for all; God wills the salvation of all, and the Gospel is offered to all; then, a "consequent will" by means of which God decides actually to grant salvation "to those whose persevering faith in Christ he had foreseen," and to prepare damnation for those who persevere in their resistance to grace.   In 1724 Mosheim declared that the Five Arminian Articles comprised the pure Lutheran doctrine. Pietism, rationalism, supernaturalism, and the entire religious tendency of the eighteenth century was unfavorable to the development of the doctrine of predestination; the antecedent will began to crowd out the consequent will; and predestination was held to imply nothing more than God's general decree to save men by means of faith in Christ. Herder considered it a blessing that the controversy concerning grace had been buried in the River of Oblivion, and exclaimed, "Wither the hand that ever raises it thence." Leibnitz still endeavored to harmonize the freedom of the will with predestination. But Kant openly declared that man still has an inclination to virtue, so that he is able to perform his duty.

### E. The Development of the Doctrine of Predestination among the Reformed:

(1) The Reformed remained true to the Pauline and Augustinian doctrine of predestination.

(2) Through the influence of Calvin this doctrine was given a place in the confessions of all Reformed churches.

(3) A great difference in the degree of emphasis upon and in the manner of approach to the doctrine of predestination is apparent in the way in which it is treated in the various confessions and by the various theologians. Some use the a priori method of approach, others the a posteriori. The former postulate predestination and derive from it the doctrine of salvation; the latter take as their starting point the doctrine of salvation and reason back to predestination. Whether predestination is discussed in Theology, (the a priori order) or in Soteriology, (the a posteriori order) does not necessarily imply an essential difference in principle.

While the Lutherans gradually sacrificed the erstwhile position of Luther and of the Reformation as a whole, those of Reformed persuasion remained faithful to it; accordingly, the parting of the ways must not be laid to their charge. Zwingli arduously defended the doctrine of predestination, basing his defense not only upon anthropological grounds but especially upon a theological foundation, i.e., upon arguments derived from the being of God. In the first edition of the Institutes Calvin expressed himself with great moderation, but his study of the epistle to the Romans, April, 1538-1541, carried on while in Strassburg, led him to accept a more and more definite view in regard to man's lack of freedom and the truth of election. Although he guarded himself against the paradoxes of Luther and Zwingli and at times rather implied than taught predestination, e.g., in the Catechism of Geneva, he nevertheless defended it with zeal wherever it encountered opposition and denial. He defended the doctrine of predestination against the attack of Alb. Pighius of Kampen, The Netherlands, in his writing: *Defensio sanae et orthodoxae doctrinae de servitute et liberatione humani arbitrii* (A Defense of the Sane and Orthodox Doctrine concerning the Slavery and Liberation of the Human Will),

1543. Against Bolsec he directed his *De aeterna Dei praedestinatione* (Concerning Eternal Divine Predestination), 1552; and against Rome his *Acta Synodi Tridentinae cum antidoto* (Acts of the Synod of Trent with an Antidote), 1547. Moreover, he did not rest until his doctrine had been accepted in every part of Switzerland, especially in Zurich, where Bullinger was advocating a moderate, infralapsarian view. Through the influence of Calvin the doctrine of predestination was given a place in the confessions of all the Reformed churches.

Nevertheless, from the beginning a great difference in the manner of approach to this doctrine was evident both in the confessions of the church and in the writings of the theologians. Apart from the Anhalt Repetition of 1579, the Confession of Sigismund of 1614, and the Colloquy of Leipzig of 1631, which do not give a true representation of the Reformed doctrine of predestination, an undeniable difference is apparent to any one who compares the symbols. Calvin's Catechism of Geneva omits this doctrine entirely; the Heidelberg Catechism merely makes mention of it in answers 52 and 54; the Anglican Articles indorse only a predestination unto life, whose objects are those whom God has elected in Christ, art. 7; the Second Helvetic Confession written by Bullinger, art. 10, and the First Scotch Confession, art. 8, present a similar view; the French Confession of Faith, art. 12, the Belgic Confession. art. 16, and the Helvetic Consensus Formula, 4-6, are definite but moderate and infralapsarian; the most Calvinistic and express statements on the subject are found in the Consensus of Geneva, the Canons of the Synod of Dort, the Lambeth Articles, written by Dr. Whitaker in 1595, the Irish Articles of 1615, and the Westminster Confession.

The same difference is apparent in the way in which this doctrine is treated by various theologians. Some, to prevent misuse of the doctrine of predestination, followed the a posteriori method of approach, i.e., they preferred to reason from effect to cause and to proceed from the fruit to the root. Instead of deriving the doctrine of predestination and election from the idea of God, according to the a priori method of approach, they followed the opposite order: given faith and conversion, they reasoned back to election and used this doctrine as a means of comfort and assurance. Bullinger, Urasinus, Olevianus, Boquinus, Hyperius, Sohnius, and others belong to this group. But this does not imply an essential difference in principle. Without exception the aforementioned theologians have repeatedly, clearly, and unreservedly declared their belief in the Calvinistic doctrine of predestination. And, on the other hand, Calvinists have always insisted that the doctrine of predestination should be handled with great prudence and caution. Calvin did not discuss it at all in the Cathechism of Geneva. The Canons of the Synod of Dort (I, 12, 14) and the Westminster Confession (ch. 4, par. 8) issue a warning against all vain attempts to investigate the secret ways of God. Many theologians of the early period discussed election in connection with the doctrine of salvation instead of in connection with the doctrine of God. In this they followed the example of the apostle Paul, who in Romans 9-11 begins with the doctrine of sin and grace and reasons back to election, and who also in Eph. 1:3 makes the blessings in Christ his point of departure. Nevertheless, just as Paul after he has once mentioned election apriorily derives all the blessings of salvation from election, Rom. 9:29 ff.; Eph. 1:4 ff.; so also among the Reformed the synthetic method of approach gradually superseded the analytical. The life of faith was indeed the condition that gave rise to the confession of the doctrine of election, but the fact of election was the source of every spiritual benefit, "the mainspring and first cause of all blessings." This was the conviction of Calvin not only, but also of Melanchton, Hamming, Bucer, Olevianus, etc. Musculus says in so many words, "We treat election after faith, not in order to indicate that the former really follows the latter, but in order that we might look up from the stream to the source itself." The systematic treatment and the theological significance of predestination demanded its inclusion in the doctrine of God. This order had been followed by scholasticism, and was still followed by some Lutheran theologians. This method of approach became customary with Reformed theologians, some of whom treated the doctrine of election as a part of the doctrine of the attributes, while others discussed it separately after the doctrine of the trinity.

Whether predestination is made a part of the doctrine of God (the a priori order) or is treated at the beginning or in the middle of the doctrine of salvation (the a posteriori order) does not necessarily imply an essential difference in principle. Nevertheless, it is a significant fact that the a priori order is usually followed by Reformed theologians; while Lutherans, Arminians Roman Catholics, and most of the more recent dogmaticians have gradually begun to adopt the a posteriori order. The reason for this difference is not that the Reformed in a speculative manner derive predestination from an a priori, philosophical, deterministic conception of the Deity; while the others adhere to God's revelation in Christ as deposited in Scripture — for even the most strenuous Calvinist, whenever he teaches the doctrine of God or of God's counsel, intends to present nothing else than the doctrine of Scripture— but the real reason for this difference is the fact that for the Reformed the doctrine of predestination has not merely an anthropological and soteriological but especially a theological significance. God's glory, not man's salvation, is considered the chief purpose of predestination. Also the synthetic, a priori order is rooted in a deeply religious motive. Hence, the assertion that this order of treatment presupposes a nominalistic conception of the Deity and that it offers a dry and lifeless dogma lacks every ground. The doctrine of predestination can be treated in a dry and abstract manner in the middle as well as at the beginning of dogmatics. To be sure, a true and saving faith is the prerequisite for the confession of the doctrine of election, but this is also required with respect to all the other doctrines, e.g., the doctrine of God, the trinity, man. If this consideration is allowed to decide the issue, every dogma would have to follow the doctrine of salvation. But in dogmatics we do not discuss the truth as it subjectively enters the consciousness of the believer but as God has objectively revealed it in his Word. The synthetic method alone is able to do justice to the glorification of God, as a religious interest.

**F. The Development of the Doctrine of Predestination among the Reformed (continued): the Controversy in regard to Infra- and Supralapsarianism:**

**(1** This controversy is rooted in the struggle between Augustine and Pelagius. According to Pelagianism both original and actual sin (unbelief) logically precede election and reprobation; according to Augustine ONLY original sin precedes predestination. According to supra, predestination logically precedes not only actual but also original sin. Hence, Pelagianism: original sin, actual sin, predestination; Augustinianism or infralapsarianism: original sin, predestination, actual sin; supralapsarianism: predestination, original sin, actual sin.

**(2)** Many followers of Augustine accepted the doctrine of twofold predestination: a predestination unto glory and a predestination unto death.

**(3)** The three Reformers: Luther, Zwingli, and Calvin, arrived at the supralapsarian view: election and reprobation are deeds of God's sovereignty, logically preceding God's decree concerning the fall. Nevertheless, Calvin often follows the infralapsarian reasoning.

**(4)** For the order of the elements of the decree see III C.

**(5)** The Synod of Dort expressed itself in an infralapsarian manner but did not in any sense condemn supralapsarianism. It rejected Arminianism.

Among the Reformed another controversy soon arose, namely, in regard to supra- and infralapsarianism. This controversy is rooted in the struggle between Augustine and Pelagius. With the Pelagians the order in the elements of God's counsel was as follows:

1. A decree to create man.

2. A decree to send Christ in order to redeem fallen humanity, to cause him to die for all and to be proclaimed to all, and to grant to all "grace sufficient" unto salvation.

> 3. A decree determining the eternal salvation of some on the ground of foreseen faith, and the eternal punishment of others on the ground of foreseen unbelief.

A totally different order was presented by Augustine. At times he makes reprobation a part of predestination, but even then he views foreknowledge not as something negative and passive but as a divine activity. For, God's will is the "necessary ground of things"; what happens "contrary to his will does not defeat his will"; when God "permits" something, this permission is positive, efficacious. "Surely, he permits willingly, not unwillingly." The supralapsarian position, viz., that reprobation is an act of God's sovereignty, is already implied in this view. Usually, however, Augustine uses the words *divine foreknowledge* and *permission* when he speaks about the fall. Augustine has the following order:

1. A decree to create man and to permit him to fall.

2. A decree to elect some out of this corrupt mass unto eternal life, and to allow others to remain in the perdition wherein they have involved themselves. Accordingly, both election and reprobation presuppose a fallen humanity, a "corrupt mass." From this it appears that Augustine usually favors the infralapsarian representation; in his reasoning he does not go back beyond the fall; he views reprobation as an act of God's justice. "God is good, God is just. Because he is good, he is able to deliver some that are undeserving of salvation; because he is just, he is not able to condemn any one who is undeserving of condemnation."

Now, although Augustine does not view the decree of predestination as preceding both original and actual sin (the supra position), neither does he place the decree of election and reprobation after both of these (the Pelagian position). According to Augustine, *only* original sin logically precedes predestination. Moreover, he considers original sin to be a sufficient ground for reprobation. Actual sins are not taken into account in the decree of reprobation although they are considered in connection with the determination of the degree of punishment. Augustine derived this order in the elements of God's counsel from Rom. 9:11, 12 (". . . for the children being not yet born, neither having done anything good or bad, that the purpose of God according to election might stand, not of works, but of him that calleth, it was said unto her, 'The elder shall serve the younger.' Even as it is written, 'Jacob I loved, but Esau I hated.' ") and from the fate of children dying in infancy unbaptized. Nevertheless, although original sin is a sufficient ground for reprobation, Augustine does not view it as the final and deepest ground. According to him God's sovereignty, as expressed in Rom. 9:18, ("So

then, he hath mercy on whom he will, and whom he will he hardeneth")
is the only answer to the question why God rejected some and chose
others, particularly, why this person was rejected and that one elected.

3. Finally, a decree determining the means whereby the end in view
will be realized.

Augustine does not directly deduce a decree establishing the means
unto perdition from the decree of reprobation as such. He does teach
that even in regard to sin God proceeds in an active and positive manner;
God is the "Disposer of sins," he deemed it right that there should be
sin, he punishes sin with sin; but Augustine generally views reprobation
negatively, i.e., as preterition or dereliction (passing by or abandonment), and he does not as a rule view it as part of predestination, but
identifies the latter with election, and subsumes both election and
reprobation under God's providence. On the other hand there is a
predestination of the means unto *salvation*. With Augustine predestination or election is always a predestination unto glory. It implies foreordination unto grace. Accordingly, foreseen faith and good works are
not the ground of election, neither is Christ the final ground. But election is foreordination unto the desired goal, hence, unto the means
whereby this goal will be realized, i. e., unto Christ who was himself
predestinated, and thus unto calling, baptism, faith, and the gift of
perseverance; predestination is a preparation for grace. Accordingly,
the elect, by way of grace in Christ, will surely obtain heavenly salvation. Therefore, in later years many followers of Augustine arrived
at the doctrine of twofold predestination: a "predestination unto death"
began to be coordinated with a "predestination unto glory." Nevertheless, the former could not be construed in the same sense as the latter;
hence, a distinction was made between a negative and a positive reprobation. The negative reprobation logically precedes the fall; it is an act
of God's sovereignty; it does not depend upon foreseen demerits any
more than election depends upon foreseen merits; it implies "the decree
to permit certain individuals to fall into a state of guilt" and it is "the
cause of dereliction." Thus many Thomists, Alvarez, the Salmanticenses,
Estius, Sylvius, etc., taught that negative reprobation precedes the fall
and that it is purely an act of God's sovereignty and good pleasure.
Nevertheless, this supralapsarian reprobation was viewed as wholly
negative, i.e., as God's purpose not to elect certain individuals, to permit
them to fall, and afterward to ordain them to everlasting punishment
(positive reprobation). *Essentially,* Luther, Zwingli, Calvin, and all
supralapsarian Reformed theologians never went beyond this point.
They neither taught a "predestination unto sins" nor did they represent
God as the author of sin, as is falsely charged by Roman Catholics, who

advance this accusation against the Predestinationists of the fifth century, Gottschalk, Bradwardina, Wyclif, and especially against the Reformers. They do this merely in order to justify their own Semi-Pelagian view, and to harmonize it with the teachings of Augustine and Thomas Aquinas.

Essentially the teaching of Augustine and Thomas Aquinas in regard to predestination was accepted by the Reformers: the modifications introduced by them were slight and unessential, if we except the doctrine of assurance. The Reformers agreed with Augustine and Thomas Aquinas on many points; viz., they, too, believed that election is not conditioned upon foreseen merits, but that it is the source of faith and good works; that predestination unto glory always implies predestination unto grace; that negative reprobation is not to be explained as an act of God's justice but as an act of his sovereignty, and that it logically precedes sin; that this negative reprobation is followed by a decree to permit sin and to allow some to remain in their fallen state; and that positive reprobation takes sin into account. To all this they added, however, that the concepts *foreknowledge* and *permission*, though not wrong in themselves, cannot and should not be interpreted in a merely passive sense; that even if they could be so construed, they would offer no real solution of the problem; and that the distinction between positive and negative reprobation has very little value. Thus, all three Reformers arrived at the so-called supralapsarian view of the doctrine of predestination, according to which both election and reprobation are to be viewed as acts of God's sovereignty, logically preceding God's decree concerning the fall, sin, and redemption through Christ. But it is especially Calvin who often purposely refuses to go beyond the secondary causes of salvation and perdition, and therefore often reasons in an infralapsarian manner. Let not the reprobate view God's decree as the cause of his perdition, but let him rather look upon his own corrupt nature with respect to which he himself is guilty. The elect and the reprobate were equally guilty but God is merciful toward the former, just toward the latter. In Romans 9:21 the "clay" indicates men in their fallen condition, of whom God elects some while he leaves others "in their own ruin, to which by nature all are exposed." The fall in Adam is the nearest cause of reprobation. God hates only sin in us. And of this representation: "that out of the race doomed in Adam God elected those whom he was pleased to elect, and reprobated those whom he willed to reprobate." Calvin says, "just as it is a great deal more suitable unto the cultivation of faith, so it is discussed with greater profit . . . is not only more conducive unto piety, but, it seems to me, more theological, more suitable to practical Christianity, and also more conducive unto edification." Nevertheless, this does not fully satisfy Calvin. Sin may be the proximate cause of perdition, it is, nevertheless, not the deepest cause. For the theory that God apart from any previous plan decided to create man, then sat down, as it were, in a watchtower to see what man would do, and having seen and foreseen this, only afterward proceeded to the act of election and reprobation, is altogether untenable. Foreknowledge and permission do not solve the problem, because God, foreseeing the fall, could have prevented it; accordingly, he voluntarily permitted the fall because it seemed good to him. Accordingly, the fall of Adam, sin in general, and all evil, were not only foreseen by God but in a certain sense were willed and determined by him. Accordingly, there must have been a reason, unknown to us, why God willed the fall; there is "a deeper divine decree" logically preceding the fall. Hence, when Pighius answers Calvin by objecting that according to the latter's view there would have been in the divine mind a "distinction between elect and reprobate previous to the fall of man," Calvin indeed answers that Pighius fails to distinguish between "proximate and remote causes," that every reprobate must consider his own sin to be the direct cause of his perdition, and that the opposite view is handicapped with the same objections, but he does not deny the validity of the conclusion drawn by Pighius; there is a "secret divine decree" anteceding the fall. The final and deepest cause of reprobation as well as of election is the will of God. Hence, with Calvin the supralapsarian and infralapsarian representation alternates. This is also true of most of the later theologians who embraced supralapsarianism. They regard the supralapsarian view to be admissible but they do not think of condemning infralapsarianism or of demanding that their view be embodied in the official confession of the church as the only standard of truth. They do not ask that their own view be *substituted* for the infralapsarian representation but they plead for *actual recognition* of both views.

According to the supralapsarian view a divine knowledge of all possibilities precedes every decree, a "knowledge of simple intelligence." According to the rule "what is ultimate in execution is first in design," supra teaches the following order in the elements of God's counsel:

(1) A decree determining the purpose for which God would create and govern all things, namely, the revelation of his virtues, esp. of his mercy and of his justice; respectively, in the eternal salvation of a definite number of men conceived as yet only as possibles, "creatable and fallible," and in the eternal punishment of another definite number. The manifestation of these virtues necessitated:

(2) A second decree determining the existence of human beings who would be so wretched and pitiable that they would be fit objects

of God's mercy and justice. The actual existence of such human beings necessitated:

(3) A third decree to create a man adorned with the image of God to be the head of humanity, and "by an efficacious permission" to allow him to fall so that he would involve his entire posterity in that fall.

(4) Finally, a decree to manifest God's mercy in the elect by providing a Mediator for them and by granting them the gifts of faith and perseverance, and to show God's justice in the reprobate by withholding saving grace from them and by giving them up unto sin.

In this order of the decrees election and reprobation precede not only faith and unbelief, regeneration and hardening, but also creation and the fall. However, one difficulty presents itself immediately: it was the established Reformed doctrine that the election of Christ and of the church are not to be separated and that both are included in one single decree that has as its object "the mystic Christ." But in the supralapsarian scheme the election of the church is separated from the election of Christ by the two decrees of creation and the fall. Comrie, however, tried to overcome this objection by teaching that before the decree of creation and the fall the believers are chosen unto union with Christ. This union is so close and unbreakable that when those chosen fall, as is determined in a subequent decree, Christ, who had been elected as Head, is now also chosen to be the Mediator of redemption. From this it is clear that Comrie understood that the election of the church as the body of Christ cannot be separated from the election of Christ as the Head of the Church. Accordingly, he placed the election of both before the decree of creation and the fall. However, in this manner not only men considered as mere possibilities but also a merely possible Christ was made the object of the decree of election.

The churches, however, always objected to this supralapsarian view. As a result, there is not a single Reformed confession that offers this representation. At the Synod of Dort there were a few adherents of this view, esp. Gomarus and Maccovius; moreover, the delegates of South Holland, Overisel, and Friesland preferred to leave the question undecided and to use an expression that would satisfy both parties. But although the "opinions" of the Dutch and of the foreign delegates, also of those from Geneva, were definitely Reformed in character, nevertheless, they were without exception infralapsarian and clothed in mild and moderate terms. And the Synod at length defined election as "the unchangeable purpose of God whereby, before the foundation of the world, he hath out of mere grace, according to the sovereign good pleasure of his own will, chosen from the whole human race, which had fallen through their own fault from their primitive state of rectitude, into sin and destruction, a certain number of persons. . . . . to salvation in Christ, whom he from eternity appointed the Mediator and Head of the elect, and the foundation of salvation." Nevertheless, the Synod purposely refused to condemn supralapsarianism; for, various theologians, among whom were Calvin, Beza, Piscator, Perkins, Hommins, Bogerman, etc., had at times used strong expression; e.g., "that some men are created in order that they may be damned; that men viewed as innocent are reprobated or damned; that God hates men irrespective of sin; that men were predestinated unto sin; that God has need of man as a sinner; that God willed and brought about the fact that men sinned; that God acted insincerely in the calling of certain persons," etc. At the conference held in the Hague the Remonstrants had made ready use of these expressions and of the difference between infra- and supralapsarianism; consequently, the members of the synod were intent on avoiding such "phrases that were too harsh." But when the delegates from England, Bremen, and Hesse insisted that these expressions be condemned, the Synod refused to grant this request. In defence of this refusal Synod stated that Scripture also uses very strong expressions at times, that such phrases may have a much milder meaning when examined in their context than they appear to have when considered apart from their context, and that the responsibility for them rests with the respective authors. In addition, Synod admonished against the use of immoderate phrases without mentioning any specifically and against "many other things of the same kind," and at a later session administered a severe rebuke to Maccovius because of the manner in which he had conducted himself. Accordingly, although the supralapsarian view was not embodied in the confession, neither was it condemned. The Westminster Assembly purposely refrained from attempting to decide this question and from siding with either the infra- or the supralapsarian party. For that reason many continued to favor supralapsarianism although the rights of infralapsarianism were at the same time recognized inasmuch as the latter view had been embodied in the confession of the churches, was zealously and ably defended by many theologians, and was usually placed in the foreground in the preaching of the Gospel.

**G. Religious Sects and Isms that have Opposed the Reformed Doctrine of Predestination:**

**(1) During the time of the Reformation this doctrine was rejected by Erasmus, Pighius, Bolsec, Castellio, and others.**

**(2) The Socinians denied predestination and even divine omniscience.**

**(3) In the Netherlands the Arminians (Remonstrants) taught election conditioned on foreknowledge.**

(4) In France, Amyraut propounded the doctrine of hypothetical universalism.

(5) Arminianism paved the way for rationalism, and during the seventeenth and eighteenth centuries the former exerted its influence upon neonomianism, deism, Quakerism, methodism, etc.

(6) Of late deistic Pelagianism has been superseded by pantheistic and materialistic determinism.

(7) At present some deny predestination entirely, others view it as God's purpose to save all people, while still others accept a predestination conditioned on foreseen faith (or unbelief).

(8) There are exceptions to this general reversion to Arminianism, e.g., Missouri Lutheran Synod.

Even this milder form of the doctrine of predestination encountered opposition. In the era of the Reformation it was disputed by Erasmus, Bibliander, Pighius, Bolsec, Trolliet, Castellio, Ochinus, and others. The Socinians rejected the doctrine of predestination in its entirety, accepted only a divine decree to grant eternal life to those who obey God's ordinances and to punish the others, and defended the free will of man even at the expense of God's omniscience. In the Netherlands objections were raised against the doctrine of predestination by many; e.g., by Anastasius, Gellius, Coolhaes, Duifhuis, Coornhert, Sybrants, Herberts, Wiggerts, and especially by Arminius. The latter defined predestination as the Divine decree to save in Christ, for Christ's sake, and through Christ, those concerning whom God foresaw that by virtue of prevenient grace they would believe and that by virtue of consequent grace they would persevere, and to punish the others who would not believe or persevere. Arminius still tried to defend the proposition that divine grace is necessary unto salvation and that faith is the gift of God. His followers tried to do the same in their Remonstrance of 1610, art. 3 and 4. But this grace was always viewed as resistible, art. 4 and 5, and the objection based on the definite and certain character of divine foreknowledge in regard to those who would believe and those who would not, as well as the acceptance of the *three universalities*: God's will desiring the salvation *of all,* Christ's death *for all,* and the offer of the means sufficient unto salvation *to all* gradually and necessarily resulted in making man the absolute Arbiter of his own eternal destiny. This is clear from the later writings of the Remonstrants, the letter of Episcopius to the Reformed in other countries, the second Remonstrance of the year 1617, the apology and confession published by Episcopius, and the theological works of Uytenbogaert, Eposcopius, and Limborch. Remonstrantism paved the way for rationalism. During the seventeenth and eighteenth centuries the former, though condemned by the Synod of Dort, gradually entered all churches and countries. On the Reformed side it was supported by the school of Saumur. Here Amyraut taught a double decree. God first decrees in general that all, without distinction, who believe in Christ will be saved; but foreseeing that no one is able to believe of himself, God now adds to this first, universal, and conditional decree a second particular and absolute decree to grant unto some the gift of faith and to save them. Of course, if the first, universal decree means anything at all, the second has no value. In spite of the fact that the Helvetic Consensus Formula of 1675 was drawn up in opposition to Amyraldism, cf. can. 4-6, this theory continued to gain ground, and under the influence of Pajon it led to the rejection of "efficacious grace." In all Reformed churches Arminianistic tendencies gained ground. All the sects and religious movements that sprang up during the seventeenth and eighteenth centuries were more or less Arminianistic in character. This is true in regard to neonomianism, deism, Quakerism, methodism, etc. Only a few theologians stood firm; e.g., Comrie, Holtius, and Brahe in the Netherlands; Boston and the Erskines in Scotland; and especially Jonathan Edwards, 1703-1758, in America.

In the present century deeper study in the fields of natural science, history, and anthropology has shown the intenability of deistic pelagianism. It was superseded by pantheistic or materialistic, by ethical or physical determinism. Of course, with a semblance ot similarity there is, nevertheless, a difference in principle between this determinism and the doctrine of predestination. Neither pantheism nor materialism leaves any room for a divine decree; they leave room only for unconscious fate, blind nature, and alogical will. Nevertheless, many have understood and interpreted the ecclesiastical doctrine of predestination in this deterministic sense. This is evident, e.g., from Von Hartmann's statement: "As surely as every person is not only predisposed but also predetermined unto evil, so surely every one is not only predisposed but also predetermined unto good. . . . . as surely as there are none that are absolutely reprobate, so surely there are none that are absolutely elect, for even the most reprobate individual has within himself a certain degree of grace, and the most highly favored individual is not wholly exempt from actual evil." Fundamentally this is also Schleiermacher's position, for although the doctrine of the church is his starting-point and although he adheres to the revelation in Christ, he distinguishes between election and reprobation only with reference to time; strictly speaking there are no reprobates: that some are not yet converted is due to unfavorable circumstances; those who are still unconverted will be converted later on.

All ideas of earlier and later periods recur in the theology of to-day. First, there are those who completely deny the decree of predestination on the ground that eternity should not be conceived of as a pre-temporal span of time; accordingly, one should not view the matter thus: that for countless ages God's decrees have been lying ready and prepared, but thus: that predestination in its broadest sense, including both election and reprobation, is nothing else than the eternal and immanent divine activity and government which is revealed in time, and that the decrees are nothing else than the facts of history. But thus every distinction between eternity and time, and between God and the universe, is lost, and theism is bartered for pantheism. Accordingly, others do accept an eternal decree, but regard it as consisting merely in the "antecedent will" whereby God sincerely desires and purposes the salvation of all. In the course of history the general decree becomes particular, at least for a time. For, in the execution of the decree God deals historically. The object of election is the church. Separate individuals do not constitute the object. God calls entire nations successively according as in the course of time and under God"s providential guidance they become receptive to the higher religion of Christendom. And within the sphere of each separate people the particular individuals are also called successively. The order in which they are called depends upon their nationality, character, and degree of culture. Accordingly, the election of one people and of one individual is not at the expense of others but in the interest of others: all cannot be first; those who have been passed now, i.e., the reprobate (rejected) nations and individuals, will come to true conversion later on, either in this life or probably in the hereafter. At any rate, there is no decree of reprobation from the side of God that would exclude certain, definitely known individuals from salvation; from the side of man a continued opposition and positive hardening resulting in eternal ruin is barely possible. Still others add to this general purpose a second decree by means of which God determines to save all those whose faith and perseverance he has foreseen and foreknown, and to punish the others eternally. All agree that the will of man is the final arbiter of man's eternal destiny. Nevertheless, all do not ascribe this authority of the human will to the same source. One holds that the power to accept or reject God's grace belongs to man by virtue of creation or of the pedagogic guidance of God's general providence; another ascribes this power to "preparatory and antecedent grace" granted unto man in baptism or in the preaching of the law and the Gospel; while a third tries to reconcile the two ideas by teaching that grace is granted unto those that use to good advantage the natural powers of the will and make earnest study of the Word of God, etc. Accordingly, Kaften was not entirely wrong when he said. "Modern German theology does not have a doctrine of election." Nevertheless, many church-members and theologians still accept and defend the doctrine of God's counsel. It is a remarkable fact that the Missouri Synod of the *Lutheran* Churches took a stand that approaches Calvinism, while, over against it, the Cumberland *Presbyterian* Church sanctioned an Arminianistic modification of the Westminster Confession. When the revision of the Westminster Confession was proposed in Scotland and America, many objections were raised against the doctrine of election and reprobation, against the belief in the perdition of heathen and of those who die in infancy, and in general against the construction of the Confession upon the exclusive foundation of God's absolute sovereignty in disregard of his universal love.

## III. God's Decree Is His Eternal Purpose Whereby He Has Foreordained Whatsoever Comes To Pass. Pelagianism Virtually Rejects This Decree. Neither Supralapsarianism Nor Infralapsarianism Does Full Justice To It. The Decree Of Predestination Includes Both Reprobation and Election.

**A. Definition and Characteristics of the Decree. God's decree is his eternal purpose whereby he has foreordained whatsoever comes to pass. It is efficacious, immutable, unconditional, eternal, all-comprehensive, and single.**

God's decree is his eternal purpose whereby he has foreordained whatsoever comes to pass. Scripture everywhere affirms that whatsoever is and comes to pass is the realization of God's thought and will, and has its origin and idea in God's eternal counsel or decree, Gen. 1; Job 28:27; Prov. 8:22; Ps. 104:24; Prov. 3:19; Jer. 10:12; 51:15; Heb. 11:3; Ps. 33:11; Is. 44:24-27; 46:10; Prov. 19:21; Acts. 2:23; 4:28; Eph. 1:11; etc. Even human deeds are based upon deliberation and consideration: in the case of rational beings thinking and purposing precede acting and doing. In a far more exalted sense this is true with respect to the Lord our God: apart from his knowledge and will nothing can ever come to pass. Accordingly, all Christians accept a divine decree as such. Objections are raised by pantheism alone, for pantheism does not recognize a distinct life and consciousness in God. Accordingly, it must choose between denying or accepting the existence of the logos in the universe: if it chooses the former alternative, this universe is the work of a blind will; if the latter, then pantheism is forced to accept a divine consciousness that contains the ideas of all things. The logos in the universe presupposes the logos in God.

Thought would be absent from creation if it were not for the fact that God in wisdom created all things. Furthermore, God's thought, embodied in creation, cannot be conceived of as an uncertain idea, doubtful of realization; it is not a "bare foreknowledge" that receives its contents from creation; it is not a plan, a project, or a purpose whose execution can be frustrated. But it is an act both of God's mind and of his will. Accordingly, Scripture speaks of God's counsel, of the thoughts of his heart, Ps. 33:11; of the counsel of his will, Eph. 1:11; of foreknowledge and foreordination, Acts 2:23; 4:28; Rom. 8:29; of purpose, Jer. 4:28; 51:12; Rom. 8:28; Eph. 1:9, 11; of good pleasure, Ps. 51:20; Is. 53:10; 60:10; 61:2; Matt. 11:26; Eph. 1:5, 9; decree, Gen. 41:32; II Chron. 25:16; Job 38:10; Ps. 2:7; God speaks and it is done; he commands, and it stands fast, Ps. 33:9. When the proper time arrives, God's decree necessarily produces the intended effect. It is efficacious, Is. 14:27; Ps. 115:3; 135:6; immutable, Is. 46:10; Ps. 33:11; Heb. 6:17; Jas. 1:17; independent, Matt. 11:26; Eph. 1:9; Rom. 9:11; 20:21. Nevertheless we should make a distinction between God's decree considered by itself, and the execution of the decree; just as we differentiate between God's being and his "outgoing works." God's decree is immanent in God; it is eternal, and exists apart from time. It is an "immanent work." The objection has been raised that eternity should not be conceived of as a pretemporal span of time, and that God's counsel and election must not be construed as a decree made many ages ago. By itself this remark is correct. Eternity differs essentially from time. God's counsel is no more an act that pertains to the past than is the generation of the Son; it is an eternal, divine act: eternally finished, yet continuing forevermore, apart from and raised above time. Scaliger correctly observed that God's decree was not preceded by a long period of reflection and deliberation, so that for a long time God would have been without a purpose and without a will; neither is it a plan once for all completed and finished and simply awaiting execution. But God's decree is the eternally active will of God: it is the willing and purposing God himself; it is not something accidental to God, but being God's will in action, it is one with his essence. It is impossible to conceive of God as a being without a purpose and without an active and operative will. Nevertheless, all this does not conceal the fact that God's decree is an "immanent work" determined by nothing else than by God himself, and distinct in character from God's works in time, Acts 15:18; Eph. 1:4.

Whatever object comes into existence or whatever event comes to pass in time is included in this counsel of God. His decree has as its content and object the idea of the universe, "the totality of ideas." This concept of the universe is closely related to God's being, but must not be identified with God's being nor with the Son or with the Logos. The same relation exists between the idea of the universe and the being of God as between God's *world*-consciousness and his *self*-consciousness. God's self-knowledge is not exhausted in the universe any more than is his power or any of his attributes. Nevertheless, the universe is a proper instrument for the manifestation, in creaturely fashion, of all God's attributes. The idea of the universe was by God so conceived that it is able to reveal his glory and to show forth his excellencies in a manner suited to the creature. It is a mirror in which God reflects his image. It is the creaturely reflex of his adorable being; it is a finite. limited. inadequate, yet true and faithful reproduction of God's self-knowledge. Accordingly, with reference to the universe itself this divine decree is both "efficient" and "exemplary" cause. It is efficient cause, for no creature can ever come into existence apart from God's will and decree. The decree brings forth all things, Zeph. 2:2. "God's good pleasure" is the final ground of all things. Beyond this we cannot go. The final answer to the question why a thing is and why it is as it is must ever remain: "God willed it," according to his absolute sovereignty. But the divine decree is also the exemplary cause (or pattern) of whatever is and comes to pass. For our human consciousness a thing first comes into existence, afterward we obtain an idea about it; with God, however, the idea is first; afterward and in accordance with this idea the thing comes into existence, the event occurs. Just as Moses was "warned of God . . . to make the tabernacle . . . according to the pattern that was shown to him on the mount," Heb. 8:5; and just as "every fatherhood in heaven and on earth is named from the Father," Eph. 3:15; in like manner, whatsoever is temporal is an image of that which is eternal; whatsoever exists is a shadowing forth of that which was conceived in thought, and in the final analysis whatsoever is and comes to pass is a reflection of God's being. Accordingly, the statement of Thomas Aquinas "God is the similitude of all things according to his essence" — to which statement an objection has been raised because the idea of the universe does not coincide with God's being — when rightly interpreted, is correct.

Hence, God's counsel must needs be conceived of as a single decree. The Westminster Synod discussed the question whether the word *decree* should be used in the singular or in the plural. The Westminster Confession uses the singular only. The idea of the universe is in fact one single conception in the divine consciousness. Just as Minerva comes full-grown from the head of Jupiter, and just as a genius suddenly and completely grasps the idea of a work of art, in like manner throughout all eternity the idea of the universe is fully and completely present in the divine self-consciousness. But just as in the case of an artist the execution of his conception must needs be gradual, in like manner there is a temporal and piecemeal visible unfoldment of the one and only, all-comprehensive divine decree. The idea of the universe is single, but when it is realized, it unfolds itself in all the riches of its beauty in the forms of space and time. Just as *outwardly,* i.e., to the eye of the creature, God's love and all his virtues must needs be revealed by means of the forms of breadth and length and height and depth, Eph. 3:18, 19; and we thus obtain some knowledge concerning his manifold wisdom and unsearchable riches, in like manner the one and only and eternal decree of God is gradually and little by little unfolded before the eye of the creature, unfurling itself in many events and happenings, each of which in turn points back to a definite moment in the single decree of God, so that in our human language we speak of decrees of God in the plural. This manner of speech should not be condemned as long as we maintain and recognize the close relation that obtains between the several decrees, and the fact that in God the decree is one.

B. **Pelagianism's virtual denial of the decree:**

(1) **Pelagians separate the natural from the moral sphere: in the interest, supposedly, of human freedom they withdraw the moral world-order, the sphere of right and wrong, from the province of God's decree.   Objections:**

a. **The natural and the moral world-order should be distinguished, indeed, but never separated.**

b. **According to Scripture both good and evil deeds are included in God's decree.**

c. **The Pelagian position banishes God from the universe and via deism leads to atheism.**

(2) **In particular, man's eternal destiny is withdrawn from the province of God's decree:  predestination is conditioned on foreseen persevering faith or unbelief.   Objections:**

a. **If God's decree applies to a person's temporal affairs, it applies equally to his eternal destiny, for the two are very closely related.**

b. **According to Scripture faith and unbelief are not merely foreseen but included in God's decree.**

c. **According to Scripture faith is not of human but of divine origin, I Cor. 2:14;  it is not the root but the fruit of election, Rom. 8:29; Eph. 1:4, 5;  Acts. 13:48.**

d. **According to the unanimous testimony of Christian experience, salvation is entirely God's work:  in prayer every Christian is Augustinian.**

e. **A definite and certain foreKNOWLEDGE implies foreORDINATION:  predestination.**

(3) **Pelagianism attacks every single phase of the doctrine of predestination.  It teaches:**

**a.** A CONDITIONAL antecedent decree to offer ALL men grace sufficient to be saved.  Objections:

1. Then why does God not cause the Gospel to be proclaimed to ALL individuals?

2. If the conferment of initial grace is CONDITIONAL, i.e., if it is conditioned upon merits, and it is agreed that infants lack these merits, then why do some infants die baptized, others unbaptized?

**b.** A predestination unto efficacious grace also CONDITION-AL in character, i.e., conditioned upon merits:  God purposed to give efficacious grace to all who make good use of initial grace.  Objections:

1. According to Scripture man is by nature unable and un-willing to accept the Gospel;  whence, then, does he derive the power to make good use of initial grace?

2. Scripture teaches that faith is not conditioned upon merits but an unmerited gift of God's grace.

3. The Roman Catholic doctrine of a merit of congruity is anti-Biblical, cf. Matt. 21:31.

**c.** A CONDITIONAL predestination unto glory:  a decree to grant salvation to those whose PERSEVERANCE in faith God has foreseen.  Objections:

1. God's decree, thus interpreted, is nothing more than a wish, whose fulfilment is very uncertain.

2. According to Scripture predestination unto grace implies predestination unto glory, Rom. 8:29, 30.

3. This Pelagian doctrine is a denial of GOD'S work in the salvation of sinners.

In God's counsel we distinguish first of all that decree which used to be indicated by the name "providence." Formerly, the word *"pronoia"* "providentia," "providence" was given the literal meaning of foresight, forethought, forepreparation. This used to be its connotation also in theology. Accordingly, God's providence was discussed in connection with the doctrine of God's counsel and of his will. It was defined as "that activity of God's mind and will whereby from eternity he has arranged all things in such a manner that they will work together for the accomplishment of a divinely predetermined purpose." As such it should of course be distinguished from the execution of God's counsel in time. To the latter the term "government" was applied. Thus the word providence is used to indicate God's decree or counsel. Many Roman Catholics interpret the word in that sense, and formerly also many Reformed theologians. In this sense God's providence is the ex-emplar (or pattern) in accordance with which God in time preserves and governs all things. Later on, however, it became customary to employ the term *providence* to indicate the divine activity of preserva-tion and government itself, which interpretation was already given to it by Zwingli, Calvin, Polanus, the Synopsis, etc., when they discussed it after the doctrine of creation. The name is of very little importance, but of great significance is the fact that all things are included in the decree: not only the determination of the eternal destiny of rational creatures (predestination), but the arrangement and ordination of all things without any exception. Now the term *providence* was formerly used to emphasize this all-comprehensive character of God's decree. Accordingly, predestination was not something considered entirely apart from everything else, but it was considered a phase of God's decree concerning whatever comes to pass, a distinct application of God's counsel. Hence, Zwingli said, "Providence is as it were the parent of predestination." Predestination is God's providence with a view to the eternal destiny of men and angels. Reformed theologians, on the whole, preferred to speak of God's counsel or decree, because these terms are Scriptural, which cannot be said of the term *pronoia*. God's decree is all-comprehensive and therefore applies first of all to the universe as a whole. Everything exists and takes place in accordance with God's decree: this is true with respect to the inorganic as well as the organic realm. All things rest upon God's ordinances. Heaven and earth, light and darkness, day and night, summer and winter, seed-time and harvest, both in their unity and in their diversity are ordered by God, who is wonderful in counsel and excellent in wisdom, Gen. 1:14, 26, 28; 8:22; Ps. 104:5, 9; 119:91; 148:6; Job 38:10 ff.; Is. 28:29; Jer. 5:24; 31:25 ff.; 33:20, 25.

God's decree with respect to the physical sphere is admitted by nearly all except the Manichaeans, etc. Even with respect to a divine decree referring more definitely to rational creatures in general there is great unanimity. All admit that God's will is the deepest ground of the creation of the human race, Gen. 1:26; of the distribution of the nations, Gen. 11; of the determination of their appointed seasons and of the bounds of their habitation, Acts 17:26; of the difference in gifts, talents, rank, social position, and degree of riches, existing between individuals and nations, Deut. 32:8; Prov. 22:2; Matt. 25:15; and even of the inequality and diversity of charismata in the church, I Cor. 4:7; 12:7-11; Rom. 12:4 ff. God's good pleasure is the only thing that accounts for all being and for all diversity of being. The reason for the existence and for the manner of existence of all things rests in God alone. The fact that a thing exists, and that it is what it is and not something else; that there is a variety of being and of life; that among creatures there is an endless diversity in kind, gender, duration, rank, social position, wealth, etc., is rooted in God's good pleasure. Moreover, this divine good pleasure does not presuppose but creates its object. According to Augustine if animals could speak and could argue with their Creator because they differ from men, everybody would consider this absurd. Indeed, the only attitude that becomes any creature is submission to God's good pleasure. Either a creature must be its own creator, and therefore cease to be a *creature,* or it must be and remain a creature from beginning to end, and depend for its existence and manner of existence upon God alone.

As soon, however, as this decree of God is applied also to the moral sphere, objections are raised from every side. It is argued that God's counsel has nothing to do with the moral sphere, which is held to be the special domain of man, a domain in which man works out his own destiny. Pelagius and his followers emphasize the difference between the natural and the moral sphere, between "potentiality" and "will"; and in the interest, supposedly, of human freedom, responsibility, guilt, etc., they exclude the moral sphere, either in part or as a whole, from the province of God's decree. However, even apart from further examination and because of objections that lie wholly on the surface, this attempt to make the moral sphere independent of God must be repudiated. In the first place it is contrary to Scripture. Scripture, to be sure, sets forth man's moral nature in no uncertain terms, but it never does this by creating an antithesis between the natural and the moral sphere, neither does it ever exclude the latter from the decree of God. Scripture very clearly maintains that all things are included in God's counsel, also those which pertain to the moral sphere, the evil as well as the good. Moreover, the procedure does violence to the very close connection and interrelation existing between the physical and the moral order: the two are inseparable. The idea of the universe is one organic whole. The two spheres exist distinctly, not separately. One can never say: this or that particular point marks the end of God's counsel and government and the beginning of man's will and deed. Especially during this century the study of nature and history resulting in an organic view of life has served to disprove this Pelagian separation in every respect. Furthermore, by means of this dualism the most extensive and important part of the universe is withdrawn from the province of God's decree and given into the hands of chance and fortune. Even more: the universe is withdrawn to a large extent not only from the sphere of God's will and decree, but also from the province of his knowledge. If God and his creature must needs be viewed as rivals or competitors so that freedom and distinct existence for the one can be obtained only at the other's expense, God's knowledge and will must be reduced to a minimum: the Pelagian position banishes God from the universe and via deism leads to atheism, while at the same time it enthrones the caprice and foolishness of man. Hence, the solution of the problem must be sought in another direction, namely, in the fact that God, because he is God and the universe is his creation, by his infinitely majestic activity of knowing and willing, does not destroy but rather creates and maintains the distinct existence and freedom of the creature.

However, Pelagianism does not raise its main objection against "general and special providence." To a certain extent it accepts this decree of God. But more than anything else God's decree with respect to the eternal destiny of rational creatures, predestination proper, is the target for the arrows of Pelagianism. Now predestination is merely a phase, a particular application, of God's decree or providence. Just as the natural sphere cannot be separated from the moral sphere, in like manner that which pertains to the temporal affairs of rational creatures cannot be separated from that which pertains to their eternal destiny. Yet with respect to the latter, foreknowledge is substituted for foreordination, and predestination is defined as "that divine decree whereby God, on the ground of foreseen persevering faith on the part of some, or foreseen, persevering unbelief on the part of others, has ordained the former to eternal salvation, and the latter to eternal punishment." Notwithstanding the fact, however, that this Pelagian representation is generally accepted—it is the confession of the Greek Church, of Roman Catholics, Lutherans, Arminians, Anabaptists, Methodists, etc. — it is contradicted by Scripture, religious experience, and theological reflection. In the first place Scripture very clearly teaches that faith and unbelief, salvation and damnation, are the object not merely of God's foreknowledge but of his will and decree. The word *prognosis*, foreknowledge, used in Rom. 8:29; 11:2; I Pet. 1:2; cf. Acts 2:23; does not indicate a merely passive foreknowledge, a mere condition of the mind, but just like the Hebrew word, *ydh'*, Hos. 13:5; Am. 3:2; etc., it signifies a self-determination on the part of God—preceding its realization in history—whereby he assumes a definite relation to the objects of his foreknowledge; it is most closely connected with God's "purpose," "foreordination," and "election," and it is an act of his "good pleasure." Secondly, it is the doctrine of Scripture that faith can never proceed out of the heart of man as it is by nature, I Cor. 2:14; that faith is a gift of God, Eph. 2:8; Phil. 1:29; I Cor. 4:7; and that it is not the root but the fruit of election, Rom. 8:29; Eph. 1:4, 5; Acts 13:48. Thirdly, according to the unanimous testimony of all Christian experience, salvation, not only in the objective but also in the subjective sense of the word, is only and entirely God's work. A person may be Pelagian in doctrine; in the experience and practice of Christian life, especially in prayer, every Christian is Augustinian. Then he excludes all glorying in self and glories in God only. Accordingly, Augustine was correct when he remarked that the faith of the ancient church in God's grace had expressed itself "in prayers rather than in pamphlets." Fourthly, "God's foreknowledge" is of such a character that its object is fore-known with absolute certainty, and then it is identical with predestina-tion. On the other hand, if the object of foreknowledge is viewed as being entirely arbitrary or accidental, it cannot have been foreknown. According to the doctrine of the Greek, Roman Catholic, and Lutheran churches and even according to the "Remonstrance" of the Arminians, all of whom try to substitute foreknowledge for predestination, the number of those who will believe and will be saved is just as certain and definitely fixed as it is according to Augustine and the Reformed theologians. Said Augustine, "The number of the elect is certain; it can neither be increased nor diminished." This is also the teaching of Lombard, Thomas Aquinas, and all Roman Catholic theologians, even though they differ in this respect: that some derive this certainty of the result from the will, while others, e.g., Molina, derive it from the knowledge of God. Later Lutheran theologians have made predestina-tion dependent upon foreknowledge, but they have never expressed any doubt concerning the certainty and immutability of the result, for on this point Scripture expresses itself in so many passages and in lan-guage so clear and definite that all possibility of doubt is excluded, cf. Dan. 12:1; Matt. 24:24; 25:34; John 10:28; Rom. 8:29; 30; I Pet. 1:2-4. Both "formally and materially" both quantitatively and qualitatively, the number of the saved is unalterably fixed according to the confessions of all Christian churches. But when this fact is realized in its full significance, it will be understood that "foreknowledge" is equal to "providence" and "predestination." God has foreknown with eternal and immutable certainty that certain definite persons are going to believe. But if that is true, then these individuals will also most certainly believe and be saved. On this basis there is nowhere any room for freedom in the sense of chance or fortuitousness. Fore-knowledge implies predestination. If one maintains with Castellio that God has foreknown fortuitous events in their fortuitous character, he has returned to Augustine's line of thought and is able to harmonize freedom with predestination. The question is this: Can those free and fortuitous events be known from eternity with infallible certainty? If so, Augustine is right and the doctrine of foreknowledge is unnecesary. If not, not only predestination but also foreknowledge must be denied; in that case the result of the history of the universe is a matter of mere conjecture; it remains incalculable and unknowable. Cicero al-ready saw this, and therefore denied foreknowledge also. He was fol-lowed by the Socinians, the Remonstrants, Vorstius, and many recent theologians, all of whom accepted a divine self-limitation in knowl-edge, will, and power, in order that they might maintain the freedom of the creature. Nevertheless, the Christian Churches did not dare to accept this logical conclusion as their own position. All confess God's providence (decree) and foreknowledge. All things come to pass in time in accordance with God's eternal foreknowledge. But the final result and the means that lead to this result are definitely fixed in God's foreknowledge. Thus interpreted, the doctrine of predestination is not a confession of the Reformed Church only; it is not merely the opinion of Augustine and Calvin; but it is the dogma of all of Christendom. There is difference with respect to the name that is given to this doc-trine and the manner in which it is presented, but there is *material* correspondence; i.e., all Christian Churches and theologians confess that all things exist, happen, and reach their destination in strict ac-cordance with God's eternal knowledge. In that sense Augustine was right when he said, "There has never been a time when the Church of Christ did not have the belief in this predestination, which is now de-fended with new solicitude against new heretics." Although the con-fessions differ in the degree of emphasis with which they discuss this doctrine, they all have it. Indeed, whether one thinks in the manner of Pelagius or in the manner of Augustine, the facts remain unaltered. History does not change. Facts and their interrelation in the history of the universe exist as they are, and are not dependent upon the true or false conception one may entertain in regard to them. The dif-ference lies in this: on the basis of Scripture and after the example of Augustine, Reformed theologians go beyond the secondary causes and arrive at the first cause, i.e., at the will of God in which alone they find rest for heart and mind. The invincible strength and severity of the doctrine of predestination is manifested in the facts of history which are interpreted by Scripture as the execution of God's eternal decree. It is not the doctrine of predestination itself that is harsh and severe, but the *facts* upon which this doctrine is based are horribly severe. Pelagianism, moreover, fails to satisfy for this reason: that at every point of the life and history of mankind it is in conflict with awe-inspiring reality. It is a superficial varnish, that deceives man but does not change reality.

Finally, Pelagianism, already shown to be untenable in its general position, attacks not only the doctrine of predestination as a whole but also and specifically every distinct phase of this doctrine. In the first place it accepts a conditional, antecedent divine decree to offer to all fallen men grace sufficient to be saved. An appeal is made to such passages as: Is. 5:3; Jer. 51:9; Ezek. 18:23, 32; 33:11; Matt. 23:37;

John 3:16; Rom. 11:32; and especially I Tim. 2:4 and II Pet. 3:19. This antecedent, general decree was accepted by Pelagians, Semi-Pelagians, Roman Catholics, Lutherans, Arminians, Universalists of early and later date, and among the Reformed, by the Amyraldists. However, it immediately clashes with reality. Throughout' the centuries the Gospel has been proclaimed to only a small portion of humanity. In reality, throughout history grace is particular, not universal. To be sure, many attempts have been made in order to harmonize this fact with the universal decree. Pelagians have erased the boundary-line between nature and grace, and have discovered a way of salvation in "the law of nature." Many Roman Catholic theologians are of the opinion that grace is or will be granted to all those who make proper use of the light and power of nature. Lutherans formerly maintained that at the time of Adam, of Noah, and of the apostles, Rom. 10:18, grace was universal, but that it was afterward restricted because of man's sin. More recently, theologians have begun to teach that the Gospel of grace will be proclaimed after death to all "negative infidels" (i.e., such as have not heard the Gospel). But all these hypotheses ignore Scripture, and are not able to nullify the fact that grace is particular. Once this fact is established, the question now arises: Why is the Gospel proclaimed to one and not to another? Why is one person born in a heathen land and another in a Christian country? Pelagians and Semi-Pelagians try to justify this by observing that God's "predestination unto initial grace" is conditioned on the natural merits of the individual, and on the use which he has made of the powers that are his by nature. Augustine, however, correctly refuted this Pelagian error by stating that this "predestination unto initial grace which is conditioned on foreseen merits that rise out of the will as it is by nature" does not explain why among infants—who, of course, lack these natural merits—some die after they have received the sacrament of baptism while others die unbaptized. Accordingly, Roman Catholics have always objected to this tenet of Pelagianism, have retained the doctrine of prevenient grace, and have called initial grace unmerited. Indeed, Augustine's objection referring to infants is insurmountable. "Predestination unto initial grace," e.g., the fact that one is born in a Christian country or later on becomes acquainted with the Gospel, is absolutely unmerited and unconditional. Here, at the beginning and in connection with the antecedent decree predestination must needs be viewed as absolute and unconditional. There is nothing in man that will answer the question why the Gospel is revealed to one and concealed from another, why the opportunity of eternal salvation is granted to one and not to another. The only answer to this question, an answer that must be accepted by every one, is this: *God has willed it thus.*

Secondly, Pelagianism seeks to uphold itself by means of its idea of "predestination unto efficacious grace." Reality shows that not all those who hear the Gospel accept it with a true faith. Whence the difference? Now Pelagianism teaches that the will of man determines whether the grace which he has received—a grace in itself "sufficient" unto salvation—will also be and remain efficacious unto salvation; in reality, therefore, Pelagianism has no decree which follows that concerning the universal offer of grace. Thereafter everything is left to man's decision. God has done his part: "to be able" is God's gift; "to be willing" is man's contribution. Nevertheless, not a single Christian confession has ever accepted this position. More or less clearly they all teach an "efficacious grace" and a "gift of faith" and therefore distinguish a second decree in the counsel of predestination. The question remains, however, to whom is this "efficacious, habitual, infused grace," i.e., true faith, granted? The answers given to this question are not clear but confusing. Nevertheless, among Roman Catholics, Lutherans, Arminians, etc., the doctrine was gradually developed that the grace of faith is given to those who make a good use of "initial grace," i.e., of the Gospel which has been proclaimed to them, of the illumination by the Holy Spirit which they have received, etc. In other words, this efficacious grace is granted to those "who do their very best." To be sure, the merit upon which the conferment of efficacious grace is conditioned is not a "merit of condignity," (i.e., a merit which contains in itself the title to the recompense); nevertheless, it is considered to be a "merit of congruity," (i.e., a merit *suitable* for an amount of recompense). In the bestowment of the gift of faith God takes into account the earnestness of a person's zeal and striving. The "predestination unto further grace" is an act of God's justice and fairness; it is not an act of his sovereignty. It is no more than fair that God would grant faith and foregiveness to those who have done their very best. Nevertheless, also this representation is contradicted both by Scripture and by actual religious experience. To be sure, man is obliged to faith and conversion, and is admonished thereto by the preaching of the Gospel. But the obligation does not imply the power: "thou shalt" is not to be identified with "thou canst." We ask: Whence does sinful man derive the power to accept the Gospel and to make good use of initial grace? From his own sinful heart? From the operation of the Logos within Him? From baptismal grace? Those who teach the doctrine of sufficient grace offered to all are puzzled whenever these questions are asked, and are not able to give a clear answer. Besides, Scripture teaches very plainly that man is by nature entirely unwilling and unable to accept the Gospel. It also clearly states that faith is an unmerited gift of God's grace, and that subjective — as well as objective — salvation is God's work. The fact that there is a relation between nature and grace does not mean that the two blend into one: there is an essential difference between the two. Neither Scripture nor reality lends support to the doctrine of a "merit of congruity"; on the contrary, according to Matt. 21:31, "the publicans and the harlots go into the kingdom of God before the chief priests and the elders"; and according to Luke 10:21, Christ says, "I thank thee, O Father, Lord of heaven and earth, that thou didst hide these things from the wise and understanding, and didst reveal them unto babes. . . ."

Thirdly, Pelaginanism seeks to maintain its position by means of its idea of "predestination unto glory." According to Pelagianism a person may believe the truth and may receive forgiveness and the right to life, but it is not at all certain whether he will keep his faith and will obtain salvation. Hence, on the part of God a third decree is necessary: to grant salvation to those whose perseverance *in* the faith he has foreseen from eternity. But the same objections which have already been mentioned in connection with initial grace and efficacious grace may be advanced with even greater force against this doctrine. God's decree, thus interpreted, is made conditional from beginning to end; it is no longer a "decree" in any proper sense of the word. It is nothing else than a wish, whose fulfilment is very uncertain: God looks on and takes a passive attitude; man decides and determines. Everything is left to chance and uncertainty; the final destiny, even of believers, is entirely uncertain; saints may fall away from grace at any moment. Furthermore, this view: that a man may be the object of "predestination unto grace" and at the same time not the object of "predestination unto glory," is entirely in conflict with Scripture. In Rom. 8:29, 30 we read, "For whom he foreknew, he also foreordained to be conformed to the image of his Son; . . . . . and whom he foreordained, them he also justified; and whom he justified, them he also glorified." This chain must not be broken as is done by Pelagianism, which denies the unity of God's redemptive work, and breaks it up into a series of human deeds and actions, unrelated, unconnected, and discontinuous. Finally, this Pelagian doctrine is a complete denial of *God's* work in the salvation of sinners. Scripture everywhere emphasizes God's faithfulness and immutability, the eternal character of his covenant, the certain fulfilment of his promises; but the Pelagian loses sight of all this. According to his position, the Lord does *not* know his own;

God's covenant and lovingkindness do *not* stand fast; it is *not* true that no one snatches the sheep out of the hand of the Good Shepherd; God does *not* glorify those whom he has foreknown, called, and justified. Pelagianism, logically pursued, is the overthrow of all Christianity and of all religion. Hence, not any of the Christian Churches have accepted Pelagianism proper. Though it is true that, due to Semi-Pelagian intermixture, the doctrine of predestination is no longer presented in its original purity by the Roman Catholic and Lutheran churches, nevertheless, all confess to believe in this doctrine. In essence predestination is a dogma accepted by all of Christendom.

C. **The supralapsarian and infralapsarian interpretation of the decree:**

(1) **Points of agreement.** Both agree:

(a) That God is not the Author of sin (supra as well as infra).

(b) That Scripture (not philosophy) is the only source of our knowledge of God's decree (supra as well as infra).

(c) That man's fall and punishment is not merely the object of God's foreknowledge but of his decree and foreordination (infra as well as supra).

(d) That faith is not the cause of the decree of election, neither sin the cause of the decree of reprobation (infra as well as supra).

(2) **Points of disagreement:**

(a) In general, supralapsarianism places the decree of predestination proper above (supra) the decree to permit the fall (lapsus); while infralapsarianism places the decree of predestination proper below (infra) the decree to permit the fall (lapsus). Hence:

Supralapsarianism:
        predestination
        fall

Infralapsarianism:
        fall
        predestination

(b) From this general differentiation it becomes clear that supra and infra differ in regard to their presentation of the order in the elements of God's plan. The logical order according to supra:

1. a decree determining the purpose of all things, namely, the revelation of God's virtues; specifically, the revelation of his mercy in the salvation of a definite number of possible men; and the revelation of his justice in the perdition of another definite number of possible men.

2. a decree to create the men thus elected and reprobated.

3. a decree to permit them to fall.

4. a decree to provide a Mediator for the elect and through him to justify them, and to condemn the reprobate.

The logical order according to infra:

1. a decree to create man in holiness and blessedness.

2. a decree to permit man to fall.

3. a decree to elect some out of this fallen multitude and to leave others in their misery.

4. a decree to bring about the salvation of the elect through Christ. See II, F.

(c) From this again it is apparent that according to supra men viewed as possible or creatable and fallible are the objects of the decree; while, according to infra men viewed as fallen are objects of the decree.

(3) Objections:

(a) To infra:

1. God's justice does not explain the decree of reprobation. The ultimate ground of reprobation is God's sovereign will.

2. In order to maintain reprobation as an act of God's JUSTICE infra places reprobation after the FALL as if in the decree of reprobation God figured only with ORIGINAL sin and not also with ACTUAL sins.

(b) To supra:

1. Supra is correct when it maintains that God's glory is the final goal of all God's works, but the manner in which that goal will be realized is not thereby given; it is incorrect to say that in the eternal perdition of the reprobate God reveals his justice only and that in the eternal salvation of the elect he reveals his mercy exclusively.

2. According to supra the decree of predestination has for its object possible men and a possible Redeemer; but just how are we to conceive of a decree concerning possible men whose actual future existence has not even been determined?

3. Supra makes the damnation of the reprobate the object of the divine will IN THE SAME SENSE as the salvation of the elect. This position is not sustained by Scripture.

(c) To both infra and supra:

1. It is incorrect to define the final goal of all things as the revelation of God's mercy in the elect and of his justice in the reprobate.

2. It is incorrect to represent the lost condition of the reprobate in hell as an object of predestination.

3. Predestination unto eternal death should not be coordinated with predestination unto eternal life, for while certain individuals constitute the object of reprobation, the human race under a new Head, even Christ, is the object of election.

4. Both supra and infra err when they regard the various elements of God's counsel as subordinately related to each other.

5. Both are one-sided: supra emphasizing God's sovereignty; infra, God's righteousness, holiness, and mercy.

(4) The author's conclusion in regard to the whole matter: "God's decree should not be exclusively described . . . as a straight line to indicate a relation merely of before and after, cause and effect, means and goal; but it should also be viewed as a system the several elements of which are coordinately related to one an-

other. . . . As in an organism all the members are dependent
upon one another and in a reciprocal manner determine one
another, so also the universe is God's work of art, the several
parts of which are organically related."

The word "predestination," has been used in more than one sense:
it has been given a broad and a narrow meaning. According to Pelagianism it is merely the decree whereby God, on the ground of foreseen
faith and perseverance on the part of some, and foreseen sin and unbelief on the part of others, has determined to give to the former
eternal salvation and to the latter eternal punishment. According to
this conception, creation, the fall, Christ, the proclamation of the
Gospel and the offering of grace to all, persevering faith and unbelief
precede predestination and are not included in it but excluded from
it; the decree of predestination is no more than the assignment to
eternal life or eternal punishment. In this way the most restricted
meaning is given to the word predestination, which is then made
entirely dependent upon "the bare foreknowledge of God," is a matter
of uncertainty, and is not worthy of the name predestination. In that
case not God but man is the maker of history and the arbiter of its
destiny. This error has been sufficiently refuted in the former paragraph. The important difference between infra- and supralapsarianism,
however, must be given more detailed discussion. At bottom this difference consists in a broader or a more restricted definition of the
concept "predestination." Augustine accepted a twofold restriction
of this concept: in his system the decree of predestination follows that
concerning creation and the fall, and he generally used the term "predestination" in the favorable sense, as a synonym for "election," while
he gave the preference to the term "foreknowledge" to indicate reprobation: predestination, then, is what *God* does, namely that which is
good; while "foreknowledge" refers to what *man* does, namely evil.
In general, scholasticism, Roman Catholicism, and Lutheranism, accepted this interpretation of the term predestination. Also in the
writings of Reformed infralapsarian theologians the decree of creation
and of the fall precedes that of election and of reprobation; but while
most of them were willing to look upon reprobation as a part of predestination — just so the decree of predestination follows that of the
fall — and to speak of a twin or double predestination, others considered it better to conceive of predestination as a synonym for election, and
to discuss reprobation separately and under a different name. Now, if
the term "foreknowledge" is not used in a Pelagian sense, and if the
decree of reprobation is not withdrawn from the province of the will
of God, as was done by later Roman Catholic and Lutheran theologians,
the difference is not essential but merely verbal. But it is characteristic

of infralapsarianism that, in the decree, creation and the fall precede election and reprobation; while supralapsarianism's concept of pre-destination is broad enough to include creation and the fall, which are then looked upon as means to an end: the eternal destiny of rational creatures. In the Reformed Church and in Reformed theology equal recognition has always been given to both supra- and infralapsarian-ism, viewed as interpretations of the decree of predestination. To be sure, the Dutch confessional standards are infralapsarian; nevertheless, no ecclesiastical assembly, not even the Synod of Dort, has ever troubled the supralapsarians. The Lambeth articles of Confession, purposely leave the question unanswered. Reformed theologians have always granted charter privileges to both conceptions. Spanheim used to say that in the cathedra he was supra, but when he was teaching his congregation he was infra. On the one hand, supralapsarians as well as infralapsarians teach that God is not the Author of sin, but that the cause of sin lies in the will of man. Though, as the Omnipotent One. God predestined the fall, and though, as Supreme Ruler, he executes his plan even by means of sin; nevertheless, he remains holy and righteous; of his own accord man falls and sins: the guilt is his alone. "Man falls according to the appointment of divine providence, but he falls by his own fault." Also, the supralapsarians did not arrive at their conception by means of philosophical speculation, but they presented their view because they considered it to come closer to the teaching of Scripture. Just as Augustine arrived at the doctrine of predestination through his study of Paul, so Calvin became convinced of the truth of supralapsarianism by means of his reflection on the Scriptural doctrine of sin. According to his own statement he was not giving a philosophy but the truth of God's Word. On the other hand, Reformed infra-lapsarian theologians are fully agreed that man's fall, sin, and the eternal punishment of many was not the object of "bare foreknowledge" but of God's decree and foreordination. Hence, the difference does not concern the content of God's counsel. Both infra- and supralapsarianism deny the freedom of the will, reject the idea that faith is the cause of election and that sin is the cause of reprobation, and thus oppose Pelagianism; both in the final analysis pay homage to God's sovereignty. The difference concerns only the order of the decrees. Infralapsarians prefer the historical, causal order; supralapsarians defend the ideal, teleological order. The former give a more limited meaning to the concept predestination, and exclude from it a preceding creation, fall, and providence; the latter subsume all the other decrees under pre-destination. The former emphasizes the manyness, the latter the oneness, of the decree. With the former each of the several decrees has significance by itself; with the latter all the preceding decrees are subordinate to the final decree.

The problem is not solved by means of an appeal to Scripture. Whereas infralapsarianism is supported by all those passages in which election and reprobation have reference to a fallen universe, and are represented as deeds of mercy and of justice, Deut. 7:6-8; Matt. 12:25, 26; John 15:19; Rom. 9:15, 16; Eph. 1:4-12; II Tim. 1:9; supralapsarianism seeks its strength in all those texts that declare God's absolute sovereignty, especially with reference to sin, Ps. 115:3; Prov. 16:4; Is. 10:15; 45:9; Jer. 18:6; Matt. 20:15; Rom. 9:17, 19-21. The fact that each of the two views leans for support on a certain group of texts without doing full justice to a different group indicates the one-sided character of both theories. Though infralapsarianism deserves praise because of its modesty — it abides by the historical, causal order — and though it *seems* to be less offensive and though it shows greater consideration for the demands of practical life, it fails to give satisfaction. It is just as difficult to conceive of *reprobation* as an act of God's justice as it is thus to conceive of election. Faith and good works, to be sure, are not the cause of election, but neither is sin the cause of reprobation; God's sovereign good pleasure is the cause of both; hence, in a certain sense, the decree of reprobation always precedes the decree to permit sin. Moreover, if in the divine consciousness the decree of reprobation follows that to permit sin, the question cannot be suppressed, "Then why did God permit sin?" Did this permission consist in a "bare foreknowledge" and was the fall in reality a frustration of God's plan? But no Reformed theologian, even though he be an infralapsarian, can ever or may ever say this. In a certain sense he must include the fall in God's decree; he must conceive of it as having been foreordained. But why did God "by an efficacious permission" foreordain the fall? Infralapsarianism can answer this question only by referring to God's good pleasure, and then it agrees with supralapsarianism. Reprobation cannot be explained as an act of God's justice, for the first sinful deed at any rate was permitted by God's sovereignty. Reasoning backward, infralapsarianism finally arrives at the position of supralapsarianism; in case it should be unwilling to admit this, it would have to resort to foreknowledge. Add to all this the fact that infra places the decree of reprobation *after* the fall, but just where? Is *original* sin the only sin that is taken into account by the decree of reprobation, and in making this dreadful decree does God leave *actual* sins entirely out of consideration? If, as infra insists, reprobation must be referred to God's justice, then instead of placing this decree immediately after the entrance of original sin, why not place it after the complete accomplishment — respectively by each reprobate person — of all actual sins? This is exactly what was done by Arminius — who also included the sin of foreseen unbelief — but such a procedure would never do on the part of a Reformed theologian. Reprobation would then become dependent upon bare foreknowledge, i.e., upon man; man's sinful deeds would then become the final and deepest cause of reprobation; hence, in order to avoid this error the decree of reprobation was placed *immediately* after the fall. But by doing this infra becomes supralapsarian with respect to all *actual* sins: reprobation does not precede original sin, but it does precede all other sin. At first glance infralapsarianism seems to be more moderate and less offensive than supralapsarianism, but deeper study reveals the fact that appearances deceive.

Accordingly, supralapsarianism undoubtedly has in its favor the fact that it refrains from every attempt to justify God, and that both with respect to reprobation and with respect to election it rests in God's sovereign, incomprehensible, yet wise and holy good pleasure. Nevertheless, it is at least just as unsatisfactory as is infralapsarianism, and perhaps even more so. It wishes to pass for a solution, but in no sense whatever does it give a solution of even a single problem. In the first place, to say that the manifestation of all God's excellencies is the final goal of all of the ways of God is indeed correct; but when supra includes in that goal the manner in which this divine glory will be revealed in the eternal destiny of rational creatures, it errs. For, the eternal state of salvation or of perdition is not in itself the goal, but one of the means employed in order to reveal God's excellencies in a manner suited to the creature. It would not do to say that God would have been unable to manifest his glory by saving all men, if this had been his pleasure. Neither is it correct to say that in the eternal state of the reprobate God reveals his justice *exclusively*, and that in the eternal state of the elect he manifests his mercy *exclusively*. Also in the church, purchased with the blood of the Son, God's justice is revealed; and also in the place of perdition there are degrees of punishment and sparks of divine mercy. The final goal of all God's work's must needs be his glory, but the manner in which that glory will shine forth is not thereby given, but has been determined by God's will; and although there were wise and holy reasons why God purposed the perdition of many and not the salvation of all, nevertheless these reasons, though known to him, are not known to us: we are not able to say why God willed to make use of this means and not of another. A further objection to supralapsarianism is the fact that according to this view the objects of the decree of election and reprobation are men considered merely as possibilities and — as Comrie added — a Christ viewed as a mere possibility. To be sure by some this element has been eliminated from the supralapsarian scheme. But the principle which gave rise to this error still remains. Logic requires that a possible Christ should be added to possible men as the object of election, for in the decree of election the church and its Head, i.e., the saved and the Savior cannot be separated.

But even aside from this, the decree of election and reprobation which has for its object "creatable and fallible men" is not the real, but merely a tentative decree. In the end supralapsarianism is forced to proceed to the infralapsarian order in the elements of the decree. For, following the decree concerning the election and reprobation of these possible men comes the decree to create them and to permit them to fall, and this must be succeeded by another decree respecting these men, who are now no longer viewed as mere possibilities but as realities — even in the decree — viz., to elect some and to reprobate others. The logic of the supralapsarian scheme is very weak, indeed. Supralapsarianism really differs from infralapsarianism only in this respect, viz., that after the manner of Amyraldism, it prefixes a decree concerning possibilities to the infralapsarian series of decrees. But just how are we to conceive of a decree respecting *possible* men, whose *actual* future existence has as yet not been determined? In the consciousness of God there is an infinite number of "*possible* men," who will never live. Hence, the decree of election and reprobation has for its object "nonentities," not definite persons known to God by name. Finally, there is this difficulty connected with supra, viz., that it makes the eternal punishment of the reprobates an object of the divine will *in the same manner and in the same sense* as the eternal salvation of the elect; and that it makes sin, which leads to eternal destruction, a means *in the same manner and in the same sense* as the redemption in Christ is a means unto eternal salvation.

Now Reformed theologians all agree that the entrance of sin and punishment was willed and determined by God. It is perfectly true that words like "permission" and "foreknowledge" do not solve anything. The difficulty remains the same, and the same questions arise; viz., why, if God foreknew everything, did he create man fallible, and why did he not prevent the fall? Why did he allow all men to fall in Adam? Why does he not grant to all men faith and the blessing of hearing the Gospel? In brief, if God foreknows and permits something, he does this either "willingly" or "unwillingly." The latter is impossible. Accordingly, only the former remains: God's permission is an "efficacious permission," an act of his will. Nor should it be supposed that the idea of permission is of any force or value over against the charge that God is the Author of sin; for he who *permits or allows* someone to sin and to perish in his sin although he was able to prevent him from sinning is just as guilty as he who incites someone to sin. On the other hand, however, all agree that although sin is not *"excluded"* from the will of God it is, nevertheless, *"contrary"* to his will; that it is not merely a means to the final goal, but a disturbance in God's creation; and that Adam's fall was not a step ahead but a fall in the real sense of the word. It is also a fact that admits of no doubt that, however much logical reasoning may demur, no one is able to suggest other and better words than "permission, foreknowledge, preterition, dereliction," etc. Even the most outspoken supralapsarian is not able to dispense with these words, neither in the pulpit nor in the cathedra. For, although it be admitted that there is a "predestination unto death," no Reformed theologian has ever dared to speak of a "predestination unto sin." Without any exception all (i.e., Zwingli, Calvin, Beza, Zanchius, Gomarus, Comrie, etc.) have rejected the idea that God is the Author of sin, that man was created unto damnation, that reprobation is the "cause" of sin, and that sin is the "efficient cause" of reprobation; and all have maintained, that the inexorable character of God's justice is manifest in the decree of reprobation, that reprobation is the "accidental cause" of sin, and that sin is the "sufficient cause" of reprobation, etc. Accordingly and happily, supralapsarianism is always inconsistent: it begins by making a daring leap, but it soon retreats and returns to the previously abandoned position of infralapsarianism. This is very evident from the works of supralapsarians. Nearly all of them hesitate to place the decree of reprobation in its entirety and without any restriction before the decree to permit sin. The Thomists differentiated between a "negative and a positive reprobation"; the former was made to precede creation and fall, the latter was made to follow them. This same distinction, be it in a modified form, recurs in the works of Reformed theologians. Not only do all admit that reprobation should be distinguished from condemnation, which is the execution of that decree, takes place in time, and has sin for its cause; but in the decree of reprobation itself many differentiate between a preceding, general purpose of God to reveal his excellencies, especially his mercy and justice, in certain "creatable and fallible men"; and a subsequent, definite purpose to create these "possible men," to permit them to fall and to sin, and to punish them for their sins.

Accordingly, neither supra- nor infralapsarianism has succeeded in its attempt to solve this problem and to do justice to the many-sidedness of Scripture. To a certain extent this failure is due to the one-sidedness that characterizes both views. In the first place it is incorrect, as we stated before, to define the "final goal" of all things as the revelation of God's mercy in the elect, and of his justice in the reprobate. God's glory and the manifestation of his excellencies is, to be sure, the final goal of all things; but the double state of salvation and damnation is not included in that final goal, but is related to it as a means. No one is able to prove that this double state must of necessity constitute an element in the final goal of God's glory. In all his "outgoing works" God always has in view his own glory; but that he seeks to establish this glory in *this* and in no other way is to be ascribed to his sovereignty and to nothing else. But even aside from this, it is not true that God manifests his justice only in the damnation of the reprobate, and his mercy only in the salvation of the elect, for also in heaven God's justice and holiness shines forth, and also in hell there is a remnant of his mercy and compassion. Secondly, it is incorrect to represent the lost condition of the reprobate in hell as an object of predestination. To be sure, sin should not be referred to "bare foreknowledge and permission"; in a certain sense, the fall, sin. and eternal punishment are included in God's decree and willed by him. But this is true *in a certain sense* only, and not in the same sense as grace and salvation. These are the objects of his delight; but God does not delight in sin, neither has he pleasure in punishment. When he makes sin subservient to his glory, he does this by means of the exercise of his omnipotence, but to glorify God is contrary to sin's nature. And when he punishes the wicked. he does not take delight in their sufferings as such, but in this punishment he celebrates the triumph of his virtues, Deut. 28:63; Ps. 2:4; Prov. 1:26; Lam. 3:33. Accordingly, though on the one hand, with a view to the all-comprehensive and immutable character of God's counsel, it is not wrong to speak of a "twofold predestination" (gemina praedestinatio) ; nevertheless, on the other hand, we must be careful to keep in mind that in the one case predestination is of a different nature than in the other. "Predestination is the disposition, goal, and ordination of the means with a view to a goal. Since eternal damnation is not the goal but merely the termination of a person's life, therefore reprobation cannot properly be classified under predestination. For these two things are in conflict with each other : to ordain unto a goal and to ordain unto damnation. For, by reason of its very nature, every goal is the very best something, the perfection of an object ; damnation, however, is the extreme evil and the greatest imperfection ; hence the expression 'God has predestinated some men unto damnation' is incorrect." Hence, no matter how often and clearly Scripture tells us that sin and punishment were ordained by God, nevertheless, the words "purpose" (*prothesis*), "foreknowledge" (*prognosis*) and "foreordination" (*proorismos*) are used almost exclusively with reference to "predestination unto glory." In the third place, there is still another ground for the assertion that those err who co-ordinate "predestination unto eternal death" with "predestination unto eternal life," and view the former as a goal in the same sense as the latter; while it is true that certain *individuals* constitute the object of reprobation, *the human race* under a new Head, namely Christ, is the object of election; hence, by grace not only certain individuals are saved, but the human race itself together with the entire cosmos is saved. Moreover, we are not to suppose that merely a few of God's virtues are revealed in this salvation of the human race and of the universe, so that in order to reveal God's justice the state of eternal perdition must needs be called into being; on the contrary, in the consummated Kingdom of God all of God's virtues and excellencies are unfolded: his justice and his grace, his holiness and his love, his sovereignty and his mercy. Hence, this "state of glory" is the real and direct end of creation, though even this goal is subordinate to the exaltation of God. In the fourth place, both supra and infra err when they regard the various elements of the decree as standing in subordinate relation to each other. Now it is true, of course, that the means are subordinate to the final end in view, but from this it does not follow that they are subordinate to one another. Creation is not a mere means toward the fall, neither is the fall a mere means toward grace and perseverance, nor are these in turn merely means toward salvation and perdition. We should never lose sight of the fact that the decrees are as rich in content as the entire history of the universe, for the latter is the unfoldment of the former. The history of the universe can never be made to fit into a little scheme of logic. It is entirely incorrect to suppose that of the series: creation, fall, sin, Christ, faith, unbelief, etc., each constituent is merely a means toward the attainment of the next, which as soon as it is present renders the former useless. As Twissus already remarked, "The different elements of the decree do not stand to one another in a relation merely of subordination, but they are also coordinately related." It is certainly wrong to suppose that the sole purpose of creation was to produce the fall; on the contrary, by means of God's creative activity a universe that will remain even in the state of glory was called into being. The fall took place not only in order that there might be a "creature in the condition of misery," but together with all its consequences it will retain its significance. Christ not merely became a *Mediator,* which would have been all that was necessary for the expiation of sin, but he was also ordained

by God to be the *Head* of the church. The history of the universe is
not a mere means which loses its value as soon as the end of the age is
reached, but it has influence and leaves fruits, for eternity. Moreover,
here on earth we should not conceive of election and reprobation as
two straight and parallel lines; on the contrary, in the unbeliever there
is much that is not the result of reprobation, and in the believer there
is much that should not be ascribed to election. On the one hand, both
election and reprobation presuppose sin, and are deeds of mercy and
of justice, Rom. 9:15; Eph. 1:4; on the other hand both are also deeds
of divine right and sovereignty, Rom. 9:11, 17, 21. So, Adam even
before the fall is a type of Christ, I Cor. 15:47 ff.; nevertheless, in
Scripture the fact of the incarnation always rests upon the fall of the
human race, Heb. 2:14 ff. At times Scripture expresses itself so
strongly that reprobation and election are coordinated, and God is
represented as having purposed eternal perdition as well as eternal
salvation, Luke 2:34; John 3:19-21; I Pet. 2:7, 8; Rom. 9:17, 18, 22,
etc.; but in other passages eternal death is entirely absent in the
description of the future; the victorious consummation of the kingdom
of God, the new heaven and earth, the new Jerusalem in which God
will be all and in all is pictured to us as the end of all things, I Cor.
15; Rev. 21, 22; the universe is represented as existing for the church,
and the church for Christ, I Cor. 3:21-23; and reprobation is completely
subordinated to election.

Accordingly, neither the supra- nor the infralapsarian view of predestination is able to do full justice to the truth of Scripture, and to
satisfy our theological thinking. The true element in supralapsarianism is: that it emphasizes the unity of the divine decree and the fact
that God had one final aim in view, that sin's entrance into the universe was not something unexpected and unlooked for by God but
that he willed sin in a certain sense, and that the work of creation was
immediately adapted to God's redemptive activity so that even before
the fall, i.e., in the creation of Adam, Christ's coming was definitely
fixed. And the true element in infralapsarianism is: that the decrees
manifest not only a unity but also a diversity (with a view to their
several objects), that these decrees reveal not only a teleological but
also a causal order, that creation and fall cannot merely be regarded
as means to an end, and that sin should be regarded not as an element
of progress but rather as an element of disturbance in the universe so
that in and by itself it cannot have been willed by God. In general,
the formulation of the final goal of all things in such a manner that God
reveals his justice in the reprobate and his mercy in the elect is too
simple and incomplete. The "state of glory" will be rich and glorious

beyond all description. We expect a new heaven, a new earth, a new humanity, a renewed universe, a constantly progressing and undisturbed unfoldment. Creation and the fall, Adam and Christ, nature and grace, faith and unbelief, election and reprobation — all together and each in its own way—are so many factors, acting not only subsequently to but also in coordination with one another, collaborating with a view to that exalted state of glory. Indeed, even the universe as it now exists together with its history, constitutes a continuous revelation of God's virtues. It is not only a means toward a higher and richer revelation that is still future, but it has value in itself. It will continue to exert its influence also in the coming dispensation, and it will continue to furnish material for the exaltation and glorification of God by a redeemed humanity. Accordingly, between the different elements of the decree—as also between the facts of the history of the universe—there is not only a causal and teleological but also an organic relation. Because of the limited character of our reasoning powers we must needs proceed from the one or from the other viewpoint; hence, the advocates of a causal world and life-view and the defenders of a teleological philosophy are engaged in continual warfare. But this disharmony does not exist in the mind of God. He sees the whole, and surveys all things in their relations. All things are eternally present in his consciousness. His decree is a unity: it is a single conception. And in that decree all the different elements assume the same relation which a posteriori we even now observe between the facts of history, and which will become fully disclosed in the future. This relation is so involved and complicated that neither the adjective "supralapsarian" nor "infralapsarian" nor any other term is able to express it. It is both causal and teleological: that which precedes exerts its influence upon that which follows, and that which is still future already determines the past and the present. There is a rich, all-sided "reciprocity." Predestination, in the generally accepted sense of that term: the foreordination of the eternal state of rational creatures and of all the means necessary to that end, is not the sole, all-inclusive and all-comprehensive, purpose of God. It is a very important part of God's decree but it is not synonymous with the decree. God's decree or counsel is the main concept because it is all-comprehensive; it embraces all things without any exception: heaven and earth, spirit and matter, visible and invisible things, organic and inorganic creatures; it is the single will of God concerning the entire universe with reference to the past, the present, and the future. But predestination concerns the eternal state of rational creatures, and the *means* thereto: but not *all* things that ever come into being nor all events that ever happen can be included in these means. Hence, in a previous paragraph we discussed "providence" as a thing by itself, although the relation between it and predestination was clearly shown. In the doctrine of God's decree common grace should receive a much more detailed discussion than was formerly the case, and should be recognized in its own rights. Briefly stated, God's decree together with the history of the universe which answers to it should not be exclusively described— after the manner of infra- and supralapsarianism—as a straight line indicating a relation merely of before and after, cause and effect, means and goal; but it should also be viewed as a system the several elements of which are coordinately related to one another and cooperate with one another toward that goal which always was and is and will be the deepest ground of all existence, namely, the glorification of God. As in an organism all the members are dependent upon one another and in a reciprocal manner determine one another, so also the universe is God's work of art, the several parts of which are organically related. And of that universe, considered in its length and breadth, the counsel or decree of God is the eternal idea.

### D. The parts of predestination: reprobation.

(1) Scripture teaches reprobation, especially as this decree becomes evident in the facts of history.

(2) According to Scripture, reprobation is both negative (God's purpose to pass by some men in the bestowment of regenerating grace) and positive (his purpose to ordain them to eternal punishment for their sins), cf. Acts 14:16 (negative) with Rom. 11:8, etc., (positive).

(3) The facts of history point back to reprobation as well as election and are inexplicable upon any other basis.

(4) On the other hand, with a view to God's sovereignty and to the all-comprehensive character of his decrees, reprobation (as well as election) is fully included in the counsel of predestination.

(5) Nevertheless, reprobation is not in the same sense a part of God's decree and an object of his will; for (a) while faith is not the meriting cause of the salvation of the elect, sin is indeed the meriting cause of the eternal perdition of the reprobate; (b) God takes delight in that which he accomplishes according to the decree of election, but that which he effects according to the decree of reprobation (eternal punishment and suffering) is not in and by itself an object of his rejoicing.

From the foregoing it has become evident in which sense reprobation must be viewed as included in the decree of predestination. Viewed in the light of the all-comprehensive character of Gods counsel, it is perfectly proper to speak of a "double predestination." Sin, unbelief, death, and eternal punishment are the object of God's government as well as are all things. Not only is it true that reducing "predestination" at this point to a mere "foreknowledge and permission" avails nothing, but it is also a fact that Scripture speaks very plainly and positiv̌ely. It is true that the Bible does not make frequent mention of reprobation as an eternal decree. All the more, however, is reprobation represented as an act of God which becomes manifest in the history of the world. God rejects Cain, Gen. 4:5; curses Canaan, Gen. 9:25; sends Ishmael away, Gen. 21:12; Rom. 9:7; Gal. 4:30; hates Esau, Gen. 25:26; Mal. 1:2, 3; Rom. 9:13; Heb. 12:17; suffered the nations to walk in their own ways, Acts 14:16. Even within the circle of special revelation mention is often made of God's rejection of his people and of certain definite persons, Deut. 29:28; I Sam. 15:23, 26; 16:1; II Kings 17:20; II Kings 23:27; Ps. 53:5; 78:67; 89:38; Jer. 6:30; 14:19; 31:37; Hos. 4:6; 9:17. But in that negative act of rejection, a positive divine deed often reveals itself. This positive deed is described as: hatred, Mal. 1:2, 3; Rom. 9:13; cursing, Gen. 9:25; hardening, Ex. 7:3; 4:21; 9:12; 10:20; 10:27; 11:10; 14:4; Deut. 2:30; Josh. 11:20; Ps. 105:25; I Sam. 2:25; John 12:40; Rom. 9:18; obduration, I Kings 12:15; II Sam. 17:14; Ps. 107:40; Job 12:24; Is. 44:25; I Cor. 1:19; blinding and deafening, Is. 6:9; Matt. 13:13; Mark 4:12; Luke 8:10; John 12:40; Acts 28:26; Rom. 11:8. God controls all things, even the evil deeds of men. He puts a lying spirit in the mouth of false prophets, I Kings 22:23; II Chron. 18:22; through Satan moves David to number Israel, II Sam. 24:1; I Chron. 21:1; and proves Job, chapter 1; calls Nebuchadnezzar and Cyrus his servants, II Chron. 36:22; Ex. 1:1; Is. 44:28; 45:1; Jer. 27:6; 28:14; etc.; and Assyria the rod of his anger, Is. 10:5 ff.; delivers Christ into the hands of enemies, Acts 2:23; 4:28; sets him for a falling and a rising, for a savor unto death and unto life, for a stone of stumbling and a rock of offense, Luke 2:34; John 3:19; 9:39; II Cor. 2:16; I Pet. 2:8. He gives men up in the lusts of their hearts unto sin, Rom. 1:24; sends a working of error, II Thess. 2:11; raises up Shimei to curse David, II Sam. 16:10; cf. Ps. 39:10; and Pharaoh to show his (God's) power, Rom. 9:17; and the man born blind that the works of the Lord should be made manifest in him. When we speak of these divine acts, we must of course not forget to take into account man's own sinful deeds. Divine hardening implies human hardening, Ex. 7:13, 22; 8:15; 9:35; 13:15; II Chron. 36:13; Job 9:4; Ps. 95:8; Prov. 28:14. Heb. 3:8; 4:7. Jesus speaks in parables not only *in order that* but also *because* unbelievers see not neither hear, Matt. 13:13; cf. Mk. 4:12. God gives men up unto sin and error because they merited this punishment, Rom. 1:24; II Thess. 2:11. Moreover, believers do not clearly see God's controlling providence over the evil deeds of enemies until these crimes have been perpetrated and this wickedness has been revealed, II Sam. 16:10; Ps. 39:9. Nevertheless, in all these things God's will and government also become manifest, and his absolute sovereignty is disclosed. He makes peace and creates evil; he forms the light, and creates darkness, Is. 45:7; Am. 3:6; he creates the wicked for the day of evil, Prov. 16:4; doeth whatsoever is pleasing to him, Ps. 115:3; doeth according to his will among the inhabitants of the earth, turneth the heart of every person whithersoever he will, Prov. 16:9; 21:1; directs all our goings, Prov. 20:24; Jer. 10:23; makes from the same lump of clay vessels unto honor and vessels unto dishonor, Jer. 18; Rom. 9:20; hath mercy on whom he will and hardeneth whom he will, Rom. 9:18; appoints unto disobedience, I Pet. 2:8; ordains (or designates beforehand) unto (this) condemnation, Jude 4; and has excluded many names from the book of life, Rev. 13:8; 17:8.

Such and similar strong expressions of Scripture are confirmed and corroborated by the facts of daily experience, by the history of mankind. Those who accept the decree of reprobation always appeal to the terrible facts of history—an abundance of material. Round about us we observe so many facts which seem to be unreasonable, so much undeserved suffering, so many unaccountable calamities, such an uneven and inexplicable distribution of destiny, and such an enormous contrast between the extremes of joy and sorrow, that any one reflecting on these things is forced to choose between viewing this universe as if it were governed by the blind will of an unbenign deity as is done by pessimism, or, upon the basis of Scripture and by faith, to rest in the absolute and sovereign, yet — however incomprehensible — wise and holy will of him who will one day cause the full light of heaven to dawn upon these mysteries of life. Accordingly, the acceptance or the rejection of a decree of reprobation should not be ascribed to a smaller or greater measure of love and sympathy in a person. The difference between Augustine and Pelagius, Calvin and Castellio, Gomarus and Arminius, does not consist in this: that the latter were possessed of a greater degree of kindness, tender-heartedness, and sympathy than the former; but the difference consists in this: that the former accepted Scripture in its entirety, hence, also this doctrine; that they were and always wanted to be theists; that even in those shocking events of history they discerned the will and the purpose of God; and that they were not afraid to look grim reality in the face. Pelagianism strews flowers over a grave, changes death into an angel, looks upon sin as mere weakness, discusses the uses of adversity, and regards this world as the best world possible. Calvinism eschews all such flimsy "toying and trifling." It refuses to be hoodwinked, to worship a creature of its own imagination, and to labor under a delusion; it takes into account the full seriousness of life, stands up for the rights of the Lord of lords, and humbly kneels in adoration before the sovereign and incomprehensible will of God Omnipotent. And for that very reason it is really much more merciful than Pelagianism. How deeply Calvin felt the gravity and earnestness of what he was saying is apparent from his "awful decree." With gross injustice this expression has been charged against him. It does not plead *against* Calvin, but pleads *for* him. The "decree" regarded as Calvin's teaching, is not "awful" (horribile); but awful, indeed, is the reality which is the manifestation of that divine decree; a reality which is revealed by Scripture and by history, remains unchanged whether one chooses to agree with Pelagius or with Augustine, and is not destroyed by any delusion. Now in the midst of this terrible reality Calvinism does not come forth with a solution, but it offers this comfort: that, in whatsoever happens, it recognizes the will and the governing hand of an omnipotant God, who is at the same time a merciful Father. Calvinism does not offer a solution, but it causes man to rest in him who dwelleth in light unapproachable, whose judgments are unsearchable and whose ways are past tracing out. That was Calvin's comfort. "For the Lord will be my witness, to whom I surrender my conscience, that I daily consider his judgments so wonderful that no curiosity tempts me to know any thing in addition to them, that no sinister suspicion of his incomparable justice creeps upon me, in fine, that no desire to murmur rankles in my breast." And in that rest of soul he awaited the day in which he would see face to face and would receive the solution of these riddles.

Although, as we have seen, it is entirely true on the one hand that reprobation should be subsumed under predestination, nevertheless, the former is not in the same manner and in the same sense included in the divine decree as is election. The defenders of a "twofold" predestination" have always admitted this. Whenever any one challenged the sovereignty of God, the positive and unambiguous testimonies of Scripture, and the facts of history (incapable of being set aside), they were as uncompromising as was the apostle Paul and at times used hard expressions not pleasing to the heart of man, inclined as it is, to Pelagianism. Thus, Augustine once made the remark that even if God had willed to damn some men who were innocent, he could not be accused of sin: "If the human race, which as created in the beginning out of nothing so exists, were not born under the guilt of death and with original sin, and, nevertheless, the omnipotent Creator should have wished to condemn some unto eternal perdition, who would say unto the omnipotent Creator, "Wherefore hast thou done thus?" And other theologians, also a few Reformed, have expressed themselves similarly. Whosoever perceives anything of the incomparable greatness of God and of the insignificance of the creature, and at the same time considers the fact that we so often regard with mere indifference the most severe suffering of men and animals—especially when such suffering is in our own interest or for the benefit of art or science—will hesitate to pass censure on Augustine and others because of such an expression, and will not think of calling God to account. If the question at issue is purely one of *rights,* what *rights* can we claim over against him who formed us out of clay, and to whom we are indebted for all that we are and possess? Nevertheless, although momentarily one may speak in this manner to one who thinks that he has a right to accuse God of injustice, Calvin and nearly all Reformed theologians have positively rejected and frowned upon such "absolute domination." Although the reason why God willed one thing and not another, why he elected the one and rejected the other, is entirely unknown to us, nevertheless his will is ever wise and holy and good, so that God has just reasons for whatever he does. His power and justice are inseparable. Just so God's honor and sovereignty were first recognized, all Reformed theologians advised the most careful and delicate treatment of the doctrine of predestination, and warned against all vain and useless speculation. "It is not proper for us to be too severe; if only we do not meanwhile either deny the truth of that which Scripture clearly teaches and experience confirms, or venture to carp at it as if it were less becoming to God." Although the Lord knoweth them that are his and we are told that the number of the elect is small, "nevertheless, we should cherish a good hope concerning every one, and we should not rashly reckon any one among the reprobate."

Furthermore, all maintained that although sin is not "excluded from" or "beyond" God's will, it is, indeed, "contrary to" God's will. Sin cannot have been the "efficient and moving cause" of the decree of reprobation—for it followed the eternal decree in time, and, if it had been the cause, all men would needs have been reprobated—but it was, indeed, "its sufficient cause" and definitely "the meriting cause" of eternal punishment. For, there is a difference between the decree of reprobation and reprobation itself. The will of God is the final and deepest cause of the former, while the latter takes sin into account. The decree of reprobation is realized by means of man's own guilt. Therefore, it is neither a blind "fate," pushing men on against their own will, nor a sword of Damocles, suspended threateningly over their head; but it is the divine idea of reality itself. The concatenation of cause and effect, condition and fulfilment, etc., as we see it in reality, answers to precisely the same arrangement in the decree of God. The same relation which we observe between sin, guilt, misery, and punishment, exists between them in the decree. Before our eyes the decree —hitherto unknown—is unfolded in all its fulness in the history of the world. Hence, in our thinking, the decree is and must be the exact reflex of reality. We view things *after* they have come into being. But in the mind of God the decree is the eternal idea of reality, as it is gradually unfolded in time. He thinks objects *before* they exist. Accordingly, the decree of reprobation means only this: that the final cause of all of sinful reality, of the entire history of the world, together with all the interrelations existing between the events, is not inherent in reality itself—for how would that be possible?—but lies outside of it, in the mind and will of God. The decree does not change reality in the least; the latter is and remains entirely the same whether one agrees with Augustine or Pelagius; but because of this decree the believer confesses that even those dreadful events which are by the Manichaeans ascribed to an "antigod" and by pessimism to a blind, malevolent will, happen according to the will of him who now causes us to walk by faith, but who will one day justify himself before the eyes of all creatures.

Accordingly, those who misrepresent God's counsel in general, and the decree of reprobation in particular, as if it were merely the divine purpose respecting a person's eternal destiny, are guilty of a serious error. No one has a right to interpret the decree of reprobation as an iron decree, determining only the final destiny of the lost, who are then viewed as inexorably shut up to this eternal state of perdition, no matter what penitent efforts they may put forth. The decree is as rich in content as is reality itself. God's decree (in the full sense of God's counsel) is the fountain-head of *all* reality. In a single conception it embraces the end together with all the ways, the goal together with all the means. It is not a transcendent power, intervening now and then at random, and pushing things on toward their appointed goal; but it is the divine, immanent, and eternal idea, manifesting its fulness in the forms of space and time, and successively (i.e., in length and breadth) unfolding to our limited view that which in the mind of God is a unity. Accordingly, we should not thus conceive of the purpose of reprobation, as if it were a decree all by itself, sustaining no relation to the other decrees in general, nor to the decree of election, in particular. In reality there is not such a dualism between sin and grace, punishment and blessing, justice and mercy, as if the reprobate were visited only with sin and punishment, and the elect only with grace and blessing. Is it not true that even believers sin every day, and that they stumble in many things? Nevertheless, is there any one foolish enough to maintain that these sins of believers are the result of election? All deny this. To be sure, God renders even these sins subservient to the salvation of his children, so that to them that love God all things work together for good, even to them that are called according to his purpose, Rom. 8:28; but this is not due to anything inherent in the nature of sin itself, but only to the omnipotence of God whereby he overrules evil for good. Sin is not a means unto salvation as is regeneration and faith. It is not "a preparation for grace" but is in and by itself a "negation of grace." Hence, the law is still of value for the believers; hence, they are admonished to give the more diligence to make their election sure with fear and trembling; and hence also, Scripture sometimes speaks of a temporal hardening and rejection of believers. And on the other hand, the reprobate receive many blessings, which do not result from the decree of reprobation, but from the goodness and grace of God. They receive many natural gifts: life, health, strength, food, happiness, etc., Matt. 5:45; Acts 14:17; 17:27; Rom. 1:19; Jas. 1:17; etc.; also with respect to the reprobate, God does not leave himself without witness. He endures them with much longsuffering, Rom. 9:22. He causes the Gospel of his grace to be proclaimed to them, and he has no pleasure in their death, Ezek. 18:23; 33:11; Matt. 23:27; Luke 19:41; 24:47; John 3:16; Acts 17:30; Rom. 11:32; I Thess. 5:9; I Tim. 2:4; II Pet. 3:19. Pelagians interpret these passages as if they meant that it is God's real desire that every single human individual be saved, and that there is no decree of reprobation. But this is not what these passages teach. They do teach, however, that it is God's will that all the means of grace be also used in behalf of the reprobate, with a view to their salvation. Now these means of grace do not as such flow forth from the decree of reprobation. They can be misused to that end: they can serve to render a man inexcusable, to harden him, and to make his condemnation heavier; just as the sun operates in two ways: it fosters and warms, but it also scorches and sears. But in and by themselves these means are not "means of reprobation" but "means of grace unto salvation." Accordingly, though election and reprobation culminate in a final and total separation, here on earth they repeatedly crisscross. This points to the fact that in and by itself neither of them constitutes a final goal, and that in the mind of God they were never a "final cause." Both are means unto God's glory, which is both the final goal and, for that very reason, also the deepest cause of all things. The beginning and the end, the reason and the purpose of all existence is something that is good in itself. Sin and punishment, considered in and by themselves, can never have been willed by God. They are in conflict with his nature. He is far removed from wickedness, and he doth not afflict willingly: he does not do it "from the heart." Hence, sin and punishment were willed by God in this sense only as means unto a different, better, and greater good. There is even an important difference between election and reprobation. Whatsoever God does, he does unto his own glory. Accordingly, the cause and purpose of election lies also in God. But God takes delight in the work he accomplishes by means of election. In that work he sees his own virtues reflected as in a mirror. But that which God effects according to the decree of reprobation is not in and by itself an object of his rejoicing. Sin is not a good in itself. But it becomes a good when by the omnipotent God it is rendered subservient to his glory, however much sin in itself endeavors to thwart God's glory. In a secondary sense sin is a good; because it is put in subjection, restrained, and conquered, and thus reveals God's greatness, power, and justice. For herein does God's sovereignty become most brilliantly apparent, that he knows how to overrule evil for good, Gen. 50:20; and how to render sin subservient to the salvation of his church, Rom. 8:28; I Cor. 3:21-23; to the majesty of Christ, I Cor. 15:24; Eph. 1:21, 22; Phil. 2:9; Col. 1:16; and to the glory of his own name, Prov. 16:4; Ps. 51:5; Job 1:21; John 9:3; Rom. 9:17, 22, 23; 11:36; I Cor. 15:28.

**E. The parts of predestination: election.**

(1) The decree of election should be viewed against the dark background of the decree of reprobation.

(2) The ground of the decree of election is not man's merit but God's sovereign grace. Hence this decree is a source of great comfort for God's people, while Pelagianism is guilty of merciless cruelty.

(3) Objects of the decree of election are (a) elect people (considered individually, yet as constituting the body of Christ: the Church); (b) elect angels; and (c) Christ.

Thus, predestination finally culminates in election; in this it reaches its zenith and becomes fully realized. Predestination in its highest form is the decree of God with respect to the revelation of his virtues in the eternal, glorious state of rational creatures and the appointment of the means that lead to that goal. Even when thus considered we should not lose sight of reprobation. It is only when viewed against this dark background that the decree of election shines forth most brilliantly. It is a matter of solemn significance that also in this highest sphere, which concerns the eternal weal and the eternal woe of rational creatures, the day arises out of the blackness of night, and the light out of the darkness. It seems as if the rule: many are called, but few chosen, holds everywhere. The saying: "One man's death is another man's breath," contains a deep truth. There is a sense in which Darwin's doctrine of the survival of the fittest has universal application. A thousand blossoms fall in order that the remaining few may ripen into fruit. Millions of living beings are born, but only a few remain alive. Thousands of people labor in the sweat of their brows in order that a few may be able to wallow in gold and swim in wealth. Riches, wealth, art, science, and whatsoever is high and noble is built upon a foundation of poverty, deprivation, and ignorance. The equal distribution of the socialists is entirely absent from the universe. In not a single sphere is there equality. Everywhere we find election against the dark background of reprobation. The world is not ordered according to the pharisaic law of work and wages; merit and riches have nothing to do with each other. So also in the highest sphere it is God's grace that effects a separation. All the decrees — hence also the decree of election — have for their deepest cause the good pleasure of God. Pelagians of every description have always tried to view the decrees as manifestations of God's justice in which man's merit was taken into consideration. According to them God's decrees are conditioned on the foreseen behavior of the creature. God offers salvation to all, and grants faith to those who avail themselves of this offer, whether they do so in their own strength or by means of supernatural strength which they receive. He saves those who persevere in faith unto the very end. Now it is true that a certain order is apparent among the decrees. They embrace both the final goal and the means that lead toward the realization of that goal. In God's decree the prayer of his children and the hearing of their prayer are closely related. When God decided to give rain in a dry season, he at the same time decided that his people would pray for it and that he would send rain as an answer to their prayer. In his decree he established a relation between sunshine and warmth, sowing and harvest, laziness and poverty, knowledge and power, etc., and thus also between sin and punishment, unbelief and destruction, faith and salvation. The harmony between the phenomena and happenings in the world of reality is a perfect reflex of the harmony in the sphere of God's ideas and decrees. Scripture often limits itself to a discussion of these "secondary causes" and Reformed theologians have accepted them in their full significance. But these secondary causes do not constitute the final and deepest cause. And the question: What is that deepest cause? forces itself upon us from every side. It is inescapable. Why *is* there that relation between the events and phenomena which we observe round about us? An appeal to the nature or character of these things is not a satisfactory answer, for also that nature has been determined by God. Science can tell us *that* things are as they are, but it cannot tell us *why* they are as they are. The created universe gives no answer to the question why there is a causal relationship between creatures, why each creature is what it is, why there is among creatures variety in unity, an infinite diversity in character, nature, sex, genus, power, intellect, riches, honor, etc. The same thing holds in the realm of rational creatures. Why were some angels predestined to eternal glory, while the perdition and damnation of the others are both foreseen and foreordained? Why did Christ assume *that* human nature which was thus honored, and not rather another? Why is one man born within the pale of Christendom, and another outside of this sphere? Why does one individual have so many advantages over another in character, mien, disposition, and education? Why does one child die in early infancy, and why does it enter heaven as a covenant-child; while the other dies outside of the covenant, and without grace? These are so many questions to which no creature can give an answer. The decrees of God are not to be viewed as manifestations of a justice which operates according to works and merits. When we think of the angels, it becomes especially apparent that the final cause of election and reprobation must needs be the will of God. For even when one resorts to foreknowledge and says that God has foreseen the perseverance of some and the fall of other angels, the fact still remains that this foreknowledge preceded their creation. Why, then, did God create those angels whose fall he had foreseen? Why did he not give to them as well as to the others sufficient grace to remain obedient? We have here a clear instance of a reprobation based only and exclusively upon God's sovereignty. And just as reprobation should not be interpreted as if it were merely an act of God's righteousness, so also election must not be viewed as if it were in and by itself always an act of divine mercy. In the election of Christ and of the good angels sin and consequent mercy are altogether out of the question. And the election of men is indeed a deed of mercy, but it is not only a deed of mercy for in that case it would have been necessary for God to show mercy to all, whereas all were wretched. In like manner, reprobation is indeed an act of divine justice, but it is not an act of justice only, for in that case all would have been reprobated.

Accordingly, though it is perfectly true that a certain relation obtains between the different decrees; nevertheless, as divine acts these decrees are not conditional but absolute; they are manifestations of God's absolute sovereignty. God established a causal relation between sin and punishment, and he maintains this relation in the conscience of every man; nevertheless, the deepest cause of the decree of reprobation is not sin and unbelief but the will of God, Prov. 16:4; Matt. 11:25, 26; Rom. 9:11-22; I Pet. 2:8; Rev. 13:8. Similarly, there is a causal relation between faith and salvation; but the decree of election was not caused by foreseen faith; on the contrary, election is the cause of faith, Acts 13:48; I Cor. 4:7; Eph. 1:4, 5; 2:8; Phil. 1:29 It is even wrong to regard Christ as being "the cause of election" though a good interpretation can be given to this expression. Thomas Aquinas is correct when he says that Christ is the cause of our predestination when the latter is viewed not as an act or as a decree but with a view to its purpose and goal. Similarly, some Reformed theologians spoke of Christ as the "cause or foundation of election" or they spoke of our election "through and on account of Christ." Now Christ is indeed the "cause or foundation of election," inasmuch as election is realized in and through him; he is also the meritorious cause of salvation, which is the purpose of election; he is also the Mediator and the Head of the elect. It is also true that the counsel of election was made with a view to the Son, because of love toward him. Christ and the church were chosen together by means of one decree, in communion with each other, and for one another, Eph. 1:4. But this does not make Christ, as Mediator, the "actuating, moving, and meritorious cause" of the decree of election. In that sense Christ has indeed been called the cause of election by many Roman Catholics, Remonstrants, Lutherans, and many modern theologians. But Reformed theologians have always opposed this view. For, Christ is himself an object of predestination, so that he cannot at the same time be its cause. He is a gift proceeding from the Father's love, which precedes the sending of the Son, John 3:16; Rom. 5:8; 8:29; II Tim. 1:9; I John 4:9. The Son did not move the Father to love, but predestinating love arose out of the wellspring of the Father's own spontaneity. Accordingly, Scripture teaches everywhere that the cause of all decrees is not inherent in any creature but lies only in God himself, in his will and good pleasure, Matt. 11:26; Rom. 9:11; Eph. 1:4. And for that very reason the doctrine of election is for the believer and even for the unbeliever a source of unspeakable comfort. If predestination were founded on human merits, all would be lost. But because election is a matter of grace, there is hope even for the most wretched one. If work and wages were the standard of admission to the kingdom of heaven, no one would ever enter. If Pelagianism were true, and the virtuous would be elected because of their virtue and the Pharisees because of their righteousness, poor publicans would be barred. Pelagianism is guilty of merciless cruelty. But believers in the decree of election look upon the most unworthy and degraded of men as a creature of God and an object of his eternal love. The doctrine of election should not be preached in order to terrify many — as is often done — but in order to bid all to partake of the riches of God's grace in Christ. No one *has a right* to believe that he is a reprobate, for every one is earnestly and unfeignedly called and is in duty bound to believe in Christ unto salvation; no one *can* believe it, for his very life and whatever makes life dear to him is an evidence of the fact that God has no pleasure in his death; no one really *believes* it, for in that case he would have hell on earth. But election is a source of comfort and strength, of meekness and humility, of trust and confidence. Man's salvation is established firmly and immutably upon the rock of God's grace and omnipotent good pleasure.

Finally, this glorious character of election shines forth even more brilliantly when we consider its object and goal. Formerly, it was customary to particularize with respect to that object. Accordingly, angels, men and Christ were discussed separately. All are agreed that men are the object of election and predestination; whether they be regarded as fallible or fallen, as believers or as those who are going to believe. Of course, this must not be interpreted in this sense: as if mankind in general, or nations, tribes, or even the church, merely in general, as contrasted with individuals and definite persons, were the object of election, as was erroneously held by Schleiermacher, Lipsius, Ritschl, and others. This representation is merely an abstraction, for mankind, a nation, a tribe, and the church, have no existence apart from individual persons. It is also contradicted by Scripture, which teaches a personal election, mentioning Jacob, Mal. 1:2; Rom. 9:10-12; "as many as," Acts 13:48; "whom," Rom. 8:29; "us," Eph. 1:4; Paul, Gal. 1:15; and tells us that the names of the elect are written in the book of life, Is. 4:3; Dan. 12:1; Luke 10:20; Phil. 4:3; Rev. 3:5; etc. Nevertheless, it is true that in Scripture these elect are not viewed separately and atomistically, but as constituting an organism. They are the people of God, the body of Christ, the temple of the Holy Spirit. They are elect *in Christ,* Eph. 1:4; chosen to be members of his body. Accordingly, both Christ and the church are included in the decree of predestination. Hence, Augustine said, "Just as therefore, that one man was predestinated to be our Head, so we, being many, are predestinated to be his members." The Synod of Toledo expressed itself similarly, and scholasticism discussed in detail the doctrine of the election of Christ, especially on the basis of Rom. 1:5. The Lutherans denied this fact because they viewed predestination as an election from sin unto salvation through the mercy of God. Reformed theologians, however, very strongly defended the doctrine of Christ's foreordination and the fact that Christ together with the church constitutes the object of election. They even argued the question whether Christ was an object of predestination only or also of election. Some, as Calvin, Gomarus, Marck. and De Moor held that Christ was foreordained to be Mediator in order to bring about the salvation of his people: the election of believers was by them looked upon as logically preceding the foreordination of Christ as Mediator. Others, however, as Zanchius, Polanus, and the Synopsis, regard Christ as being an object of election also, whereas he was foreordained to be not only the Mediator but also the Head of the church: thus the election of Christ was viewed as logically preceding the election of the church.

Now it is true, indeed, that Christ was ordained to be the Mediator in order to do whatever was necessary for man's salvation; and it is equally true that Christ was not elected by God's mercy from sin and misery unto glory and blessedness. Nevertheless, Scripture often makes mention of the election of the Messiah, Is. 42:1; 43:10; Ps. 89:3, 20; Matt. 12:18; Luke 23:35; 24:26; Acts 2:23; 4:28; I Pet. 1:20; 2:4. This has rightly been called election, because from eternity the Father appointed the Son to be the Mediator, and especially because, by grace only and exclusive of any merit, Christ's human nature was foreordained to the office of Mediator and was destined to become united with the Logos. But strictly speaking, Christ is thereby made an object of predestination only, whereas predestination differs from election in this respect, viz., that the former embraces especially the arrangement of the means toward the end. Nevertheless, Scripture asserts with equal emphasis that the church was chosen in and for Christ, to be conformed to his image and to behold his glory, John 17:22-24; Rom. 8:29; Christ was foreordained to be not only the Mediator, but also the Head of the church; and all things were created not only through him but also unto him, I Cor. 3:23; Eph. 1:22; Col. 1:16 ff. Nevertheless, Christ is not thereby made the ground and foundation of election; but the election of the church is the first blessing for the church, and even this blessing is bestowed in union with Christ. Moreover, not the ground but the purpose of this election is that all the other blessings — regeneration, faith, etc., — are through Christ given unto the church. In that sense Christ's election logically precedes our election. But no matter how this logical order was viewed, all Reformed theologians maintained that Christ together with the church — called "the mystic Christ" — was the real object of election. "By one, indivisible decree we were all elected: both Christ and we." But the scope of the object of election was widened even more when the angels were also included in the decree of predestination. This was the view of Augustine, of the

Scholastics, and of the Reformed theologians, but not of the Lutherans. Scripture leads the way in representing the angels as objects of predestination, I Tim. 5:21; II Pet. 2:4; Jude 6; Matt. 25:41; and the example of Christ teaches that election does not always presuppose a condition of sin and misery. Accordingly, although the elect are viewed in Scripture as a separate people, Gen. 12:1; Deut. 7:6; 30:3; Jer. 29:14; 51:45; Ezek. 11:17; Hos. 11:1; Acts 2:40; Phil. 2:15; I Pet. 2:9; etc., and the number of elect is said to be very small, Matt. 7:14; 22:14; Luke 12:32; 13:23, 24; in that elect assembly the world is saved. Not a few people but the world itself is the object of God's love, John 3:16, 17; 4:42; 6:33; 12:47; II Cor. 5:19. In Christ all things in heaven and on earth are reconciled unto God; in him all things are summed up, Eph. 1:10; Col. 1:20. The world, created through the Son, will also become the possession of the Son, who will be the Heir of all things, Col. 1:16; II Pet. 3:13; Rev. 11:15. Hence, the object of God's election and of the salvation that is in Christ is not an unknown mass, but an organic whole. "A reconciled mankind will be delivered from a hostile mankind. The Church without spot and wrinkle, gathered out of all nations and destined to reign forever with Christ, is itself the land of the blessed, the land of the living." And because the object of election is a perfect organism, for that very reason election itself cannot be conceived of in any other way than as being a firm and definite divine decree. In a mere *aggregate* the number of parts is entirely immaterial. But an *organism* is based on number and measure. Christ was by God chosen to be the Head of his body, the church; and together they must grow up into a fullgrown man, in such a manner that every member has its own place, and performs its own task. Election is the divine idea, the eternal plan of that temple which is being built by God throughout the ages. Of this temple God is himself the Builder and Architect. Everything is subservient to its erection. Just as all God's decrees culminate in that of God's glorification, so the entire history of mankind and of the universe cooperates to usher in the Kingdom of God. Says Calvin: "Even those who are not citizens of that kingdom are born with a view to the salvation of the elect." Creation and the fall, preservation and government, sin and grace, Adam and Christ, all contribute — each in his own way — to the construction of this divine edifice. And this building is itself erected unto the honor and glorification of God. "For all things are yours, and ye are Christ's, and Christ is God's," I Cor. 3:21-23.